MAINSTREAMING OUTSIDERS:

The Production of Black Professionals

SECOND EDITION

MAINSTREAMING OUTSIDERS:
The Production of Black Professionals
SECOND EDITION

James E. Blackwell
University of Massachusetts/Boston

GENERAL HALL, INC.
Publishers
5 Talon Way
Dix Hills, New York 11746

MAINSTREAMING OUTSIDERS
The Production of Black Professionals
Second Edition

GENERAL HALL, INC.
5 Talon Way
Dix Hills, New York 11746

Publisher: Ravi Mehra
Editor: Eileen Ostermann
Composition: *Graphics Division,* General Hall, Inc.

LIBRARY OF CONGRESS CATALOG CARD NUMBER: 87-080426

ISBN: 0-930390-76-8 [cloth]

Manufactured in the United States of America

For my parents, Edward and Celia,
whose love, motivation, strengths, and dreams
were the sources of an enduring inspiration...

Contents

Foreword   xv

Preface   xvii

Acknowledgments of Data Sources   xix

1 Historical Context of Mainstreaming   1

A Definition of Mainstreaming 2, Mainstreaming during the Reconstruction Era 3, The DuBois–Washington Controversy 6, Black Professional Schools and Mainstreaming 7, Legal Attacks on "Separate but Equal" 8, U.S. Supreme Court Cases 8, Impact of the Civil Rights Movement 13, Career Choices of Black Students 15, Economic Barriers to Higher Education 17, The 1970s and 1980s 23, Notes 26

2 Methodological Issues and Reference Points   29

Objectives of the Study 29, A Theoretical Viewpoint 30, The Universe of the Study 35, Data-Collection Procedures 35, Description of the Survey Inventory 35, Other Sources of Data 38, Limitations of Data 44, Operational Definitions 44, Data Analysis 46, Notes 47

3 Data Analysis of Survey Findings   48

Correlates of Total Black Student Enrollment 51, Identification of Most-Powerful Predicators 56, Black Student Enrollment in Professional Schools 56, First-Year Enrollment 56, Total Enrollment 60, Black Students graduated from Professional Schools 60, Notes 64

4 The Current Crisis in Higher Education   65

Curriculum Content and Quality 65, Criticisms of New State Policies 68, Admissions Programs 69, The Patterns of Financial Assistance 71, Notes 73

5   The Medical Education of Black Americans   74

Howard University and Meharry Medical College 75, The Role of Professional Associations 76, The *DeFunis* and *Bakke* Cases 85, Traditional and Nontraditional Admissions Criteria 88, Applicant Activity in the 1970s and 1980s 92, Enrollment in the 1970s and 1980s 97, Total Enrollment 102, Sex Ratio 104, The Graduation of Black Students 106, Problem Areas in the Medical Education of Black Students 107, Black Faculty 109, Notes 111

6   Mainstreaming Black Americans in Dentistry   113

The Historical Context 113, Professional Associations and the Training of Black Dentists 115, Applicant Activity in the 1970s and 1980s 117, Admissions Criteria 118, Enrollment of Black Dental Students 119, Enrollment in 1970s 119, First-Year Enrollment Trends 121, Enrollment in the 1980s 131, Factors Affecting Enrollment 133, Availability of Financial Aid 133, Recruitment Programs 142, Graduation Profiles 144, The Sex Variable 147, Notes 152

7   Mainstreaming Black Americans in Optometry   153

The Historical Context 154, Recruitment and Enrollment of Black Students 155, Admissions Criteria 158, Enrollment Trends 162, Male-Female Ratios 166, Retention 166, Black Graduates in Optometry 167, Major Problems 168, Notes 172

8   The Recruitment and Enrollment of Black Students at Schools of Pharmacy   173

Recruitment 173, Admissions Requirements 180, Enrollment: B.S. in Pharmacy Programs 186, Enrollment in the "*Adams* States" 188, Sex Ratio 191, Enrollment: Pharm.D. and Graduate Programs 193, Financing One's Education 196, Black Graduates in Pharmacy 198, Xavier University College of Pharmacy: A Case Study of Success 200, Sex Ratio 203, Notes 206

9   Blacks in Veterinary Medicine   208

Tuskegee Institute: Pioneer in Veterinary Medicine 208, Recruitment at Tuskegee 209, Admissions Policy and Practices 213, Enrollment at Tuskegee's School of Veterinary Medicine 214, Graduation 215, Financial Aid 217, Impact of the *Bakke* Decision 217, Desegregation Trends 218, Role of Associations 219, Admissions Criteria 223, Enrollment 226, Graduation 229, Problem Areas 229, Notes 231

10   Engineering and Architecture: Pathways to Progress   233

The Production of Black Engineers Before 1970: Black Schools of Engineering 233, The Role of the Corporate Structure 236, Minority Education Engineering Effort 238, The 1973 National Academy of Engineering Conference 239, National Advisory Council on Minorities in Engineering 239, Committee on Minorities in Engineering 241, Supportive Organizations 241, The Recruitment of Black Students 243, Institutional Strategies 243, Admissions Criteria 245, Undergraduate Admissions 245, Graduate Admissions 246, Enrollment of Black Students 246, Undergraduate Enrollment Trends 247, Total Enrollment 249, Enrollment in Graduate Programs 252, Retention 256, Finance 259, Self-Confidence 261, Estrangement 261, Graduation Rates 262, Graduate Degrees 264, Problem Areas 266, Architectural Education 268, Notes 270

11   The Legal Profession and Black Americans   272

A Historical Overview 272, The Impact of Professional Associations 274, Council on Legal Education Opportunity 278, The Recruitment of Black Students 281, Admissions Requirements 283, Responses to the *Bakke* Decision 287, Enrollment of Black Students in Law Schools Since 1970 288, First-Year Enrollment 288, Total Enrollment 289, Enrollment in Historically Black Law Schools 291, Special Programs 292, Problem Areas 293, Notes 295

12   The Social Work Profession: Parity Attained and Lost   297

Historical and Societal Contexts 297, The Berkeley Model 299, Recruitment, Admissions Criteria, and Special Admissions 302, Financial Assistance 305, Enrollment of Black Students 306, First-Year Enrollment

307, Total Enrollment 307, The *"Adams* States" 310, Enrollment in Doctoral Programs 311, The Production of Black Social Work Professionals 315, Black Faculty 317, Problem Areas 319, Notes 321

13 The Production of Black Doctorates 322

An Overview 323, Doctorates Awarded to Black Americans 327, Distribution by Field 330, Sources of Funds for Graduate Education 333, Graduate and Professional Opportunities Program 336, Time Lapse between the Baccalaureate and the Doctorate 339, Special Problems and Issues 340, Notes 345

14 Policy Implications in Mainstreaming Outsiders: Outlook for the Future 347

Needed Policy Changes (How to Succeed by Really Trying) 351, Beyond Tokenism: Five-Year Plans 357, Notes 361

Bibliography 362

About the Author 368

Name Index 369

Subject Index 371

List of Tables

Table 1	Annual Average Unemployment Rates for Black and White Americans Age 16 and Over, 1950–1980	19
Table 2	Distribution of Families by Race and Income, Selected Years, 1953–1983	20
Table 3	Black and White Median Family Income, Selected Years, 1953–1984	21
Table 4	Participation Profile by Field in Response to Survey Inventory	37
Table 5	Pearsonian Correlations of Total Black Student Enrollment with All Predictors, 1971, 1975, 1979	52
Table 6	Pearsonian Correlation Matrix, Year 9: Total Black Student Enrollment with All Variables	54
Table 7	Regression of First-Year Black Student Enrollment in Professional Schools with Most-Significant Variables, All Cases, Years 1, 5, 9	58

Table 8 Regression of Total Black Student Enrollment in Professional Schools with Most-Significant Variables, All Cases, Years 1, 5, 9   61

Table 9 Regression of Total Black Students Graduated from Professional Schools with Most-Significant Predictor Variables, All Cases, Years 1, 5, 9   62

Table 10 Total National Medical Fellowship Awards Approved for 1982–1983, All Minorities and Institutions Combined   81

Table 11 Applications to U.S. Medical Schools by Race, 1970–1984, All Institutions Combined   94

Table 12 Applicants, Acceptances, and Acceptance Rate of Black First-Year Enrollees in U.S. Medical Schools, 1974–1984   96

Table 13 First-Year Medical School Enrollment by Race, 1970–1984, All Institutions Combined   98

Table 14 New Entrants and First-Year Enrollments in U.S. Medical Schools by Race, Sex, Number, and Percentage, 1981–1982 and 1983–1984   99

Table 15 Medical School Repeaters by Race, Year, Class, and Percentage, 1974–1984   101

Table 16 Total Enrollment in U.S. Medical Schools by Race, 1970–1984 All Institutions Combined   103

Table 17 Total Enrollment in U.S. Medical Schools by Race and Sex, 1981–1982 and 1983–1984   105

Table 18 Total Graduates from U.S. Medical Schools by Race, 1970–1985, All Institutions Combined   106

Table 19 Applicants and First-Year Enrollment in Dental Schools, 1975–1984   117

Table 20 Black Student Dental School Enrollment, October 1970   120

Table 21 First-Year Enrollments in Dentistry Programs, All Institutions Combined, 1968–1986   123

Table 22 Student First-Year Enrollment in Schools of Dentistry in "Non-*Adams* States," by School, Sex, and Year, 1974–1984   124

Table 23 First-Year Black Student Enrollment in Schools of Dentistry in First-Tier "*Adams* States," by School and Sex, 1974–1984   126

Table 24 First-Year Enrollment in Dental Schools in Second-Tier "*Adams* States," by School and Sex, 1980–1984   128

Table 25 Total Enrollment, All Classes and Institutions, in Dental School Programs, 1968–1984   132

Table 26 Total Black Student Enrollment in Schools of Dentistry in First-Tier "*Adams* States," by School and Sex, 1974–1984   134

Table 27 Total Enrollment in U.S. Dental Schools in Second-
Tier "*Adams* States," by School, and Sex, 1980–1984   136
Table 28 Financial Assistance Awarded to Predoctoral Dental
Students in the United States, 1982–1983   138
Table 29 Total Dentistry Degrees Conferred, All Institutions
Combined, 1968–1984   145
Table 30 Black Dental School Graduates from Institutions in
the First-Tier "*Adams* States," by School and Sex,
1974–1984   148
Table 31 Number of Black Graduates from Dental Schools in
Second-Tier "*Adams* States," by School, and Sex,
1980–1984   149
Table 32 Total Black Dental School Graduates in "Non-
Adams States" by School, Sex, and Year, 1974–1984   150
Table 33 Profile of 1984 Entering Class in Colleges of
Optometry by Institution, Gradepoint Average, and
Mean OCAT Scores   161
Table 34 Total Enrollment in Colleges of Optometry, by
School and Race, 1970–1984   164
Table 35 Total Enrollment of Black Students in Schools and
Colleges of Optometry, by Sex and Institution, 1979
through 1984   167
Table 36 Tuition and Fees, Schools and Colleges of
Optometry, Fall 1984   171
Table 37 Black Student Enrollment in First Professional
Degree Programs in Pharmacy, 1979–80 to 1984–85   181
Table 38 Average Total Enrollment of Black Students in
Schools of Pharmacy in "*Adams* States," 1979–1984
(first professional degree)   189
Table 39 Black Student Enrollment in Schools of Pharmacy,
by Sex, 1979–1984 (first professional degree)   191
Table 40 B.S. Pharmacy Degrees Awarded in "*Adams* States,"
1974–1984   192
Table 41 B.S. Pharmacy Degree Graduates by Race, 1972 to
1984   199
Table 42 Graduate Degrees in Pharmacy, by Race, Selected
Years 1974–1984   199
Table 43 Enrollment by Race at Xavier University of
Louisiana, College of Pharmacy, 1968–1984   204
Table 44 Enrollment by Sex, Xavier University, College of
Pharmacy 1979–1984   204
Table 45 First-Year Enrollment, Tuskegee School of
Veterinary Medicine, 1970–1984   215
Table 46 Number of D.V.M. Degrees Awarded by Tuskegee
Institute, 1969–1985   216

Table 47   Recruitment Activities, Colleges of Veterinary
           Medicine, 1984   224
Table 48   Total Enrollment in Doctor of Veterinary Medicine
           Programs, by Race, 1969–1985, All Institutions
           Combined   228
Table 49   First-Year Enrollment in B.S. in Engineering
           Programs, by Race, 1968–1984, All Institutions
           Combined   248
Table 50   Total Engineering Enrollment, by Race, 1970–1984,
           All Institutions Combined   251
Table 51   Current Rank of "*Adams* States" by Number of
           Blacks Enrolled in Engineering Schools, 1983–1984
           All Institutions Combined (and Percent Blacks in
           State Population)   253
Table 52   M.S. Degree Full-Time Enrollment in Engineering,
           1969–70 — 1983–84 All Institutions Combined   254
Table 53   Doctoral Degree Enrollment in Engineering, by
           Race, 1969–1984   255
Table 54   Bachelor's Engineering Degrees Awarded, by Race
           1970–1984, All Institutions Combined   263
Table 55   Black Engineering Baccalaureates Awarded by
           Predominantly Black Colleges, 1984   263
Table 56   Engineering Baccalaureates Awarded in 1984, by
           Race, in "*Adams* States" and the District of Columbia   264
Table 57   Masters's Engineering Degrees Conferred,
           1970–1984, by Race, All Institutions Combined   265
Table 58   Engineering Doctorates Conferred, by Race,
           1970–1984, All Institutions Combined   267
Table 59   First-Year Enrollment in J.D. Programs, Approved
           Law Schools, by Race, 1968–1984, All Institutions
           Combined   288
Table 60   Total Enrollment in J.D. Programs, Approved Law
           Schools, by Race, 1968–1985, All Institutions
           Combined   290
Table 61   First-Year Enrollment M.S.W. Programs, Schools of
           Social Work, by Race, 1969–1983, All Institutions
           Combined   308
Table 62   Total M.S.W. Enrollment in Schools of Social Work,
           By Race, 1969–1983, All Institutions Combined   309
Table 63   First-Year Black Student Enrollment, M.S.W.
           Programs, Twenty-Five Largest Schools of Social
           Work, Selected Years, 1970–1981   310
Table 64   First-Year Enrollment in Primary Public Institutions,
           Schools of Social Work, "*Adams* States," by Race,
           1970–1979   312

Table 65 Full-Time M.S.W. Enrollment, Institutions in
          "*Adams* States," by Race, 1981, 1982, 1983   313
Table 66 Enrollment in Doctor of Social Work Programs, by
          Race, 1970–1983, All Institutions Combined   314
Table 67 M.S.W. Degrees by Race, 1970–1984, All
          Institutions Combined   315
Table 68 Doctor of Social Work Degrees Awarded, by Race,
          1970–1984, All Institutions Combined   316
Table 69 Number of Full-Time Black Faculty in Schools of
          Social Work, 1970–1984, All Institutions Combined   318
Table 70 Full-Time Black Faculty, Schools of Social Work in
          "*Adams* States," 1981–1983   320
Table 71 Doctorates Awarded to Black Americans,
          1973–1979   328
Table 72 Doctorates Awarded U.S. Black Citizens by Field,
          Percent of Total Doctorates, Percent of Total
          Awarded Black Americans by Years, 1973–1984   329
Table 73 Sources of Support for Doctoral Students, by Race,
          1974–1984, and Percentage Using Sources   334
Table 74 Median Age at Doctorate and Median Time Lapse
          from Baccalaureate to Doctorate, by Race,
          1973–1984   341

List of Figures

Figure 1 Dual–Degree Programs in Engineering at Historically
          Black Colleges in 1984–1985   235
Figure 2 Cooperating Traditionally White Institutions
          Dual–Degree Programs in Engineering with
          Historically Black Institutions, 1983–1984   236
Figure 3 Leaders in the Enrollment of Black Undergraduates
          in Engineering   251

Foreword

The first edition of *Mainstreaming Outsiders: The Production of Black Professionals* grew out of the mutual and special interest of the author and the Southern Education Foundation in the problem of the underrepresentation of black Americans in graduate and professional education. As a result of that sustained interest, and consistent with the research goals of the Southern Education Foundation, the foundation agreed to sponsor the survey research on which this book is based. Because of the interest expressed by many scholars in the data presented in the first edition, SEF, a public charity foundation, responded favorably to the reqeust to sponsor further research in this area. The data contained in this book are a result of the commissioned study, one of 20 sponsored since 1978 under SEF's Higher Education Program. A major function of this program is to monitor desegregation efforts in states that historically have operated dual systems of public higher education and ultimately to inform the public of the issues that affect equal opportunities for minorities in higher education.

Since its incorporation in 1937 and the establishment of its initial fund by George Peabody in 1867, SEF has been concerned with issues related to race and education. Specifically, the issues that surfaced in the *Adams v. Richardson* case, filed in 1970 and charging that the U.S. Department of Health, Education, and Welfare had defaulted on its obligation to enforce Title VI of the Civil Rights Act of 1964, began to shape the foundation's program in higher education. The foundation recognized that the issues obviously affected black access to, and graduation from, postsecondary institutions in the South. Consequently, funds were provided to support black coalitions, regionwide conferences, the commissioning of studies, and the publication of other materials. As stated by a former board member, the *Adams* case "will affect hundreds of institutions, tens of thousands of employees, faculty administrators, hospital workers, workers in experiment stations, cafeteria employees, etc., and millions of students. . . ." Within this context, the foundation made a decision to allocate resources to explore further the status of blacks in public higher education institutions. This support of projects has continued over the past 12 years and has been the core of the Higher Education Program.

It is our hope that readers will look closely at the data and use the information as benchmarks while attempting to resolve the issue of educational equity for minorities. Both editions of *Mainstreaming Outsiders* will serve as a challenge to those in policymaking positions to effect change where needed in the present decade. James E. Blackwell is not new to the Southern Education Foundation. We have enjoyed a close working relationship over the past 11 years. Dr. Blackwell has assisted the foundation with several of its conferences, addressing desegregation of public higher education systems, and has prepared several publications for the foundation. He has served since 1978 as chairman of the Higher Education Program Research Task Force, which primarily has coordinated higher education research for SEF.

The board and staff are delighted that SEF, a public charity foundation, has been able to sponsor the research that resulted in the second edition of *Mainstreaming Outsiders*. The support was made possible as a result of SEF's receiving a grant from the Ford Foundation for its Higher Education Program and activities related to higher education desegregation. This book contains significant documentation for policy analysts; the trend noted by Dr. Blackwell should not be ignored. For those who are concerned with the issue of underrepresentation of black Americans in graduate and professional schools, *Mainstreaming Outsiders* surely will be a useful document.

Eldridge W. McMillan
President
Southern Education Foundation

Preface

Mainstreaming Outsiders is a product of my long-standing professional interest in the dynamics and complexities of intergroup relations, and of the conditions in the social structure that perpetuate patterns of group dominance and group subordination. One of the most effective strategies employed by dominant groups to protect their control over the highly prized values and rewards within a society is to manipulate and limit access to these values and rewards. High educational attainment is one example of a highly prized value in a modern, industrialized, and technological society, since the society places a great premium on expert knowledge, competence, training, and skills. Inequities in access to education generate other forms of structural inequality. As a result, it becomes even more difficult for subordinate groups, who are characteristically outside that reward structure, to alter their status within the social system.

As was the case when this book was first published in 1981, this second edition is an examination of the efforts to fulfill what appeared to have been a national commitment during the civil rights era to eliminate structural inequalities and to mainstream blacks through expanded access and equity in educational opportunities. Although the primary focus here is on the experiences of black Americans in their efforts to move into the educational mainstream through the acquisition of graduate and professional degrees since 1970, much of what is said is generally applicable to Puerto Ricans, Mexican Americans, Native Americans, and Asian Americans. Nevertheless, the nature of this book does not permit as much attention to those minority groups as would have been desired.

This second edition extends the data base for the trend analysis from 1970 to 1984–1985; consequently, an additional five years of data are used in the analysis of trends in enrollment, retention, and graduation or production of blacks with graduate and/or professional degrees. Similarly, this edition examines the degree to which national conditions, influences at the federal level, and changing commitments at the institutional level have had an impact on the overall process of access, recruitment, matriculation, and production of blacks from graduate and professional institutions. As was done in the previous edition, the position of blacks in the educational structure is compared with the progress and advances made by the white population and with national totals. The fields covered remain those of medicine,

xvii

dentistry, law, engineering, pharmacy, optometry, social work, veterinary medicine, and graduate education. A new chapter focuses on barriers that restrict the movement of blacks through the educational pipeline, and, like the findings from the survey research portion of the study, it provides a substantive basis for the subsequent trend analysis.

I am indebted to several persons who assisted me in the various stages of this project. I express my sincere gratitude to my colleagues Siamak Movahedi, Russell Schutt, and Philip Hart for their advice on methodological issues raised during the research, and to the late T. Scott Miyakawa for his invaluable and constructive criticisms made after throughly reading the manuscript in its early stages; other professional colleagues who read part or all of the manuscript and offered constructive criticisms: Marie Haug (Case Western Reserve University), Cameron Fincher (University of Georgia), Wiley Bolden (Georgia State University), Anne S. Pruitt (Ohio State University), Edgar Epps (University of Chicago), and William Curlette (Georgia State University); my research assistants for the second edition: Richard Lunden, John Sherwood, Zaki Sakin, William J. Stracqualursi, Pauline Young, and Margueye Seck; my research assistants on the first edition: Kathleen Leon, Charlotte Craig, and Jeanne O'Neill; John Murphy, Dianne Horabik, and Tom Marx of the Computer Center of the University of Massachusetts at Boston for special assistance in data processing; the extraordinary typing services provided by Anne Foxx, Barbara Saulnier (who typed the first manuscript), DeAnna Eaton, Patricia Garrity, and Suzanne Bellotti; Mrs. Karima Al-Amin, director of the Higher Education Program, and President Eldridge W. McMillan of the Southern Education Foundation for their support and sponsorship of this project.

Above all, I am especially grateful to Myrt, my wife, for the myriad roles she played not only in the development of this project but in the advancement of my work as a sociologist. Her contributions and support as an objective concerned critic and research assistant, and her abiding faith in the ultimate value of this undertaking, combined with humaneness and understanding, will always be of inestimable importance to me.

James E. Blackwell

Acknowledgments of Data Sources

Although I do not cite their names here, I am deeply indebted to the administrators and institutional research staff of participating graduate and professional schools for their survey inventory responses, which were a rich source of immensely important data. A special note of gratitude is expressed to the organizations and individuals listed below; their generous assistance provided so much of the data upon which this study is based:

    Association of Colleges of Pharmacy: Dr. Lars Solander and Dr. Richard Penna

    American Association of Dental Schools: Dr. James K. Walker

    American Bar Association: Dean James White

    American Dental Association: Dr. James W. Graham and Dr. Gene A. Kramer

    Association of American Law Schools: Dr. Millard Rudd and Prof. Derek Bell

    Association of American Medical Colleges: Dr. Davis G. Johnson, Dario Prieto, Lillye Mae Johnson, and Mary Cureton

    Association of American Veterinary Medical Colleges: Dr. W. M. Decker

    Association of Schools and Colleges of Optometry: Lee Smith

    Committee on Minorities in Engineering: Levoy Spooner

    Council on Legal Education Opportunity: Wade Henderson, Esq., and Lawrence Dark, Esq.

    Council on Social Work Education: Ruth Posner

    Engineering Manpower Commission: Patrick Sheridan and Barbara Ann Supple

    National Architectural Accrediting Board: Dr. Hugo Blasdel

    National Fund for Minority Engineering Students

    National Advisory Council on Minorities in Engineering (NACME): Dr. John O. Stevenson, Dr. Robert Finnell, and Dr. Luis Mirandi

    National Medical Fellowships, Inc.:

National Optometric Association: Dr. Edwin Marshall and
Dr. Charles Comer
National Research Council: Dorothy Gilford, Peter D.
Syverson, and Susan Coyle
The National Center for Educational Statistics
The U.S. Office of Civil Rights
The U.S. Office of Education
Tuskegee Institute: President Benjamin Payton and Dr. Ellis
Hall, and President Emeritus Luther Foster
Xavier University of Louisiana: President Norman Francis, Dean
of Pharmacy, Dr. Marcellus Grace, and former Dean of
Pharmacy Warren McKenna

Chapter **1**   HISTORICAL CONTEXT
OF MAINSTREAMING

The mainstreaming of outsiders is deeply rooted in American history. The association of the concept with non-European racial and ethnic groups is, however, a relatively recent phenomenon. If mainstreaming is conceptualized as one of the many dimensions of assimilation into American life, the differences in the applicability of the idea to the actual experiences of European white ethnic groups, when compared with those of Third World minority groups are apparent. Almost from the inception of the first wave of European immigrants during the colonial period, it was assumed that these groups, as well as the Europeans who followed them, would be assimilated into the mainstream of American society after an unspecified period of time. With each successive group, it may be argued, the time frame for their becoming mainstreamed was longer, but the inevitability of attainment of equal access to the opportunity structure of American life was never in doubt.

This view was not the case for Third World groups. Most assuredly, during the antebellum days of the American Deep South, the prevailing sentiment, the result primarily of the subhuman characteristics attributed to black persons, was that they could not and should not be brought into the mainstream of American life. After slavery, in all parts of the nation, all sectors of the society heatedly debated whether or blacks could be brought into the mainstream and whether they indeed had a right to those privileges reserved for the dominant group. Today, racist individuals and groups and ultra-right-wingers in American society deny such rights; others demand them, while still others raise the issue of mainstreaming at whose expense. Further, the Reagan administration has implemented policies and initiated practices that may seriously undermine a substantial amount of the progress achieved in the two decades before 1980.

What do we mean by mainstreaming? How is the process applied to the experiences of black Americans in graduate and professional education? And how is it related to the concept of blacks as "outsiders" in American society? What social, political, and economic conditions or factors have facilitated or restricted the mainstreaming of outsiders in recent years? These are some of the salient questions addressed in this chapter.

1

A Definition of Mainstreaming

The term *mainstreaming* refers to a process by which an unfavored racial or ethnic group is provided opportunities to fulfill occupational roles in the same manner as members of the more favored or dominant group in a desegregating American society. Those in the unfavored group are generally regarded as outsiders or peripheral to the American society because of previous conditions of servitude, or are ascribed lower status based on racial identification, ethnicity, or their disfavored position in the overall social structure, which has been relatively frozen by law and social custom. Members of this group are subjected to categorical discrimination and exclusionary policies.

The primary mechanism for mainstreaming is an expansion of the educational opportunity structure. However, broad educational opportunities as a social process are contingent on the degree to which such persons either have suffcient economic means to take advantage of new educational opportunities or the degree to which financial resources are made available to them from external sources. Access to the widening educational opportunity structure also depends on the internal and external political climate of an institution, the dynamics of institutional behavior, and the quality of social and political pressure brought to bear on a state or the nation as a whole, particularly in terms of responses to pressures for enduring social change that will elevate the overall status of the unfavored group.

It should be noted here that it is not always a compelling necessity for the expansion of educational opportunities to take the form of new positions or seats for unfavored members of the society. This fact applies to institutions previously closed to them and institutions that offered only token representation to members of outside groups. It may mean locating special programs or strengthening those already present in institutions established primarily for members of the outsider group because of de jure or de facto segregation and customary policies of discrimination and exclusion.

Hence, to mainstream black Americans is to remove restrictions and barriers constructed against their entry, individually or collectively, into the central fabric or into the educational, economic, and political life of a desegregating American society.

As a process, mainstreaming requires all the characteristics that social scientists have come to label *cultural assimilation*. At the outset, implicit in mainstreaming is the notion that individuals partaking of the process can and do speak the language of the dominant group. They have incorporated much of the dominant group's cultural norms, values, and social expectations as their own. Or, at least, these persons submit to both expediency and reality, since behaving, as dominant-group mandates require, is the most efficacious method of being mainstreamed.

Nevertheless, persons who seek to enter the mainstream of American society confront, at minimum, two options. In the first instance, they can attempt to behave precisely as the mainstream of the dominant group behaves; that is, they must use the dominant-group life patterns as a model or as normative guidelines and, as anglo-conformity philosophy demands, in the process, divest themselves of their original culture. In the second instance, such persons may compartmentalize their actions, as do individuals and groups who practice cultural pluralism. In this way, they follow dominant-group expectations in language, values, social expectations, and customs regarding the world of work and in the educational process, but adhere to the cultural mandates of their ancestral culture in other aspects of daily life. In either case, the quid pro quo involved in mainstreaming exacts a price that those who seek to be mainstreamed must be willing to pay. Depending on the degree of compatibility between the culture and the values of the outsiders and of the dominant group, a certain amount of cultural loss is involved for the outsiders. However, it is assumed that the cultural, economic, social, and political gains achieved by being mainstreamed more than adequately compensate for cultural loss. In fact, being mainstreamed is a sine qua non for upward mobility, for social acceptance by the dominant group and members of the influence establishment of the outsider group. It is the key to access, privilege, and highly prized rewards of the total society.

In the case of black Americans as outsiders, the process of mainstreaming is continuous and has a long but episodic history. This situation reflects the fact that black Americans have remained a minority group longer than any other group in the United States except the indigenous Native American population. A brief examination of that historical experience is instructive with respect to current efforts to incorporate blacks into the American mainstream.

Mainstreaming during the Reconstruction Era

The importance of higher education as a mechanism for mainstreaming blacks was recognized several years before the Civil War began. Law excluded blacks who sought a college or university education in the southern portions of the United States, and blacks were restricted by social custom in all other sections of the country. Occasionally, a few institutions, such as Berea College and Oberlin College in Ohio, admitted blacks on a selective basis. Before the Civil War began and ended, two black colleges were established to Christianize blacks and to provide them with an education in the liberal arts. These were Wilberforce University in Ohio and Lincoln University in Pennsylvania.[2] Between 1854 and 1952, some 123 colleges were established to serve black students who did not have access to "white institutions" because of de jure and de facto discrimination.

As the Civil War was drawing to a close, and as Reconstruction began, attention was given to the responsibility of the federal government to provide educational programs for the newly emancipated blacks. That responsibility was implicit in President Lincoln's Emancipation Proclamation of September 22, 1862; the passage of the Fourteenth Amendment, which in 1868 assured "due process"; and the Fifteenth Amendment, which in 1870 extended the franchise to black males. The federal government's role in accelerating access to education for blacks was made even more explicit in 1865 with the establishment of the Freedman's Bureau. This agency used its authority to found Howard University in 1867 as the only federally sponsored college or university for black Americans in the United States.[3]

Federal intervention in efforts to ensure the expansion of educational, economic, social, and political opportunities for the newly emancipated black Americans was enhanced by the enactment of Civil Rights Bills in 1866 (passed by Congress over President Andrew Johnson's veto), by the Civil Rights Bill of 1875, and by the radical reconstruction program, in general, that Thaddeus Stevens constructed. As a result, blacks entered grade school and secondary education programs at a comparatively rapid pace, while Howard University became one of an increasingly large number of colleges established for black students in a continually segregated society.

Almost all the black colleges founded during Reconstruction (1865–1877) were established by or with the assistance of northern white philanthropists who committed themselves to the educational advancement of 4 million newly freed slaves and about one-half million free blacks classified as "free men of color" before the Civil War. Many of these philanthropists were affiliated with religious bodies that were also instrumental in the founding of black colleges. Among such religious organizations and missionary groups were the American Missionary Association, the Congregational church, Baptists, Methodists, and Presbyterians. Hence, the majority of the earliest black colleges were private institutions founded either by blacks or by and with the assistance of white citizens.

Among the earlier private black colleges were Fisk University (Tennesee, 1866), Morehouse College (Georgia, 1867), Talladega College (Alabama, 1867), Atlanta University (Georgia, 1867), and Hampton Institute (Virginia, 1864).[4] According to Frank Bowles and Frank A. DeCosta, 16 of the 34 historically black public colleges now in existence were established between 1866 and 1890. Only Cheyney State College (1837) in Pennsylvania was founded before the Civil War.[5] All but two of these institutions, however, were listed as normal or industrial schools and did not confer bachelor degrees. Four of them were affiliated with a religious body and came under public control after 1890. The two public institutions permitted to offer a college degree did not confer their first degrees until 1884 and 1895.[6]

Seventeen public black colleges now in existence were established under the so-called second Morrill Act of August 30, 1890. This act paved the way for the development of legally separated black and white land-grant public institutions in various states. As a result, within a nine-year period between 1890 and 1899, one land-grant college for black students was either established or planned in each of the 17 southern and border states.[7] They were separate, unequal, and, for the most part, could not award baccalaureate degrees at that time. The legacy of industrial, mechanical, and agricultural education, often associated with publicly supported historically black colleges, can be traced to this period. Liberal arts education was presumed by many to be the domain of the private institutions for black college students. Importantly, despite the predominance of normal schools and elementary and secondary programs at institutions called colleges, between 1865 and 1895 more than 1100 black Americans received college degrees.[8] Hence, black institutions of higher education were in the forefront of efforts to bring black Americans into the mainstream of American life. Their first graduates, like many of those who followed, were the vanguard of leadership in the segregated black community at the turn of the twentieth century.

Dual systems of education for black and white Americans were stimulated by the 1896 U.S. Supreme Court decision *Plessy* v. *Ferguson*. This case clearly established the principle of separate-but-equal regarding all aspects of American life. Under this decision, states were not compelled to construct even the rudimentary components of an integrated and desegregated society. In fact, they were permitted to rigidify segregated structures, since they had only to satisfy the mandate of establishing separate facilities that could be labeled equal. Suffice it to say, such facilities were indeed separate but never equal. White privilege prevailed in every aspect of American life and notably in higher education. The proliferation of both private and public colleges for black students was a reaction to the stark reality that excluded indigenous black Americans from the rights enjoyed by all other citizens of the United States and by European foreigners who desired to attend American colleges and universities.

The advent of *Plessy* v. *Ferguson* was certainly signaled by the Compromise of 1877, followed by the withdrawal of federal troops from the South and the reestablishment of "home rule," and state actions to circumvent the Civil Rights Bill of 1875. Nevertheless, the successes of the black colleges during Reconstruction were the first systematic attempts to assure the mainstreaming of a very select group of black Americans.[9]

The DuBois–Washington Controversy

Ideological and philosophical differences among black Americans over what were assumed to be appropriate strategies for mainstreaming surfaced in the DuBois–Washington controversy. Booker T. Washington, educated at Hampton Institute and eminent president of Tuskegee Institute in Alabama, had become the most widely known and influential black American in the United States by 1895. Thus, the entire nation listened with special attention when in 1895 at the Atlanta Exposition he gave his famous "Let down your buckets where you are" address. In this speech, Washington pointedly advocated racial separation; the cultivation of friendship with white southerners; and industrial, agricultural, and practical education. As John Hope Franklin points out in *From Slavery to Freedom,* this speech pleased especially Southern whites who were suspicious and distressed over the classical education advocated for blacks by various northern white persons and groups.[10] It also pleased accommodationists among the northern white leadership undisturbed by new social boundaries between the races. Clearly, Booker T. Washington saw industrial education not as a means of propelling blacks into the mainstream of the total American society but as a mechanism through which some could be of special service to the growing black communities around the nation. Washington, then, became an apostle of accommodation and separation. W. E. B. DuBois, on the other hand, was cut from an entirely different intellectual frame. Born in Massachusetts, educated at Fisk, Harvard, and Berlin, he envisioned a qualitatively different future for American blacks. In 1903 he published one of his several important books, *The Souls of Black Folk.* In one of the essays in this book, entitled "On Mr. Booker T. Washington and Others," DuBois leveled severe criticisms at Washington's "Tuskegee machine," Washington's own role in which he viewed as that of an apostle for injustice to black people, his disregard of the debilitating consequences of the caste structure in American society, and his relegation of higher training for the brighter minds among black youth to a level of impracticality and secondary importance. DuBois advocated training what he called a "talented tenth" of black intellectuals who could not only assume positions of academic and professional responsibility but who could provide sufficient leadership for rescuing blacks from the pitfalls of racial segregation and discrimination. This "talented tenth" could organize blacks to attack racial injustice as well as the devastating impediments that the caste system imposed on any effort to mainstream black Americans.[11]

These were two diverse approaches to mainstreaming; one centripetal, the other centrifugal. One advocated turning inward toward the black population while accommodating the harsh realities of an openly segregated and overtly discriminating society. The other admonished blacks to recognize their twoness of being black and American and prepare to claim those rights and privileges assured and safeguarded under the Constitution of the United States. It is in DuBois that the idea of preparing black Americans for occupational roles and leadership positions in the American society as a whole takes form. Blacks nurtured and developed this idea in parallel institutions of a segregated society even as laws, social customs, and categorical discrimination prevented them from open access to the institutional fabric of American society.

Black Professional Schools and Mainstreaming

Between 1896 and 1954, black professional schools assumed the responsibility of providing professional education for black Americans. Once again, their role in this endeavor was imperative, since blacks could not receive professional training at most historically white institutions in the country. Obviously there were major exceptions, exclusively in the North, since some black students received graduate and professional training from institutions such as Harvard, the University of Wisconsin, and Yale.

In the early part of this period, especially at the turn of the century, a half dozen medical schools were established at historically black institutions. While they existed, they trained almost all black physicians, dentists, nurses, pharmacists, and other health-care professionals. The implementation of *Plessy* v. *Ferguson's* mandate for separate-but-equal assured re-segregation, pernicious discrimination, and racial isolation in higher education. Philanthropic contributions declined during the first two decades of the twentieth century. Consequently, such instititions as Shaw University in North Carolina and Virginia Union University, both church-dominated, were compelled to discontinue their professional schools in medicine and law.[12] Negative recommendations from the Flexner Commission resulted in the demise of others. By 1915, Meharry Medical College (Tennessee) and Howard University in the District of Columbia remained as the two historically black professional schools that offered medical and dental degrees. These institutions provided excellent training in the health professions and scientific fields for black students. Attestation to this fact is evident in the observation that for a better part of this century, a distinct majority of blacks in positions of significance in medical and dental fields, either as practitioners in all-black or predominantly white settings, in all parts of the nation, received their medical and dental school training at one of these institutions. More than 80% of all black physicians and dentists up until 1968 were graduates of these two institutions.

Inasmuch as no historically black college offered a doctoral degree or very much of a graduate education program in general before 1954, blacks who lived in the South were forced to travel North or West for this training. Similarly, black residents of northern states confronted quota systems that seriously restricted the number of blacks who could be admitted at any given time. This limitation helps explain the paucity of blacks who received doctoral degrees, as well as other professional degrees, before 1970. For example, only 57 doctorates were conferred on black Americans between 1930 and 1939.[13]

Legal Attacks on "Separate but Equal"

The underrepresentation of blacks in the professions not only meant the inability of blacks to take advantage of whatever opportunities for professional roles opened to them in unsegregated situations, it also meant that they could not possibly meet the needs of a segregated black community.

As more and more black lawyers were trained, however, sufficient legal resources were mounted for attacks against de jure segregation in higher education. The legal route was arduous, time-consuming, and laden with psychological stress for plaintiffs involved in each suit filed before local, district, appeals, and Supreme Court. In the forefront of this attack against racial injustice and in an effort to assume equality of opportunity for black Americans were the National Association for the Advancement of Colored People (NAACP) and the NAACP Legal Defense and Educational Fund (hereafter referred to as the LDF). The NAACP had already attacked discrimination in housing and in the political arena with notable success, before the initiation of its work during the mid 1930s on graduate and professional education. Individuals had also sued for access to professional education as early as 1933 when Thomas Hocutt unsuccessfully sued officials of the University of North Carolina for entrance into that institution's School of Pharmacy. The technicality that led to the dismissal of his case against the University was his inability to establish "eligibility."[14]

U.S. Supreme Court Cases

Given the de jure restrictions against admission of black students to graduate and professional schools in the 17 southern and border states, as well as only token inclusion in northern institutions, it is not without significance that the NAACP and the LDF directed primary and initial attention to discrimination in public institutions. To combat the assault against "separate and unequal," it should be noted, several of the 17 states responded, first, by constructing "separate but equal" professional schools for black students, and, second, by establishing out-of-state tuition grants for black students. Both measures were calculated to circumvent efforts by blacks to gain admission to historically white public institutions. By 1933, black college graduates increasingly demanded access to professional school education. During that same year, some 97% of the approximately 38,000 black students enrolled in colleges were studying at historically black institutions.[15]

Between 1935 and 1954, five Supreme Court cases that addressed the problem of equality of educational opportunity for black Americans received national attention and illustrate the issues raised by the LDF. These five cases were *University of Maryland* v. *Murray,*165 Md. 478 (1935); *Missouri ex rel Gaines* v. *Canada* (1938); *Sipuel* v. *Board of Regents of the University of Oklahoma* (1948); *Sweatt* v. *Painter* (Texas, 1950); and *McLauren* v. *Oklahoma Regents* (1950). All these cases were a prelude to *Brown* v. *Board of Education of Topeka, Kansas* (1954). Yet each is significant for special reasons, and all are important for their collective attack against categorical discrimination in graduate and professional schools.

The *Murray* case in Maryland attacked both the principle of "separate but equal" and the policy of out-of-state tuition grants to black students as a means of excluding them from the publicly supported professional schools within the state of their residence purely because of their race. Murray had applied to the School of Law at the University of Maryland but was offered out-of-state tuition to a law school of his choice in another state. He refused; ultimately his case reached the U.S. Supreme Court where the court ruled in his behalf. The Court stated that, since no separate School of Law was established for blacks in Maryland, and because attending a law school other than in Murray's home state of Maryland would result in undue hardship on him, the University of Maryland was compelled to admit him to its School of Law.

Similarly, the University of Oklahoma was ordered to enroll Ada Lois Sipuel in its law school. The state also was told to desist in compelling its black students who desired graduate and professional education to accept out-of-state tuition grants in lieu of admission to a state-supported graduate or professional school.

Perhaps the most significant aspect of the *Gaines* case in Missouri was the success realized by the LDF in establishing the doctrine that separate-but-equal could not fully satisfy the demands of dual protection; that only actual *identity* of facilities and shared use of the *same* public institutions would suffice.[16] A hurriedly constructed law school at all-black Lincoln University was not equal. As a result of this case, the U.S. Supreme Court once again voided out-of-state tuition grants as a mechanism for excluding blacks from all-white law schools. Although the state was compelled to admit Lloyd Gaines to the University of Missouri School of Law, he disappeared before he was formally admitted and was never heard from thereafter.[17]

The attack on separate facilities achieved a new significance and added momentum in the *Sweatt* case in Texas. Heman Sweatt applied for admission to the all-white University of Texas School of Law and was denied. Instead, he was expected to attend the makeshift law school that the state of Texas had established for black students under the auspices of all-black Texas Southern University. He sued, and when his case reached the U.S. Supreme Court, the Court agreed that these makeshift facilities were indeed unequal and absolutely unacceptable. Therefore, the University of Texas was ordered to admit Mr. Sweatt to its law school. However, the fundamental question underlying the *Plessy* v. *Ferguson* decision was not addressed: Are state mandated, racially separate educational facilities and programs *inherently* unequal?

That question was not resolved to any degree of satisfaction even when the University of Oklahoma admitted George McLauren to its doctoral program in education. The university had subjected him to demeaning segregated facilities *within* the institution; however, the U.S. Supreme Court ordered the university to desist in these practices. In so doing, the Court articulated the principle that when black students are admitted to a traditionally all-white institution, the right to equal and fair treatment within these institutions must not be violated. Blatant resegregation of students *within* desegregated institutions was intolerable.

These five cases brought national attention to state and institutional behavior that collectively impeded efforts by black students to enter the mainstream of educational opportunity, as well as to the legal successes of the LDF in attacking institutional discrimination. Nevertheless, forcing the LDF to file state-by-state suits time and time again seemed to have been the strategy of resistance to desegregation and for the preservation of the policy of "whites only" at the major public graduate and professional schools. As a result, the practice of out-of-state tuition grants continued in several states not previously subject to litigation.

In some states, trepidation arose over the litigation successes of the LDF—a concern heightened by every new evidence that the Supreme Court was becoming impatient with each state's calculated resistance to equal educational opportunities for black residents. Nine years before the famous *Brown* decision, the conference of Deans of Southern Graduate Schools concluded in one of its studies that the black Americans' demand for equal educational opportunities within their own home state was exceptionally strong and that positive response was imperative. The conference suggested the construction of "regional" graduate and professional schools for black students in which each state would contribute its share to cover operational, management, and educational costs of these institutions. Again, this was a strategy to prevent blacks from entering the all-white state-supported institutions within the 17 southern and border states. The conference report was issued in 1945, and by 1947 this idea was widely accepted by the white educational leadership but had garnered little support from black Americans.[18] Inasmuch as the Supreme Court decisions in *Murray, Sipuel, Sweatt, Gaines,* and *McLauren* during this period were favorable to blacks, there seemed to be no need to think seriously about regional schools for blacks. They did not need to embrace a diversion from the ultimate goal of a fully integrated society.

On May 17, 1954, the U.S. Supreme Court ruled in the case of *Brown* v. *Board of Education of Topeka, Kansas,* that the principle of "separate but equal" was unconstitutional. The Court pointed to injustices inherent in racial separation in public institutions and in 1955 ordered the various jurisdictions to embark on desgregation in education "with all deliberate speed." The relentless pressure by the NAACP and the LDF had finally paid off, since that greatly needed sweeping decision against the "separate but equal" principle had been won. Now the problem was implementation. What was meant by "all deliberate speed?" By its reluctance to provide more specific implementation guidelines for its unanimous decision in the *Brown* case, the Supreme Court left the doors of resistance open. Philosophies of "nullification" and "gradualism," among others, followed. Nevertheless, a few blacks enrolled in graduate schools of the 17 southern and border states immediately affected by the decision. Their representation in the all-white professional schools of these States was minuscule, however, and tokenism in its worst form.

Although no state-controlled medical schools were established by the southern states for black students before this decision, this was not the case regarding law schools. Faculties or schools of law had been established at all-black Texas Southern University, Southern University (Louisiana), North Carolina Central University, Florida A & M College, and at South Carolina State Agricultural and Mechanical College.[19] Black students continued to be excluded from the all-white pharmacy, optometry, veterinary medicine, social work, architecture, and other professional schools. These exclusionary policies were the major factor in the underrepresentation of blacks in the high-status professions.

In order fully to comprehend the mounting demand for inclusion and mainstreaming of black Americans since the late 1960s, the issue of "underrepresentation" must be addressed. The basis for determining both representativeness and underrepresentation in enrollment is the proportion of blacks in a state's population. Therefore, in this view, blacks are not adequately represented in a graduate or professional school until their enrollment approximates their proportion in the state's population. There is, of course, a controversy over parameters of "underrepresentation" and "representation." In fact, other measures may be utilized.

Representation is inextricably related to all the processes that influence access, as well as to efforts to meet a compelling social need. The latter is tied to proportionality. Hence, the issue is not simply a question of the available pool of blacks, which usually implies those who have completed a baccalaureate degree with certain majors. Strict reliance on this factor is frequently a rationalization for inaction. It is a justification for doing so little to recruit more black students at college and precollege levels. It is a position that underscores a compelling urgency to train a sufficient number of black students at every level of education and to eliminate all social, economic, political, and institutional barriers to access so that black students can be admitted with the same regularity and expectations of accomplishments as other students admitted to graduate and professional schools. Hence, underrepresentation is a reflection of horrendous political, economic, academic, and institutional behavioral barriers that continually exclude black students from equal access to graduate and professional schools.

Although some of these barriers are discussed in greater detail in a following section, the point should be reiterated here that the barriers of economic deprivation, racism, and particularly racist admissions policies helped foment the accelerating demand for social change witnessed during the 1960s and 1970s. Unquestionably, the collective force of such barriers explain the underrepresentation of blacks in the major professions.

Previous studies on this subject are instructive at this point. For instance, Dietrich C. Reitses reported that the proportion of blacks in medical schools remained at about 2.5% of total enrollment for the decade, 1947–1956. In 1947–1948, the 588 black medical school students in U.S. medical schools constituted only 2.59% of total enrollment in all U.S. medical colleges. Of that number, all but 93 were enrolled at either Meharry or Howard University medical colleges.[20] At the same time, Sorenson pointed out that at least 26 medical schools officially excluded blacks from admission.[21]

There was a 24% decline in the proportion of black students enrolled at predominatly white medical schools between 1955 and 1962. Up to 1969, black student enrollment in U.S. medical schools never exceeded 2.8% of total enrollment in all U.S. medical schools, and the overwhelming majority of those students continued to be enrolled at the two historically black medical colleges. By 1969, however, the proportion of blacks in first-year medical school classes had reached 4.2% in that category.[22]

In the field of law, black students constituted a mere 2% of the 65,000 law students enrolled in ABA approved schools of law in 1964—a decade after the historical *Brown* decision. Black student enrollment in graduate schools and in such professional degree programs as architecture, engineering, pharmacy, and optometry was 1% or less in 1964. Graduate and professional school educational opportunities for black students were literally a sham. Admissions policies and practices were antithetical to the spirit of the *Brown* decision.

Impact of the Civil Rights Movement

The civil rights movement of the 1960s was undoubtedly the most significant social protest movement for racial justice; for social, political, and economic equality; and for change in the pattern of race relations that this country has ever known. Consequently, special attention is given to the role of students in stimulating social and educational change, the impact of federal government policies and civil rights legislation, and external factors that influenced the major educational institutions to respond in positive ways to the pressures and demands for change.

Before the first publicized sit-ins staged by college students at a luncheon counter in Greensboro, North Carolina, the wall of racial segregation in higher education had already been cracked by court-ordered admission of a few black students to professional schools in a handful of southern states. Similarly, a few all-white universities had permitted black undergraduates to enroll. For instance, the University of North Carolina admitted a black student for the first time in its 162-year history in 1951. The University of Tennessee followed a year later with its first black student. Under court pressure, the University of Alabama admitted its first black student, Autherine Lucy, in 1956 but suspended her 4 days later following a campus riot and finally expelled her on February 29, 1956.[23] These were responses to external pressure and political forces rather than an expression of positive institutional behavior.

The first sit-ins were a demand for social rights and privileges, such as eating without discrimination at lunch counters or swimming in the same pools as those used by the white population. The Student Nonviolent Coordinating Committee (SNCC), formed at Shaw University as an interracial body in 1960, took the leadership in organizing this aspect of the civil rights movement. But, the objectives of the SNCC-sponsored sit-ins changed over the course of the decade. So did the fundamental aspirations of black students in general change, whether the students were located on campuses of historically black institutions or historically white colleges.

For example, in 1962 demonstrators at the University of Chicago charged that university with operating 100 segregated apartment houses. During the same year, the federal government had to deploy federal troops to the University of Mississippi to safeguard James Meredith, who had enrolled in the School of Law under a court order. The governor of Mississippi, Ross R. Barnett, in defying the federal government, stated, "There is no case in history where the Caucasian race has survived social integration."[24]

This fear of social integration connoted the racism involved in resistance to equality of access to higher education. Black students, however, showed as much concern about overall quality of life on black college campuses as they did about gaining access to the historically all-white professional schools.

The shift toward concerns other than opposition to segregated housing and the ability to drink at the same water fountains or eat at the same lunch counters as whites was first observed on campuses of black colleges and universities in 1968. During that year, black students either demonstrated or seized buildings and hostages at such predominantly black institutions as Alcorn A & M College in Mississippi, Cheyney State College in Pennsylvania, Tuskegee Institute in Alabama, and Bowie State College in Maryland. Their demands included campus reforms and a black-oriented curriculum.[25]

These demonstrations, political and social statements as they were, provided models for similar activities at such predominantly white institutions as San Francisco State College, Boston University, Northwestern University, Trinity College, Columbia University, Brandeis University, University of California/Berkeley, Cornell University, and Queens College — all of which were struck by major student revolts during 1968 and 1969. By this time, the impetus for student sit-ins had assumed a character altogether different from their thrust in 1960. The students of 1968 and 1969 demanded courses in Afro-American Studies, the establishment of black Student Unions, changes in admissions policies concerning the use of standardized tests, the recruitment of more black students, and the hiring of more black faculty on predominantly white college campuses. In effect, not only did these students demand curriculum reforms but significantly greater access to diverse programs of study than those in which many black students traditionally enrolled. As Harry Edwards points out, these students sought "freedom . . . educational opportunity," and it did not matter whether it was gained through integration or through separation within the institutions."[26]

But the students seemed ambivalent about "mainstreaming." A part of them cried out for the educational skills needed to be competitive in the larger society, and a part of them insisted on a curriculum that would help them be more effective in serving the black community. And some of them observed that the same kind and quality of training that would make them more effective in the black community were precisely the things required for wider participation in the mainstream of American society. Albeit, student pressures from inside the universities and colleges were also instrumental in extracting positive responses from institutions to increase the presence and participation of black students in graduate and professional schools. Their movement helped transform the racial composition of colleges and universities throughout the nation.

The Civil Rights Act of 1964, which many claim the U.S. Congress enacted as a final tribute to the late President John F. Kennedy, contained the legal basis for "affirmative action" in higher education. Other legal justifications were based in Executive Orders issued by President Lyndon Johnson and requirements for federal contracts mandated by the U.S. Department of Labor and Equal Employment Opportunity Commission (EEOC). Its Title VII challenged the constitutionality of many requirements for access to jobs and admissions policies then in effect in various institutional structures. Title VII provided the statutory prohibition against discrimination in admissions on the basis of race, religion, or creed. The power of the federal government to cut off funds to educational systems not in compliance with federal policy regarding desegregation was provided by the Elementary and Secondary Education Act of 1965. The Equal Employment Opportunity Commission began to issue various guidelines for conformance to federal statutes and brought pressure to bear on educational institutions to expand educational opportunity to blacks and other disadvantaged minorities. Clearly, some faculty members and administrators demonstrated a commitment to the democratization of graduate and professional education. Consequently, they helped to reformulate recruitment and admissions policies that would lead to changes in the racial composition of many institutions in all parts of the nation.

As succeeding chapters amplify, the private sector has been influential in efforts to increase the presence of black students in graduate and professional schools since the mid-1960s. Major corporations, responding to pressures from the federal government to hire more blacks, realized that the paucity of blacks in such fields as engineering and architecture could be relieved only by dramatic changes in the rate of participation of black students in academic programs that prepared them for occupational roles in the corporate structure. Groups like the Association of American Medical Colleges, the Association of American Law Schools, and the Council on Social Work Education, among others, enunciated policies that demonstrated a firm commitment to *include* blacks rather than drive them away from these professions.

Career Choices of Black Students

The success of the efforts of groups such as those mentioned in the previous section was and continues to be determined in part by the shifting career choices of black students as a greater array of options becomes available to them. The black population, regardless of social class, has always stressed education as the primary avenue to upward mobility. The black middle class, particularly, has consistently given high priority to the acquisition of postsecondary education not only for its economic benefits, but for its social rewards in terms of status, prestige, and presumed cultural attainment. As long as de jure segregation was supported and as long as de facto segregation and systematized patterns of discrimination persisted, the skills obtained through postsecondary and professional education largely served a black population in a segregated racial community. The primary career open to black college graduates was teaching. A selected few could enter medicine and dentistry; fewer entered law because the opportunities for practicing that profession were seriously wanting. Entry into such professional fields as optometry, pharmacy, and veterinary medicine is a relatively recent phenomenon compared to entry into the teaching profession. But orientation to social welfare services is of long standing.

Career choices made by black Americans, therefore, reflect their historical experiences with racial isolation and oppression, exclusionary policies of higher education, economic deprivation, and discouragement from considering the possibilities of other options. Given these conditions, the black community was limited in the variety of professional role models that it could provide to black youth. Because of the proportionately higher number of educated blacks who lived in this closed community, however, it is important to observe that the segregated southern black communities had a far greater number of highly visible role models than did black communities outside the South. Nevertheless, even before 1954, when desegregation was constitutionally sanctioned, innumerable poor, working-class black fathers and mothers impressed on their children the importance of "being better educated than they were," of "making something out of yourselves," in order to obtain higher-status jobs, a significantly improved economic condition, and more effective means of coping with racial injustice and discrimination.

Shifts in career choices of black students began in the late 1950s and have continued to the present time. As previously indicated, before the 1950s, black college students focused almost exclusively on teaching and social service as career choices. With the implementation of desegregation, black students were exposed to considerably more information about career possibilities. They encountered counselors who had the information to impart and who could advise them on how to obtain financial resources when needed. They were in contact with academic advisers who could suggest courses appropriate for their new career objectives. They also benefited from social encounters with peers interested in a full range of career possibilities that black students dared not dream about before desegregation. Their level of aspiration rose appreciably in this context. Consequently, distribution patterns in career choices began to change.

Studies by such researchers as Robert L. Crain and Patricia Gurin and Edgar Epps substantiate the thesis of shifts in career patterns consequent to desegregation. Crain observed that black students in a desegregated school setting increased their level of aspiration for a variety of careers far beyond the level of aspiration for careers demonstrated by black students in predominantly black institutions.[27] In a survey of 535 black college seniors from six institutions in 1964 and 536 black college seniors in 1970, Gurin and Epps found a continuing commitment to the professions but notable shifts in career aspirations. For instance, the proportion of black males and females who in 1964 aspired to be physicians declined by 50% in 1970 (i.e., from 8% to 4% and from 2% to 1%, respectively). The proportion of men who aspired to be public school teachers dropped from 22% of the total in 1964 to 13% in 1970. In contrast, the proportion of black college seniors who aspired to be accountants doubled among men and tripled among women.[28] Similarly, increasing numbers of black college seniors aspired to be lawyers, engineers, architects, and public advisers, and to acquire other kinds of professional careers.

From the late 1960s and onward the career choices of black college students, as well as black high school students, were undoubtedly influenced by environmental cues over and beyond those found in the immediate family or school situation. Information obtained from printed and electronic media provided secondary role models and subtle cues, if not subliminal suggestions about career possibilities. The United Negro College Fund's advertising campaign showed black students in a variety of settings; commercials from oil companies, engineering and computer firms, and business and industry in general began to depict blacks in diverse occupational roles. Some commercial television programs utilized black actors in what was for the industry "nontraditional" occupational characterizations. Hence, some blacks were physicians, dentists, nurses, lawyers, as well as athletes. All these factors contributed heavily to the changing career choices of black students. While they may help explain the entry of a greater number of blacks into diverse professional programs, they do not explain the continuing dominance of education as a major among black recipients of the doctoral degree. That choice is apparently explained by other factors. This exception notwithstanding, the evidence shows that black students entered into more diverse professional fields in the late 1960s and 1970s than at any time in their history. They did so despite their continuing condition of economic deprivation, discrimination, and suspicious institutional behavior.

Economic Barriers to Higher Education

The five economic barriers to higher education are (1) high rates of unemployment; (2) inadequate income to support students in higher education programs; (3) low occupational status; (4) limited access to scholarships and fellowships; and (5) fear of excessive indebtedness resulting from loan programs. Specific attention is given in this section to the first three barriers; the remaining two, which are more specifically student related, are discussed in subsequent chapters.

For more than 30 years, the unemployment rate among black Americans has been consistently about twice that of the white population. As indicated in Table 1, the unemployment rate among white Americans was 4.9% in 1950 but 9.0% for blacks and other races. In 1954 white unemployment rose to 5.0% while the rate for blacks went to 9.9% or a black to white ratio of 2:1. That ratio remained at 2:1 or higher for every year thereafter, except for a few years in the 1970s when it dipped to 1.8:1 among known job seekers. When the number of discouraged workers is added to this figure, however, the ratio climbs far beyond 2:1. In addition, black teenagers are three times more likely to be unemployed than white teenagers; consequently, they cannot save as much to support a college education. In 1984, one of every five black workers was unemployed.

Unemployment inevitably means low income, and this situation indicates that impoverished people, who barely have sufficient income to meet daily basic and survival needs, will have little or no funds to support a college or professional education. As shown in Table 2, black families are paid less than 60% of the income paid to white families in the United States. Only in 1969 did the median family income of black families exceed more than 60% and black families are receiving proportionately less income today than they did a decade ago. Even though the dollar income of blacks and whites is increasing, the gap between the median income of whites and blacks is also widening at an alarming rate (see Table 3).

Low income and unequal income reflect low occupational positions held by black Americans compared to positions held by whites, as well as the persistence of institutional racism in hiring practices. Although substantial improvements took place in the occupational position of black Americans between the 1950s and 1980s, blacks continue to be overrepresented in lower-status positions compared to white Americans. According to the most recent data released by the U.S. Department of Commerce, blacks constitute 18% of all service workers and 14% of all operators, fabricators, and laborers. Blacks make up 54% of all private household cleaners and servants; one-third of all the maids, housemen, and garbage collectors; and approximately one-fourth of all nurse's aides, orderlies, and attendants. At the upper level of the labor force, blacks are decidedly underrepresented. For example, blacks represent about 3% of all the "experienced physicians, lawyers, and engineers"; 4% of the nation's managers and administrators; and only 6% of the clergy, judges, and computer programmers.[29]

Table 1
Annual Average Unemployment Rates for Black and White Americans
Age 16 and Over, 1950–1980

Year	Unemployment Rate Black and Other Races	White	Ratio of Black and Other Races to White
1950	9.0%	4.9%	1:8
1951	5.3	2.1	1:7
1952	5.4	2.8	1:9
1953	4.5	2.7	1:7
1954	9.9	5.0	2:0
1955	8.7	3.9	2:2
1956	8.3	3.6	2:3
1957	7.9	3.8	2:1
1958	12.6	6.1	2:1
1959	10.7	4.8	2:2
1960	10.2	4.9	2:1
1961	12.4	6.0	2:1
1962	10.9	4.9	2:2
1963	10.8	5.0	2:2
1964	9.4	4.6	2:1
1965	8.1	4.1	2:0
1966	7.3	3.3	2:2
1967	7.4	3.4	2:2
1968	6.7	3.2	2:1
1969	6.4	3.1	2:1
1970	8.2	4.5	1:8
1971	9.9	5.4	1:8
1972	10.0	5.0	2:0
1973	8.9	4.3	2:1
1974	9.9	5.0	2:0
1975	13.9	7.8	1:8
1976	13.8	7.0	1:9
1977	13.1	6.8	1:9
1978	12.4	5.5	2:3
1979	11.5	5.6	2:1
1980	14.2	7.8	1:8
1981	15.6	6.7	2:3
1982	20.2	9.3	2:1
1983	20.6	8.7	2:3
1984[a]	14.6	6.0	2:4

Source: Adapted from Table 47 in *The Social and Economic Status of the Black Population in the United States: An Historical View, 1790–1978*, Current Population Reports, Special Studies Series P-23, No. 80; and Robert Hill, *The Illusion of Black Progress* (Washington, D.C.: National Urban League, 1979), p. 33; and ch. 2 in James E. Blackwell, *The Black Community: Diversity and Unity* (New York: Harper & Row, 1985).

[a]Seasonally adjusted for fourth-quarter rates.

Table 2

Distribution of Families by Race and Income, Selected Years, 1953–1983

Percentage of Families in Each Income Bracket, by Year and Race

Income	1953		1959		1964		1969		1974		1983	
	Black	White	Black	White	Black	White	Black	White	Black	White	Black	White
Under $1,500	16	7	14	4	8	3	5	2	4	2	—	—
$ 1,500– 2,999	16	7	19	6	13	5	10	3	10	3	—	—
$ 3,000– 4,999	23	11	19	10	20	9	15	7	17	7	21.7	7.7
$ 5,000– 6,999	18	16	16	12	18	10	15	8	14	8		*
$ 7,000– 9,999	16	26	17	23	18	18	19	14	16	14	10.8	12.8
$10,000–11,999	6	13	7	16	8	13	9	11	8	11		**
$12,000–14,999	9	3	5	12	7	15	12	16	11	15	15.2	12.9
$15,000 and over	2	11	4	19	8	28	17	40	19	42	42.8	66.7

Source: Adapted from Table 15 in The Social and Economic Status of the Black Population in the United States: An Historical View, 1970–1978, p. 32; and Bureau of Labor Statistics data, 1983.
* In 1983, income categories were collapsed so that the first figure includes income bracket $3,000—$6,999. The second figure includes $7,000—11,999.

Table 3
Black and White Median Family Income, Selected Years, 1953–1984

Year	Income Black (percentage of white income in parenthesis)	White
1953	4,547 (56)	8,110
1959	4,931 (52)	9,547
1964	5,921 (54)	10,903
1969	8,074 (61)	13,175
1974	7,808 (58)	13,356
1976	9,242 (59)	15,537
1979	11,650 (57)	20,520
1980	12,674 (57)	21,904
1982	12,353 (56.4)	21,902
1984	15,432 (56.0)	27,686

Source: Adapted from Table 19 in *The Social and Economic Status of the Black Population in the United States: An Historical View, 1790–1978*, p. 36; and data supplied by the Boston office of the U.S. Department of Commerce.

By contrast, white Americans constitute only 12.2% of all service workers; 35% of private household cleaners and services; 86% of all administrators and officials; 92.2% of all financial managers; about 90% of all engineers, computer specialists, physicians, lawyers, and dentists; and almost 90% of all registered nurses.[30]

Black males earn only two-thirds of the income received by white males when all occupations are combined. According to Robert Hill's analysis, black male professionals earn about 73% of the income received by white professionals, while black managers are paid 77% of the amount of income received by white managers. In contrast, black laborers are paid approximately 10% more than white laborers.[31] The fact that black females are currently achieving greater parity with white female workers in the same occupational areas does not obfuscate the reality that black workers, in general, are in lower-status occupations with lower incomes. This situation results in untoward economic disabilities that dramatize the need for greater financial assistance to black students who wish to enter college and graduate and professional schools. It is estimated that over three-quarters of all black students come from families whose median family income is less than $18,000 and 40% from homes where it is less than $12,000 at a time when the costs of graduate and professional education continue to climb out of the reach of lower-income families.[32]

The mainstreaming of outsiders is not solely dependent on the removal of economic barriers; it is also conditioned by the systematic removal of serious educational barriers to college, and graduate and professional school enrollment. For instance, increasing the available pool necessitates a major curtailment of the high school attrition rate and a substantial increase in the number of both college-going and college-completion rates among black students. Although significant progress has been accomplished even since 1970 with respect to the college-going and college-completion rates of black Americans, the available pool for graduate and professional school participants can be expanded. The issue may be framed by the following data: The median number of years of schooling is 12.2 for blacks and 12.6 for whites. As of 1982, among persons between the ages of 25 and 34, the percentage of black high school graduates climbed from 53.4% in 1970 to 79.3% in 1982. Among whites, these figures were 76.1% and 87.2% for 1970 and 1982, respectively. Within the same age cohort, 15.0% of blacks had attained one year or more of college training, compared to 31.2% for whites, in 1970. By 1982, more than one-third (35.8%) of blacks and amost half (46.2%) of whites had achieved this level of formal education. Within that 12-year period, the college completion rates of blacks more than doubled, from 6.1% in 1970 to 12.6% in 1982. By contrast, the college completion rates for whites rose from 16.6% in 1970 to 24.9% in 1982.[33]

Nevertheless, in 1985 demographers observed a disturbing trend in college-going rates among black high school graduates. Specifically, while the number of high school graduates among 16- to 24-year-old blacks reached unprecedented heights, the actual proportion of college-going blacks in this age cohort continued to decline. For instance, between 1976 and 1983, the proportion of black high school graduates entering college dropped from 34% to 27%. Significantly, the number of blacks graduating from high school in 1983 was about 500,000 more than in 1976. But 8000 fewer blacks entered college than did so in 1976.[34] Such losses obviously reduce the number of blacks eligible for graduate or professional school enrollment, even though the absolute number of blacks eligible for this level of formal education has climbed dramatically since 1970.

Yet, some 426,000 more blacks enrolled in college in 1975 than in 1970. By 1979–1980, the number of blacks enrolled in college exceeded 1.2 million, but by 1984, the absolute number of blacks in college was 996,000—but only 95% of colleges reported. The enrollment profile is complicated, however, by the relatively low persistence rate for black college students and by the approximately 50% of blacks matriculated in two-year community colleges, most of whom are in technical programs that restrict their eligibility to transfer to four-year colleges and universities. This low persistence rate explains why blacks constitute only 8 or 9% of all college seniors. Nevertheless, the steady rise in the college completion rates among blacks, from 4.0% in 1960 to 10.4% in 1984 (among persons age 25 and older) provides concrete evidence for the existence of an expanded pool of potential enrollees in graduate and professional schools.

The 1970s and 1980s

Many of the conditions previously described continued to affect the overall participation of black students in graduate and professional schools in the 1970s. Other social, political, and economic conditions have exacerbated efforts to stimulate increased enrollment and graduation rates among black students at these levels.

Three sets of litigation during the 1970s are important for clarifying the access issue but for entirely different reasons. These cases are *Adams* v. *Richardson, DeFunis* v. *Odegarrd,* and *Regents of the University of California* v. *Allan Bakke* case.

Adams v. *Richardson,* also known as *Adams* v. *Califano and Adams* v. *Bell,*[35] dates back to 1969 when a suit was filed with the assistance of the LDF against the Office of Civil Rights and the Department of Health, Education, and Welfare for not enforcing those provisions of Title VI of the Civil Rights Act of 1964 applicable to dual systems of higher education. Nine southern states and the State of Pennsylvania were charged with continually operating dual systems of higher education that effectively channeled black college students into predominantly or historically black colleges and white students into historically white institutions.

On June 12, 1973, the Department of Health, Education, and Welfare was ordered by Judge John Pratt of the U.S. District Court of the District of Columbia to terminate federal funds to those states that continued to violate the Civil Rights Act of 1964. The 10 states involved were Arkansas, Florida, Georgia, Louisiana, Maryland, Mississippi, North Carolina, Oklahoma, Pennsylvania, and Virginia. Collectively, these states became know as the "*Adams* states." (Tangentially, the ruling affected all 17 southern and border states in which a historically black college is located.) These states were required to submit plans for dismantling their dual systems and demonstrating substantial movement toward assuring equality of opportunity in access, distribution and retention of students, faculty, and administrators in state systems. For most of the 1970s, because of various legal challenges, the focus of attention was on 7 states: Arkansas, Florida, Georgia, Maryland, North Carolina, Oklahoma, and Virginia.

The desegregation plans submitted by these states were rigorously scrutinized by the LDF, the courts, the U.S. Department of Justice, and statewide coalitions that monitor desegregation progress in the various states. Two states, North Carolina and Maryland, have achieved a separate status since 1973, either because of agreements worked out with the Reagan administration (North Carolina) or because of a suit against the federal government (Maryland). Nevertheless, they are still under a federal court order to dismantle dual systems of higher education, an order that also mandates increases in black student enrollment at all levels of postsecondary education, and their progress is still monitored carefully. Extensions were granted to the remaining "first tier states" to complete the dismantling process by 1986. The unresolved questions focus on the degree to which these states and other affected states, which now include a total of 18 jurisdictions consequent to actions taken by the Carter administration, are complying with specific aspects of the court order pertaining to enrollment of black students in traditionally white institutions, the enrollment of white students in historically black institutions (HBIs), the enhancement of HBIs, the strengthening of the curricula at HBIs, the equitable distribution of academic programs in public colleges and universities, and the desegregation of faculty, executives, administrators, managers, and other staff in colleges and universities supported fully or in part from state funds. Advocates of this dismantling and equalizing process envision the enforcement of court orders in the *Adams* case as a powerful instrument for accelerating the pace of recruitment, enrollment, and graduation of blacks from publicly controlled institutions and their subsequent admission to graduate and professional schools.

Both the *DeFunis* and *Bakke* cases challenged the legitimacy of special programs designed to bring relief to black students through rectification of the consequences of past patterns of discrimination. Both cases arose in nonsouthern states and both raised questions about the utilization of subjective criteria, such as racial and ethnic designation, as opposed to the so-called neutral or objective criteria in admissions decisions. Both argued that the utilization of subjective criteria in ways that granted special favor to black applicants for admission to the professional school of law and medicine constituted what has come to be characterized as "reverse discrimination." The plaintiffs further challenged admissions quotas for minority students in general and "set aside" programs that guaranteed a specific number of seats to minority students. There did not appear to be any concern in these cases for rectification of past policies of categorical discrimination that excluded black students from graduate and professional school programs.

These two suits, *DeFunis* in Washington and *Bakke* in California, focused national attention on the myriad problems inherent in the assumption that objective or neutral criteria for college and professional school admission, such as MCAT, LSAT and GRE test scores, gradepoint averages, and rank in class, are free from bias and select only the most meritorious from among any group of students. The arguments heard in these cases, especially *Bakke,* illuminate the many instances of exceptionality regarding merit when these standards are applied to white students, as well as their abuses when applied to black and other minority students. This debate provided disturbing evidence that many persons had now taken the position that "blacks had had their chance," that "they should not get ahead at the expense of whites," and, that whatever commitment any number of individuals, organizations, and to some degree the federal government, had in the past to aggressive equal educational opportunity programs had all but dissipated. While the *Bakke* case was in litigation, between 1974 and 1978, institutions seemed to have been in a holding pattern. The question here is to what degree is this period characterized by changes in recruitment and enrollment patterns of black students in graduate and professional schools?

The decision reached by the Supreme Court in the *DeFunis* case did not resolve the issue, since by the time the case reached this Court, it was moot: DeFunis was already enrolled in law school. The decision reached in the *Bakke* case was significantly more far-reaching in its implications, and is discussed in Chapter 5.

In addition to allegations of reverse discrimination and challenges to special admissions and recruitment programs, the 1970s were characterized by fluctuations in financial aid and scholarship programs, the development of retention programs to influence educational outcomes, and escalating attacks on standardized tests that culminated in the enactment of a "truth in testing law" in New York State. The debate on the efficaciousness of coaching to raise test scores reached the U.S. Congress. Admonitions that retrogression was occurring in efforts to safeguard what limited access to graduate and professional schools blacks had experienced were sounded in all parts of the nation.

The same issues are of equal concern in the 1980s. In fact, because of the policies and practices of the Reagan administration, the devastating effects of the recession of 1981–1983 on the black community, and the continuing controversy over the injudicious uses of objective tests, some of the issues are of even greater importance for blacks in the 1980s than in previous decades. For instance, Reagan administration reductions in financial aid programs and the unsuccessful effort to eliminate completely the Graduate and Professional Opportunities Program (GPOP) in 1983 signal to blacks a high degree of insensitivity and indifference, among President Reagan and members of his administration, to the special needs of blacks, other minorities, and the working poor in general for financial assistance.

Further, the escalation of competency examinations, either for exit from high school or as a criterion for admission to certain college programs, has already reduced drastically the access of black students to higher education.

Clearly, the political climate has changed from the upheavals of the 1960s and the progressive orientation toward the resolution of social, economic, and political injustices that these upheavals spawned. A new conservatism has indeed appeared and misconceptions about access of black students to the detriment of white applicants are encouraged by both printed and electronic media. Our evidence in succeeding chapters demonstrates that, just as enrollment among black students increased during the 1970s, overall enrollment rose in significant leaps for American students as a whole. Succeeding chapters address these issues with greater depth and specificity.

In addressing the problems elaborated in this book, it must be stressed that all black and all minority students do not fall into the category of "underprepared, underfinanced and problem-inflicted" students. A significant percentage of these students is more than adequately prepared, often exceptionally well prepared for graduate and professional school programs regardless of the field of study. It is a tragic mistake to assume that blacks and other minority students represent a homogeneous type, and it is decidedly worse to treat them as if all required special, and all too frequently demeaning paternalistic, attention. These students simply want equality of opportunity, a fair and equal chance, respect for themselves as the individuals they are, the same quality of training offered to others, and unbiased evaluations of their performance.

Notes

1. Milton Gordon, *Assimilation in American Life* (New York: Oxford University Press, 1964).
2. James E. Blackwell, *The Black Community: Diversity and Unity* (New York: Harper & Row, 1985).
3. Lerone Bennett, *Before the Mayflower: A History of Black America* (Chicago: Johnson Publishing, 1969), pp. 400–403.
4. Ibid.
5. Frank Bowles and Frank A. DeCosta, *Between Two Worlds: A Profile of Negro Higher Education* (New York: McGraw-Hill, 1971), p. 32 and Appendix B-34.
6. Ibid.
7. Ibid.
8. Blackwell, *Black Community*, pp. 5–10.
9. John Hope Franklin, *From Slavery to Freedom* (New York: Alfred Knopf Co., 1952), pp. 385–387.
10. W. E. B. DuBois, *The Souls of Black Folk* (Chicago: 1903).
11. Op. Cit., p. 538

12. Commission on Human Resources, *Minority Groups Among United States Doctorate Level Scientists, Engineers and Scholars,* 1973 (Washington, D.C.: National Academy of Sciences, 1974).

13. John Hope Franklin, *From Slavery to Freedom,* p. 541.

14. Ibid., p. 538.

15. Richard Bardolph, *The Civil Rights Record* (New York: Thomas Y. Crowell, 1970), p. 271.

16. Ibid.

17. Op. Cit., p. 542.

18. Cf. Bennett, *Before the Mayflower,* p. 204. It is somewhat ironic that South Carolina had moved so deeply into rigid segregation, since its major all-white university had been desegregated during Reconstruction. In 1873, Richard T. Greener, the first black graduate of Harvard University, was named professor of metaphysics at the University of South Carolina—a university that then had a racially integrated student body and Board of Trustees. By the turn of the century, with the re-establishment of home rule and the advent of *Plessy v. Ferguson,* the nation once again experienced a triumph of white supremacy in all aspects of day-to-day living. The action of South Carolina, therefore, in establishing a makeshift law faculty for black students was characteristic of the time.

19. Dietrich C. Reitzes, *Negroes and Medicine* (Cambridge, Mass.: Harvard University Press, 1958).

20. A. A. Sorenson, "Black Americans and the Medical Profession, 1930–," *Journal of Negro Education* 41 (Fall 1972): 337–342.

21. Cf. James E. Blackwell, *Access of Black Students to Graduate and Professional Schools* (Atlanta: Southern Education Foundation, 1975), and James E. Blackwell, *The Participation of Blacks in Graduate and Professional Schools: An Assessment* (Atlanta: Southern Education Foundation, 1977).

22. Bennett, *Before the Mayflower,* pp. 420–423.

23. Ibid.

24. Harry Edwards, *Black Students* (New York: The Free Press, 1970).

25. Ibid.

26. Robert L. Crain, "School Integration and Occupational Achievement Among Negroes," *American Journal of Sociology* 75 (1970): 593–606.

27. Patricia Guren and Edgar Epps. *Black Consciousness. Identity and Achievement* (New York: Wiley, 1975), pp. 39–43.

28. *The Social and Economic Status of the Black Population in the United States: An Historical View,* 1790–1978 (Washington, D.C.: Department of Commerce, Bureau of the Census, Special Studies Series 23, No. 80, 1979), p. 218.

29. U.S. Department of Commerce, *America's Black Population: A Statistical View* (Washington, D.C.: Bureau of the Census, Special Publication PIO/POP–83–1, 1983), p. 11.

30. James E. Blackwell, *The Black Community: Diversity and Unity, 2d ed.* (New York: Harper & Row, 1985), Tables 2–1 and 2–2.

31. James E. Blackwell, "Social Factors Affecting Educational Opportunity for Minority Group Students," Chapter 1 in College Board, *Beyond Desegregation: Urgent Issues in the Education of Minorities* (New York: College Entrance Examination Board, 1978), pp. 1–12.

32. Income data.

33. U.S. Department of Commerce, *Population Profile of the United States: 1982* (Washington, D.C.: Bureau of the Census, Current Population Reports Special Studies Services 23, No. 130, 1983), p. 22.

34. Gaynelle Evans, "Social, Financial Barriers Blamed for Curbing Blacks' Access to College," *Chronicle of Higher Education,* August 7, 1985, p. 1.
35. In 1981 this suit was again renamed to become *Adams* v. *Bell;* thus it recognizes a new secretary of Education. Bell was secretary of the U.S. Department of Education during the first term of the Reagan administration.

2 METHODOLOGICAL ISSUES AND
REFERENCE POINTS

This study has two basic components. This first component is based on an analysis of exploratory survey data on 743 cases (i.e., professional schools) covering eight professional fields of study offered at one or more of 427 institutions in the United States. The eight professional fields are (1) dentistry; (2) engineering; (3) law; (4) medicine; (5) optometry; (6) pharmacy; (7) social work and; (8) veterinary medicine. The disparity between cases and numbers of institutions is attributed to the fact that some institutions offered multiple opportunities for professional education. The second component of the study is a trend analysis of first-year enrollment, total enrollment and graduation rates of black students from professional schools during the 1970s and 1980s. In fact, the time covered by both components of the study is 1970 through 1984. In addition to the eight professional fields included in the first component, the trend analysis also includes selected data on architectural education and the production of doctoral degrees by race. In both instances, comparative data, especially between blacks and whites, are presented.

Objectives of the Study

The principle objective of this study is to ascertain answers to the following questions:

1. What changes occurred between 1970 and 1985 in the access of black students to graduate and professional schools? Has access improved, remained static, or retrogressed?
2. To what extent were the observed changes influenced by such factors as special recruitment and special admissions programs, quality of financial aid and scholarships offered to black students, the number of black faculty in the professional school, the presence of a minority affairs officer, the presence of a retention program, the number of professional schools within the state, the proportion of blacks in the state population, the presence or absence of a black college in the state, whether or not the State is under litigation to dismantle a dual system of

higher education (i.e., the "*Adams* states"), the location of the institution, and the type of institution (e.g., private, public, or state-assisted).

3. What happened in the "*Adams* states" with regard to increasing access of black students to graduate and professional schools? Were the observed changes in access and production in those states different from patterns noted in other parts of the nation? If so, what factors appear to account for those differences?

4. To what degree can role-model theory be tested through an empirical analysis of recruitment, admissions, enrollment, and graduation rates at selected institutions?

5. What appear to be the major impediments to increasing equality of educational opportunity in graduate and professional schools? How can these problems be alleviated?

6. To what degree did the U.S. Supreme Court decisions in the *DeFunis* and *Bakke* cases have a "chilling effect" on the recruitment and enrollment of black students in graduate and professional schools?

7. How salient are such factors as institutional commitment and behavior, assistance from the private and corporate structures, and governmental intervention for facilitating matriculation of black students and their graduation from graduate and professional schools?

8. How can the responses to the above sets of questions instruct us as to what factors appear to be the most salient predictors of enrollment and graduation and what policies appear to be successful in fostering minority-student enrollment and graduation from graduate and professional schools? And, finally, what do responses to such questions as those raised above suggest as future courses of action in the 1980s and beyond for achieving the goal of equality of educational opportunity for all Americans?

A Theoretical Viewpoint

This research was not undertaken to garner support for a specific theoretical perspective. Nor was it intended to justify the overarching utility of a single-factor theoretical approach as opposed to employing several macrotheories to explain social phenomena. The relative strengths of both approaches are demonstrated in sociological literature.

A case can be made for approaching the experiences of black students in attempting to gain access to graduate and professional schools from either a functionalist or a Marxist–conflict theoretical perspective. Functionalist proponents would likely argue that changes in access of minority students to professional education occurred through a series of necessary evolutionary stages, beginning with a denial of opportunity to these students, toward a more advanced state of limited and imperfect access, and finally, if the system required it, the attainment of a mature stage of complete equality for black Americans. Since functionalists would probably perceive some form of discrimination as a functional imperative in order to make the social system work, it is doubtful whether blacks or any other racial minority would ever reach the final or mature stage of complete equality. In my view, this approach is not only static and supportive of the status quo, as so many of its critics have maintained, but it underestimates the potential influence of disruption in the social system generated by both internal and external forces in creating major changes in the educational sub-system.

Neo-Marxists and class-conflict theorists would undoubtedly conceptualize the problem strictly in terms of a struggle between classes. In this view, inequality of access may be perceived as evidence of the purposeful utilization of education as a means to solidify and rigidify class inequality. In this view, since black Americans are overrepresented in the lower income classes and since upward mobility for them proceeds at an intolerably slow pace in a racist society, the continued denial of equality of access to the educational opportunity structure assures a prolonged state of occupational servility and overall subordination to the dominant group. Although both models, functionalism and conflict theory, contain attractive elements, neither is as totally adequate nor sufficiently encompassing of the critical factors that explain inequality of access as is power theory![1]

Consequently, for purposes of this study, certain sociological concepts have a higher degree of salience in facilitating understanding of access as a process (e.g., *equalizing* educational opportunities between minorities and majorities). Of special importance are such concepts as structural inequality, norms, authority, power, and social status. As a personal choice, greater attention is given to the theoretical notions of power to explain the process of access and outcomes (e.g., enrollment through graduation from graduate and professional schools) than to other perspectives.

Chapter 1 cast efforts to propel black Americans into the mainstream of higher education in terms of legalistic attacks against discrimination that culminated in the civil rights movement of the late 1950s and of the 1960s. A central goal of that movement, which the student movement subsequently re-articulated, was to eliminate structural inequality and change institutional norms. Pressures for these changes in higher education arose from evidence that prevalent institutional policies resulted in discrimination against blacks and other minorities and did not promote democratic participation in decision-making processes. Hence, it was imperative for colleges, universities, and their graduate and professional schools to overhaul or transform substantially their racial composition and to revolutionize those methods of making decisions that impacted on the lives of matriculated students and on the very nature of the labor force itself. In this context, concepts such as "shared authority" and "participatory democracy" achieved widespread popularity.

These movements also sought to break through the demeaning stereotypes about black Americans and other minorities that were sufficiently prevalent in graduate and professional schools to influence decisions regarding the admissibility of these students. For example, one may conclude that some selection or admissions officers held stereotypes concerning the "educability"of black students or about presumed intellectual differences between blacks and whites. If those stereotypes were strongly believed, then decisions on admissions would reflect that belief system. Those officials were likely to consider only those blacks who were clearly superior to all candidates, for that was the only way that they could be regarded as "equal" to white candidates whose objective scores were at the lower end of admissions cutoff points. Assuming a certain ubiquity of these kinds of stereotypes as normative in educationl institutions, we need to focus also on institutional behavior regarding the access process.

Institutional behavior is an intervening variable of special significance for any theory advanced to explain the process involved in creating greater equality of educational opportunity. It is a multidimensional variable that embraces such components as commitment, authority, power, sanctions, and a concern for status and image within the network of institutions of higher education. Strong and positive institutional behavior regarding access of black students is indicated by forceful leadership, the allocation of resources to achieve articulated goals, and modifications in policies proven to be impediments to equality of opportunity.

The authority validating institutional behavior may be either centralized or decentralized. Centralized authority is likely to be more effective in inducing sustained change under certain circumstances. For example, it is a function of the degree of commitment of the decision makers in the hierarchy of authority to the primary goal and the willingness of that authority to invoke institutional sanctions against those units within the university that do not comply with mandates to recruit, admit, and enroll more black students.

It is also highly probable that certain decentralized units within the institutional community (e.g., a school, college, or department) may be considerably more inclined to take steps in the direction of educational change than are the leaders at the top of the authority structure. In such instances, it is necessary for them to have at least a tacit agreement that the top echelons of the leadership structure will not undermine or subvert their efforts to achieve this goal. Support or lack of support for this endeavor may be a function of the leaders' perceptions as to whether or not a significant change in the racial composition of the department, college, school, or university will alter their statuses or rankings within the network of educational institutions or in the eyes of the public.

Similarly, formal organizations and associations, such as accrediting bodies and coordinating functionaries, have a great deal of both manifest authority and power, as well as implied authority and latent power. Transformations in institutional behavior may be related to the kind of pressure brought to bear on institutions by related associations as well as by an even more external structure—the federal government. The former may use their influence, persuasive powers, and overall organizational support to encourage changes in institutional norms. Some are in a position to invoke sanctions to assure compliance, such as loss of accreditation or some forms of financial support that may be obtainable only though associational approbation.

In the case of the federal government, informal strategies of persuasion may be employed as a means of fostering greater equality of educational opportunity. Nevertheless, the federal government alone has at its disposal the ultimate weapon of power—a cutoff of all financial support from the government—against institutions whose behavior violates established governmental norms and policies. That action is, perhaps, its most obvious manifestation of power. But, power may take many forms and routes to social change. Just as the government has maximum power in certain critical areas, the power and authority of institutions and their units may also be quite broad regarding the processes of access and graduation from graduate and professional schools. Institutions may use their discretionary authority in the area of admissions as manifestations of their power either to *exclude* or *include* certain groups of students.

Power may be conceptualized as the ability to control decision-making processes regarding access to and distribution of social, educational, economic, and political rewards offered within a social system. In societies characterized by dominant and minority groups, that ability to control is vested primarily in the hands of the dominant group. Members of the dominant group, irrespective of social class and position in the social structure, regard themselves as more worthy and more entitled by virtue of their membership in the dominant group to a greater share of this control than are members of subordinate or outsider groups. Dominant-group members come to believe in their entitlements and actualize their claims over them. Consequently, they are not prepared to share their access to social rewards, economic gains, or opportunities in the educational and political subsystems without pressure.

Dominant-group elites, leaders and decision makers are in a unique position, since they have the power to deny outsiders sufficient access to scarce values that foster social, political, and economic equality, as well as educational parity with dominant-group members. They not only institutionalize their own standards of conduct as normative but they use their influence and authority to regulate normative behavior for members of the social system as a whole. A subordinate group is not entirely powerless, however, since it may possess one or more of those three sources of power described by Robert Bierstedt. These sources are (1) the size of the group; (2) the degree of social organization within a specific group; and (3) the group's resources.[2]

The size of a group is not a necessary precondition for gaining access to scarce resources or highly prized values. The quality of a group's social organization and it ability to capitalize on its own sense of social cohesion may be of far greater salience for changing power relations. Possessing resources alone is not adequate; it is the ability to mobilize successfully those resources—ultimately a manifestation of sophisticated social organization—that becomes paramount. As Hubert M. Blalock asserts, the resources are not only expressed in terms of money, status, and property but may be of one of two kinds—pressure or competitive resources. The pressure resources possessed by a group refer to its ability to use coercive techniques to exact rewards from another (i.e., a boycott in order to obtain jobs), whereas competitive resources are exemplified in the expertise needed by the dominant group.[3]

Just as dominant groups have control over opportunities to improve their members' conditions in the economic structure through provisions of better jobs, equal wages, and a reduction in unemployment, they also have control over decisions on admissions to graduate and professional schools. During the 1960s, blacks employed both pressure and competitive resources in order to transform the traditional admissions practices and alter institutional norms. Even though the ultimate responsibility for admissions decisions in graduate and professional schools remained in the hands of the dominant group, the pressure of blacks on admissions committees did result in positive changes. These outsiders discovered firsthand evidence of the ability of dominant-group decision makers to modify traditional admissions criteria and make "adjustments in objective assessments" for both purposes of selectivity and preferential treatment for members of the *dominant* group.

Whenever dominant-group members feel threatened by the encroachments of subordinate-group members on their perceived entitlements, they increasingly resist the organized efforts undertaken by subordinate-group members to achieve greater gains. That resistance takes any number of forms, such as new legislation that regulates "normative behavior" as defined by the dominant group, systematized attacks on subordinate-group member in terms of attributed negative traits and their presumed inadequacies, denial of privilege or alterations in requirements for admission to the mainstream itself, and allegations of "reverse discrimination."

Resistance, as evidenced perhaps in legal assaults, may result in retrogression or retardation of subordinate-group advances. Consequently, the struggle for equal opportunity through changes in power relationships seems continuous for outsiders.

The Universe of the Study

An initial goal for the first component of this study was to include all institutions in the United States that offer a professional degree in the fields selected for analysis. This objective would have meant including all 102 schools of architecture, 124 schools of medicine, 168 American Bar Association approved schools of law, 59 schools of dentistry, 13 colleges of optometry, 80 colleges of pharmacy, 287 schools of engineering, 22 colleges of veterinary medicine, 88 schools of social work, and some 220 institutions listed by the American Council on Education as Ph.D. granting institutions. This would have yielded a statistical universe of 1162 professional and graduate degree programs or cases.

The constraints of manageability, feasibility, and the likelihood of institutional responses ultimately required modifications in the original goal for an inclusive universe of the study. Preliminary testing indicated major difficulties in obtaining data directly from institutions on doctoral students by field primarily because of the tremendous amount of labor required by each institution. That idea was abandoned, and selected institutional data were obtained from other sources. Interviews with key individuals knowledgeable about architectural education suggested extreme difficulty in obtaining data of sufficient quality from schools or colleges of architecture for the time frame covered by the study. Hence the attention given to architectural education was reduced. Consequently, the major fields of study covered by the survey research portion of this analysis included a potential total of 840 cases. Selected institutional data, coupled with information obtained through personal interviews and data from governmental sources, constitute the limited data sets on architectural education.

Data-Collection Procedures

Description of the Survey Inventory

Data for this study were collected in two overlapping phases. Phase 1 of the study consisted of data collection through a mailed survey. A survey inventory was constructed for distribution to the deans of the colleges or schools of specific professional programs (e.g., the dean of the School of Law, the dean of the School of Medicine, the dean of the School of Dentistry, and so on, were each forwarded a copy of the instrument even though all may have been physically located at the same university). Each dean was requested to complete only those sections of the 23 items in the inventory that were pertinent to his or her specific professional school.

The survey instrument asked for (1) institutional identification data, including the name, location, and type of institution; (2) numerical data by race on applications, acceptances, and enrollment for the study period; (3) place of undergraduate degrees of full-time black graduate or professional degree students (i.e., whether received from an historically black college or from a predominantly white college, aggregated by year); (4) number of students graduated by year, profession, and race for each year during the study period; (5) number of students graduated by year, profession, race, and sex for each year of the study period; (6) number of doctoral degrees conferred by year, field, and race for each year during the study period; (7) number of masters degrees conferred by year, field, and race for each year during the study period; (8) number of full-time faculty by year, degrees, and race; (9) number of part-time faculty by year, degree, and race; (10) tenured faculty by year, degree, and race; (11) distribution of black faculty by teaching fields or discipline; (12) description of minority recruitment program; (13) description of special admissions program; (14) description of program admissions requirements; (15) costs of graduate or professional education by year; (16) description of academic support services; (17) description of nonacademic support services; (18) explanation of goals for enrollment of black students; (19) discussion of the impact of the *Bakke* decision on admissions policies, financial aid programs, and retention; (20) financial support programs by year, type, and racial distribution; (21) views of major problems in the recruitment and enrollment of black graduate and professional school students; and (22) general comments about the project and its goal.

Two mailings of this inventory were sent to the deans of each program. These two mailings yielded responses from 117 programs and/or institutions that indicated inability to participate in the study and from 141 active participants in the study. The pattern of participation and nonparticipation by field is described in Table 4.

Even though returns from the mailed survey were considerably less than anticipated, usable data were obtained from both the correspondence indicating inability or unwillingness to participate and from the completed inventories. Much of the correspondence was supportive, thoughtful, and explicit in explanations for nonparticipation. The responses to the completed surveys tended to be careful, analytical, and of inestimable value in understanding problems of access.

Table 4

Participation Profile by Field in Response to Survey Inventory

Program / Field	Number of Participating Schools	Number of Nonparticipating Schools
Dentistry	13	3
Engineering	20	14
Law	15	16
Medicine	30	21
Optometry	6	1
Pharmacy	16	2
Social work	8	9
Veterinary medicine	11	2
Architecture	2	6
Ph.D granting institutions Arts and sciences	20	43
Total	141	117

Nonparticipants offered a variety of explanations. In general, reasons for refusing to participate can be categorized, in descending frequency as follows: (1) Information requested is not available for the time period needed; (2) to complete the inventory would be too time-consuming; (3) available personnel is too limited to complete the inventory acceptably; (4) most of the information has already been reported to professional associations and can be obtained directly from them; (5) budgetary resources are too limited to do the computer search and analysis required by the inventory; (6) state approval is required to release some of the data requested; (7) it is against institutional policies to participate in studies of this type; and (8) "other" reasons.

Selected comments from the refusals correspondence illustrate this range of responses and reveal some of the problems in collecting this type of institutional data:

One writer stated: "After examining the specific information being sought, I am afraid we are not able to be of much help. We have only very recently been recording many of the items about which you seek information at all or in a form which would allow reasonable retrieval."

Another wrote: "The ADA has been collecting identical data to that which you request for many years. It has been tabulated and widely published. If after contacting the ADA you still find that you need additional information from ———, I will be more than happy to see if I can gather it."

Another wrote: "We are making headway to attract more black undergraduate students for our various engineering programs. Hopefully, in years to come, some of the better graduates will decide to continue their education at the graduate level. The prospects are dim, since graduate stipends of some $460 per month cannot at all compete with lucrative salaries of $1500–$1800 offered by industry."

Still another: "This questionnaire is not relevant to ——— College since we do not have a separate graduate school with that name generally used."

Another wrote: "This college does not maintain records on minorities, the university does but not by major department. We do not actively recruit any students. All students meeting minimum admission standards are admitted. ——— The questionnaire is not applicable to this college."

Another wrote: "Our records are inadequate."

Still another: "The data you request has not and is not maintained. I am sorry we cannot assist you with your research in this matter."

And another: "I regret to inform you that we will not be able to collect the data you need since it would involve a major amount of time and effort on the part of this office. I simply do not have the resources available."

And finally: "If, however, in your project funding you have the resources which could be used to provide us with a graduate assistant to help us with the project on our campus we would be delighted to coordinate this activity for you."

This range of response also illuminates some of the limitations of the survey data, which are discussed in greater detail later in this chapter. They also underscore the necessity of continuing to obtain data from other sources, especially in projects of this type.

Other Sources of Data

Because of the limited number of institutional responses to the survey inventory, it was necessary to obtain data from other sources. Hence, the second phase of the data-collection process consisted of interviews with administrators, data analysts, and other key informants of the professional associations with whom the various institutions and their programs had some formal affiliation. Through these key informants, the major portion of the data utilized in the statistical analysis of this study were collected. These formal organizations collect data on an annual basis from all institutions that have specialized programs in one or more of the professional fields selected for study here. The institutional data reported to these professional associations form the primary data source for this study. These sources are as follows:

1. *The Council on Social Work Education,* located in New York, collects and publishes statistical data on social work education on an annual basis. These data are included in *Statistics on Social Work Education.* All schools of social work are included in the statistical analysis. The volume includes descriptive statistics on the following areas: student enrollment, institutional characteristics with special attention to student enrollment, ethnic characteristics of students and faculty, admissions data, tuition charges, degrees awarded, applications for admissions to first-year master's degree programs, number of full-time students receiving financial grants in graduate school by institution, and characteristics of doctoral degree students. The council also publishes additional documents that provide data on special programs and services offered by schools of social work.

2. *American Dental Association* (Chicago) *and the American Association of Dental Schools* (Washington, D.C.). The American Dental Association publishes an annual volume called *Dental School Trend Analysis; Minority Report: Supplement to the Annual Report Dental Education,* and *Annual Report: Dental Education.* These volumes provide comprehensive statistical data, both historical and current, on dental education, advanced specialty education, levels of predental education, and dental licensure results. They also contain enrollment data for each institution by sex, minority status, graduation data by sex and minority status, tuition data, academic programs and admissions policies, faculty by institutions (but not disaggregated by race), minority recruitment, financial assistance, special programs (if any), and such admissions requirement data as Dental Aptitude Test, gradepoint average, residency, and general information about the institution's curriculum. General characteristics of entering class by race and sex for institutions are also given. Selection factors are discussed in one or more of these volumes.

3. *Association of American Medical Colleges* (Washington, D.C.). This association publishes annually *Minority Student Opportunities in United States Medical Schools,* which contains statistical data on minority applications, acceptances, enrollees, and faculty by institution. It has a thorough description of medical school programs for disadvantaged students in the areas of recruitment, admissions policies and procedures, and financial assistance.

Another publication is *Minority Student Information on Individual Medical Schools*. This volume identifies the contact person for minority students at each medical college and depicts first-year and total enrollment data on specific minority-group students by institution.

The Participation of Women and Minorities in United States Medical School Faculties contains aggregate data on minority faculty at U.S. medical schools. In December of each year, the *Journal of Medical Education* publishes "Medical Education in the United States," which provides graduation statistics that can be disaggregated for minority-group descriptions.

The Division of Student Services of the Associations of American Medical Colleges, under the leadership of Dr. Davis G. Johnson, publishes annually *U.S. Medical School Enrollments by Race and Ethnicity*.

The National Medical Fellowships provide financial data on scholarship awards by institution and year.

4. *Engineering Manpower Commission* (New York City). This association[4] has two major annual publications: *Engineering and Technology Enrollments* and *Engineering and Technology Degrees*. A major function of the commission is to collect, analyze, and publish significant data on engineering manpower. It collects data on institutions accredited by the EPCD, and these data are displayed by school, curriculum, enrollment, degrees, and race. The enrollment documents provide enrollment by year, program, and race for each institution so that an examination of these data will enable one to construct a profile of how many blacks, for instance, are enrolled in the first, second, third, or fourth year at a given institution. The annual publication of *Engineering and Technology Degrees* cites the number of degrees conferred, first professional, M.S., and Ph.Ds., by institution, program, and race.

The National Research Council publishes information on the activities of the Committee on Minorities in Engineering. Among these activities are the collection and dissemination of information on special recruitment and admissions programs for minority students. The Conference Board's publications also provide qualitative and quantitative data on engineering programs and on the work of the Committee on Minorities in Engineering. The College Board has sponsored a Minority Engineering Scholarship Program and an Upper Division Scholarship Program designed to increase minority-student access to colleges of engineering. Major sources for financial data were publications and other materials provided by the National Fund for Minority Engineering Students.

5. *A Review of Legal Education* is published annually by the Section on Legal Education of the American Bar Association. This document contains:

(*a*) law school admissions requirements; (*b*) a list of ABA-approved law schools; and (*c*) for each approved law school, enrollment statistics, a survey of minority-group students enrolled in J.D. programs, admissions requirements, number of degrees conferred, law school enrollments since 1950, and tuition and fees data and related data. Its annually updated report on minority-student enrollment by year and class permits the reader to develop an immediate perspective on enrollment trends for each minority group.

In addition to data obtained from interviews at the national headquarters of the Association of America Law Schools (Washington, D.C.), considerable data were obtained from an examination of the *Proceedings: Report of Committees and Projects* of its annual meetings. Important committees for purposes of this examination were the AALS Special Committee on Effective Use of Legal Education, Committee on Admissions Standards, Council on Legal Eduction Opportunity (CLEO), and the Committee on Minority Groups. These reports contain data on recruitment, admission, financial support, enrollment, and minority faculty in law schools. Persons associated with those committees were also interviewed.

Other information on the distribution of black and other minority faculty in law schools was obtained from Derek Bell of the Harvard University School of Law (former dean of the law school at the University of Oregon). Data on CLEO were obtained from Wade Henderson, then director of CLEO in Washington, D.C.

Educational Testing Service Publications were invaluable for their analysis of institutional data, performance on the Law School Admissions Test by race, and in the presentation of impediments to the growth and retention of minority students in schools of law.

6. *Association of American Veterinary Medical Colleges* (Washington, D.C.). This Association collects enrollment data from all colleges of veterinary medicine in the nation. Before 1974, these data were categorized by race and disaggregated by minority group. Beginning in 1975, an agreement was made that these data would no longer be published in a way that identifies specific institutions. Instead, aggregate data on minority groups, foreign students, and Caucasian students would be reported annually. Hence, the data from the AAVMC are useful for developing a trend of total Caucasian, minority, and combined enrollment for the period since 1973. This had to be supplemented by data from other sources, such as the HEGIS Reports, which provide racial composition by school, and personal interviews. Data for the profile on Tuskegee Institute's School of Veterinary Medicine were provided by Dr. Ellis Hall, who also made available a number of conference reports that contained institutional data.

Interviews were conducted by phone with the deans of four colleges of veterinary medicine who also chair important committees of the association that have an impact on the enrollment and graduation of black students.

7. *Association of Collegiate Schools of Architecture* (Washington, D.C.). This association publishes *Architectural Schools of North America,* which includes information on its 102 schools. For example, it provides descriptions of departments and colleges of architecture, type of program offered, admissions requirements, enrollment data by race, degrees conferred, ethnicity and sex of students, and financial data. These data were supplemented by interviews with key informants in the Washington office and by data from the National Center on Educational Statistics and Office of Civil Rights Publications.

8. *American Association of Colleges of Pharmacy (AACP)* (Bethesda, Md.). This association has a number of publications used in this research. The more relevent ones were the annual *Reports on Graduate Enrollment Data and Graduate Study in Member Colleges.* These documents contain yearly enrollment and graduation data by race and by first professional and graduate degree programs. They provide information on teaching assistantships, nonservice stipends, general financial support for pharmacy students, and admissions requirements. Other reports provide faculty distribution data and information on recruitment and special programs.

The material used for the development of the Profile on the Xavier University School of Pharmacy was provided by Dr. Warren McKenna, former dean of the School of Pharmacy, Dr. Marcellus Grace, dean of the School of Pharmacy, and by Dr. Norman Francis, president of Xavier University of New Orleans.

9. *Association of Schools and Colleges of Optometry* (Washington, D.C.). This association annually publishes *A Survey of Optometric Educational Institutions.* This survey includes institutional data on student characteristics, enrollment by year, retention and withdrawal data, minority-group student enrollment characteristics, faculty characteristics, annual student expenditures, financial aid data, and admissions/selection factors. The association also publishes *Information for Applicants to Schools and Colleges of Optometry* each year. This document includes a general survey of the academic requirements for admission to each of the 13 schools and colleges of optometry in the United States, and financial aid data.

As in all of the above professional degree programs, these data were enriched by personal interviews with key informants of the association, additional brochures and publications (e.g., journal articles), and data obtained from the National Center for Educational Statistics, the Higher Education General Information Survey (HEGIS), and publications of the U.S. Office of Civil Rights.

10. *Graduate Education in the Arts and Sciences.* Enrollment and degree data were obtained from the National Center for Educational Statistics; publications from the Department of Health, Education and Welfare, especially its *Racial and Ethnic Enrollment Data from Institutions of Higher Education* (published biennially), which now provides institutional data by ethnicity (HEGIS Reports), and from the National Academcy of Science and the National Research Council.

11. The National Academy of Sciences publishes an *Annual Summary Report: Doctorate Recipients from United States Universities.* This report presents tables that depict ethnic characteristics of doctoral degree recipients by field of study. It also contains historical data and data on methods of financial support, plans for employment after the completion of the doctoral degree, and time lapse between the undergraduate degree and the completion of the doctorate.

12. General: In addition to these basic data sources, a major search of the literature on graduate and professional education was undertaken. This revealed support for the specific observation made through the analysis of primary and secondary data. Other agencies and bureaus in Washington, such as the Department of Health, Education and Welfare, the U.S. Office of Education, and the Health Manpower and Resources Agency, provided significant data on financial aid and scholarship programs.

Data from all these sources were matched and discrepancies in statistical presentations reconciled, reorganized for presentation with the survey inventory described in Phase 1, and prepared for computer processing. As a result, data were obtained on 427 institutions and 743 professional school programs (cases) to be used in analysis. The following distribution of these cases by field shows the actual number of schools in that field plus the percentage that number is of the total N of 743 computerized cases (percentages exceed 100% due to rounding):

1. Dentistry = 59 cases, or 8%
2. Engineering = 235 cases, or 32%
3. Law = 161 cases, or 22%
4. Medicine = 108 cases, or 15%
5. Optometry = 13 cases, or 2%
6. Pharmacy = 74 cases, or 10%
7. Social work = 84 cases, or 11%
8. Veterinary medicine = 9 cases, or 1%

Limitations of Data

Just as no statistical technique for data analysis is infallible, so no data-collection strategy is without problems. This study is based on data collected from institutions through a survey inventory and, principally, from institutional and state data collected from a variety of primary and secondary sources. The major problem presented by this approach lies in the tremendous effort required to reconcile differences and to match data reported from diverse sources. This difficulty involves some institutions whose records are sketchy and whose data have never (or only recently) been computerized, and for which reconstructuring time sequences of data becomes problematic. This problem is overcome in those cases in which reporting of institutional data to their accrediting agency or to the Office of Civil Rights in the Department of Health, Education, and Welfare has become regularized for a substantial period of time.

A problem could arise from the tendency of most institutions not to collect data by race before 1972. Despite legal constraints to the contrary, some institutions, especially for their professional programs, collected such data and reported them with regularity to their respective national association as early as 1964. Matching data from a variety of sources reconciles whatever degrees of inconsistency may exist in quantitative data and provides greater numerical precision.

Even with the most careful reconstruction, however, the data are uneven for some fields for certain years. The reason is that some institutions either did not report data for those specific years or omitted selected items for that particular year. As a result, missing data for some years reduce the number of cases below the total N of 743 for certain specific years and items. This is no different from the occurrence of usable and nonusable responses to forced-choice and open-ended questions in survey research. As long as a sufficient number of cases are present in the sample to render statistical analysis appropriate, these omissions do not present irremediable problems.

The availability of data from the professional associations and from both the National Center for Educational Statistics and the Office of Civil Rights assures more effective reconciliation and checks on the accuracy of institutionally reconstructed data reported in a survey inventory. These sources enabled the collection of usable data on 743 programs and most professional schools. In all, more than 98% of the institutions are presentated in the discussion of specific professional fields.

Operational Definitions

1. The term *access* refers to the enrollment of black students in graduate or professional schools. Access may be conceived as existing in

one of three possible levels: Level 1 is called "weak or limited access," in which very small numbers of black students are enrolled in relation to their proportion in the state or national population. Level 2 is labeled "approximate access," in which the enrollment is in excess of one-half the proportions. The third and most desirable level or form of access, Level 3, is referred to as "equal access." In this final stage, which happens to be the goal of equality of opportunity proponents, the proportion of black students enrolled is the same or slightly higher than the proportion of black persons in the state or national population.

2. *Distribution* refers to actual dispersion or concentration of black students in various graduate or professional fields. This term encompasses a quantitative spread or concentration relative to enrollment and graduation rates.

3. *Outcome* is a term that applies to the number or proportion of black students who actually receive degrees in a given field. It is expressed quantitatively as the actual number of black graduates and/or the proportion of black students graduating with graduate or professional degrees in a field.

4. *Retention program* means any organized or formally constituted activity, the specific purpose of which is to retain students until they successfully complete degree requirements (e.g., tutorials, counseling and guidance, academic advising, financial aid programs), as well as informal associations (e.g., Black Student Association) and black faculty who may provide psychosocial support for black students during various stages of the educational process.

5. *Quality of financial aid* and *quality of scholarship aid* refer to the dollar amounts awarded to students from all sources and to the proportion of black students receiving financial assistance. On the basis of total information available (e.g., dollars awarded, financial resources), these variables were trichotomized as follows: good, adequate, or little or no assistance provided.

6. *Presence or absence of special admissions programs* is self-explanatory. That is, a determination was made as to whether or not an institution had ever used any form of special admissions program for minority students during the 1970's. Similarly, a determination was made as to whether an institution had established a *special minority recruitment program* and a *minority affairs office.*

7. *The presence or absence of a black college in the state* simply refers to the state locations of the 107 historically black colleges and whether a specific professional or graduate school is located in one of the states in which these institutions are located.

8. Use was made of the latest Bureau of the Census data to make a determination of the *proportion of black persons in the total population* of the state. The precise percentage of black persons was entered into the computations.

9. The actual *number of black faculty* employed full-time in a given institution was also entered into the data base for analysis. Hence, this definition does not refer solely to whether black faculty are present but to the size of the black faculty cohort as well.

10. *Litigation status* refers to whether the institution or professional school is located in a state that is either currently covered by litigation in the *Adams* v. *Califano* case, *or* may be covered by this litigation because of the presence of a historically black college within the state, *or* is not likely to be under litigation due to the presumption of innocence regarding the perpetuation of a dual system of higher education. Although 10 states in 1980 were involved in the *Adams* case, in 1984 an additional 8 states could be sued by the *Adams* case.[6]

11. *Location of the institution* is a trichotomized variable. For purposes of this study, institutions are located in one of the three following locales: (1) rural area or small town; (2) city; (3) large metropolitan area.

12. *First-year black student enrollment*[7] refers to the number of black students who entered the first-year class of a graduate degree or professional school class in each specific year of the decade.

13. *Total black student enrollment* means the combined enrollment of all black students in a given professional degree program for each year.

14. *Total black students graduated* refers to the actual number of black students reported as degree recipients for each year of the study.

Data Analysis

The first stage of data analysis concerns the exploratory survey research that characterized Phase 1 of the study. It involves regression analysis between one or more of three dependent variables (i.e., first-year enrollment of black students, total enrollment of black students, and graduation rates of black students) and the independent or predictor variables (i.e., quality of financial aid, quality of scholarships, presence or absence of a special recruitment program, presence or absence of a special admissions program, presence or absence of a minority affairs office (officer), number of black faculty, presence or absence of a retention program, type of institution (e.g., public, private or state-assisted), number of professional schools within the state, proportion of blacks in the state population, presence or absence of a black college in the state, whether the state is currently or may be under litigation in the future to dismantle a dual system of higher education, and location of the institution. The Statistical Package for the Social Sciences (SPSS) was used for this analysis.

The second stage in the data analysis involves the development of trends in enrollment and graduation by race. These trends are presented in six separate ways: (1) total professional school enrollment or graduation by field and race; (2) enrollment of first-year black professional school students by field and by year for the study period; (3) enrollment and graduation data by sex on a selective basis; (4) participation of black students by field and state (in order to plot changes and make comparisons between states in access of black students to professional schools); (5) enrollment and graduation activity in the "*Adams* states" by selected fields of study; and (6) trends in the production of black students with doctoral degrees in selected fields.

In succeeding chapters, the findings are presented first in terms of the 743 cases; that is, as a summary of findings for all cases and for all fields combined, and for all measures. This analysis is followed by specific chapters for major professional fields and doctoral-level education.

Notes

1. For further discussion of one or more of these positions, see Randall Collins, "Some Comparative Principles of Educational Stratification," *Harvard Educational Review* 47, no. 1 (February 1977): 1–29; and notes 2, 3, and 4.
2. James E. Blackwell, "The Power Basis of Ethnic Conflict in American Society," in Lewis A. Coser and Otto N. Larsen, eds., *The Uses of Controversy in Sociology,* (New York: Free Press, 1976), Chap. 10.
3. Robert Bierstedt, "An Analysis of Social Power," *American Sociological Review* 15 (December 1950): 730–738.
4. See Hubert M. Blalock, "A Power Analysis of Racial Discrimination," *Social Forces* 39 (1960): 53–69 and *Toward a General Theory of Intergroup Relations* (New York: Wiley, 1967).
5. The Engineering Manpower Commission works cooperatively with a number of agencies, societies and associations, located in the same building, that have a collective interest in facilitating broader participation of minority groups in the engineering profession. Among these are the Engineering Joint Council and the American Society of Engineers.
6. Enrollment data only in schools of law were not always disaggregated by race. It is estimated that black students comprise about 90 per cent of minority enrollments for this field reported in survey data.
7. By January 1981, Alabama, Texas, West Virginia, Delaware, Ohio, Kentucky, South Carolina, and Missouri were added to this group by the U.S. Department of Justice.

Chapter   **3**   DATA ANALYSIS OF
                                     SURVEY FINDINGS

The mainstreaming process discussed in this book is based upon an analysis of two sets of data. The first type of data refers to information obtained using the institutional profiles constructed both from survey reports from the participating institutions and supplemental data on those institutions gained from other sources. This survey and supplemental process yielded 743 professional school programs or cases that could be subjected to statistical analysis utilizing the criterion and predictor variables.

The second type of data is constructed for a trend analysis of the process of mainstreaming black professional school students and for ascertaining the factors that appear to be associated with these trends. Hence, this second level of analysis builds on the first presentation. The trend analysis is integrated into the discussions within subsequent chapters covering the full range of processes involved in mainstreaming black students, from access to graduate and professional schools through the actual number graduated; and it is addressed in Chapters 4 through 13. This second edition updates trend data in relevant categories for the period from 1980 to 1984. Wherever obtained, post 1984 data are also used.

Our primary concern here is an analysis of the findings of data obtained on the 743 cases resulting from the institutional surveys. In order to address the issues posed at the beginning of Chapter 2, 3 dependent variables and as many as 13 predictor variables were identified.

The three dependent variables employed in this exploratory study are (1) the first-year enrollment of black students; (2) the total enrollment of black students; and (3) the total number of black students graduated. These three variables were subjected to statistical analysis for every year of the 1970s. The variables were selected on the basis of the current assumption that they are the primary manifestations of access and outcomes (graduation rates).

The following variables were selected as possible predictors of one or more of the three dependent variables:

1. *Quality of financial aid* was selected because the literature is replete with *assertions* that black students require substantial amounts of financial assistance due to the impoverished economic backgrounds of

the majority of black students. (Assigned score: 2 = good; 1 = adequate; 0 = poor or none.)

2. For basically the same reason, *quality of scholarship aid* was selected as a possible predictor variable for determining access and graduation (Assigned score: 2 = good; 1 = adequate; 0 = poor or none.) As with the quality of financial aid, these scores were arbitrarily assigned based on available information from all sources. This information consisted of institutional survey and catalogue data, foundation reports, governmental data, and the like.

3. *Special admissions program* was selected because of the suggestions made that these programs have enabled a significant number of black students to matriculate in graduate or professional schools. It has also been suggested that it would not have been possible for many of them to enroll had it not been for the establishment of special admissions programs. (Assigned score: 1 = yes; 2 = no.)

4. The same can be said of *special recruitment programs.* The essential question here is to what extent has the presence or absence of special minority recruitment programs either facilitated or retarded the enrollment of black students in graduate and professional school. (Assigned score: 1 = present; 2 = absent.)

5. Conventional wisdom has similarly permitted many to assume that the access of black students is a function of the presence or absence of either a *minority affairs officer* or a *minority affairs office,* which presumably is the conscience of the institution regarding the implementation of equality of opportunity programs in higher education through a broad range of affirmative action mandates. (Assigned score: 1 = present; 2 = absent.)

6. The *number of black faculty* in the graduate or professional school was employed to test the various assumptions of role model theory. One of the central assumptions, explicit in the socialization literature, is that role models provide a standard of possible achievement of conduct and serve as sources of inspiration regarding alternative career choices or avenues for upward mobility. An important question emerges: Does the presence or absence of black faculty serve either as a facilitator of black student matriculation or as a barrier to access? (The assigned score is the actual number of black faculty reported.)

7. *Presence or absence of retention program* is presumed to be a significant correlate of outcomes (graduation). It is also assumed to be a factor on which some students may rely in making a decision as to whether or not to enroll in graduate or professional degree programs. (Score: 1 = present; 2 = absent.)

8. The *number of professional schools in the state* may be a determinant of the range of opportunities for gaining access available in a given state.

It can be assumed that the greater the number of professional schools within a state, the greater will be the enrollment of black students in that type of professional degree program within the same state. On the other hand, a small number of professional schools may be restrictive and, therefore, serve as an obstacle to access. (Score: 1 = 0 – 3; 2 = 4, 5; and 3 = 6 + professional schools.)

9. Another assumption that may be made on the basis of *historic patterns of college enrollment* is that the presence or absence of a black college in a state may be associated with success in increasing black students' access to postcollege programs. Underlying this assumption is the notion that these institutions may serve as quasi-feeder institutions to the graduate and professional schools within the same state and may be a primary site for recruitment. (Score: 1 = present; 2 = absent.)

10. Inasmuch as enrollment may be a function of the students in the available pool, an important question that arises is the degree to which the *number of black students enrolled in these programs is a function of the percentage of black persons in the state's population.* Is it appropriate to assume that the larger the black population in the state, the greater will be the percentage of black students matriculated in the graduate and professional schools of that state? (The assigned score here was the actual percentage of blacks in the population.)

11. The most fundamental rationale for including *litigation status* as a predictor variable was to attempt a determination of whether being under a court order to desegregate higher education actually makes a difference in the type of access that black students experience. (Score: 1 = yes; 2 = maybe; 3 = no or not likely.)

12. The black population in the United States is predominantly an urban population. Hence, an interesting question arises as to whether the *physical location of an institution* makes a difference in its success in recruiting and enrolling black graduate or professional degree students. Are black students more prone to select institutions located in large metropolitan communities similar to their homes, or are they attracted to this type of study to institutions located in smaller cities or communities? (Based on U.S. census definitions, this variable was scored: 1 = up to 50,000; 2 = 51,000 to 999,999; 3 = 1 million and above.)

13. Finally, there has been some suggestion that *private institutions,* especially in the early part of the 1970s, *were more aggressive in the recruitment of black and other minority students.* There is also some evidence that private institutions draw the lion's share of financial resources and can award more financial aid and scholarship assistance to deserving black students. Therefore, it has been assumed that

private institutions are more successful in both enrolling and graduating black students. Hence, this variable was selected as a predictor in
order to ascertain possible associations between institutional types
and the criterion variables. (Score: 1 = private; 2 = public; 3 =
state-assisted.)

Correlates of Total Black Student Enrollment

In order to ascertain possible relationships between the criterion and
the predictor variables, and in the interest of parsimony, a decision was
made to test these relationships by examining "total black student enrollment" and the predictor variables in two ways. First, Pearsonian correlations
were calculated for three different points in the decade: year number 1, year
number 5 (or the middle part of the decade), and year number 9, the last
year on which the most complete data are available. The second step was an
examination of the Pearsonian correlation matrix for a single time frame;
year number 9 was selected for this purpose.

According to Table 5, in year 1, which was 1970–1971, the most
powerful predictor of total black student enrollment in graduate and professional schools is the presence of black faculty ($r = .82$; $p < .001$). Explaining
65% of the variance in enrollment, the magnitude of this correlation lends
support to the theoretical premise that the presence of role models serves to
attract black students to institutions and that presence may raise the level of
aspiration among this group of students for a professional career.

Other important correlations observed for the first year were between
total black student enrollment and quality of financial aid ($r = .21$, $p <$
.001); quality of scholarship assistance ($r = .21$, $p < .001$); special admissions programs ($r = -25$, $p < .001$);[1] special recruitment programs (r
$= -.18$, $p. < .001$); percentage of black persons in the state's population
($r = .32$, $p. < .001$); location of the institution ($r = .15, p < .001$); and
retention programs ($r = -.25$, $p < .001$). Taken singly, only the percentage of blacks in the state population explains more than 10% of the
variance (see Table 5).

These correlations lead to the conclusion that the greater the financial
and scholarship assistance provided to black students, the larger will be the
number of black students enrolled in graduate and professional schools.
The *absence* of a special admissions and recruitment program is a deterrent
to enrollment. Similarly, the *absence* of retention programs does not persuade
black students to enroll in graduate or professional schools. In contrast, the
larger the number of black persons in the state population, the larger is the
total enrollment. This suggests that the most successful institutions in attracting black students are those institutions located in states having a

Table 5
Pearsonian Correlations of Total Black Student Enrollment with All Predictors, 1971, 1975, 1979

Criterion and Year						Variables							
	Fin/ Aid	Sch/ Aid	Sp/ Admiss	Sp/ Recruit	Min/ Office	Blk Fac	N/Prof Sch	% Blk Pop	Blk Col/State	Litigation Status	Loc/ Inst	Inst Type	Retention
Total Enrollment 1971	r=.21 **	r=.21 **	r=-.25 **	r=-.18 **	r=-.15 **	r=.82 **	r=.08 **	r=.32 **	r=-.10 *	r=-.00 *	r=.15 **	r=-.01 *	r=-.25 **
Total Enrollment 1975	r=.33 **	r=.31 **	r=-.26 **	r=-.19 **	r=-.13 **	r=.84 **	r=.11 **	r=.32 **	r=-.08	r=.01	r=.22 **	r=-.00	r=-.19 **
Total Enrollment 1979	r=.37 **	r=.35 **	r=-.14 **	r=-.15 **	r=-.08 *	r=.83 **	r=.13 **	r=.29 **	r=-.10 *	r=-.01	r=.16 **	r=-.04	r=-.17 **

$* \ p < .05.$
$** \ p < .01.$
Not significant when no star is given.

significant black population. The correlation between location of the institution and total enrollment suggests that black students are less frequently attracted to institutions located in large metropolitan areas, presumably similar to those of the place of their home residence. The absence of a black college in a state seems to have made a difference in 1970–1971. This may be explained by the tendency of institutions to draw on black colleges as the primary source of their recruitment for graduate and professional education. However, these findings are cautioned by the generally weak associations observed.

According to these data, being under litigation to desegregate higher education did not make an apparent difference in the total number of black students enrolled. In other words, institutions that were to be subjected to this litigation were not any more successful than institutions that were not under litigation in enrolling black students.[2] Neither did the type of institution make an apparent difference. Private institutions did not apppear to be any more successful in attracting black students than either public or state-assisted institutions in 1970–1971. Private institutions may have been more successful in this endeavor in the late 1960s but this did not appear to be the case in 1970. It is possible that in a more rigorous assessment of possible relationships between these two variables, type of institution might emerge as a significant variable. That is not the situation at this point.

In the middle of the 1970s and in the last year of the analysis, the same forms of correlation emerged. Of primary importance here, however, is the power of the black faculty variable as a predictor of total enrollment. In every year, the correlation between these two variables is substantially stronger than is the correlation between total enrollment and any of the remaining predictor variables.

The Pearsonian correlation matrix tables present intercorrelations between the predictor variables. In some instances, these intercorrelations are both strong and significant. Although this particular group of variables taken collectively appears to have a high degree of salience in influencing access of black students to professional schools, these findings are tentative and must await more refined analysis.

The high correlation between some of the variables suggest that they may, in fact, be measuring the same phenomenon. That is to say, the correlation between quality of financial aid and quality of scholarships awarded to black students may reflect the strength of institutional commitment to provide a sufficient amount of financial assistance that enables black students to pursue a professional degree. Similarly the correlation between "being under litigation to dismantle dual systems of higher education" with the "presence of a black college within the state" is not unexpected. It is precisely in states under litigation that all of the historically black colleges are located (Table 6).

Table 6
Pearsonian Correlation Matrix, Year 9:
Total Black Student Enrollment with All Variables

Variables

	Total Blk Enroll	Fin/Aid	Sch/Aid	Sp/Admiss	Sp/Recruit	Min/Office	Blk Fac	N/Prof Sch	% Blk Pop	Blk Col/State	Litiga Status	Loc/Inst	Inst Type	Retention
Total Blk Enroll	1.000													
Fin/Aid	r=.37**	1.000												
Sch/Aid	r=.35**	r=.59**	1.000											
Sp/Admiss	r=-.14	r=-.12	r=-.21	1.000										
Sp/Recruit	r=-.15*	r=-.23**	r=-.19**	r=.25**	1.000									
Min/Office	r=.08	r=-.18**	r=-.16*	r=-.06	r=.18**	1.000								
Blk Fac	r=.83**	r=.21**	r=.30**	r=-.27**	r=-.11*	r=-.09	1.000							
N/Prof Sch	r=.13*	r=.08	r=.07	r=.12*	r=-.08	r=-.04	r=-.10	1.000						
% Blk Pop	r=.29**	r=.11*	r=.11*	r=-.03	r=-.11*	r=.05	r=.34**	r=.00	1.000					
Blk Col/State	r=-.10	r=-.02	r=.00	r=-.01	r=.10*	r=-.05	r=-.19**	r=.06	r=.48**	1.000				
Litigation Status	r=-.01	r=.01	r=.03	r=-.12*	r=.08	r=-.08	r=-.00	r=.05	r=-.27**	r=.86**	1.000			
Loc/Inst	r=.16*	r=.16*	r=.18**	r=-.13*	r=-.04	r=.04	r=.08	r=.19**	r=.14**	r=.03	r=.10	1.000		
Inst Type	r=-.04	r=.00	r=.04	r=-.02	r=-.08	r=.04	r=.10*	r=.19**	r=.03	r=.01	r=-.00	r=.25**	1.000	
Retention	r=-.17**	r=.02	r=-.18**	r=.21**	r=.42**	r=.11*	r=-.13*	r=-.08	r=-.12*	r=.05	r=.03	r=-.12*	r=-.02	1.000

*p < .05.
**p < .01.
Not significant when no star is given.

Equally important to observe is the predictive power of the "presence and size of the black faculty" in relation to this criterion variable. While high correlations between this predictor and this criterion variable may, indeed, be particularly supportive of role model theory, the probability that something else is at work in this relationship is certainly worth noting. The presence of a substantial number of black faculty and a fairly large black student enrollment in the same professional school may also be strong indicators of an institutional commitment and a racial climate within the institution sufficiently positive so as to both facilitate the hiring of black faculty and promote the matriculation of black students beyond token levels.

Conversely, the absence of black faculty and black students, or their token approximations in professional schools may suggest lack of institutional commitment to equality of employment and educational opportunity as well as a negative institutional climate. Yet, the presence of black faculty predictor variable is illuminating for understanding institutional success or failure in the enrollment and production of black professionals and remains preeminent.

Given these considerations, it can be argued that the factors treated as predictor variables in this research could be conceived as dependent variables if "institutional commitment" and "institutional climate" are regarded as dependent variables. Indeed, in subsequent chapters, such inferences occur from time to time, but without regard to a direct statistical analysis. In effect, enrollment and graduation of black students from graduate and professional schools attest to degrees of institutional behavior and the willingness of black faculty and students to engage in the learning and teaching process of a given institution because the overall institutional milieu is not viewed as an impediment of significant consequence to them. Notwithstanding, for purposes of this analysis, first-year black student enrollment, total black student enrollment, and number of black students graduated are treated as dependent variables. The probability that they, as a group of variables, might reflect special actions taken or not taken by an institution to promote equality of opportunity is amplified in subsequent chapters. It should also be reiterated here that all the variables treated in this analysis as predictors may be regarded as explicit manifestations of institutional policy and behavior.

Again, it is important to note that these interactions occur within a dynamic system characterized by constant feedback between variables over time; consequently, the technical distinction between independent and dependent variables may, in the long run, be meaningless.

Retention programs appear to be most successful when they include a good quality of scholarship monies, are associated with organized special recruitment and special admissions programs, and are located in institutions with minority affairs officers or offices. They are also more likely to be present in institutions located in large metropolitan communities and in states with a substantial proportion of black persons in the total population. Irrespective of location, the very existence of retention programs is a response to a clearly defined need. This suggests that many schools have not done a particularly good job in providing basic educational skills to their pupils and/or that the quality of the learning environment creates a need for various kinds of support services.

Identification of Most-Powerful Predictors

The next step in this analysis was an attempt to isolate the most powerful set of predictors of first-year enrollment, total enrollment, and of total black students graduated. To accomplish this task, a stepwise regression method was employed.[3] Given the magnitude of the data collected over 9 or 10 years time, the principle of parsimony was once again applied. Hence, a decision was made to illustrate the outcomes of the stepwise regression by reporting on last step findings for Years 1, 5, and 9. In this manner, patterns or trends and inconsistencies in the predictive power of certain variables could be specified.

It should be stressed that this study is not confirmatory; rather it is exploratory. Therefore, the observations made regarding the power of predictor variables should be regarded as primarily heuristic in that the statistical analysis may shed light on relationships between variables, which could have an impact on the professional education of black students. Although a stepwise-regression technique was employed in the analysis of data, for purposes of this study, a decision was made to focus exclusively on the last step in the equation and to report betas, R^2 for the equation as a whole, F scores, and level of significance. The general rule of thumb for including variables in the tables was that they appeared significant at least at the .05 level. Exceptions to this general criterion were made when the correlation between an independent variable and one or more of the criterion variables was significant at an earlier step at least at the .05 level and was only slightly different at the last step of the equation. Consequently, a table may sometimes include a variable with a relationship that is significant at the .07 level.

Black Student Enrollment in Professional Schools

First-Year Enrollment

During the first year covered by the study, this analysis shows that the most important predictor of first-year enrollment of black students in professional schools was "the number of black faculty" in the professional school (Table 7). The salience of the black faculty variable for predicting first-year black student enrollment was observed once again in the fifth year as well as in the ninth year. During the fifth year, however, "the proportion of Blacks in the state's population" was also significantly correlated with first-year black student enrollment. In both years, the correlations between these two independent variables and the dependent variable, first-year black student enrollment, met the criterion for determining the most important and powerful predictors. This situation was observed when the betas, R^2s, Fs, and significance levels were examined (Table 7).

In year 9, four variables met the criterion for selection as the most powerful predictors. These were (1) number of black faculty in the professional school; (2) quality of financial aid; (3) number of professional schools within the state; and (4) litigation status. In addition, two variables were included in the table because they had appeared as significant at least at one earlier step in the stepwise-regression analysis, even though their level of significance at the last step varied slightly from the .05 level of confidence. These variables were type of institution and presence or absence of a black college in the state.

According to this analysis, the number of black faculty in the professional schools appears to be consistently correlated with first-year enrollment of black students in professional schools. The persistence of this variable as the most powerful predictor suggests that those institutions seriously committed to improving the level of enrollment of black students in professional schools might be more successful in achieving that objective by hiring more black faculty. One can also speculate that a more detailed analysis as directed to other minority groups might show a similar relationship between the presence of faculty members of those groups and first-year professional school enrollment of minority students from the same groups. This is, of course, speculation; however, it is informed by impressionistic evidence observed in certain professions (e.g., law and social work).

The correlation between a good quality of financial aid and significant first-year enrollment is not unexpected. As previously discussed, a disproportionate number of black students come from a household with a median family income that is only about 57% of that of the white population. We have also pointed out that a large proportion of these families subsist at or near the poverty level. Since the costs of professional school education often exceed the median family income of black Americans, and given the extreme difficulties that blacks encounter in finding other sources of financial support, some form of financial aid is required to assure their enrollment and retention. This analysis suggests that those institutions with a better quality of financial aid programs do a better job of enrolling black students at the first-year level of professional school training. Although this variable

Table 7
Regression of First-Year Black Student Enrollment in Professional Schools with Most-Significant Variables, All Cases, Years 1, 5, 9

Year	Variable	Beta	F	Significance
1	*Number of black faculty in the professional school	.50	5.61	.03

R^2 for the equation as a whole = .32
F for the equation as a whole = 13.53,
Significance = .001

Year	Variable	Beta	F	Significance
5	*Number of black faculty in the professional school	.86	92.20	.00
	*Proportion of blacks in the state's population	.30	7.00	.00

R^2 for the equation as a whole = .49
F for the equation as a whole = 73.13,
Significance = .003

Year	Variable	Beta	F	Significance
9	*Number of black faculty in the professional school	1.67	105.63	.00
	*Quality of financial aid	7.60	5.41	.02
	*Number of professional schools in the state	4.98	4.65	.03
	*Litigation status: "Adams states"	− 13.12	4.57	.03
	*Type of institution	− 7.66	3.19	.07
	*Presence or absence of black college in state	19.93	3.35	.07

R^2 for the equation as a whole = .62
F for the equation as a whole = 23.75,
Significance = .000

*Most-significant predictor variables in the equation.

appears to be more powerful in the ninth year of this analysis, it did appear as an important variable at earlier steps in previous years.

Similarly, one should expect that the greater the number of professional schools within a state, the more likely are black students to be enrolled in professional schools. Having more professional schools means, obviously, an enlarged amount of space. In turn, these states provide more opportunities, at least in theory, for students of all races to be included. This expanded opportunity seems to be the case, since it appears that those states with several professional schools are more likely to enroll a larger number of black students in their first-year professional school classes.

The anticipated impact of *Adams* v. *Califano* has not been achieved so far. This failure may be attributed to lack of rigorous enforcement of court orders, especially the reluctance of the federal government to utilize its power to cut off funds from noncomplying states. According to these findings, the most effective states, regarding the enrollment of black students in professional schools, are states outside the 17 southern and border states, which are not likely to be included under the *Adams* litigation. It must be stated, however, that in some professional schools, significant increases in first-year professional school enrollment have occurred in states that are at present under litigation or in states likely to be included under such litigation. These increases may be a direct response to *Adams* litigation. This finding may also suggest that effective enforcement of the legal mandate to desegregate higher education is required to accelerate the process of enrolling larger numbers of black students in all professional schools in states under *Adams* litigation.

During the 1960s, it was generally assumed that private institutions were more effective in enrolling black students in professional schools. While that conclusion may have been valid for the 1960s, the situation during the 1970s appeared to be episodic. The findings in this investigation suggest that publicly supported and state-assisted institutions began to enroll more black students than private institutions. But, in the last year of the 1970s private institutions appeared to have been more successful. One reasonable explanation for this change lies in the exorbitant costs of private school education. When that fact is coupled with the uncertainties of financial assistance programs, speculations about the correlations or relationships between type of institution and black student enrollment achieve a new reality. However, the reported confidence level is weaker than the level reported for correlations between other variables in the equation.

Similarly, the confidence level of the correlation between the presence of a black college in the state and first-year black student enrollment in professional schools is weaker than that for other correlations reported. Nevertheless, some support can be made for the position that, at least with regard to the 743 cases in this study, states in which no black college is located were more effective in the 1970s in enrolling black first-year professional school students than states in which black colleges were located. That is precisely why the *Adams* suit was necessary -- to move those institutions beyond the levels of limited tokenism in the desegregation of higher education. This conclusion may be borne out by the trend analysis presented in subsequent chapters when institutional and state-by state data are discussed.

Total Enrollment

To discover the most important predictors of total black student enrollment in professional schools, the same procedure was followed as that presented in the discussion of first-year black student enrollment. The regressions for years 1, 5, and 9 are presented in Table 8. According to this analysis, the number of black faculty in the professional school was consistently the most powerful predictor of total black student enrollment in each of the years selected for analysis. In addition, three variables that were also correlated with first-year enrollment were correlated with total enrollment. These were (1) quality of financial aid (fifth and ninth year); (2) number of professional schools in the state (fifth year); and proportion of blacks in the state population (fifth year). Still another predictor appeared (in both the first and fifth years) to be correlated with total enrollment. This variable was the presence or absence of special admissions programs. Only in the fifth year, however, did that correlation meet our criterion for unqualified inclusion as a powerful predictor. It appears that institutions with special admissions programs are more successful in enrolling black students than are those institutions without them.[4] The comparatively stronger level of confidence shown in the fifth year in relationship to the relatively weaker confidence level displayed in the first year may be important. For instance, it might suggest that in 1970 a larger number of institutions utilized special admissions programs to attract black students. By the fifth year, however, when organized attacks against special admissions programs proliferated and achieved nationwide publicity, professional schools were less likely to admit the utilization of these programs (see Table 8).

Black Students Graduated From Professional Schools

When similar procedures for data analysis were applied to correlations between total numbers of black students graduated and the predictor variables, the number of black faculty once again appeared as the most significant predictor in every year selected for analysis (see Table 9). It was the only variable that met the criterion for acceptability during the first

Table 8
Regression of Total Black Student Enrollment in Professional Schools
with Most-Significant Variables, All Cases, Years 1, 5, 9

Year	Variable	Beta	F	Significance
1	*Number of black faculty in the professional school	2.51	52.93	.00
	*Presence of special admissions programs	21.89	3.70	.07

R^2 for the equation as a whole = .74
F for the equation as a whole = 18.30
Significance = .000

Year	Variable	Beta	F	Significance
5	*Number of black faculty in professional school	1.33	22.83	.00
	*Proportion of blacks in state population	.87	5.72	.01
	*Presence of special admissions program	−17.79	4.31	.03
	*Number of professional schools in state	6.81	3.78	.05
	*Quality of financial aid	9.38	3.31	.07

R^2 for the equation as a whole = .35
F for the equation as a whole = 15.70
Significance = .000

Year	Variable	Beta	F	Significance
9	*Number of black faculty in professional school	1.95	16.15	.00
	*Quality of financial aid	20.30	4.10	.04

R^2 for equation as a whole = .32
F for the equation as a whole = 21.32
Significance = .000

*Most-significant predictor variables in the equation.

Table 9
Regression of Total Black Students Graduated from Professional Schools
with Most-Significant Predictor Variables, All Cases, Years 1, 5, 9

Year	Variable	Beta	F	Significance
1	*Number of black faculty in professional school	.15	7.8l	.01

R^2 for the equation as
a whole = .4l
F for the equation as a whole = 19.48
Significance: = .000

Year	Variable	Beta	F	Significance
5	*Number of black faculty in professional school	.37	54.43	.00
	*Presence of a retention program	−1.8l	3.38	.06
	*Proportion of blacks in state population	.41	5.84	.01
	*Presence of special admissions program	−3.38	4.16	.04

R^2 for equation as a whole = .43
F for equation as a whole = 27.82
Significance: = .000

Year	Variable	Beta	F	Significance
9	*Number of black faculty in professional school	1.41	34.59	.00
	*Presence of special admissions program	−5.79	6.18	.0l

R^2 for equation as a whole = .4l
F for equation as a whole = 31.80
Significance: = .000

*Most-significant predictor variables in the equation.

year. In fact, only two predictor variables attain unqualified acceptance in subsequent years selected for analysis, namely (1) presence or absence of a special admissions program; and (2) proportion of blacks in the state population. The presence of a retention program achieved a level of confidence only slightly varied from the previously stated criterion for acceptance. It should be pointed out that rigid adherence to the .05 level of confidence is not intended to communicate something sacred about that level. It is only a criterion established for the sake of statistical analysis. There are instances, of course, when conventional wisdom might be highly salient for understanding the relative importance of the effect of an independent variable on a dependent variable, even though the correlation does not fall within narrowly defined parameters of acceptance. Such is the case with the retention variable and its correlation with black student graduation in the fifth year. Although most black students do not require "special retention" programs (e.g., tutorials, traditional academic support services), all benefit, directly or indirectly, from the presence of other components of a broadly defined retention program. That program includes the presence of black faculty, a critical mass of black students, formal or informal psychological support structures, and a positive learning environment. These features may not be reflected in simplistic correlational analysis.

In sum, the analysis of the data on the 743 cases suggests that the most powerful predictor of first-year black student enrollment, total black student enrollment, total number of black students graduated from professional schools is, first and foremost, the presence of black faculty members in professional schools in the state. Others are the presence or absence of special admissions programs, proportion of blacks in the state population, presence or absence of a retention program, type of institution, and litigation status with regard to the *Adams* v. *Califano* case. Once again, it is possible that all these predictors may be a manifestation of the same thing: institutional commitment. What is therefore needed, is another construction that permits a more detailed investigation that specifies institutional commitment as the dependent variable.

The question may be raised whether the findings are repeated if each dependent variable is tested against all the predictor variables employed in this study within the context of specific professional fields, as opposed to the aggregate of all cases. An attempt at that analysis failed because of the paucity of cases per year in relation to the large number of predictors attempting to enter the regression equation. In other words, the number of cases, when disaggregated by professional field for every year of the study, was not adequate for the type of analysis desired. Hence the findings reported in this exploratory study apply to the aggregate of cases. Without a more complete data set, it may be premature to make unqualified or grandiose generalizations about a particular field.

Nevertheless, some of the data utilized in the trend analysis are, in fact, more complete and do permit more definitive statements about the relationships between one or more of the dependent variables and such predictors as the number of black faculty and quality of financial aid. Clearly, there is a need for even more complete data on all variables included in this analysis and, perhaps, a sharper statistical model to move this analysis beyond its heuristic level.

Notes

1. Negative correlations refer to the "absence" of these special services.
2. This situation may be attributed to the fact that the first federal court order in the *Adams* case to dismantle publicly supported state systems of higher education was not issued until 1973. Potentially affected states had not anticipated the demands to be imposed by the Court.
3. The strengths and weaknesses of the stepwise regression technique is discussed in Maurice G. Kendal and A. Stuart, *The Advanced Theory of Statistics, vol. 2* (London: Charles Griffin, 1961).
4. The minus signs for beta scores are simply a function of the way in which the variable is coded.

Chapter 4 THE CURRENT CRISIS IN
HIGHER EDUCATION

A major recommendation of this study of blacks in graduate and professional schools is that it is absolutely imperative to begin preparation for postsecondary education in the early years of a person's life. Early childhood education and the quality of learning experienced in the precollege years necessarily influence subsequent educational outcomes. Blacks and other minority students have been shortchanged by educational systems throughout most of American history. The benefits of high-quality public education have not been uniformly shared across racial and class lines. One major consequence of this systematic neglect is the inadequate preparation of all too many youngsters, irrespective of race, for participation in postsecondary education.

The next nine chapters are devoted to a critical examination of trends in the recruitment, enrollment progression, and production of blacks in graduate and professional education as observed for the 15 years between 1970 and 1985. This selection provides a more detailed assessment of a full range of often interrelated factors that affected the nature, scope, and character of the participation of blacks in higher education, and of the socioeconomic and political conditions that influenced the degree or magnitude of change in that participation experienced by blacks.

Given the premise that access to colleges and graduate or professional schools is strongly influenced by variables such as the quality of precollege training and by patterns of systematic discrimination experienced by blacks before college, it is important to examine some aspects of precollege education. This introduction to the next nine chapters serves that function.

Curriculum Content and Quality

Profound changes occurred in literally all aspects of American education during the time frame of this study. For example, the movement toward equal educational opportunity observed during the 1960s meant significant changes in the racial and ethnic composition of many schools, colleges, and universities. The demand for "relevance" resulted in major transformations in curriculum content and quality, as well as in teaching methodology and pedagogy. During the latter part of the 1970s and the first half of the 1980s, national concern over the consequences of uncritical change in schooling and in expectations for the bachelor's degree was expressed in a plethora of reports issued by blue-ribbon panels and national commissions. Highly influential reports, most of which were particularly critical of public school education and inappropriate changes in the quality of higher education, were issued by the College Board, and the National Commission on Excellence in Education.[1] In 1984 and 1985, reports critical of higher education were released by the National Institute of Education, the National Endowment for the Humanities, and the Association of American Colleges.[2]

The first set of reports raised alarm over what was viewed uniformly as a steady decline and erosion of the quality of education provided by the nation's public school system. Confirmation of that decline was observed in the 16-year downturn in scores achieved on the Scholastic Aptitude Test (SAT); a decrease in the number of units of academic subjects required for high school graduation; a watered-down curriculum that was so weak it failed to prepare young people adequately either for successful college work or for acceptable performance in the world of work; a high school curriculum which permitted excessive freedom among students to make educational decisions which should have been the responsibility of teachers and administrators; too many "frill" courses; grade inflation; the high rate of functional illiteracy among high school graduates; the inability of far too many pupils to demonstrate a mastery of the most rudimentary expectations in such basic skills as reading, comprehension, writing, computation, and oral expression in the English language.

The deteriorated conditions of physical plants, outdated and outmoded equipment, and critical shortages of facilities vital to learning and teaching demanded urgent attention. This combination of weaknesses in the curriculum, lowered academic expectations and performance, inadequate physical plants, and lack of interest in learning displayed by many pupils led to a conclusion that the nation was, indeed, at risk. "Perilous" referred to the condition of public schools and their incapacity adequately to prepare and produce a sufficient number and variety of individuals capable of fulfilling future requirements for an informed citizenry.[3]

As stated earlier, in 1984 and 1985, similar assessments and criticisms were made of baccalaureate-degree-granting institutions. It was asserted that the quality of education offered at this level had also declined. For example, the Association of American Colleges noted in *Integrity in the College Curriculum* that responsibility for this dilution of the overall quality of the bachelor's degree rested squarely on the shoulders of college and university professors. This report charged that college academians were too often so preoccupied with their own research and career advancement that effective teaching was sacrificed.[4]

The watering down of the curriculum was a pattern noted not only in precollege education; it was viewed as a universal characteristic of higher education. This situation was manifested in lowered academic standards; reduced requirements for majors; and acquiescence to internal and external pressures for a more vocationally oriented curriculum to the point that high-order cognitive skills and a commitment to intellectual rigor were being abdicated. Further, basic liberal arts education, through which students learn critical thinking and an appreciation for art, literature, world history, basic values, and the need to learn how to live in a multicultural world, had been sacrificed on the altar of expediency and relevance for the intended vocational pursuit. As a result, the nation's colleges and universities produced too many graduates who were without a sense of history, linguistically illiterate, and devoid of aesthetic appreciation.

Reports on the condition of precollege education and the quality of postsecondary education agreed that the most effective way of addressing the problems identified was to raise standards in the pursuit of excellence in education. One major shortcoming of almost all those reports was their failure to give even a modicum of attention to the need to pair equity with excellence in education. The major exception to this observation was the initiation of Project Equality (EQ) in 1981. This 10-year commitment by the College Board was designed to achieve a greater degree of excellence in education without sacrificing equity, in order to assure maximum benefits for racial and ethnic minorities generally locked out of the educational pipeline.[5]

A national consensus emerged near the mid 1980s which noted the urgent need to improve the overall quality of precollege and higher education. No such national agreement existed, however, with respect to identifiable responsibility for that developmental education so imperative for a substantial proportion of college students who continually entered institutions of higher learning without adequate preparation.

In fact, some states and some systems seemed to have taken a more or less calculated position that developmental education in colleges and universities could be all but effectively eliminated if standards were raised in high schools and if higher requirements for high school graduation were implemented. One popular method for accomplishing that goal was the institutionalization of minimal competency examinations as a requirement for graduation or for advancement from lower to higher divisions in the system (e.g., achievement of junior standing in high school or college). By 1985, some 38 states had adopted such practices. Satisfactory completion of competency examinations, therefore, was a graduation requirement. Southern states, which formerly operated de jure segregation and unequal school systems, were in the forefront of this movement. The full impact of these new standards, exemplified in examinations and standardized tests, was noted almost immediately in states such as Florida.

Florida's examinations, mandated by its Raise Bill and its College Level Achievement Skills Test (CLAST), had devastating consequences for black pupils. The impact was noted by the declining proportion of blacks in the state system of higher education, the inordinately high failure rate of blacks on the examinations, and the relative paucity of blacks who progressed through community colleges into four-year colleges and universities. By way of illustration, one major report indicated a decline in the proportion of blacks in higher education in Florida from 13.8% in 1976 to 10.2% in 1981. Further, a significant proportion of the 8000 students lost to higher educational institutions in Florida between 1979 and 1983 were black. Much of that attrition can be directly attributed to failures on competency examinations. For example, in 1983, 56% of all blacks, compared to 33% of Hispanics and 17% of whites, failed Florida's CLAST. In addition, Florida had a 42% dropout rate among pre-high-schoolers in 1983. A disproportionate number of those dropouts were black, a fact which further depressed the potential pool of blacks for college admission, graduation, and entry into graduate or professional schools in that state.[6]

Criticisms of New State Policies

Paralleling the proliferation of minimum competency requirements was the implementation of state-mandated policies whereby school systems were required to raise academic standards by *expanding* high school graduation requirements. This change usually meant an increase in the number of courses required in basic science, biology, chemistry, physics, mathematics, English and composition, and social studies. Several problems emanated from the new policies. First, in the mid 1980s, there was a critical shortage of adequately trained teachers available for several of the new courses required. Specifically, the situation was especially acute with respect to the availability of suitably trained teachers for courses in basic science, mathematics, biology, chemistry and physics, computer literacy, and computer application.

One central explanation for this shortage was, and remains, the failure of teacher-training institutions to produce sufficient numbers of teachers with these kinds of competencies. That failure may be directly attributed to the fact that teacher education or training programs, colleges, and schools are not attracting students who major in these fields as they may have done in the past. Majors in the biological and physical sciences tend to be oriented to much more lucrative positions than the relatively limited financial rewards provided by the teaching profession. Further, many academically able students are persuaded to seek positions of much higher status than can be provided by teaching, a profession that has been steadily devalued by American society, especially for persons teaching in the K–12 levels.

A major criticism of the new policies devised to achieve excellence and higher standards is the failure of public school systems to provide the human and financial resources necessary to achieve that goal at the moment such policies are put into effect. Consequently, it may be argued that this movement toward higher standards may be counterproductive in terms of generating higher performance by the systems' pupils on the standardized tests employed as measures of goal attainment. Insufficient resources and inadequately prepared teachers may still produce pupils who are unsuccessful at achieving high test scores. Clearly, the goals for higher academic standards and a greater degree of excellence in education at all levels are laudatory and uniformly embraced. Nevertheless, maldistribution of resources and properly trained personnel usually results in gross inequities between school districts and widens the educational gap between various groups of students.

Findings from examinations of correlates of performance on the SAT are instructive on this point. While the SAT scores of blacks improved significantly between 1981 and 1984, overall performance on the SAT, irrespective of race, depends on a number of factors. In general, higher group mean scores are positively correlated with high median family income, more academic subjects taken in high school, career aspirations, and educational tracks.[7] Students in the academic track perform better than those in the vocational one. If parental income is viewed as a proxy for social class, then it may be concluded that group mean scores will be higher in the upper-income than in the lower-income brackets. Although some blacks whose parental income is at the lower end of the spectrum achieve high test scores, they, not unlike any other group similarly circumstanced, tend to produce higher test scores if their parental income is at the higher end of the income scale.[8] This fact suggests that a family's ability to provide educational tools, reading materials, and early exposure to intellectually challenging materials in an environment conducive to learning augments a student's capacity to perform well on standardized tests.

There is also evidence to suggest that performance on standardized tests may be significantly improved through coaching, test familiarity, and test readiness. If students do not have the financial resources to receive coaching, they may be at a decided disadvantage when compared with the wealthier but not necessarily more intellectually gifted student who is able to pay enormous sums for coaching and thereby raise test scores.

Admissions Programs

The situation regarding test scores achieves a special salience at a time when postsecondary institutions are raising standards and using higher cutoff scores for college admission. Fluctuations in admissions requirements for colleges and graduate and professional schools persisted between 1970 and 1985. At the beginning of this period, special admissions programs were established as one method of including larger numbers of students who had been denied equal access to colleges and graduate or professional schools. As elaborated in succeeding chapters, special admissions programs coexisted with "regular" admissions requirements. Many black students entered postsecondary education programs under both arrangements. The advent of the *DeFunis* and *Bakke* cases, however, began a relentless attack on special admissions and minority recruitment programs, as well as on all programs characterized as "preferential treatment" for selected groups.

Decreases in the enrollment and progression of blacks through graduate and professional schools correspond with those attacks. Some institutions responded to such attacks by eliminating so-called special programs and by publicly asserting that the most significant admissions criterion was performance on standardized tests. The demand for a meritocracy received a new momentum in 1978 when the U.S. Supreme Court declared illegal rigid set-aside programs under which institutions specified a finite number of places in professional schools for minority groups and for which non-minorities could not compete. One outcome of this decision was an attack by opponents of testing on the abuses of testing and on all institutions that used a single criterion as the principal determinant of eligibility. Significantly, the College Board and the Educational Testing Service (ETS) also decried test abuses and the use of a single criterion for admissions. Nevertheless, the battle over test use and the efficacy of coaching continues in the mid 1980s and is likely to persist.

The pool of potentially eligible candidates for admission to a graduate or professional school is not only affected by the students' ability to perform well on objective criteria for admissions but also on the absolute number of persons who actually complete various levels in the educational pipeline. The graduate–professional pool is largely constructed from those who successfully complete college. In turn, the number entering college is a function of the number who graduate from high school or who receive a high school equivalency certificate. And the number completing high school reflects the ability of secondary schools to control or reduce the high school dropout rate.

For a time, it seemed that the high school dropout rate among blacks was under control. Indeed, between 1970 and 1980, the percentage of black 17-year-olds who had dropped out fell from 22.2% to 16.0%. These figures compared to 11.9% and 11.3% for whites in 1970 and 1980, respectively. In 1981, the dropout rate continued to decline among blacks and whites. Among blacks, it fell to 15.4% of all 17-year-olds in the population, while among whites it remained steady at 11.3%[9] By 1984, however, the high school dropout rate among blacks was 15.8%; it had begun to rise again.[10]

Between 1960 and 1981, blacks made significant gains in college attendance. For instance, among 18- to 24-year-olds in the population in 1960, 18.4% of all blacks, compared to 24.2% of all whites, were enrolled in college. A decade later, in 1970, the percentage of black enrollees climbed to 26.0%, while that for whites in that age cohort increased to 33.2%. Five years later, primarily due to affirmative efforts in the recruitment of blacks for colleges and their increasing access to financial assistance, 32% of all blacks between the ages of 18 and 24 were enrolled in colleges; the percentage of whites remained relatively constant at 32.4%. Blacks had closed the gap between themselves and whites. Both groups showed a downturn in the proportion of persons in that age cohort enrolled in college in 1980. Specifically, the college-going rates fell to 27.8% for blacks and 32.0% for whites. In 1981, however, a slight upturn was registered, 28.2% for blacks and 32.8% for whites.[11] The situation worsened in 1983 when 8000 fewer blacks enrolled in college than in 1976; 500,000 more blacks received high school diplomas. This situation may be attributed largely to the financial aid policies imposed by the Reagan administration, more stringent college admissions policies, less than aggressive recruitment of black students and to the economic problems experienced by a substantial segment of the black population.

College completion rates have also improved significantly among black Americans in recent years. For example, among blacks 25 years and older, 3.1%, compared to 7.7% of whites, had completed four or more years of college in 1960. By 1970, the rate among blacks rose modestly to 4.5%, while that for whites increased to 11%. By 1980, due largely to the unparalleled increase in college access experienced by blacks, the growth in college-going rates among them, and increased federal financial aid, blacks had made significant gains in college completion. In 1981, 8.2% of all blacks and 17.1% of all whites in this age cohort had completed four or more years of college.[12]

The steady expansion of high school and college graduate pools means an expansion of the potential pool for admission to graduate or professional schools. While significant increases in the absolute numbers of blacks matriculated in some professional schools and graduate programs were noted during the early 1970s, major problems were observed after 1975. The next nine chapters address this issue and discuss a number of interconnected factors that have curtailed the advancements made by black Americans during the early 1970s.

The Patterns of Financial Assistance

While some impediments to the continued access, progression, and production of black professionals seem to be unique to specific disciplines or professions, certain barriers are common to all fields. One barrier commonly experienced is shrinking financial assistance for students enrolled in postsecondary education. This problem is especially acute for black and other minority students who come from families whose median family income is only 55% of that of the white population. It is particularly severe for students whose family income is at the lower end of the middle-income spectrum and for those from working-class and poverty families.

Large-scale federal contributions to financial aid for postsecondary education students began in 1955 with the enactment of the National Defense Education Act (NDEA). Since that time, federal intervention and contributions to college and graduate–professional education have expanded enormously through the development of an immense variety of programs and legal statutes. Among these are Pell Grants, also known as Basic Education Opportunity Grants, or BEOGs; Supplemental Education Opportunity Grants (SEOGs); the SSIG, or Social Security Insurance Grants; College Work Study (CWS); Graduate Student Loans (GSLs); specially directed programs for social security beneficiaries veterans, and persons who qualify for grants and loans; and other programs encompassed by the Middle Income Assistance Act of 1978. While institutional funds and contributions to postsecondary education from the private sector grew at unparalleled rates during the 1960s and 1970s, the major sources of such assistance were federal programs. For example, in the early 1960s, less than 40% of total dollars supporting college and postcollege assistance were federal in origin. By 1983, approximately 80% of all student financial assistance came from federal sources. Federal support for higher education declined significantly, however, during the first term of President Ronald Reagan. In fact, there was a $2 billion drop in total aid between 1981–1982 and 1983–1984. This loss can be attributed to Reagan administration imposed restrictions on eligibility for GSLs, the phasing out of student benefits previously guaranteed to social security beneficiaries, and the steady decline in veterans benefits.[13] Clearly, student aid, whether at the college or graduate–professional school level, has not kept pace with inflation.

Student aid has also been affected by inflation and shifts in the allocation of aid through grants and loan programs. After adjustments for inflation, even increases in absolute dollars to such popular programs as Pell Grants were valued at less than their dollar worth in the late 1970s.[14] Moreover, total financial assistance awarded through grants and loans was 48% each in 1984, compared to 80% awarded in grants in 1975–1976 and only 17% received through loans. Thus, under the Reagan administration, the *pattern* of financial aid to students changed dramatically. This is especially noticeable with respect to the proportion of students who must assume heavy financial burdens through loan programs in order to finance education.

As amplified in subsequent chapters, this necessity to depend heavily on repayable loan programs may be a serious deterrent to many students, especially blacks and other minorities, from pursuing advanced, graduate, or professional degrees. Yet blacks are more likely than whites to be compelled to support their graduate–professional education through loans; especially in graduate programs, whites are more likely to be awarded fellowships and graduate and teaching assistantships than are black students. Were it not for significant financial contributions through grants and special scholarships from the private sector to blacks and other minority students, the absolute numbers would have been reduced even more drastically in several graduate–professional fields of study. This situation is especially noteworthy in medicine, engineering, dentistry, and law.

In sum, the numbers and percentages of blacks who complete graduate or professional school training are affected by a great array of factors. Many factors are systemized in the educational enterprise. Some result from variations in federal, state, and private-sector intervention or neglect in ways that either advance or impede access and progression. Some are structural in the sense that they result from economic deprivation. Others are motivational and depend on the individual's own determination to surmount apparently insurmountable barriers in order to obtain educational goals.

Notes

1. See College Board, *Academic Preparation for College* (New York: College Board, 1983); idem, *Report of the National Blue Ribbon Panel on Declining Test Scores* (New York: College Board, 1979); National Commission on Excellence in Education, *A Nation at Risk* (Washington, D.C.: U.S. Government Printing Office, 1983).
2. National Institute of Education, *Involvement in Learning* (Washington, D.C.: National Institute of Education, 1984); William Bennett, *To Reclaim Legacy* (Washington, D.C.: National Endowment for the Humanities, 1984); Association of American Colleges, *Integrity in College Curriculum* (Washington, D.C.: Association of American Colleges, 1984).
3. National Commission, *A Nation at Risk*.
4. Association of American Colleges, *Integrity in the College Curriculum*.
5. College Board, *Project Equality* (New York: College Board, 1983).
6. James E. Blackwell, *Desegregation of State Systems of Higher Education: An Assessment* (Atlanta: Southern Education Foundation, 1984).
7. _____, "Correlates of the Scholastic Aptitude Test" paper presented at the Annual Forum of the College Board, Dallas, Texas, October 1983.
8. Ibid.
9. James E. Blackwell, *The Black Community: Diversity and Unity*, 2d ed. (New York: Harper & Row, 1985), p. 164.
10. Data provided by Wendy Bunno of the U.S. Bureau of the Census, August 28, 1985.
11. Op. Cit., p. 183.
12. Ibid., p. 184.
13. Donald A. Gillespie and Nancy Carlson, *Trends in Student Aid: 1963–1983* (Washington, D.C.: College Board, 1984), p. v.
14. Ibid.

Chapter 5 THE MEDICAL EDUCATION OF BLACK AMERICANS

Few issues in graduate and professional education created as much controversy, political enmity, personal dilemmas, and social strains among the nation's citizenry as did that of the admission of black and other minority students to medical colleges during the 1970s. Most of the litigation during that period regarding access to professional schools involved either medicine or law, but the most celebrated cases were in medical education.

The dilemmas unearthed during the controversy over the medical education of black Americans in the 1970s revealed problems considerably more fundamental in nature and scope than suggested by specific observations. For instance, whether the nation listened or not, Americans were informed of the critical nationwide shortage of black and other minority-group physicians in general and, most especially, in underserved areas. Paucity of black physicians coincides with other health-related problems. This shortage of physicians and other health-care personnel dramatizes the gross inadequacies in the delivery of health-care services to those groups in the population whose needs are most pronounced.

It is clearly not a problem of the quality of training but, most fundamentally, a manifestation of the limited number of individuals and appropriate facilities available to provide the services required. As a result, disproportionate numbers of black Americans needlessly die each year of hypertension, cardiovascular disorders, malignant neoplasms, early childhood diseases, lead poisoning, influenza, and cirrhosis of the liver. Inordinate numbers of black Americans continually suffer from serious and incapacitating mental health problems because of inabilities to develop the kinds and quality of coping strategies obtained through proper psychiatric care. This, too, is a manifestation of both shortage and maldistribution of physicians and other health-care professionals.

This chapter focuses on those efforts mounted between 1970 and 1985 to alleviate the problem of underrepresentation, as well as on programs designed to utilize medical education as one strategy for mainstreaming black Americans in the professions. It devotes special attention to some of the major dilemmas and social conflicts of the 1970s that affected the implementation of those programs and the ultimate realization of their goal—the production of larger numbers and percentages of black physicians.

74

Howard University and Meharry Medical College

In terms of history, no two institutions have played such a pronounced and vitally important role in the training of black Americans in the health-care professions as have Howard University in Washington, D.C., and Meharry Medical College in Nashville, Tennessee. During Reconstruction and post-Reconstruction, eight medical schools opened for the training of black physicians, dentists, and other health specialists. Of those schools, only the College of Medicine at Howard, established in 1867, and Meharry Medical College, founded in 1876, remain.[1]

Howard, largely federally funded, and Meharry, heavily subsidized by the federal government although privately established, assumed the responsibility for medical education among black Americans at a time when, as policy, blacks were excluded from other medical colleges. Their responsibility encompassed far more than formal coursework in medical schools. It was necessary for these institutions to provide clinical training, internships, and residencies for blacks. That type of training was unavailable to blacks throughout southern "whites only" facilities and only minimally and selectively open to them in other parts of the country.

Because of the deepening patterns of segregation, discrimination, and rampant racism which followed the legalization of the "separate but equal" philosophy and its dispersion among all forms of institutional life, opportunities for medical training for black Americans were universally restricted. Clinical training was confined to historically black hospitals because of the refusal of white hospitals to accept even those black students graduated from historically white medical schools. Meharry and Howard graduates shared the same experience.[2] Racism, segregation, discrimination, and absolute necessity account for the establishment of the teaching hospitals associated with the two black medical colleges. Freedmen's Hospital was founded at Howard University, and Hubbard Memorial Hospital was established at Meharry. They provided a large share of the spaces required for black interns and residents. Other historically black hospitals that played an early role in this endeavor included Homer G. Phillips (St. Louis), Provident (Chicago), and Flint Goodrich (New Orleans). Others operated in Detroit, Philadelphia, Greensboro, and elsewhere.

Similarly, blacks were not permitted to hold faculty positions in historically white medical colleges because white students objected. Blacks were barred from administrative positions in medical schools because of institutionalized patterns of racism and racial discrimination. Few practicing black physicians were permitted to join local, state, or national medical associations and societies. Consequently, they were prohibited from influencing health-care policy that affected the lives of American citizens. In essence, black Americans were relegated to what Montague Cobb calls "The Negro medical ghetto."[3]

Howard University and Meharry Medical College assumed the responsibility of meeting the needs of black Americans not only in a medical ghetto but in preparing their graduates to fulfill a leadership role in the medical community of the larger American society. The magnitude of their success can be gleaned from the fact that as late as 1967, approximately 83% of the 6000 black physicians in practice received their training at either Meharry or Howard.[4] Despite increases in the absolute numbers of black students enrolled in historically white medical schools and the growing numbers of black faculty in these institutions in 1979, Howard and Meharry accounted for 23% of black first-year enrollees in U.S. medical schools; about 22% of total black students enrollment, and approximately 26% of all blacks holding faculty positions either in the basic sciences or as clinical appointees.[5] And it is their graduates who hold leadership roles today, as in the past, in the National Medical Association (the black counterpart to the largely white American Medical Association was founded in 1895) as well as in policymaking roles in the broader medical community. Hence, Meharry and Howard continue to play a major role and to perform an important service in the American society as a whole. During the 1970s, two additional, predominantly black medical colleges opened, in Atlanta at Morehouse College and in Los Angeles at the Charles Drew Medical Center at UCLA). Undoubtedly, their presence also helped depress the percentage of black medical school students enrolled at Meharry and Howard University. Further, it is probably safe to assume that the distribution of black medical faculty was also somewhat affected by the establishment of these two institutions.

The Role of Professional Associations

The centerpiece of the civil rights movement of the 1960s was "access" —opening up opportunities to better jobs, public accommodations, political rights, and equality of educational opportunity. Since it encompassed all aspects of social life in the American society in which blacks were categorized as "outsiders," medical education could not escape its thrust. As the student sit-in movement shifted from public accommodations toward gaining other dimensions of structural equality, a primary target was defined as access to graduate and professional schools, especially in medicine and law. These were high-status professions presumed to produce lucrative financial rewards and be the source of tremendous power, influence, and prestige in the community.

Any assessment of the percentages of blacks or of their absolute numbers in the medical profession leads to the inevitable conclusion that black Americans not only are underrepresented but have been shortchanged. Prior to the escalation of the civil rights movement, there was no substantial evidence of serious commitment by the white medical establishment to the medical education of black and other minority students. The overall shortage of black physicians is suggested by the fact that as the 1970s began, black Americans represented approximately 11.1% of the total U.S. population but only 2.1% of all practicing physicians in the nation.[6] The paucity of black applicants to medical schools exacerbated the situation. This was indeed an intolerable disparity—a situation that begged rectification. This dearth of black physicians, the recognition of the inadequacies in the delivery of health-care services to underserved areas, pressures from the civil rights movement, and consciousness raising among some medical school faculties and administrative leadership coalesced to produce major policy decisions by the power structure of the medical profession.

In response to this situation, a number of efforts, aimed at rectification of past and current injustices and inequities in medical education, were initiated either jointly or independently by a variety of professional organizations in the health-care field. Among these were the Association of American Medical Colleges (AAMC), the National Medical Association (NMA), the American Medical Association (AMA), and the American Hospital Association (AHA). Policy statements of major foundations also signaled increasing commitment to accelerate the mainstreaming process of black students in the field of medicine. This list included the Ford Foundation, Carnegie Foundation, Alfred P. Sloan Foundation, Josiah T. Macy Foundation, Rockefeller Foundation, Robert Wood Johnson Foundation, and many others. As we shall see, the federal government became more aggressive in its efforts to stimulate greater equality of access through a variety of enabling scholarship programs and direct financial assistance to medical and dental schools. The combined activities and programmatic developments fostered by these groups were directed at changing the racial and class composition of medical schools and toward reducing their long-standing characteristic as the bastions of white male privilege and opportunity.

One of the prime movers in these endeavors was the AAMC, whose leaders, with the enouragement and support of its membership institutions and through policies enunciated at annual meetings, embarked on a program of significant change in 1968. In that year, the AAMC publicly expressed its endorsement of a position previously taken by some of its member institutions to move toward increasing diversification of students of medical colleges. This move meant effectuating changes that would lead to more aggressive recruitment, selection, admission, and enrollment of larger numbers of students from varied ethnic, racial, and economic backgrounds and from different geographic areas of the country.[7]

In 1969, in cooperation with the National Medical Association, the AMA demonstrated its changing commitment through the endorsement of resolutions which stressed wider participation of all outsider groups in the health-care fields. They supported greater use of equivalency and proficiency tests in order to provide a more systematic method of evaluating previous education and experience. This policy assured recognition of the value of on-the-job experience for academic credit should such persons decide to seek professional training in medical colleges.[8]

The AAMC, also in 1969, obtained its first major grant (approximately $1.5 million) from the U.S. Office of Economic Opportunity (OEO) for the purpose of facilitating equal access to educational opportunities for minority students in health-care fields. As a result of this grant, and others that followed, the AAMC established national projects that have proven indispensable for increasing access to medical schools. Among these projects are the AAMC's Office of Minority Affairs, the Medical Minority Applicant Registry (also known as Med-Mar), and the publication *Minority Student Opportunities in United States Medical Schools*. The Office of Minority Affairs, located at the AAMC national headquarters, is an invaluable link in the recruitment process. The grants received from OEO were also a prime source of funds utilized for the development of about 50 minority programs at colleges and professional schools.[9] These concerted actions represented early manifestations of a strong commitment to attack head-on the problem of underrepresentation of minorities in medicine.

Pursuant to that commitment, the AAMC was also troubled by both underrepresentation and maldistribution of blacks in the medical profession. The primary responsibility for the training of black students was, and had been, assumed for almost 100 years by Meharry and Howard. As a consequence of racism, segregation, and discrimination, by 1970 black students represented only a paltry 2.8% of total enrollment in all U.S. medical schools, and Howard and Meharry accounted for about 50% of all blacks in medical colleges. To address this problem of opening up more of the historically white medical schools and, thereby, distributing new enrollees throughout medical colleges, the AAMC organized the first of two Task Forces on Minority Student Opportunities in Medicine in 1970. This task force was funded by the Alfred P. Sloan Foundation and was chaired by Dr. Bernard M. Nelson.

Principal objectives of the task force included a delineation of the barriers which militated against full participation of minority groups in medical education, the identification of programs and strategies that could facilitate increases in access of minority students to medical schools, and the recommendation of concrete proposals that would assist in that process.[10] In April 1970 the task force presented its findings and recommendations to the Inter-Association Committee on Expanding Educational Opportunities in Medicine. One of its more highly publicized recommendations was to increase minority-group representation to 12% of total enrollment in U.S. medical colleges by 1975–1976. Implementation programs regarding this recommendation, coupled with a recommendation to establish regional career informational and tutorial centers, drew widespread attention under the National Medical Association's banner "Project 75."[11]

In view of the immediate action taken on them, at least four additional recommendations from the 1970 Task Force had long-term implications. It was recommended that (1) a central national organization be identified that would have the primary responsibility for coordinating the solicitation and distribution of all financial aid to minority-group medical students; (2) an educational opportunity bank be established as a more permanent solution to the problem of financial aid; (3) regional centers be set up throughout the United States which could more effectively disseminate essential information about opportunities in the health professions as a career; and (4) the AAMC be urged to seek funds from external sources that would enable it to expand the Office of Minority Student Affairs to broaden the scope of its services.[12]

Support for these recommendations was immediate and broad. The medical colleges endorsed the recommendations, as did the leadership structure of the AAMC. The proposals were also accepted by the American Medical Association, the National Medical Association (which is the leading historically black organization of physicians), the American Hospital Association, the federal government, and several major foundations.

The organization selected to coordinate the solicitation and distribution of scholarship monies to minority-group medical students was the National Medical Fellowship (NMF), headquartered in New York City. This strategy proved highly successful, especially in the early 1970s. For example, in 1970–71 the NMF awarded 588 fellowships, valued at $923,750, to minority students. In 1973–74 the total number of recipients tripled to 1760, while the dollar value of the awards more than doubled to $2,393,800. The total number of medical colleges had increased from 82 to 110 between 1971 and 1973, however, while the number of minority students had climbed from 808 to 1301. Thus, significantly more students needed financial aid. The peak year for total number of awards given to minority students was 1974–75 when 1840 minority medical students received NMF scholarships. Between 1975 and 1984, the total number of awards granted by the NMF dropped precipitously, from 1551 in 1975–76 to 836 in 1979–80, but the downward trend was reversed in 1981–82 when 1122 awards totaling $1,484,170 were distributed. That upward trend continued through 1983–84 when 1152 awards with a total value of $1,878,236 were allocated to minority students. In 1984–85, NMF Awards were granted to only 985 students.[13]

From the inception of these grants, the majority of the minority-group recipients of NMF awards have been black students. This distribution is not unexpected given the fact that the vast majority of underrepresented minorities in U.S. medical colleges are black Americans. This situation may be briefly illustrated by comparing minority first-year enrollments for the years 1970–71 and 1983–84. In 1970–71, of the 808 minority students enrolled in the 82 medical colleges, 697 were blacks, 73 were Mexican Americans, 3 were mainland Puerto Ricans, and 3 were Native Americans (Indians). By 1983–84, first-year minority-student enrollment had more than doubled to 1658 students. Equally dramatic increases were experienced in absolute numbers for blacks (1173), Mexican Americans (301), mainland Puerto Ricans (109), and Native Americans (7).[14] Of the 588 awards to first-year medical students distributed in 1982–83, for example, 428 were received by blacks, 98 by Mexican Americans, 54 by mainland Puerto Ricans, and 8 by Native Americans.

Another method of assessing the real magnitude of NMF awards is the percentage of first-year students assisted from this source. Again, 1982–83 may be employed for illustration. In that year, 37.3% of first-year black students, 32.1% of Mexican Americans, 47.3% of mainland Puerto Ricans, and 12.9% of Native Americans received NMF awards. In 1984–85, however, of the 504 NMF awards to first year medical students, 70.6% were received by blacks, 18.5% by Mexican Americans, 8.5% by mainland Puerto Ricans, and 2.4% were received by Native Americans.

As suggested by the data presented in Table 10, the total number of recipients per state is, in part, a reflection of the total number of alleopathic and osteopathic colleges of medicine within a state. The 109 recipients in California were enrolled in 10 institutions, while the 130 New York recipients matriculated at 13 institutions. Nevertheless, the smaller number of California residents received $150,160 compared to $117,575 received by students from New York. Hence, factors other than the number of institutions are apparently related to the amount of award received.

The majority of NMF award recipients tend to come from New York (130), California (109), Pennsylvania (85), Tennessee (83), District of Columbia (78), Michigan (66), Texas (60), Massachusetts (56), Ohio (56), Illinois (54), and New Jersey (50). Of this group, only Pennsylvania, Texas, and Ohio are among the "*Adams* states." In the District of Columbia, Howard University, a historically black institution (HBI), accounted for 64 of the 78 recipients. In Tennessee, 78 of the 93 recipients came from Meharry Medical College (another HBI). Other "*Adams* states" represented among the recipients were Alabama (10), Arkansas (16), Florida (13), Georgia (24), including 15 recipients from the newly established college of medicine at Morehouse, (an HBI), Kentucky (7), Louisiana (17), Maryland (12),

Table 10
Total National Medical Fellowship Awards Approved for 1982–1983, All Minorities and All Institutions Combined

State	N of Institutions	N of Recipients	Amount Granted
Alabama*	2	10	$ 7,500
Arizona	1	7	5,900
Arkansas*	1	16	11,500
California[a]	10	109	150,160
Colorado	1	3	3,300
Connecticut	2	9	9,100
District of Columbia	3	78	68,935
Florida*[a]	4	13	8,500
Georgia*	4	24	20,350
Illinois*[a]	8	54	45,900
Indiana	1	9	5,700
Iowa[a]	1	2	1,500
Kentucky*	2	7	5,675
Louisiana*	3	17	13,500
Maryland*	2	12	11,825
Massachusetts	4	56	57,750
Michigan[a]	4	66	57,550
Minnesota	3	12	17,250
Mississippi	1	8	4,600
Missouri*[b]	4	24	19,800
Nebraska	2	10	9,810
New Hampshire	1	7	5,800
New Jersey[a]	3	50	59,260
New Mexico	1	7	4,700
New York	13	130	117,575
North Carolina[a]	4	30	25,400
North Dakota	1	1	1,700
Ohio*[a]	6	56	43,400
Oklahoma*[a]	3	8	6,200
Pennsylvania*[a]	8	85	96,949
Rhode Island	1	9	9,450
South Carolina*	2	4	2,900
Tennessee*	4	83	74,510
Texas*[a]	7	60	40,600
Utah	1	2	1,650
Virginia*	2	6	5,200
Washington	1	10	12,600
West Virginia*[a]	2	3	2,500
Wisconsin	2	46	41,650
Hawaii	1	1	500
Puerto Rico	2	2	2,000
Total	**128**	**1146**	**$1,090,649**

Source: *National Medical Fellowship Annual Report, 1983,* pp. 22–27.
* = an "Adams state"; [a] = 1 college of osteopathic medicine; [b] = 2 colleges of osteopathic medicine.

Missouri (24), North Carolina (30), Oklahoma (8), South Carolina (4), Virginia (6), and West Virginia (3).[15] See Table 10.

As of 1985, the NMF was supported by more than 150 corporations and foundations, by private contributors, and by former recipients. The largest foundation support continues to be the Robert Wood Johnson Foundation, which pledged $2 million to NMF over a four-year period from 1982 to 1986. Other major contributors are the Henry J. Kaiser Family Foundation ($300,000); the Commonwealth Fund ($260,000 between 1982 and 1984); and the Andrew Mellon Foundation ($250,000 between 1982 and 1985). In addition, the William T. Grant Foundation awarded the NMF a $60,000 grant in support of a behavior development research fellowship for black and other minority students.[16]

Almost from the beginning of the national effort to expand opportunity for medical education to blacks and other minority students, the Robert Wood Johnson Foundation was a major financial supporter. This organization gave some $10 million to American medical schools between 1971 and 1975 as loans or scholarships for minority, female, and rural medical students. The federal government was also involved early on, with the establishment of the Health Professions Scholarship and the Health Professions Loan Program.[17] In addition, several institutions received capitation grants from the federal government based on the number of target-group students recruited and enrolled in the professional school.

Expeditious action on the 1969 resolutions paved the way for significant recruitment programs to be established at the nation's medical schools and by professional organizations such as the National Medical Association. As a component of Project 75, in 1970 the NMA embarked on a program of establishing counseling and tutorial centers in various regional areas throughout the country. This project was supported through funds obtained from the Office of Economic Opportunity (OEO). A major initial purpose of these centers was to assist prospective applicants to improve their academic skills in preparation for possible medical school training and to achieve a better understanding of their own commitment to the medical and health-care professions. Subsequent evaluation of Project 75 revealed extensive shortcomings and inadequacies in the academic preparation of many of the students, who sought assistance especially in the basic sciences. It was soon evident that the kinds of services provided through Project 75 should, in fact, be incorporated in early training programs, even in elementary school level.[18] The Department of Health, Education, and Welfare provided additional monies for recruitment activities and programs developed for increasing access to health-care fields through its newly created Office of Health Professions Scholarship Program.

Participants were also exposed to a number of role models at these regional centers who provided information about medical careers and often tutored in the basic sciences. Any number of black physicians, scientists, and health-care practitioners offered their services at these centers on a regular basis. Informed encounters also more effectively socialized potential applicants into the world of medical education.

The AAMC was able to obtain sufficient funds to permit expansion of its Office of Minority Affairs. As a result, three major activities of that Office have continued and broadened their scope. The first of these is Med-Mar. This is a Medical Minority Applicant Registry, which is a mechanism through which minority-student applicants to medical colleges may have pertinent biographical data circulated to the admissions offices of various medical colleges and other health-service organizations without cost. Participation in this program is voluntary after a request for minority identification is provided on the Med-Mar Questionnaire. This is completed at the time the MCAT or the New MCAT is taken. The Med-Mar lists are circulated in July and November of each year for the benefit of both the applicant and interested medical colleges. After medical colleges make assessments of the biographical data submitted by the applicant, interested institutions may contact the applicant or the institution may request additional information from Med-Mar.[19]

The second service provided by the AAMC Office of Minority Affairs is the Minority Student Information Clearinghouse, which furnishes information of all types that is of special interest to minority-group medical school applicants and students as well as to institutions. This service included information about the application process, programs of specific medical institutions, fee waivers, and so forth. The third related service to minority affairs is the continued publication of *Minority Student Opportunities in U.S. Medical Schools*. This book has been published almost annually since 1969. Its functions are described in Chapter 2. It is a comprehensive document containing an impressive collection of information of value to anyone interested in medical education. The AAMC also participates in a centralized application service (which is explained in a subsequent section(and provides pertinent data on "fee waiver" programs of participating medical colleges.

Despite these activities, and for reasons to be amplified in a subsequent section, the goals of Project 75 and the AAMC of achieving a 12% minority-student enrollment by 1975–1976 were not attained. In fact, the enrollment of minority groups peaked in 1974, and for some groups there has been a noticeable continuing decline in their proportionate representation in medical colleges. This trend is especially true of black student enrollment, despite increases in their absolute numbers.

Given this situation, the Executive Council of the AAMC established a second Task Force on Minority Student Opportunities in Medicine in February 1976. The essential charges to the task force were to obtain information, to analyze and assess problems that impede efforts to enroll more minority students in medicine, to explain the difficulties encountered by applicants from these groups in attempting to gain access, to investigate how minority-group students within medical institutions themselves have responded to the challenges posed by a changing racial composition, and finally to shed light on the perceptions that minority-group students may have of the desirability of medical careers when other alternative choices are available to them.[20]

The second task force identified seven major goals in response to its charges. In the order of importance as a guideline to the AAMC's interpretation of problems encountered in providing greater access to minority-group students, they are:

Goal 1.   Increase the pool of qualified racial minority applicants to levels equivalent to their proportion in the U.S. population with progress toward that goal reviewed on a biennial basis.

Goal 2.   Enlarge the number of qualified racial minority students admitted to medical school through improvement of the selection process.

Goal 4.   Emphasize the importance of financial assistance for racial minority students pursuing careers in medicine.

Goal 5.   Increase the representation of racial minority persons among basic science and clinical faculty.

Goal 6.   Encourage the establishment of faculty development programs aimed at fostering an understanding of the history and culture of racial minority groups and at improving the quality of medical school instruction.

Goal 7.   Ensure that graduate and medical education needs and opportunities for racial minority students are met.[21]

After more than two years of investigation, analysis, and evaluation of all the issues related to its charges and its seven goals, the task force made some 34 recommendations in its report of June 1978. These recommendations, which influenced many recommendations made in this study, reveal the immense difficulties encountered in sustaining overall commitment to increase equality of opportunity in medical education. They also point to the fluctuations in patterns of enrollment and the retrenchment in financial as well as public support for programmatic efforts to expand the racial composition of medical schools beyond mere tokenism. By 1978 the mood of the nation had shifted dramatically from a manifest concern for improving the status of minority groups in the direction of self-centered dominant-group prerogatives. Individual members of the majority group had challenged the legitimacy and constitutionality of special programs designed to attain the goals articulated by both the first and second task force reports.

Coalitions forged during the civil rights period of the 1960s were now dissolved as former partners took opposing and often acrimonious positions during the debates over admissions policies, practices, and procedures in graduate and professional schools.

The *DeFunis* and *Bakke* Cases

Although the *DeFunis* and *Bakke* cases emerged as symbols of resistance to efforts to achieve equality of educational opportunity, other court cases that challenged affirmative efforts in the professional schools arose with less public notice and fanfare during the 1970s. It should be borne in mind that about 50% of U.S. medical schools initiated special recruitment programs in 1969. By 1975, 89 of the 112 medical institutions that responded to a special questionnaire in a study conducted by John S. Wellington and Pilar O. Gyorfy indicated that they had established special recruitment programs for minority students.[22] Frank Atelsek and Irene L. Gomberg reported in 1978 that of the institutions they studied, 45% that awarded graduate and professional degrees had at least one program designed specifically for minorities and women; 30% had special recruitment programs; 35% offered academic assistance, and schools of medicine and law were considerably more active in these endeavors than were other professions.[23]

This study shows that, for 1975, 66% of the medical schools had special recruitment programs; 55% had special admissions programs of some type; 85% had minority financial aid programs; and 50% had special academic assistance or retention programs. Without questions, these programs played a major role in whatever increases in the enrollment of black and other minority-group students occurred during the 1970s. But the legal challenges to modest successes boldly asserted that minority-group students were entering medical schools at the expense of white students.

Between 1970 and 1976, aside from the challenge mounted by Marco DeFunis, Jr., the constitutionality of these special efforts and preferential admissions, in particular, was raised in several lower courts. These reached the court of appeals of New York, for instance, which raised the question of the constitutionality of the minority programs at the Downstate Medical Center. Also, a challenge to the admissions policy of the Sophie Davis Center for Biomedical Education of the City University of New York reached a federal court in New York. Similarly, the financial aid program of the Law School of Georgetown University had to be defended in a federal court.[24] But the two most important and far-reaching cases with national implications were *DeFunis* v. *Odegaard* (1974) and *Regents of the University of California* v. *Allan Bakke* (1978).

Certain features of the *DeFunis* case were described in Chapter 1. An excellent account of the DeFunis family and educational history is presented in *Bakke, DeFunis, and Minority Admissions: The Quest for Equal Opportunity* by Allan P. Sindler.[25] This reference also provides a cogent analysis of the *DeFunis* case from its origins through the decision by the U.S. Supreme Court that the case was moot and without legal merit.[26] Just as this case was particularly significant as a precursor to the *Bakke* case, it had the immediate effect of identifying central issues germane to mainstreaming in professional school education. The case showed how many former partners in civil rights struggle against racial injustices during the 1960s found themselves in an explosively contentious relationship.

For example, DeFunis gained support from such groups as the AFL–CIO and the National Association of Manufacturers. Strong support for his case came from the Anti-Defamation League of B'nai B'rith, the American Jewish Committee, the American Jewish Congress, and the Jewish Rights Council. Opponents to the position taken by DeFunis included the National Organization of Jewish Women, Harvard University, the Massachusetts Institute of Technology, Rutgers University, the Law School Association, the AAMC, the NAACP–LDF, the National Urban League, and major civil rights organizations that represented the black, Puerto Rican, Mexican American, and Japanese American communities.[27] Essentially, then, battle lines were drawn and positions staked out in preparation for forthcoming cases in this issue.

In 1973, Allan Bakke, a white male of Norwegian ancestry and a resident of California, applied for the first time to the Medical College of the University of California at Davis. He was rejected and applied for the second time to UC–Davis in 1974, only to be rejected for a second time. Like DeFunis, Bakke had strong academic credentials and had performed well on all objective measures of evaluation. The UC–Davis Medical School enrolled 100 students in its first-year class, but through its special admissions programs, 16 of the 100 seats were specified exclusively for minority students. As a result of its special admissions program, the medical school had become one of the more successful nonblack medical colleges in enrolling minority-group students.

By 1974, as in the case of law schools and despite the expansion of the number of medical colleges since 1964, competition for positions in medical school classes had become keen and severe. Admissions standards were indeed raised, and even though there may have been an increasing tendency to assign greater weight to objective measures of evaluation, many medical schools required personal interviews to enable them to develop a more acceptable assessment of subjective or nontraditional factors employed in evaluation of criteria for admission. Allan Bakke was interviewed at UC–Davis with mixed results. He considered options of suing

Stanford University to test the constitutionality of its special admissions programs, which set aside 12 seats for minority-group students. He was assisted in his decision about options available to him by a person who was then a staff member of the UC–Davis Admissions Office. Ultimately, in 1974, following his rejection from the UC–Davis Medical School (as well as rejection from 11 other medical colleges), he sued and attacked the constitutionality of preferential admissions programs.

The case attracted more national attention than perhaps any other ethnic case that reached the Supreme Court of the United States since *Brown* v. *Board of Education.* It was followed with exceptional interest as it made a way through the lower courts. The California Supreme Court supported Bakke, but the Regents of the University of California decided to appeal the decision, which led the case to the U.S. Supreme Court for resolution. Many persons questioned the motives of the University of California in pursuing what was described as a weak case supported by a weak legal defense at the state level. One persistent question was whether or not some form of collusion existed to eliminate special admissions programs based on racial or ethnic preference. Hence, the university was placed in a double bind of defending both its program and its legal course of action.

Some 57 *amici* briefs were filed in this case. Supporters of Bakke advocated an end to what they defined as "reverse discrimination," preferential treatment for minority groups and quotas. Opponents to Bakke argued against the legitimacy of the concept "reverse discrimination" and for recitification of past and present acts of discrimination that resulted in inequitable treatment between the races, secondary citizenship for minorities, and relegation of minority groups to the status of outsiders in the American society. They insisted on parity in all aspects of social, economic, political, and educational life, social justice, and equality of opportunity. They took the position that race is a necessary variable in consideration of past patterns of discrimination and genuine efforts to eradicate every vestige of such behavior. They warned, and justifiably so, of the chilling effects of a decision totally in support of Bakke since the evidence indicated that the institutions, federal, state, and local governments had already begun to return to the preaffirmative era in their treatment of minority groups in any number of ways.

The printed and electronic media dutifully reported public opinion polls and the results of various studies on the attitudes of the American public regarding the critical issues in the *Bakke* case. In the opinion of many, the electronic media seemed to have demonstrated a definite pro-Bakke bias that was persuasive in shaping public sentiment in his behalf.

Perceptions, no matter how unreal they were in terms of what objective data show, were pervasive that women and minorities received preferential treatment in jobs and income and that the white male was paying an unnecessary and unconstitutional price for their gains. Racism was displayed in an increasingly common assumption that all minorities were "less qualified" than whites for whatever position was in question—whether in terms of admissions to graduate and professional schools, the acquisition of jobs, salary increases, or promotions. This was and is today the social milieu in which the *Bakke* decision was rendered and in which it at present operates.

On June 28, 1978, the U.S. Supreme Court rendered a two-part decision in the *Bakke* case. The first part of the decision, on a 5–4 vote, ordered Bakke to be admitted to the UC–Davis School of Medicine and rejected as unconstitutional "set aside" programs specifically for minority students. Since four associate justices abstained on the second part, the Court voted 5–0 in favor of the use of "race" as a positive factor in making decisions in certain circumstances. It should be stressed that the court *did* support the consideration of race or ethnicity in college and professional school admissions decisions; it *confirmed* the authority of colleges and universities to invoke discretionary powers in the formulation of admissions policies and in the implementation of admissions procedures; it *did* support the utilization of flexible goals (but *rejected* the employment of rigid, fixed quotas) so long as flexible goals are not in violation of Title VI of the Civil Rights Act of 1964.

The decision *does permit* the continuation of voluntary affirmative action practices designed to provide a diversified academic community that includes students, faculty, administrators and/or executives from different racial and ethnic groups. The Court warned, however, that "race conscious" programs formulated to meet the social goal of diversity must satisfy compelling state interests. Therefore, one can read the decision as positive support for special admissions programs not involving arbitrary, fixed quotas and not deliberately racially exclusive. The question remains nonetheless whether the *Bakke* case has indeed produced a chilling effect on the admission and retention of black students in graduate and professional schools. The analysis of data collected for this study may be illuminating on this point. However, it may be argued that UC–Davis has already felt the impact of the decision, since not a single black student enrolled in its 1980 first-year medical school class.[29] Since 1981, only 14 blacks have enrolled in that medical college. The Total black student enrollment in fall 1984 was 10.

Traditional and Nontraditional Admissions Criteria

Admissions personnel in medical colleges (as well as in other professional fields) agree that institutions have always drawn on some combination of traditional (so-called objective) criteria and nontraditional (or "subjective" factors) in making assessments of eligibility for entry into medical colleges. The relative weight assigned to each component varies over time, under special circumstances, and from institution to institution in various jurisdictions.

Objective criteria include such variables as score or performance on the Medical College Aptitude Test (MCAT or new MCAT), college gradepoint average (GPA), the quality of the undergraduate college attended, and references. Many have argued that in some institutions ability and willingness to make a substantial financial contribution to the medical college is viewed as an objective factor. One characteristic that distinguishes objective measures from subjective measures is the case by which the former are subject to quantification or the arbitrary assignment of numerical cutoff points.

Of the institutions participating in the survey component of this study, all say that they relied on objective criteria in determining eligibility for admissions. Nevertheless, all admitted the use of subjective measures in their overall evaluation of candidates. Between 1974 and 1978, as competition for space increased and with the uncertainty of Supreme Court action on the *Bakke* case, greater reliance on gradepoint average and new MCAT scores was discernible. It should also be pointed out that the proportion of first-year medical school students with college gradepoint averages of *A* increased from 19.7% in 1970 to 39.5% in 1973. The proportion of such students reached 44.2% in 1974 and a high of 50.4% in 1977. It showed a slight decline just below the 50% mark (48.6%) in 1978–1979. The proportion of first-year students who entered medical colleges with a gradepoint average of *B* dropped significantly from 73.3% in 1970 to 50.8% in 1974 and continued to decline to 46.9% in 1978–1979. Students with C averages declined from 7.0% in 1970 to 1.8% in 1978–1979.[29] The most recent data on this subject are for 1984 when the mean gradepoint average for black first-year entrants was 3.01, while that for first-year entrants as a whole is 3.48 on a 4.0 scale.[30]

Clearly, the level of academic competition has sharpened dramatically during the past 15 years. Similarly, MCAT and new mean MCAT scores have climbed and become more competitive. In general, white students have scored considerably higher than black students on such tests. In some institutions, the performance of white students on such tests has been made as much as 2.5 points higher than the average mean score[31] presented by black students.

This disparity is not explainable by greater intellectual ability or reasoning capacity of the one group over the other, as some have indeed asserted, but more so by cultural factors and the socioeconomic condition or milieu from which the majority of black students in medical colleges are drawn. The majority of white students have had long-standing experience with the kinds and quality of questions encountered in aptitude tests and are therefore psychologically prepared to answer them. Most are middle- and upper-middle-class students who have also had continual reinforcement in home, school, and peer-group environments of the kinds of verbal skills required for success on these tests. A distinct majority of white medical school students come from homes with family earnings equal to or above the median family income of white families, in contrast to the overrepresentation of black students with low-income origins. Some persons argue that white students are financially more able to attend "coaching schools" and thereby raise their scores on MCATs. The effectiveness of coaching is a matter of continuous and heated debate in educational communities.[32]

Subjective factors, in contrast, are not easily amenable to quantification or precise statistical abstraction. One must rely often on personal hunches, judgments informed by experience, and astute observations, as well as good common sense, in making subjective appraisals of a candidate's merit. The institutional participants in this study uniformly agreed that some form of subjective or nontraditional factors played an important role in their admissions decisions. These nontraditional factors included such things as personal interviews; motivation for medicine as demonstrated, for instance, by work experience, membership in a premedical organization, community and volunteer work; personal characteristics evaluated in interviews by members of the admissions committee (faculty and student members); communication skills; working while carrying a full academic load as an undergraduate; maturing; sense of direction; promise for becoming leaders and contributors to the field of medicine; integrity; personal stability; commitment to service; ability to relate to people; awareness of world events; disadvantaged background; and race.

Of special importance to note is that literally all institutions utilize a combination of cognitive and noncognitive factors. During the early 1970s, a significant proportion of the medical colleges did overweight the noncognitive or nontradition/subjective factors in ways that permitted compensation for poorer test scores among black students as a group in contrast to whites as a group. *However, it must also be reiterated that most black students did not enter medical colleges exclusively through special admissions programs. They had high MCAT scores and exceptionally high GPAs, often considerably higher than many of their white classmates.*

Medicine is a "people oriented" and people-contact profession. It requires individuals who have not only excellent mental and intellectual capacities but are sensitive to the problems of others and have the personality to work toward the accumulation of understandings of diverse personalities. Medical schools cannot and should not rely solely on performance on objective measures of evaluation, for to do so results in mistaken assumptions about the kind of person who can be the most effective physician or health-care specialist. Consequently, noncognitive factors have come to occupy a position of paramount importance in admissions decisions. This practice is so despite the tendency to use rigid cutoff points when confronted with difficult choices. All medical colleges insist that they wish to train the most well-rounded person to deliver effective health-care services. Such a person is not necessarily the person with the highest MCAT score or with an *A* average from a prestigious undergraduate college. Nor does this mean that a *C* student with a "good personality and high motivation" is, ipso facto, such a person. A good balance must be made somewhere in between, and that is undoubtedly why so many medical colleges suggest or insist on personal interviews on all applicants.

A substantial proportion of the medical institutions employed some form of special admissions program both before and following the decision in the *Bakke* case. Special admissions programs obviously take a variety of forms. They include the set-aside programs established by the University of California at Davis and Stanford, as only two examples prior to 1978, in which minority students are guaranteed a specific number of seats in each entering class. They also take the form of separate admissions committees, in which all decisions on minority-group applicants are rendered by this group. Some take the form of subcommittees of the Admission Committees in which the subcommittee considers minority applicants and reports their findings and recommendations to the parent committee. Often the parent committee merely rubber-stamps subcommittee recommendations.

A few committees were labeled for "disadvantaged students"— often a euphemism for minority students. Frequently, unitary admissions committees attempted to assure that minority faculty and/or students were members of the admissions committee in order to guarantee the minority perspective in the decision-making process. Less than 25% of the institutions surveyed indicated that they never employed any special admissions committee, subcommittee, or minority membership on the parent committee during the 1970s. However, by 1978, most institutions had modified their "special character" of admissions to be in conformance with the *Bakke* decision. The evidence clearly supports the argument that those institutions that have employed aggressive recruitment and sensitive admissions programs have been the most successful institutions in enrolling black students in medical colleges.

An analysis of 1983 data[33] showed that the 127 U.S. schools and colleges of medicine use a broad mix of factors in determining eligibility for admission. Of the 127 institutions, only about 25 (19.6%) actually specify a minimum GPA for admission. The minimum GPA is expressed, however, in terms of a mean GPA for new entrants. It ranges from a 3.0 to a 3.7 on a 4.0 scale. Another 29 institutions (22.8%) require a "strong" but undefined

GPA. Five indicate "flexibility" with respect to GPA requirements; however, 65 institutions (51.1%) do not specify a GPA for admission to medical school.

With respect to MCAT scores, almost all institutions indicate that applicants are required to take this test as a prerequisite for consideration. Nevertheless, they differed significantly in terms of the minimum score required as well as the use made of scores reported. Only 12 institutions (9.4%) required a mean MCAT score of 8 or above. Thirty-four, or 26.7% mandated a "strong" MCAT performance. Sixty-six institutions (51.9%) did not specify a minimum MCAT score.

In 1985, 72 of the 127 institutions (56.6%) inserted antidiscriminatory clauses in their publications. In general, the statement insists that the institution either does not discriminate on the basis of race, sex, national origin, or religion in making admissions decisions or that these factors are not given consideration. However, 105 medical colleges (82.6%) explicitly state that "disadvantaged students" are "encouraged" to apply. Few institutions indicate a program of "fee waivers" for minority applicants. Several clearly state a commitment to affirmative action and describe active recruitment, summer enrichment, opportunity award, and other programs available for black and other minority students. These programs include Med-Mar, ASEP, MEDREP, MEDPREP, EOP, and RAR. The remaining institutions are either silent about assistance or encouragement for minority students or say that they have no special programs for minority students or that enrichment–academic support services are available to "all" students.

It seems that many medical colleges have indeed withdrawn or disbanded special admissions programs. Further, while special recruitment does not appear to be as aggressive as it was before the *Bakke* case, institutions as a rule have at least one central contact person for minority affairs, and several institutions make concerted efforts to attract black and other minority students to medical colleges.

Applicant Activity in the 1970s and 1980s

Opponents of special admissions programs and affirmative efforts in higher education insist that black and other minority students are entering medical colleges at the expense of white students. The underlying assumption seems to be that so very few blacks are deserving of admissions and that all whites who are turned away are considerably more deserving than the black and other minority students who successfully enroll in medical colleges. Common sense should inform us of the erroneousness of such assumptions. But gaining admission to a professional school is such an emotionally charged phenomenon that "rejects" must identify scapegoats to rationalize their presumed failures. Nevertheless, these erroneous assumptions are often conveyed, wittingly or unwittingly, by the press and television. To establish truth or falsity of such assertions in a truly scientific way it would be necessary to examine every applicant, case by case, total score by total score, on both objective and subjective measures, at every institution, and to make comparisons over every time span. That is neither a practical nor a sensible undertaking.

The controversy over who gets into medical school may be viewed in the context of overall application and applicant activity. As the 1960s began, some 14,397 persons filed 54,662 applications to the 86 existing medical colleges in the United States. That equation represented a rate of 3.8 applications per person. At that time, the medical college at Howard University and Meharry Medical College enrolled approximately 83% of all black medical school students. This, of course, meant that the remaining 17% of black students were scattered in 84 institutions and several of that 84 had no black students. As the 1960s closed, there was a 59% increase in the total number of applicants, which almost tripled the number of applications from 54,662 to 133, 822 by 1969–1970 (see Table 11).[34]

A pattern of escalation in the number of applicants and applications filed was well established by then, at precisely the moment that the movement for promoting greater access of black students to nonblack medical institutions achieved its greatest momentum. The two movements coincided: the escalation of white students' interest in the field of medicine and the push for more black and other minority students in this field. The attraction of white students to medicine may be partially explainable by some students selecting medicine who might have chosen high-technology fields like engineering had it not been for the temporary decline in the hiring of engineers at this time. It is also explainable by the influence of numerous publications that advertised the critical shortage of physicians, who of course enjoy exceptionally high social status, prestige, and power, as well as excellent remuneration. For whatever reason, the number of applicants soared during the 1970s.

It can be assumed that the establishment of the American Medical Colleges Application Service benefited black students who applied to medical colleges. This service sends all pertinent application data to a central site for computerization and distribution to member institutions. An applicant pays a single processing fee, which reduces the overall costs normally involved in applying to multiple institutions. Interested institutions then contact the applicant for scheduling possible interviews as one component in the admissions process. As a result of participation in centralized application services, one may assume that the number of applications filed by black students closely approximates the overall number of black applicants. This is in contrast to the white situation in which applications exceed applicants.

Table 11
Applications to U.S. Medical Schools by Race, 1970–1984,
All Institutions Combined

Academic Year	Applicants	Applications Filed	Applications per Person	Black Applicants	% Blacks
1970–71	24,987	148,797	6.0	1,250	5.0
1971–72	29,172	210,943	7.2	1,552	5.3
1972–73	36,135	267,306	7.4	2,186	6.0
1973–74	40,506	328,275	8.1	2,227	5.5
1974–75	42,624	362,376	8.5	2,423	5.6
1975–76	42,303	366,040	8.7	2,288	5.4
1976–77	42,155	372,282	8.8	2,523	6.0
1977–78	40,589	371,545	9.2	2,487	6.1
1978–79	36,636	335,982	9.2	2,564	6.9
1979–80	36,141	329,470	9.1	2,599	7.2
1980–81	36,100	330,888	9.2	2,594	7.2
1981–82	36,727	339,975	9.3	2,644	7.2
1982–83	35,730	334,987	9.4	2,600	7.2
1983–84	35,200	319,340	9.1	2,588	7.3
1984–85	35,944	331,937	9.3	2,620	7.3

Source: Association of American Medical Colleges.

By 1970–71, some 24,987 persons filed an average of 6.0 applications per person, resulting in a total of 148,797 applications. Only 1250 applicants or 0.8% of applicants were blacks. The following year, applications exceeded the 200,000 level, and the ratio of applications reached 7.2 per person. However, black applicants increased by only 302. Black students obtained only a 33% rate of acceptance, compared to 38.1% for the applicant population as a whole. In the same year that Bakke filed his suit against the University of California (1974), some 42,624 persons filed 362,372 applications. By that time, the number of applications from black Americans had climbed by a mere 1173 over the 1970 figure, compared with an overall increase of approximately 16,000 in the four year period.

By 1974, 11 new medical colleges had opened, an increase from 103 to 114 institutions. Not only were more applications made but the space available in medical schools had increased, although not sufficient to accommodate all applicants, deserving or not. In 1974, 43% of all black applicants were accepted to medical school, in contrast to 38.3% of the total number of applicants. This disparity suggests that a special effort was being made to accommodate more qualified black applicants than that black students received preferential treatment. Yet, if one examines the applicant characteristics very carefully, it is quite easy to discern that comparatively few black persons were then applying to medical colleges. Moreover, Howard and Meharry still accounted for a substantial proportion of all blacks who entered medical colleges. This dispersion in the historically white institutions was so minimal as to occupy only about 5 seats per entering class per 112 medical colleges.

In the fall of 1978, the year in which the U.S. Supreme Court handed down its controversial decision in the *Bakke* case, there was a decline by almost 4000 in the total number of applicants from the preceding year (40,589 to 36,636) and a precipitous drop in the total number of applications filed (from 371,445 to 335,982). Yet the number of applications filed per person was precisely the same as in 1977–78, at its highest level in the 1970s, 9.2 per person. Noticeably, the number of black applicants increased by only 77 from the 1977–78 figure (see Table 11).

A significant upswing in the absolute number of applications filed was registered in 1981–82 and the number of applications filed per person rose to 9.3. The number of black applicants increased to 2644, or 7.2% of all applicants. Since that year, however, applications to U.S. medical schools, as well as the absolute number of applicants, has been dropping at a steady pace. In fact, between 1981 and 1984, the number of applications fell by more than 20,000, and the number of applicants declined by almost 1000 potential medical students. Although the number of black applicants declined by only 56 persons, black applicants constituted 7.3% of the total number of applicants. Despite the efforts mounted to increase the number of blacks enrolled in U.S. medical schools, black applicants rose only from 1250 (1970–71) to 2620

(1984–85) (see Table 11 and 12). *There is no firm evidence to support the argument that blacks and other minority students entered medical colleges at the expense of white students.* Even without the presence of blacks and other minority-group students in the applicant pool, the overwhelming majority of rejected whites would continue to be rejected from medical colleges.

Table 12
Applicants, Acceptances, and Acceptance Rate of
Black First-Year Enrollees in U.S. Medical Schools, 1974–1984

Academic Year	Applicants	Black Students Acceptances	Black Students Acceptance Rate Percent	Enrollees, First Year	Acceptance Rate, All Applicants Percent
1974–75	2423	1049	43	1106	35
1975–76	2288	945	41	1036	36
1976–77	2523	966	38	1040	37
1977–78	2487	966	39	1085	39
1978–79	2564	970	38	1061	45
1979–80	2599	1024	39	1108	47
1980–81	2594	1057	41	1128 (1013)*	47
1981–82	2644	1037	39	1196 (1000)*	47
1982–83	2600	1001	39	1145 (961)*	48
1983–84	2558	1019	40	1173 (992)*	48.9
1984–85	2620	1049	40	1148 (994)*	52.4

Source: Office of Minority Affairs, AAMC, Dario O. Prieto, director.
* = New entrants. When "repeaters are disaggregated from first-year enrollees, it is evident that the number of black matriculants in first year medical school classes has been declining steadily since 1978."

Between 1970 and 1984, 35,145 blacks were applicants to U.S. medical colleges. This number represented a mere 6.39% of the total of 550,949 applicants during that period, and an even lower fraction of the applicants filed for medical colleges (see Table 12).

Earlier, reference was made to differential acceptance rates based on racial identification. A clearer understanding of the acceptance rate pattern may be gleaned from an analysis of Table 12. It is evident that the acceptance rate, that is, the percentage accepted to medical colleges among persons who applied, has not varied dramatically for black students since 1975. It is apparent that while the acceptance rate for black students has hovered about 39%, the acceptance rate for applicants as a whole climbed from 36% to 52.4% between 1975 and 1984. Further, the absolute number of "accepts" among blacks rose by only 94 students between 1975 and 1984; however, the total number of first-year students increased by 112 during that period (see Tables 11 and 12). The apparent discrepancy in these two figures is attributed to the over-reporting of first-year students in 1975. "New entrants" were not disaggregated; thus, "first year" enrollment of black students was actually lower than the 1975 figure.

Although the optimistic goals of Project 75 of enrolling minority students to equal 12% of total enrollment by 1975 were not attained, one cannot justifiably categorize that effort as a failure. Nor can a similar characterization be made of the conscientious recruitment efforts and substantial financial outlays from the private sector simply because comparatively few generated more black students. The number of applications from black students during the 1970s was about five times greater than the total number produced during the 1960s. During the 1970s, medicine had to compete with other career choices that were opening up for black students, some of which offered substantial financial rewards without incurring encumbrances or mounting indebtedness created by the rising costs of medical education. Some professions did not demand the continued deferring of gratifications as a prerequisite for goal attainment. Hence, the problem of underrepresentation does not imply a failure of Project 75.

Enrollment in the 1970s and 1980s

The pattern of access of black students to medical colleges during the 1970s can best be characterized by initial optimism and success, followed by declines, a leveling off and fluctuations (Table 13).

In 1968–1969, approximately 60% of the 266 first-year black students enrolled in U.S. medical colleges were enrolled at Meharry and Howard Medical Colleges. About 40% were scattered among 54 of the remaining 97 medical institutions.[35] As the 1960s ended and the 1970s opened, the 440 black medical school students, who represented 4.2% of all first-year classes combined, were still concentrated primarily at the two historically black medical colleges. Tables 13 and 14 reveal a systematic increase in the overall enrollment of first-year students as well as a climb in the proportion of first-year black enrollees. Although the proportions of black students reached a peak of 7.5% in 1973 and 1974, the same year Bakke filed his suit in California, the absolute numerical change from year to year is not that significant except in the years 1970 and 1971. For instance, the increase in first-year enrollees for black students between 1973 and 1974 was by 70 students, compared to an overall increase of 524 first-year enrollees. The following-year increase for black students was 79 students compared to an overall increase of 703. Each succeeding year thereafter shows a noticeable decline in proportionate enrollment of black students and significant reductions in absolute numbers are apparent. Hence, the overall first-year enrollment increased continually; only four more black students enrolled in first-year classes in 1976 over the 1975 figure, and a dramatic drop occurs thereafter because the reported first-year figures for black students also include first-year repeaters.

Table 13
First-Year Medical School Enrollment by Race, 1970–1984,
All Institutions Combined

Academic Year	First-Year Enrollment		
	All Students	Black Students	% Blacks
1970–71	11,169	697	6.1
1971–72	12,088	882	7.1
1972–73	13,352	957	7.0
1973–74	13,876	1,027	7.5
1974–75	14,579	1,106	7.5
1975–76	14,910	1,036	6.8
1976–77	15,282	1,040	6.7
1977–78	16,136	1,085	6.7
1978–79	16,530	1,064*	6.4
1979–80	16,930	1,108*	6.5
1980–81	17,186	1,128*	6.2
1981–82	17,268	1,196*	6.0
1982–83	17,254	1,145*	5.8
1983–84	17,150	1,173*	5.9
1984–85	16,997	1,148*	5.9

Source: Association of American Medical Colleges.
*Includes new students and first-year repeaters. If these figures were not included, the number of first-year, first-time black enrollees falls to 922 in 1978–1979, or 5.8% of all first-year, first-time enrollees.

When one removes the repeaters from first-year enrollment in 1978–1979, for instance, the number of first-time black student matriculants in U.S. medical colleges falls sharply to 922, or 5.8% of first-year enrollees throughout the nation. Hence the number of new entrants is actually less than the number enrolled in 1972, two years *before* the *Bakke* suit began, and the proportion is less than the proportion of blacks observed at the beginning of the decade. The impact of the "repeat" factor on the first-year medical college enrollment profile may be illuminated further in Tables 13 and 14. These tables reveal that in 1981–82, only 984 of the 196 black first-year students were, in fact, new entrants. Blacks constituted 5.9% of new entrants, but 6.9% of all first-year students. Among black students, black males constituted 56.3% while females represented 43.7% of new entrants. White students make up 83.5% of all new entrants and 82.4% of all first-year enrollees. Men constituted 69.2% of all new entrants. Women constituted 30.8% of all first-year matriculants and 30.7% of all new entrants.

Table 14
New Entrants and First-Year Enrollments in U.S. Medical Schools by Race, Sex, Number, and Percentage, 1981–1982 and 1983–1984

| | 1981–1982 | | 1983–1984 | |
	First-Year New Entrants	First-Year Enrollment* (N = 126 schools)	First-Year New Entrants	First-Year Enrollment* (N = 127 schools)
All students				
Total	16,644	17,268	16,480	17,150
Men	11,532	11,951	11,110	11,497
	(69.3%)	(69.2%)	(67.4%)	(67.7%)
Women	5,112	5,317	5,370	5,653
	(30.7%)	(30.8%)	(32.6%)	(33.3%)
White students				
Total	13,895	14,218	13,565	13,909
% of total	(83.5)	(82.4)	(82.3)	(81.1)
Men	9,760	9,991	9,299	9,503
Women	4,135	4,227	4,266	4,396
Black students				
Total	984	1,196	971	1,173
% of total	(5.9)	(6.9)	(5.9)	(6.8)
Men	554 (3.3)[a]	679 (3.9)[a]	527 (3.2)[a]	629 (3.7)[a]
% of black	56.3	56.8	54.2	53.6
Women	430 (2.6)[a]	517 (3.0)[a]	445 (2.7)[a]	544 (3.1)[a]
% of black	43.7	43.2	45.8	46.4

Source: Association of American Medical Colleges. Updates, December 1, 1981, and October 28, 1983.

*First-Year Enrollments include repeaters of first year, new entrants, and returning students.
[a] = Percentage of total.

In 1983–84, the actual number of black new entrants fell by 13 students, but they still represented 5.9% of all new entrants. Black men made up a mere 3.2% of all new entrants and 3.7% of all first-year enrollment. Black women, while continuing to gain ground on black men in the first-year class, constituted a mere 2.7% of all new entrants and 3.1% of all first-year medical students in 127 schools and colleges of medicine. Again, more than 8 of every 10 medical school students, either as new entrants or as first-year enrollees, were white. The actual number and percentage of women among both new entrants and all first-year matriculants increased to the point that women represented one-third of new entrants and of first-year enrollees (Table 14).

The repeat rate among black students is dramatically higher than that shown for all students combined. It varied from five to almost seven times higher than the repeat rate for all first-year students between 1974 and 1982, and from three to almost six times greater for blacks than other students in the second, third, and fourth year of medical college education (Table 15). Approximately 1 in every 6 black students will repeat the first year of medical school, compared to about 1 in 20 among all students combined. Explanations for repeating a class are not always clear. They may be found in inadequate undergraduate preparation in the basic sciences, weak self-discipline and poor study habits, insufficient time to study because of job commitments, family problems that interfere with conscientious studying, a hostile learning environment, prejudiced behavior by professors disinclined to be fair to minority students, and a whole range of adjustment problems experienced by black students in a substantially new, often overpowering and intimidating environment.

According to AAMC data, aside from Howard and Meharry medical colleges, the most successful medical institutions in enrolling black students in first-year classes during the 1970s were Temple University (282), University of Illinois (263), Harvard University (180), Wayne State University (179), University of North Carolina (169), Case Western Reserve University (163), State University of New York/Buffalo (157), State University of New York/Downstate (146), University of Cincinnati (130), University of Maryland (128), Washington University/St. Louis (125), University of California/San Francisco (124), Indiana University (120), University of Pennsylvania (118), Hahneman (117), University of Florida (117), Michigan State University (111), CMD/NJ–Rutgers (111), Ohio State University (108), Jefferson Medical College (107), and Tufts University (107).

Seven of the 23 institutions listed above are located in the "*Adams* states": Temple, University of North Carolina, University of Maryland, University of Pennsylvania, University of Florida, Hahneman Medical College, and Jefferson. Four of these are in Pennsylvania.

Table 15
Medical School Repeaters by Race, Year, Class,
and Percentage, 1974–1984

Academic Year	Black	All Students	Second, Third, and Fourth Years Combined	
			Black	All Students
1974–75	14.4	2.4	6.0	1.1
1975–76	15.4	2.3	5.8	1.1
1976–77	11.1	2.1	7.7	1.3
1977–78	12.8	2.5	6.1	1.1
1978–79	14.1	2.7	6.7	1.3
1979–80	14.1	3.0	3.5	1.1
1980–81	17.8	3.8	5.8	1.1
1981–82	16.9	3.5	5.9	1.1
1982–83	15.9	3.3	5.7	1.1
1984–85	15.9	3.1	N/A	N/A

Source: Minority Students in Medical Education: Facts and Figures (Washington, D.C.: Association of American Medical Colleges, Office of Minority Affairs, 1983), p. 14. Information for 1984–85 provided by Mary Cureton of AAMC Office of Minority Affairs.

Forty-four medical colleges that were in existence throughout the 1970s enrolled 50 or fewer black students in that decade. Although about one-third of these institutions are located in states with exceptionally small black populations (e.g., Vermont, North Dakota, South Dakota, Nevada and Utah), a clear majority with less than average black enrollments included such institutions as the University of California/Davis, Pritzker Medical College (University of Chicago), University of Kentucky, University of Louisville, University of Oklahoma, University of Tennessee, and Vanderbilt.

Between 1980 and 1984, the most successful medical colleges in enrolling black students were Howard University (411/102.5), Meharry (380/95), New York/Downstate (182/45.5), University of Illinois (163/40.7), Morehouse (118/29.5), New Jersey–UMD (105/26.2), Wayne University

(98/24.5), University of Michigan (97/24.2), University of North Carolina (89/22.2), and UCLA (79/19.7).[36]

Total Enrollment

The proportion of black students in the total enrollment in U.S. medical colleges more than doubled between 1969–1970 and 1978–1979. Increases in total enrollment can be attributed to a combination of factors that encompass institutional commitment, internal and external pressures on medical colleges, aggressive recruitment, special admissions, and federal mandates to desegregate all components of postsecondary education as dictated by the *Adams* decisions. Unquestionably, the upward climb in total enrollment of black students can also be attributed to a growing interest in medicine as an attainable career by black students from all socioeconomic statuses. This change, in and of itself, reflects a perceptual change from the viewpoint that medicine is a career choice open only to the economically affluent and socially influential.

Increasing availability of financial aid programs was a highly significant determinant of enrollment patterns during the 1970s. Recruitment itself was and continues to be affected to a large degree by the presence of adequate role models, black faculty and administrators in the university; the location of the institutions, and the type of institutions—whether private, public, or state assisted. However, it also appears that the declines in total enrollment and the leveling off of black students around 5.8% of total enrollment may reflect an actual loss of commitment to mainstream blacks through medical careers. That loss of commitment is evidenced by reductions in funds available for the recruitment and enrollment of black students. It is suggested by the eagerness with which the *Bakke* decision was received and the ensuing rapid abandonment of special admissions programs without commensurately restructuring them in ways that would assure both conformity to legal expectations and the continued commitment to racial and ethnic diversification. It is manifested in the increasingly heavier weight assigned to objective measures of evaluation and the presumed downgrading of subjective measures.

An examination of Table 16 shows that total enrollment in the nation's medical colleges has moved steadily upward. The yearly total enrollment has risen from 40,238 to 67,016 since 1970. There was an increase of more than 10,000 students in total enrollment between 1970 and 1974. In the same period, the increase in total enrollment of black students rose by approximately 1500 persons. The percentage increase may be somewhat phenomenal, but considering the low base from which the change is measured, the absolute numerical change is disappointing.

Table 16
Total Enrollment in U.S. Medical Schools by Race, 1970–1984
All Institutions Combined

Academic Year	Total Enrollment	Black Student Enrollment	Change	% Black
1970–71	40,238	1,509	-	3.8
1971–72	43,650	2,055	+ 546	4.7
1972–73	47,366	2,582	+ 527	5.5
1973–74	50,751	3,059	+ 477	6.0
1974–75	53,554	3,353	+ 294	6.3
1975–76	55,848	3,456	+ 103	6.2
1976–77	57,760	3,517	+ 61	6.1
1977–78	60,099	3,587	+ 70	6.0
1978–79	62,242	3,540	− 47	5.8
1979–80	63,800	3,627	+ 87	5.6
1980–81	65,189	3,708	+ 81	5.9
1981–82	66,298	3,884	+ 176	5.8
1982–83	66,248	3,869	− 15	5.8
1983–84	67,327	3,892	− 27	5.8
1984–85	67,016	3,944	+ 52	5.9

Source: Dario Prieto, director, Office of Minority Affairs, Association of American Medical Colleges.

Similarly, it is observed that the percentage of black students enrolled in medical colleges peaked at 6.3% in the same year that the *Bakke* suit was filed in California. The proportional decline each year thereafter is highly suspicious and suggests that a number of institutions deliberately embraced a policy of calculated cautiousness in anticipation of a pro-*Bakke* decision. Since 1974, the total yearly enrollment of all students combined climbed by approximately 14,000, that is, from 53,544 in 1974–1975 to 67,327 in 1983–1984, but dropped to 67,016 in 1984–1985. During the same period, the annual total enrollment for black students has risen by a mere 549 students, from 3353 to 3892. In fact, the total enrollment of black students dropped by some 47 students between 1977–1978 and 1978–1979, but has increased yearly since that time (Table 16).

Clearly, the fact that we now have 40 more medical colleges in 1985 than we had in 1970 has not proven a boon to the total enrollment of black students in American medical colleges. Although black students are now more widely distributed in U.S. medical colleges than ever before, when students enrolled at Howard, Meharry, Morehouse, and Charles Drew are deleted from the total enrollment figures, the problems of dispersion and concentration are readily apparent.

Meharry and Howard account for 17% of all black medical students. This means that these 2 institutions enroll as many black students as 74 medical institutions combined. According to data collected by the AAMC for fall 1984–1985 on individual medical schools, 55, or approximately 44.7% of all mainland U.S. medical schools, enroll 20 or fewer black students. More than 30 of the 123 mainland U.S. institutions enroll 10 or fewer black students. However, some 52 institutions (42%) have a total black student enrollment of between 21 and 50 students.

Only 16 of the medical colleges (13%) enrolled between 51 and 100 black students in 1984–1985. This group consists of the historically black colleges: Howard (377), Meharry (305), and Morehouse (101). It also includes traditionally white institutions: UCLA (including Charles Drew) (78), University of California at San Francisco (54), Hahnemann (56), Harvard University (61), University of Illinois (134), University of Michigan (90), New Jersey–UMDNJ (81), SUNY–Buffalo (54), SUNY– Downstate (75), University of North Carolina (82), University of Pittsburgh (53), Temple University (52), and Wayne State University (82).

Sex Ratio

An examination of the data in Table 16 amplifies the race and sex dimensions of total enrollment in U.S. medical schools. Males made up 72.1% of total enrollment in 1981–1982 but that representation declined to 69.4% in 1983–1984. At the same time, the percentage of females in total enrollment rose from 27.9% to 30.6% during that period. White males constituted 62.3% of total enrollment in 1981–1982 but only 58.7% in 1983–1984. By contrast, white females made up 21.6% of total enrollment in 1981 but continued to increase their proportion to 24.5% in 1983–1984.

Among white students, white males lost ground to white females between 1981 and 1983. The percentage of white males dropped from 73.5% to 70.6%, while the representation of white females among all white students climbed from 25.6% to 29.4% between 1981 and 1983–1984.

Black students constituted only 5.9% of total enrollment in 1981–1982 and 5.8% in 1983–1984. While black males consisted of only 3.3% of total enrollment in 1981 and 3.2% in 1983, they represented 56% of all black medical students in both years. By contrast, black females were a mere 2.6% of total enrollment but 44% of all blacks enrolled in medical school during both time periods (Table 17). *It seems evident that the most consistent beneficiaries of change in the composition of medical school enrollment between 1970 and 1985 have been white females, not racial and ethnic minorities.*

Table 17
Total Enrollment in U.S. Medical Schools by Race and Sex,
1981–1982 and 1983–1984

Category	1981–1982 (N = 126 schools)		1983–1984 (N = 127 schools)	
	N	% of Total	N	% of Total
All students				
Total	66,298	100.0	67,327	100.0
Male	47,793	72.1	46,692	69.4
Female	18,505	27.9	20,635	30.6
White students				
Total	56,201	84.8	56,167	83.4
Male	41,309	62.3	39,638	58.7
% white		(73.5)		(70.6)
Female	14,393	21.7	16,529	24.5
% white		(25.6)		(29.4)
Black students				
Total	3,884	5.9	3,892	5.8
Male	2,166	3.3	·2,144	3.2
% black		(56.0)		(56.0)
Female	1,718	2.6	1,748	2.6
% black		(44.0)		(44.0)

Source: Office of Minority Affairs' Association of American Medical Colleges; Washington, D.C.

The Graduation of Black Students

Between 1970 and 1985, 213,393 persons were graduated from U.S. medical colleges. Of that number, 9,952 (4.6%) were black Americans. Absolute numbers of black student graduates and their proportions among the total number of students who received medical degrees increased in every year up to 1977–1978. Following that year, both absolute numbers and proportion of black students graduated from medical colleges decreased, excepting 1983, and have continued on a downward trend (Table 18).

Table 18
Total Graduates from U.S. Medical Schools by Race, 1970–1985, All Institutions Combined

Year	Total All Students	Total Black Students	Change	Percentage Black
1970	8,367	165		1.9
1971	8,974	180	+ 15	2.0
1972	9,551	229	+ 49	2.4
1973	10,391	341	+112	3.2
1974	11,613	511	+170	4.4
1975	12,714	638	+127	5.0
1976	13,561	743	+ 75	5.4
1977	13,607	752	+ 9	5.5
1978	14,393	793	+ 41	5.5
1979	14,966	774	− 19	5.2
1980	15,135	768	− 6	5.1
1981	15,673	766	− 2	4.9
1982	15,985	763	− 3	4.8
1983	15,802	883	+120	5.5
1984	16,343	818	− 65	5.0
1985	16,318	828	+ 10	5.0
Totals	213,393	9,952		4.6

Source: Dario Prieto, director, Office of Minority Affairs, Association of American Medical Colleges.

The data provided in Table 18 attest to the successes experienced in the early 1970s in enrollment of black students as a consequence of institutional commitment, federal assistance, aggressive recruitment, and perhaps, flexible admissions policies. Without this combination of factors, it is highly probable that Howard University and Meharry Medical College would have continued to graduate more than four-fifths of all the black physicians in the United States. As a direct result of changes in the recruitment and enrollment patterns, larger and larger numbers of the nation's medical colleges are participating in the effort to expand equality of opportunity in medical education. The apparent loss of a substantial number of these students between the first and fourth years, however, suggests problems of serious proportions.

Problem Areas in the Medical Education of Black Students

One of the most serious problems is the comparatively high attrition rate of black students. Many of the institutions that responded to our survey referred to the lack of adequate preparation in the basic sciences as a serious weakness of most of the students who are dismissed for academic reasons or repeat a year of study. Indeed, one of the cautions about Table 12 is the fact that we are not able to identify the precise number of "repeaters" in each first-year class. Repeaters are probably included in each of the preceding years. Hence, it may be somewhat presumptious to conclude that the fallout apparent between first-year enrollment (Table 11) and the number of black students who should have graduated four years later is as great as it appears to be (Table 18).

Nevertheless, the retention problem is considerably more serious for black students than it is for white students and other minority students. The Association of American Medical Colleges reports that 38.6% of minority, compared to 13.3% for nonminority, students who interrupt their medical education do so because of academic difficulties. About 41.0% minority and 38.5% nonminority students leave medical school for a time because of personal or family difficulties. Only 7.2% minority and 4.6% nonminority students interrupt medical education because of financial difficulties.[37]

According to one study, black Americans have a retention rate of approximately 87% through four years of medical education, compared to 97% for the medical population as a whole. The retention rates for Mexican Americans (88%) and Native Americans (Indians) 89% are only slightly better. By contrast, mainland Puerto Rican Students have a retention rate of 98% which is slightly better than the national average.[38] According to Johnson and Sedlacek, however, minority group retention rates approximate those rates observed for white students a decade or so ago.[39] A primary goal of medical institutions is, of course, to raise the retention level of black and other minority-group students to approximate national retention averages.

To address this problem, most institutions provided some form of academic and nonacademic support services. In the 1970s several institutions obtained special grants through either the Health Careers Opportunity Program or Special Projects of the Department of Health, Education, and Welfare, as well as from other sources, to help finance programs designed to aid minority students who needed academic assistance to enhance their chances of success.

For instance, during the 1970s summer institutes and pre-enrollment enrichment programs were instituted at a number of institutions (e.g., Rutgers Medical School, University of California/Davis, University of Colorado Medical School, University of Kansas, and Harvard University). These summer programs provide students, with an overview of first-year medical school courses (e.g., gross anatomy) and conduct sessions that concentrate on understanding the basic sciences, the development of effective study skills, and a general orientation to the medical school.

In many instances, these initial services are followed up through organized academic support services made available to students who encounter academic difficulties or who wish to avoid them (at Michigan State University, Cornell University, University of Texas/Houston, and others). Supportive services, where provided, include such components as paid tutorial assistance, voluntary tutorial assistance by faculty members, courses on study skills, time management and test-taking strategies, assistance in selecting academic advisers, alternative curriculum planning and flexible curricula or self-paced studies, and assistance in financial aid planning. Personal counseling is frequently a component of comprehensive support services. In addition, as mentioned, mutual psychological support is gained through participation in organized student medical associations, Black Student Unions, recognition of the existence of a critical mass of students, and the presence of black faculty members. By the 1980s, many of these activities had become institutionalized and available to most students who desired assistance.

Inadequate financial assistance has exacerbated the recruitment, enrollment, and progression of blacks who may wish to be physicians. The cost of medical education has skyrocketed; the average yearly cost in 1985 is an estimated $18,210 at private medical schools and $9588 for state residents in public medical colleges. Yet the total amount of financial assistance that medical students are able to obtain continues to decline, after almost 30 years of increasing support. The National Medical Fellowship reported in 1983 that medical student financial assistance was reduced by 5.5%, or $25.4 million, in the single year between 1981 and

1982. Annual increases in excess of 14% at private medical colleges and more than 10% at publicly supported medical schools, coupled with no additional financial assistance to those who seek medical education, not unexpectedly reduce the number of actual matriculants and may ultimately lead to higher attrition rates imposed by inadequate financial support.[40]

The fact that the annual median family income of black families is substantially below the annual cost of medical education at private schools and only slightly above that at public medical institutions underscores the financial imperatives for these students. Yet, they, like all medical students, but even more so than most, must assume an enormous indebtedness in order to complete medical education. In 1983, for example, the mean indebtedness associated with medical education of all senior students was $23,914, and 13.5% of all graduating seniors had incurred indebtedness of $30,000 or more.[41] Without nonrepayable loans or scholarships, educational indebtedness for some black students could exceed $80,000 at the end of four years of medical education.

As stated in Chapter 4, the federal government under the Reagan administration has substantially reduced its financial assistance to graduate and professional school students. President Reagan has systematically undermined affirmative action programs both in higher education and in hiring and promotion. Several programs that once provided financial assistance to medical students have either been reduced or phased out under the Reagan administration. These include the Health Careers Opportunity (HCOP) program; the Bureau of Health Manpower, which has disappeared; and all capitation grants. And in 1984 President Reagan vetoed S. 2574, the Public Health Act Amendment. This act would have reauthorized health-profession programs, including Health Professions Student Loans, the National Health Services Corps Scholarships, and funds for minority students and schools. Despite the presidential veto, which would have extended federal aid beyond fiscal year 1985, health-profession aid programs for students did receive a $119 million increase in fiscal 1985 over the amount included in President Reagan's budget.[42]

Complicating the financial picture is the fact that neither states, the private sector, nor institutions have increased their assistance in amounts that would totally compensate for the financial losses inflicted by the Reagan administration. Hence, inadequate financial support persists as a major barrier to the entry of black students into medical colleges and as an impediment to their progression through to graduation from these institutions.

Black Faculty

Although the absolute number of black faculty at U.S. medical schools increased during the 1970s, about 40% of total black faculty are employed at the medical colleges of Howard University, Meharry Medical College, and Morehouse College. (When the number of black faculty of the Charles Drew Post Graduate Medical Center in Los Angeles is added to this group, that proportion is raised above 50%.)[43] When all institutions are combined, black faculty at U.S. medical schools constitute only about 2.0% of the total number of medical school faculty.[44]

Most black faculty teach in clinical programs, in contrast to the basic sciences programs of medical schools. This underrepresentation of black faculty in the basic sciences (e.g., anatomy, biochemistry, immunology, physiology, and microbiology) is attributable in part to the paucity of black Americans who hold the doctoral degree in these subjects. As discussed in Chapter 13, there is a critical shortage of black doctoral recipients in the physical and natural sciences. It is also explainable in part by the preference of black physicians who can also teach basic sciences for other medical careers.

Without black faculty to teach the basic sciences, many medical students must wait for the clinical aspects of their training before being exposed to role models. Several institutions included in this survey recognized the need for more black faculty to serve as role models in a variety of academic and nonacademic functions, but few seemed imaginative enough to decide how to attack the problem. Yet the data presented in Chapter 3 suggest that the presence of black faculty may be the most important contributor to the successful recruitment, enrollment, and graduation of black students.

Other problems cited include a lack of a critical mass of black students; emotional difficulties, at home and within the institution; and a failure to adjust to the new institutional environment. Clearly, the problem of retention is multidimensional and can be solved only through a coordinated, systematized program that adequately adresses each area specified in the preceding discussion.

The *Bakke* decision has had some subtle influences on practices in medical colleges. These influences are described in terms of "diluting forces," which arise from the tendency to lump together a variety of groups (e.g., women and the handicapped) under the rubric "disadvantaged." While the needs of these groups are compelling and legitimate, some officials argue that the apparent preference for white females places them in direct competition with underrepresented minorities and dilutes the efforts to combat the nation's historic and lingering problem of racism and racial discrimination.

Finally, it would be a tragic mistake to assume that the societal problem of a shortage of black physicians is no longer a significant issue simply because many were graduated from medical colleges between 1970 and 1984. The nation does not have a sufficient number of black physicians to meet the health needs of black communities nor the demand for medical researchers nor requirements for medical school faculty positions. Parity has not been reached in the production of black physicians in the United States. Hence, when the federal government warns of an oversupply of physicians by 1990, it is grossly misleading to assume that such a prediction assumes that the country will have an excess of black physicians. On the contrary, should the matriculation of blacks in medical colleges remain at or below its present rate, parity will not be reached in this century.

Notes

1. Karen Albarnel, "Is Relapse Ahead for Minority Medical Education?" *Foundation News,* March 1977, pp. 24–27.
2. *Minorities in Medicine: Report of a Conference* (New York: Josiah Macy, Jr. Foundation, 1977), p. 5; and James E. Blackwell and Philip Hart, *Cities, Suburbs and Blacks* (Bayside, N.Y.: General Hall, 1983), Chap. 1.
3. *Minorities in Medicine,* p.3.
4. *Report of the AAMC Task Force on Minority Student Opportunities in Medicine* (Washington, D.C.: Association of American Medical Colleges, June 1978), p. 1; *Report of the American Association of Medical Colleges Task Force,* (April 1970), pp. 1–18; and James L. Curtis, *Blacks, Medical Schools and Society* (Ann Arbor: University of Michigan Press, 1971), pp. 57–58.
5. Clinical appointments are distinguished from appointments as basic sciences faculty. The former are usually adjunct, nontenure-track appointees who work with medical students in clinical programs. A decided majority of black faculty members listed in medical colleges have these appointments. Basic sciences faculty are more likely to teach basic courses such as biochemistry and endocrinology. These faculty are likely to be on the tenure-track, have both the M.D. and Ph.D. or one of the two degrees, and are likely to be involved in medical training from the first year onward. Black faculty are less likely to teach in the basic sciences curriculum, except at Howard, Meharry, and Morehouse. It should also be pointed out that because of the nature of clinical training, the majority of medical faculty are likely to have such appointments and they are ordinarily physicians in practice, with needed specialities, and are attached to hospitals in which internships and resident training occur.
6. *Report of AAMC, 1978.*
7. Ibid., p. 4.
8. Ralph C. Kuhli, "Education For Health Careers," *Journal of School Health* 41 (January 1971): 17.
9. Davis C. Johnson *et al.,* "Recruitment and Progress of Minority Medical Schools Entrants, 1970–72," *Journal of Medical Education* 50 (1975): 721.
10. *Report of the AAMC Task Force on the Inter Association Committee on Expanding Educational Opportunities in Medicine for Blacks and Other Minority Students* (Washington, D.C., April 11, 1970).
11. Ibid.
12. Ibid.
13. National Medical Fellowships, Inc. *Information Brochure* (New York: National Medical Fellowships, Inc., 1984), p. 2.
14. Ibid.
15. National Medical Fellowships, Inc., *Annual Report, 1983* (New York: National Medical Fellowships, Inc. 1984), pp. 22–26.

16. Information provided by the National Medical Fellowships, Inc.
17. *Report of AAMC*, June 1978.
18. James E. Blackwell, *Access of Black Students to Graduate and Professional Schools* (Atlanta: Southern Education Foundation, 1975), p. 16.
19. "Information for Minority Group Students," *Medical School Admission Requirements*, 1976–77, p. 51.
20. *Report of AAMC*, p. 19.
21. Ibid., p. 3.
22. See Allan P. Sindler, *Bakke, DeFunis, and Minority Admissions* (New York: Longman, 1978), p. 18.
23. Frank J. Aselsek and Irene L. Gomberg, *Special Programs for Female and Minority Graduate Students* (Washington, D.C.: American Council on Education, 1978).
24. *Minorities in Medicine*, p. 34.
25. Sindler, *Bakke, DeFunis, and Minority Admissions* (New York: Longman, 1978), p. 36.
26. Ibid., p. 205.
27. Ibid.
28. Vertis Thompson, M.D., quoted in *The Montclarion*, (September 24, 1980), p. 12. He was 1980–81 president of NMA.
29. *Journal of the American Medical Association* 243 (March 7, 1980): 853.
30. Association of American Medical Colleges, *Minority Students in Medical Education: Facts and Figures II* (Washington, D.C.: AAMC, Office of Minority Affairs, March 1985), p. 9.
31. This refers to mean computed on the new MCAT. Previously, the number of points often averaged 200 above mean scores for blacks.
32. *Journal of the American Medical Association*, p. 853.
33. AAMC, Office of Minority Affairs, March, 1985, p. 9
34. Multiple applications simply mean that applicants file simultaneous applications at more than one institution to enhance opportunities for acceptance.
35. This distribution means that there were approximately two blacks in the first-year classes at white institutions and that 43 colleges enrolled no blacks in the first-year class.
36. The first number represents the total number of black first-year matriculants over the four-year period. The second number represents the average number of black students enrolled in each first-year medical class from 1981 to 1984.
37. Association of American Medical Colleges, *Minority Students in Medical Education: Facts and Figures, November 1983* (Washington, D.C.: AAMC), p. 14.
38. *Report of the Association of American Medical Colleges Task Force on Minority Student Opportunities in Medicine* (Washington, D.C.: AAMC, 1978), p. 40.
39. Davis F. Johnson and William E. Sedlacek, "Retention by Sex and Race of 1968–1972 U.S. Medical School Entrants," *Journal of Medical Education* (1975): 932.
40. National Medical Fellowships, Inc. *Annual Report*, 1983, p. 4.
41. Ibid.
42. College Board, *Update from Washington*, November 1984, p. 3.
43. *Participation of Women Minorities in U.S. Medical Faculties*, HEW Publication No. 76–91, 1976. Report prepared by H. P. Jolly and Thomas Larson of the AAMC. Personal interview with Daniel Wooten of the Charles Drew Post Graduate Medical Center, August 1980.
44. Field Report.

Chapter 6

MAINSTREAMING BLACK
AMERICANS IN DENTISTRY

This chapter focuses on the processes involved in the mainstreaming of
black Americans in the field of dentistry since 1970. Dentistry has never attracted as many people to it as have other scientific fields. Compared to black
Americans in medicine, fewer black Americans have become dentists during
the 146 years that dentistry has been recognized as a major profession in the
United States. However, the attractiveness of the field increased dramatically
after World War II. Many were drawn to dentistry during the 1960s when entrance into medical schools became so restrictive. As a result, many gifted individuals interested in the health-care field selected dentistry. Nevertheless,
there is a major crisis in dental education. It is not a crisis of quality in dental
education, but one of enrollment declines and fluctuations in dental schools
that began in 1976. This crisis is further evident in the continuing shortage of
black dentists, despite significant increases in the actual production of blacks
with professional degrees from the nation's 59 schools and colleges of dentistry.

This chapter calls specific attention to the serious underrepresentation of
black Americans in dentistry and to concrete efforts to increase their participation in this profession. The chapter focuses especially on the historic
roles performed by the College of Dentistry of Howard University and of
Meharry Medical College in the training of black dentists. It describes the
policy changes articulated by the American Dental Association and the
Association of American Dental Schools that have stimulated access and
reduced structural discrimination in dental education. However, the primary
emphases of this chapter are enrollment and graduation trends among black
dental school students since 1970, the salience of certain variables for
understanding why fluctuations or patterns occurred, the impact of the high
cost of dental education on the participation of blacks in dental education,
and the increasing presence of black women in the dental school population.

The Historical Context

Until the Baltimore College of Dental Surgery opened in 1840, there
was no college of dentistry in the United States. Dentistry was not regarded
as a major profession, and there was no formalized institution for training

individuals in the art of dental surgery. Persons who "extracted teeth" were viewed as technicians or artisans who learned their trade exclusively through apprenticeships under practitioners of this skill. The first college of dentistry in America discriminated on the basis of race. Although blacks could not enroll at Baltimore College of Dental Surgery, it is estimated that when that institution opened, some 120 blacks were practicing the art of dentistry.[1]

When Howard University opened in 1867, it did not establish either a department or a school of dentistry. Not until 1881 was such a "department" organized at Howard. Even then, the dentistry department did not have the same status as the School of Medicine. The low priority to which dentistry was assigned reflected its second-class status in the larger society as well.

Dentistry did not become a matter of special priority until Mordecai W. Johnson became the first black to serve as president of Howard University. In his inaugural address in 1926, Dr. Johnson committed himself to the expansion of the dental education program at Howard University. Three years later, the dentistry department was reorganized to become an independent, autonomous unit, separate and apart from the School of Medicine and headed by its own dean. Structural improvements continued to be made at Meharry also, and both institutions were able to broaden the scope of their programs in the training of dentists.[2]

Dentistry did not fare well at Meharry Medical College in the early years. Meharry was founded in 1886, some five years following the establishment of the Department of Dentistry at Howard University; so, early training of blacks in this profession lagged somewhat behind that at Howard. Even today, Meharry Medical College remains somewhat smaller than federally supported Howard University.

For more than 75 years, these two historically black colleges of dentistry trained more than 90% of all the black dentists in the United States. With the advent of *Plessy* v. *Ferguson* a pattern had already been established of developing strong parallel institutions in the black community to meet the felt needs of the population. Blacks were excluded from historically white colleges of dentistry either by de jure or de facto systems of discrimination. Many white dentists would not provide dental care to blacks who needed such health services. Hence, partially in response to recognized needs and partially as a reaction to systematic segregation, institutional racism, and persistent discrimination, the dental education programs at Meharry and Howard expanded and attracted increasing numbers of black students. Without these two institutions, the crisis in dental education and in the delivery of dental health services to the black community would be considerably more disastrous than it is in the 1980s.

By 1910, there were some 478 black dentists in the United States. Within a span of two decades, that is, by 1930, there was a 400% increase in the number of black dentists. According to the 1930 Bureau of Census report, the number of black dentists reached 1774.[3]

That progress was slowed to a trickle by the Great Depression. Since black Americans are so frequently treated as outsiders with limited access to highly prized services and the economic reward system, it is not surprising that periods of economic stress create devastating problems for black Americans. Hence, the Great Depression resulted in widespread economic disabilities for Americans in general, but had its most severe impact on black Americans, who were at the bottom of the economic ladder.

One consequence of this situation was a shocking decline in the enrollment of black students in dentistry. Such a precipitous fall in enrollment is illustrated by the enrollment of only 34 students in the College of Dentistry at Howard University and by only 3 students receiving the D.D.S. from Howard in 1934. The effects of the depression—high unemployment and absence of money income—prevented all but a very few black families from attempting to support higher education for their offspring. Many young men and women found it almost impossible to obtain even the most menial jobs that could generate income sufficient to support dental education. This situation improved only after the enactment of federal relief and work programs to combat economic stagnation. It was alleviated, too, by a wartime economy, necessitated by World War II, that expanded economic opportunity. Thereafter, both the enrollment of blacks in dental schools and their graduation from them increased. But the major responsibility for the training of blacks in dentistry was still assumed by Howard University and Meharry Medical College.

Earlier, after graduation, licensing, and entry into the profession, black dentists continued to encounter discrimination within the profession. The American Dental Association denied them membership or even attendance at workshops, lectures on scientific advances in dental specializations, and in-service training programs. Most of its component or constituent societies also excluded blacks. Because of these policies of exclusion, black dentists had to provide their own mechanisms for assuring their exposure to new knowledge, new technologies in dental education, and advances in the profession. Dr. David A. Ferguson, an 1899 graduate of the Dental School at Howard University, was instrumental in organizing a group of black dentists in 1901 that became the nucleus of what became the National Dental Association.[4]

Professional Associations and the Training of Black Dentists

Inasmuch as discrimination and segregation were widespread in dentistry, it was inevitable that the field would be forced to make radical changes. The professional associations played a profound role in inducing reforms that ultimately expanded access to dental schools. For instance, the National Dental Association joined with major formal organizations of the civil rights movement in demanding equality of access of black students to colleges of dentistry throughout the nation. It also insisted on the abandonment of policies of discrimination followed so rigidly by the American Dental Association and its affiliated societies. The American Association of Dental Schools and the American Dental Association also deliberated on the importance of structural reforms, policy changes, and the need to respond in aggressive ways to the dictates of the civil rights movement for broader participation of all Americans in professional education. The American Dental Association issued a policy change in 1965 in which it urged all its constituent and component societies to drop all barriers to membership based on race, religion, ethnicity, or creed. Some groups had already taken steps in this direction; the problem was not with groups themselves but with those within the groups who were most resistant to social change and unwilling to share rewards, power, influence, and status with members of other racial groups.

Ultimately all the societies complied, at least in principle, but many black dentists refused to join either the constituent societies or the American Dental Association. In 1985, many of them divert the money that would be paid to the ADA in membership fees to support the all-black National Dental Association's activities and other civic or social action programs in the black community.

The Association of American Dental Schools took further steps to dramatize its commitment to increasing the enrollment of black students in schools of dentistry. It urged the reexamination of recruitment, selection, and admissions policies to end the previous discriminatory practices. Black students could apply with greater assurance of being admitted to dental schools. Forty-four of the membership institutions of the ADA became early participants in the centralized admissions program that enabled black students, especially those from impoverished backgrounds, to reduce their application costs.

A variety of special programs were initiated with the encouragement of the American Association of Dental Schools in order to stimulate greater equality of opportunity. Finally, the American Dental Association and the Association of Dental Schools began to collect systematic data on minorities in dental schools. They also encouraged private and federal governmental financial support to assist in dental education in ways that would ultimately benefit impoverished students educationally qualified for dental schools. Concerted action of this type, a reflection of an early commitment to changing the racial composition of dental schools, had immediate and far-reaching results.

Applicant Activity in the 1970s and 1980s

The number of applicants to dental college has fallen sharply in recent years. In fact, between 1975 and 1984, the number of applicants fell from 15,743 to 6499. This decline represents a fallout of more than 58.6% in the number of persons applying to dental colleges over a 10-year period. Noticeably, the ratio between number of applicants and absolute number of first-year enrollees during the same period has converged (Table 19).

Table 19
Applicants and First-Year Enrollment in Dental Schools, 1975–1984

Year	Number of Applicants	First-Year Enrollment[a]
1975	15,734	5,763
1976	14,807	5,935
1977	12,835	5,954
1978	11,753	6,301
1979	10,520	6,132
1980	9,148	6,030
1981	8,852	5,855
1982	7,724	5,498
1983	7,128	5,274
1984	6,499	5,048

Source: American Association of Dental Schools, *Applicant Analysis: 1984 Entering Class* (Washington, D.C.: AADS, n.d.), Figure 1.
[a] Includes repeaters of first year.

Between 1983 and 1984, for example, applicants decreased by 8.8%, and the applicant-to-enrollee ratio dropped from 1.40 to 1.33. However, this change represented a dramatic downturn compared to the 3-to-1 ratio observed in 1975.

In 1984, less than 2,000 black students applied for admission to dental colleges. Only about 10% of black applicants actually enrolled. It is, therefore, evident that most institutions are unsuccessful in generating applicant activity from black students. In fact, less than 20 blacks applied for admission in 1984–85 to one-third of the dental schools. In more than three-fourths of dental colleges, less than 50 blacks applied for admission. Black students applied more frequently to the dental colleges of Howard University (251); Meharry Medical College (131); Georgetown University (100); University of Maryland (61); Ohio State University (55); and Emory (54 black applicants).

Even among institutions with substantial applicant activity among black students, immense variations are evident with respect to the actual enrollment of black Americans in dental colleges. For example, Howard University enrolled 59 blacks; Meharry 26; Georgetown 5; Maryland 14; Ohio State University 4, but Emory enrolled only one of its 54 black applicants.

Admissions Criteria

As with professional education in general, dental schools employ a mixture of objective (cognitive) criteria and subjective (noncognitive, nontraditional) criteria in reaching admissions decisions. As a response to both internal and external pressures for change, some institutions modified selection criteria in ways that facilitated greater access for black and other minority students. Special programs for minority students have taken diverse forms. They have varied from an open admissions format to a more rigid, highly quantified system. However, litigation against special admissions programs, as in the *Bakke* case, shows a high correspondence to the growing number of dental schools that now claim they have "no special programs for women and minority students." Nineteen of the 60 schools of dentistry in 1979 and 1984 publicly stressed the absence of specific programs for special groups of students. This is in contrast to the relative paucity of such statements in the early 1970s.

Objective admissions criteria include a Dental Admissions Test Score (DAT) of 4 or above on a 5-point scale. All U.S. schools of dentistry require the DAT, but all do not make the same use of test performance in overall evaluations of the candidate. All do not assign the same relative weight to these scores in determining eligibility. The DAT is designed to test the applicant's knowledge in the following areas: (1) knowledge of natural sciences (biology and inorganic and organic chemistry); (2) reading comprehension (natural and basic sciences); (3) verbal and quantitative ability; and (4) perceptual-motor ability (two- and three-dimensional problem solving).[5]

These components supposedly permit the student to demonstrate his or her manual and academic aptitude, as well as aptitude for science. Nevertheless, one's performance on these tests is conditioned by the same factors that affect performance on any objective test. These factors include previous experience and demonstrated skill in taking tests, the nature of the test setting, the test administrator, the student's sense of security and confidence, the student's emotional condition at the time of the test, and the student's coaching experience.[6] Other traditional factors utilized in admissions and selection decisions include college gradepoint average (GPA), gradepoint average in science, and letters of recommendation.

Since there are 16 states without schools or colleges of dentistry, these states have made cooperative arrangements, often with the nearest college of dentistry, for training students from their states. In effect, some colleges of dentistry not only give preference to residents of the state but to students from their contracting institutions or state. This policy may raise the level of competition for admission to particular institutions. In addition, some institutions assign a value to the quality of the applicant's undergraduate college that may affect acceptance irrespective of residence.

In 1985, 46 dental schools required a personal interview of the candidate by admissions committee members or their designees prior to formal acceptance. This number includes the School of Dentistry at the University of Puerto Rico. The remaining 14 institutions did not require a personal interview. During the 1970s, the number of dental schools that mandated an interview was fewer than 40. Other colleges of dentistry either did not make interviews a prerequisite for final consideration or admissions committees exercised discretionary authority in making an interview mandatory under special circumstances. One explanation for the interview is that it provides admissions committees with an opportunity to learn more about the applicant's personal characteristics, something that cannot be sufficiently detailed in autobiographical data. The interview also may reveal further manifestations of the applicant's commitment to the field of dentistry, and it permits admissions committee members greater latitude for forming an overall impression of the person.

Essentially, noncognitive criteria are examined through personal interviews, although some opportunities may be provided for the candidate to demonstrate manual dexterity and facility and artistry during time spent on campus. But a major effort is made to discern motivation, integrity, commitment, maturity, promise as a practicing dentist, and, as one institution puts it, "who are winners across the board." Several institutions that participated in the survey, such as the University of Kentucky, reported that DAT scores are considered in conjunction with other important factors. These noncognitiive variables include the applicant's background characteristics and overall record of personal achievement. Rigid cutoff points are not employed. Several institutions maintain that they seek a good balance between cognitive and noncognitive criteria in selection for admission. However, it is often difficult to unravel precisely how this balance is achieved.

Enrollment of Black Dental Students

Enrollment in 1970

Although schools of dentistry are currently experiencing a decline in applicants and applications, first-year enrollment continues to increase. For instance, between 1960 and 1977, first-year enrollment in U.S. schools of dentistry increased by some 64.1%.[7] Some of that change may be explained by the opening of 14 additional schools of dentistry since 1960. When that fact is taken into consideration, the net result is that those institutions in existence in 1960 realized a 40% growth in enrollment over an 18-year period.[8]

In 1960, total enrollment in U.S. schools of dentistry was 13,580 students. By 1970, total enrollment had climbed to 16,551 in 51 institutions located on the mainland of the U.S. plus one institution in Puerto

Rico. Total black student enrollment, not including Puerto Rico, was 451 students. About 62% of all those students were enrolled at either Howard University (169) or at Meharry Medical College (110). Only the University of Illinois (17 black students), University of California at San Francisco (13), University of Maryland (13), and University of Michigan (10) had an enrollment of 10 or more black students.

Eight of the 51 mainland U.S. dental schools did not have a single black student enrolled in 1970. These were the University of Louisville, Louisiana State University, Loyola University of New Orleans (since closed), University of Oregon Dental Schools, Baylor University College of Dentistry, University of Texas/San Antonio, Virginia Commonwealth University, and West Virginia University. Seventeen dental schools enrolled only a single black student, and there were only 10 institutions that had black students in the fourth year of dental school training. As a result, 47 of the 55 black seniors were enrolled at the two historically black dental schools in the nation. Ultimately, they graduated about 80% of black graduates in 1971 (see Table 20).

Table 20
Black Student Dental School Enrollment, October 1970

Dental School	1st Year	2nd Year	3rd Year	4th Year	Total
University of Alabama	3	—	—	—	3
University of the Pacific	1	—	—	—	1
University of California, San Francisco	6	6	1	—	13
University of California, Los Angeles	6	—	—	—	6
University of Southern California	—	1	1	—	2
Loma Linda University	—	—	1	1	2
University of Connecticut	—	1	—	—	1
Georgetown University	1	—	—	—	1
Howard University	59	52	35	23	169
Emory University	1	1	—	—	2
Medical College of Georgia	3	—	—	—	3
Loyola (Chicago)	—	—	1	—	1
Northwestern University Dental School	1	—	1	—	2
University of Illinois	9	7	1	—	17
Indiana University-Purdue University	1	3	3	2	9
University of Iowa	1	—	—	—	1
University of Kentucky	1	—	—	—	1
University of Louisville	—	—	—	—	—
Louisiana State University	—	—	—	—	—
Loyola University - New Orleans	—	—	—	—	—
University of Maryland	9	3	1	—	13
Harvard School of Dental Medicine	3	3	—	—	6
Tufts University School of Dental Medicine	2	4	—	1	7
University of Detroit	7	1	2	—	10

Table 20 (continued)

Dental School	1st Year	2nd Year	3rd Year	4th Year	Total
University of Michigan	5	2	2	—	9
University of Minnesota	1	—	—	—	1
University of Missouri-Kansas City	2	1	—	—	3
Washington University School of Dentistry	1	—	—	—	1
Creighton University School of Dentistry	1	—	—	—	1
University of Nebraska	—	—	1	1	2
Fairleigh Dickinson University	—	—	1	—	1
New Jersey College of Medicine & Dentistry	—	—	—	1	1
Columbia University	2	—	—	—	2
New York University	2	3	1	—	6
State University of New York at Buffalo	4	3	—	—	7
University of North Carolina	1	—	—	—	1
The Ohio State University	2	—	—	1	3
Case Western Reserve University	7	1	—	—	8
University of Oregon Dental School	—	—	—	—	—
Temple University	1	1	1	—	3
University of Pennsylvania	—	1	—	—	1
University of Pittsburgh	4	2	1	—	7
Medical University of South Carolina	1	—	—	—	1
Meharry Medical College	27	31	28	24	110
University of Tennessee	5	—	—	—	5
Baylor University College of Dentistry	—	—	—	—	—
The University of Texas Dental Branch	1	1	—	1	3
University of Texas at San Antonio	—	—	—	—	—
Virginia Commonwealth University	—	—	—	—	—
University of Washington	2	—	1	—	3
West Virginia University	—	—	—	—	—
Marquette University	1	1	—	—	2
University of Puerto Rico	1	—	—	1	2
Total	185	129	83	56	453
Total Dental School Enrollment	4563	4216	3979	3793	16,551
Percentage	4.1	3.1	2.1	1.5	2.7

Source: American Dental Association, "Analysis of Black Applicants to Dental Schools," 1971.

First-Year Enrollment Trends

Of special interest is the first-year enrollment pofile of black students in dental schools in 1970. According to Table 20, 185 black students were enrolled in first-year classes as the decade began. Again, Howard and Meharry accounted for a substantial portion of those students. Eighty-six of the 185 students were enrolled at these two institutions. Only 5 additional institutions enrolled more than 5 black students in their first-year classes. In fact, 16 of the 51 institutions, or almost one-third of them, did not enroll a single black student. Approximately 30% of them enrolled a single black student apiece, and another quarter of them enrolled from 2 to 5 black students in their first-year classes. What was missing from a significant majority of these institutions, inter alia, was a critical mass of black students sufficient to create a sense of mutual support and psychological well-being in an alien environment.

Fewer than 10% of the black students (19) were enrolled in those states that became known as "*Adams* states." Of that number, 4 were enrolled in Georgia, 9 in Maryland, 1 in North Carolina, and 5 in the three dental schools in Pennsylvania. Howard's first-year enrollment was more than twice the combined enrollment of black students in the "*Adams* states," and Meharry's first-year enrollment was significantly greater than their combined total enrollments of new students. This inaccessibility of schools of dentistry to black students underscores the importance of external pressure exerted by the NAACP–Legal Defense Fund on the Department of Health, Education, and Welfare (currently the Department of Health and Human Services) and its Office of Civil Rights to force those states that had historicaly operated dual systems of education to expand opportunities for black students. The various court decisions during the 1970s that ordered such expansion of educational opportunity are among the factors that account for the growth patterns observed in the participation of black students in the "*Adams* states" (see Tables 21, 22, 23, and 24).

The first-year enrollment of black students in dental schools increased in every year between 1970 and 1977. Thereafter, a downward trend began that was not reversed until 1980 when 283 black students were matriculated in first-year classes of mainland U.S. dental colleges. As with the students at medical colleges, first-year black student enrollment in the 1970s peaked in 1974 and 1975. The downturns noticed among black first-year dental students since the latter half of the 1970s reflect the inability of blacks to keep pace with the enrollment of white students in first-year classes. Between 1980 and 1984, the absolute number of black students in first-year dental classes continued to rise slowly. Because of the steady decline in overall enrollment of first-year students and the slight upturns among blacks in the same classes, blacks actually constituted a larger percentage of first-year students in 1984–85 than at any previous time. In the 11 year period from 1974 to 1985, some 3,163 black students enrolled in first-year dental classes. This number represented 4.6% of the 68,169 students of all races matriculated in first-year classes during that period. As shown in Tables 21 to 24, there has been some progress in the participation of blacks in dental education but that progress can only be described as limited access.

The combined enrollment of black students in the 13 schools of dentistry in the first-tier "*Adams* states" was 35 in 1974; 54 in 1975; 50 in 1976;

46 in 1977; 44 in 1978; and 46 in 1979. In terms of absolute numbers, the most successful institutions in the "*Adams* states," up to 1980, regarding first-year enrollment of black students, were the University of Maryland, University of Georgia, and University of Pittsburgh. Not only are sizable black colleges located in these states but they also have a substantial black population. With the exception of Oklahoma, blacks constitute a substantial proportion of the total population of all the "*Adams* states." Yet they are grossly underrepresented in their dental schools. Between 1980 and 1984, however, with respect to enrolling black students in first-year dental school classes among institutions in the first-tier "*Adams* states," the most successful institutions were University of Texas/Houston (37); Ohio State University (25); University of Alabama (20); University of Missouri/K.C. (17); Louisiana State University (16), and Case Western Reserve University (15) (Table 24).

Table 21
First-Year Enrollments in Dentistry Programs,
All Institutions Combined, 1968–1986

Academic Year	First Year Enrollments	First-Year Black Student Enrollment	% Black of First Year
1968–69	4,203	—	—
1969–70	4,355	—	—
1970–71	4,565	185	4.0
1971–72	4,745	245	5.1
1972–73	5,337	244	4.5
1973–74	5,445	273	5.0
1974–75	5,617	279	4.9
1975–76	5,763	298	5.1
1976–77	5,835	290	4.9
1977–78	5,954	296	4.9
1978–79	6,301	280	4.4
1979–80	6,132	274	4.4
1980–81	6,050	283	4.7
1981–82	5,855	299	5.2
1982–83	5,498	289	5.3
1983–84	5,274	276	5.3
1984–85	5,047	299	5.9
1985–86	4,843	281	5.8
Total	96,819	4,391	
(1970–1985)	88,261	(4,391)	(4.9)

Source: American Dental Association, *Minority Reports: Supplement to the Annual Reports of 1974 to 1984, Dental Education.*

Table 22
Student First-Year Enrollment in Schools of Dentistry in
"Non-*Adams* States," by School, Sex, and Year, 1974–1984

Dental School	1974 M	1974 F	1975 M	1975 F	1976 M	1976 F	1977 M	1977 F
University of the Pacific	2	1	0	0	0	0	0	0
University of California/S.F.	6	0	1	1	3	4	6	1
UCLA	4	0	4	6	6	5	6	9
USC	6	0	4	1	0	2	3	0
Loma Linda University	3	1	0	0	2	1	2	1
University of Colorado	0	0	0	0	1	1	0	0
University of Connecticut	0	0	2	0	1	0	0	0
Georgetown University	4	0	3	2	3	1	0	0
Howard University*	68	19	60	20	49	22	48	34
Loyola University (Ill.)	2	0	2	2	0	1	1	1
Northwestern University	0	0	0	1	0	1	0	0
University of Southern Illinois	0	0	0	0	1	0	0	0
University of Illinois	3	4	4	2	3	3	2	3
Indiana University	1	0	2	0	0	3	1	0
University of Iowa	2	0	0	1	2	1	0	0
Harvard University	2	0	2	1	1	0	2	3
Boston University	0	0	1	0	0	0	1	0
Tufts University	4	3	1	2	4	1	1	1
University of Detroit	2	3	5	3	3	0	3	0
University of Michigan	10	2	6	4	7	7	6	7
University of Minnesota	1	0	1	0	2	0	1	0
Creighton University	2	0	2	1	0	1	0	1
University of Nebraska	0	0	0	0	0	0	0	0
Fairleigh Dickinson University	4	0	0	1	0	1	1	0
New Jersey Dental College	3	0	8	2	9	2	8	5
Columbia University	0	0	0	0	0	1	0	0
NYU	0	3	4	0	1	0	4	1
SUNY/S.B.	1	2	1	0	0	0	0	0
SUNY/Buffalo	2	1	2	2	2	3	1	0
University of Oregon	0	0	3	1	2	0	2	0
Meharry Medical College*	32	8	25	16	34	10	41	11
University of Tennessee	4	0	0	1	1	1	0	1
University of Washington	2	0	2	0	2	1	2	0
Marquette University	0	0	0	0	0	0	0	0
Total by Sex	170	47	145	70	139	73	142	79
Total	217		215		212		221	

Source: American Dental Association, *Minority Reports.*
*Historically Black Institution.

Table 22 (*continued*)

1978 M	1978 F	1979 M	1979 F	1980 M	1980 F	1981 M	1981 F	1982 M	1982 F	1983 M	1983 F	1984 M	1984 F
0	0	0	0	1	0	1	0	2	0	0	0	0	0
0	2	4	1	5	3	3	6	5	3	3	0	1	2
4	9	5	3	5	2	3	2	2	1	2	0	1	0
2	0	0	0	0	1	0	1	0	0	0	1	0	1
0	0	6	0	0	0	0	0	0	0	4	0	0	0
0	0	1	0	0	0	0	0	1	0	0	0	0	0
0	0	0	0	1	0	1	1	1	1	0	0	1	2
2	6	3	2	1	1	0	2	3	2	3	2	6	1
45	22	45	28	47	39	42	40	57	28	43	35	51	25
0	4	1	1	1	2	0	0	0	0	1	2	2	1
1	0	0	0	0	0	0	0	0	3	0	0	0	2
1	0	0	1	0	1	8	1	10	1	4	1	1	3
2	2	2	3	4	2	9	4	2	3	2	3	1	1
2	0	0	0	1	0	1	0	0	0	3	2	1	3
2	0	1	0	0	0	0	0	0	0	1	1	0	0
0	2	1	0	1	0	1	1	1	1	0	0	0	1
2	1	0	1	1	1	0	0	0	2	1	1	0	2
0	1	1	1	0	0	1	0	1	1	0	0	1	2
1	1	1	1	3	0	4	0	0	0	0	0	1	2
5	5	8	5	2	2	6	6	4	5	8	4	7	2
1	1	1	0	1	0	0	0	1	0	0	0	0	0
2	0	0	0	1	0	0	1	1	1	1	0	0	0
0	0	0	0	1	0	3	0	0	0	0	0	0	0
2	0	4	2	5	0	5	6	2	5	7	5	1	1
8	4	4	1	5	3	4	0	1	0	1	1	1	2
1	0	0	1	0	0	0	1	0	2	1	0	1	1
2	4	0	1	1	0	0	1	3	3	4	1	2	5
0	0	0	0	1	1	1	0	0	1	0	0	0	0
0	0	1	2	0	0	0	0	1	0	0	0	1	0
0	0	0	0	1	0	1	0	2	0	0	0	0	0
30	18	32	19	32	21	30	20	25	21	24	24	22	20
1	1	0	1	2	1	0	2	1	1	0	0	2	2
0	1	0	0	0	0	1	1	1	0	0	0	1	0
1	0	1	0	2	0	3	1	1	2	1	3	5	4
117	84	122	74	125	80	128	97	128	87	114	86	110	85
201		196		205		225		215		200		195	

Table 23
First-Year Black Student Enrollment in Schools of Dentistry in
First-Tier "*Adams* States," by School and Sex, 1974–1984

Dental School	1974		1975		1976		1977	
	M	F	M	F	M	F	M	F
University of Florida	—	—	4	0	0	0	2	0
Emory University	—	—	1	0	0	0	0	1
Medical College of Georgia	5	1	6	2	5	3	1	1
Louisiana State University	1	1	0	2	2	1	0	3
University of Maryland	5	2	5	4	10	5	9	6
University of Mississippi	—	—	1	1	1	0	4	3
University of North Carolina	2	2	4	1	1	3	2	2
Oral Roberts University	—	—	—	—	—	—	—	—
University of Oklahoma	1	0	2	0	2	1	0	1
Temple University	2	2	2	0	3	1	2	1
University of Pennsylvania	1	0	6	3	1	2	2	0
University of Pittsburgh	4	3	3	5	4	4	4	4
Virginia Commonwealth	2	1	2	0	1	4	2	0
Medical College of So. Carolina	—	—	—	—	—	—	—	—
Total by Sex	23	12	36	18	30	24	28	22
Total Black	35		54		54		50	

Blank lines mean data unavailable or institutions had not opened.
Source: American Dental Association, *Minority Reports* for years
1974–1984.

Table 23 *(continued)*

1978		1979		1980		1981		1982		1983		1984		
M	F	M	F	M	F	M	F	M	F	M	F	M	F	Total
3	1	0	1	1	1	5	0	5	1	1	1	2	2	30
0	1	1	2	1	1	0	0	0	0	1	0	1	2	12
4	4	7	3	5	2	4	2	4	1	1	2	3	2	68
2	0	0	0	2	0	1	2	1	3	2	1	1	3	28
8	1	4	2	5	1	6	4	3	8	6	8	5	11	118
4	1	3	2	1	0	2	1	1	1	2	3	2	0	33
2	2	6	3	5	4	2	1	2	2	4	2	5	2	60
—	—	0	0	0	0	0	0	0	0	0	0	0	0	0
—	—	2	0	1	0	0	1	2	1	1	1	1	2	19
0	3	1	2	1	1	3	0	3	1	2	1	1	3	35
1	2	1	1	2	1	0	0	1	1	0	0	1	1	27
3	2	3	0	5	0	0	3	4	0	0	1	2	1	55
0	0	2	0	4	1	5	2	2	2	5	1	0	2	38
—	—	—	—	1	1	1	1	0	1	1	1	2	1	10
27	17	30	16	34	13	29	17	28	22	26	22	26	32	
44		46		47		46		50		48		58		532

Table 24
First-Year Enrollment in Dental Schools in Second-Tier "*Adams* States," by School and Sex, 1980–1984

Dental School	Fall 1980 M	Fall 1980 F	Fall 1981 M	Fall 1981 F	Fall 1982 M	Fall 1982 F	Fall 1983 M	Fall 1983 F	Fall 1984 M	Fall 1984 F	Total
U. of Alabama	3	6	3	2	1	1	0	2	1	1	20
U. of Kentucky	2	0	2	0	1	0	0	0	3	2	10
Louisville U.	1	1	1	1	2	3	0	1	1	2	13
U. of Missouri/K.C.	0	0	3	0	3	1	2	2	4	2	17
Washington U.	2	0	0	0	0	0	1	1	3	0	7
Ohio State U.	2	3	3	2	3	1	3	3	2	3	25
Case Western Reserve	3	1	1	2	0	0	3	1	3	1	15
Baylor Col. of Dentistry	0	0	0	1	1	1	0	1	3	1	8
U. of Tex./Houston	2	1	3	4	4	3	8	1	8	3	37
U. of Tex./S.A.	2	0	0	1	1	0	2	2	0	3	11
West Virginia U.	0	0	0	0	0	1	0	0	0	0	1
Total by Sex	17	12	16	13	16	11	19	14	28	18	164
Total Black	29		29		27		33		46		164

As shown in Table 21, black students constituted 4.9% of first-year enrollees in dental schools in 1971. By 1974, dental schools enrolled almost 100 more black students in first-year classes than they did in 1970–71. The 279 black students enrolled in 1974–1975 represented 4.9% of the 5617 students of all races enrolled in first-year classes. That the percentage of black students enrolled during the following year was almost identical to the 1973–74 percentage reflects the commensurate increase in first-year students in general and indicates that black students were not necessarily gaining ground at the expense of any particular group of students.

The decline in the black first-year enrollment thereafter may be explained by a combination of factors whose cumulative impact resulted in an enrollment drop. For example, the *Bakke* suit was proceeding through the lower courts. That reality may have fostered a state of uncertainty and dimmed optimism among recruitment and admissions committees concerning the constitutionality of some of their affirmative action and institutional policies. Simultaneously, the nation experienced a serious recession that had a far graver impact on the black population than perhaps any other segment of the population.

The economic crisis, combined with severe reductions in the available financial assistance, heightened suspiciousness among gifted black students about the practicality of deferring their gratifications or saddling themselves with debts of $50,000 or more in order to complete the requirements for a degree in dentistry. Consequently, some of these students who may normally have enrolled in schools of dentistry, opted for lucrative job opportunities then available to them. Further, actual institutional behavior relative to increasing weights assigned to objective measures of evaluation was of special importance in curtailing an expansion of black student enrollment in first-year dental school classes.

In "non-*Adams* states," and excluding Howard University and Meharry Medical College from the analysis, Table 22 shows that four institutions were comparatively successful in the recruitment and admission of black students in their first-year classes during the 1970s. These dental schools are the University of Michigan, University of California at Los Angeles, New Jersey Dental School, and University of Illinois. That each of these institutions is a public institution suggests that public institutions were, and are, considerably more responsive to pressures for increasing access to all students than were private dental schools. This suggestion appears to be borne out by the regression analysis, described in Chapter 3, which depicts a trend in that direction during the late 1970s.

In earlier years, private institutions had far more latitude in opening their doors to black students. The current enrollment profile suggests that this may no longer be the case. A plausible assumption is that either their commitment deteriorated; their focus was on token admission; or they have come to depend more heavily on quantitative factors in making admissions decisions; or on a combination of these factors. As a result, private institutions have not done as well as previously anticipated. Exceptions to this generalization are such institutions as Georgetown University, University of Detroit, Case Western Reserve University, New York University, Tufts University, and University of Southern California.

The success of this latter group is relative to what other institutions in their state or jurisdiction accomplished during the five-year period between 1974 and 1979. For instance, Case Western Reserve University did somewhat better than Ohio State University in enrolling black students in first-year classes. But the University of Detroit, much smaller in size, was not as successful in terms of absolute numbers as was the University of Michigan. Nor was the University of Southern California as successful as UCLA. Tufts did better than either Harvard University or Boston University, but all are private institutions located in the same city. Similarly Georgetown and Howard universities are located in the same city and both draw students from throughout the nation. Howard is historically black and federally supported, but Georgetown is not.

By contrast, during the first half of the 1980s, the traditionally white dental schools that experienced the greatest success in the recruitment and enrollment of black students in first-year classes were University of Maryland (57); University of Michigan (46); University of Texas/Houston, Fairleigh Dickinson University (each 37); University of California/San Francisco, University of Illinois, and Southern Illinois University (each 31); University of North Carolina (30); Medical College of Georgia (30); Ohio State University (25); Virginia Commonwealth University (24); Marquette University (22); and University of Alabama (20) (Tables 22 and 23).

The fact that seven among this group of "most successful" dental schools are located in states influenced by *Adams* litigation underscores the ultimate value of federal intervention to enforce compliance to court-ordered systemwide desegregation at all levels of higher education. It provides demonstrable evidence of how the enforcement of policies initiated in the 1970s, following the original *Adams* decision, and subsequent orders issued by Judge Pratt in 1978 and thereafter, persuaded many key governmental decision makers in these states to move somewhat more rapidly toward desegregation.

In terms of institutional control, this list of relatively successful institutions reveals that publicly supported institutions, whether in "*Adams* states" or outside the *Adams* jurisdiction, were more effective than private dental schools in the matriculation of black students during the first half of the 1980s. Only five private dental schools, some of which are "state affiliated," enrolled 15 or more first-year black students in dentistry: Marquette University, New York University, Case Western Reserve University, Georgetown University, and Temple University (see Tables 22, 23, and 24).

Further, support is enhanced for the hypotheses that institutional location and the size of the black population within the state influence the enrollment of black students. The most successful schools of dentistry, in this sense, are either located in areas of large population density and/or in states in which blacks constitute a significant portion of the state's population.

Whether in "*Adams* states" or elsewhere, the most important dependent variable in this analysis is, of course, first-year enrollment of black students. Obviously, if there is no, or limited, success in enrollment of black students, there will be little or no success in the production of black dentists. This is a problem of institutional behavior—recruitment selection, admission, quality of the learning environment, resources—and of the available student pool. Institutional behavior is not uniform throughout the nation.

Almost all dental schools enrolled at least one black student during the 1970s. Only Oral Roberts University and the Oregon Medical Center failed to enroll even a single black student in dentistry between 1980 and 1984. However, several dental schools never moved beyond token desegregation (see Tables 23 and 24). In view of the limited access of black students to several schools, however, it would seem that several are confronted in the

1980s with the task of whether or not *to move* beyond mere tokenism. Presence of more serious instances of tokenism in the "*Adams* states" adds further credence to the hypothesis that pressures engendered by such litigation as *Adams* v. *Bennett* are of inestimable importance in promoting equality of opportunity beyond tokenism. If that is the case, the question remains as to what precise litigation is appropriate in states not currently under litigation to desegregate but containing institutions whose policies help create widespread underrepresentation of blacks in the field of dentistry.

Enrollment in the 1980s

In 1970 the 451 black students enrolled in the nation's school of dentistry represented a mere 2.7% of all students enrolled. It is evident from Table 25 that total enrollment in dental schools increased by approximately 500 or 600 students annually. Even the absolute numbers of black students enrolled in dental schools almost doubled between 1970 and 1974. Since then, black student total enrollment has been conspicuously inconsistent. Total enrollment of black students actually peaked in 1975–1976, followed by an actual decline in absolute numbers, or a loss of some 22 students in 1976–1977 (see Table 25).

Only in 1979–1980 did total black student enrollment first exceed 1000. Even then, the 4.4% of total enrollment they represented did not approach parity—a percentage equivalent to the percentage of black people in the total U.S. population. Total black student enrollment in dentistry hovered around 1000 throughout the first half of the 1980s. This incontrovertible fact speaks dramatically to the need for major reforms in dental education policies, procedures, and activities that will significantly transform the racial composition of the dental profession. With such paucity of black students enrolled, coupled with retention problems, and despite apparent successes, it is understandable why in 1980 there were only 3000 black dentists in the United States.[9] By 1985, the number approximated 4000.

Table 26 presents total black student enrollment in dental schools located in the "*Adams* states." One illustration of activity in the "*Adams* states" may be drawn from the University of Florida in 1974, which had 2 black students out of a total enrollment of 88 students in its School of Dentistry. This number represented about 2% of total enrollment. In 1979–1980, 7 black students were enrolled out of a total of 249 students. These 7 black students represented less than 3% (2.8) of the total enrollment in that institution. By contrast, the University of Maryland had a total black student enrollment in its School of Dentistry in 1974 of 38 out of 527 students. This represented slightly more than 7% of the total enrollment. By 1979–1980 the proportion of black students in the dental school in Maryland had declined, but only by an insignificant fraction. It increased to 40 in 1984 (see Table 26).

Table 25
Total Enrollment, All Classes and Institutions,
in Dental School Programs, 1968–1984

Academic Year	Total Enrollment	Total Black Student Enrollment	% Black
1968–69	15,408	N.A.	N.A.
1969–70	16,008	N.A.	N.A.
1970–71	16,553	451	2.7
1971–72	17,505	N.A.	N.A.
1972–73	18,376	N.A.	N.A.
1973–74	19,369	N.A.	N.A.
1974–75	20,146	945	4.6
1975–76	20,767	977	4.7
1976–77	21,013	955	4.5
1977–78	21,510	968	4.5
1978–79	22,179	977	4.4
1979–80	22,482	1,009	4.4
1980–81	22,842	1,022	4.4
1981–82	22,641	999	4.4
1982–83	22,235	1,001	4.6
1983–84	21,428	1,000	4.7
1984–85	20,588	1,037	5.0

Source: American Dental Association, Minority Reports.

In North Carolina, in 1974, black students constituted slightly more than 2% of the enrollment in the University of North Carolina's College of Dentistry. By 1979–1980, the 18 black students enrolled there represented 5.7% of the total enrollment of 312 students. One could argue that the proportionate enrollment of black students had more than doubled during a five-year period. However, that assertion would be grossly misleading because, in the first instance, the initial base for comparison was so minute. Similar observations could be made about other institutions in the "Adams states." Black student total was only 1037 in 1985.

Some of the "Adams states" fare quite well when compared to "non-Adams states" in terms of the percentage distribution of black students in schools of dentistry. A detailed analysis of such findings is unwarranted, since most of the states never enrolled any more than from 2% to 7% of black student total enrollment. Even after a cursory glance at these data it strikes the astute observer that a crisis of underrepresentation of black students in the field of dentistry remains in 1985 despite corrective actions taken by some institutions, states, and representatives in public and private sectors (see Table 26).

According to the latest available data, the 1984–1985 statistics provided by the Council on Dental Education of the American Dental Association, 17.1% of the U.S. schools of dentistry did not enroll a single black student in that year. These 11 institutions were the University of the Pacific, Loma Linda University, University of Colorado, University of Iowa, University of Minnesota, Creighton University, University of Nebraska, SUNY/Stony Brook, Oral Roberts University, Oregon Health Sciences University, and West Virginia University. Some of the institutions (e.g., Colorado and West Virginia) reported in the *Admissions Requirements of U.S. and Canadian Dental Schools: 1985–1986* that they do not have specific programs oriented toward the recruitment of minorities and women. Institutions such as the University of Nebraska enrolled not a single black student in dentistry throughout the 1970s and only three so far in the 1980s.[10] The apparent absence of a strong institutional commitment for recruitment and matriculation of black students helps to account for the established pattern of underrepresentation of black students in total enrollment at most of the institutions listed above.

Factors Affecting Enrollment

An explicit assumption of this study is that first-year enrollment depends on 1 or more of 12 independent variables, the presence of which may prove to be powerful predictors of enrollment patterns or trends. Previous analyses have demonstrated that among the most powerful predictors of first-year enrollment are the presence of role models (black faculty); the quality of financial aid programs; being under litigation to desegregate higher education; the proportion of blacks in the state population; the type of institution, that is, public, private, or state assisted; and the special recruitment and admissions programs. Two of these variables are addressed below.

Availability of Financial Aid

The availability of adequate financial aid programs fluctuated during the 1970s despite increases in possible sources of financial assistance for students in the health fields and for institutions that operated such programs. Under President Reagan, financial aid programs, especially dollar amount available, declined dramatically over what was available under

Table 26
Total Black Student Enrollment in Schools of Dentistry
in First-Tier "*Adams* States," by School and Sex, 1974–1984

Dental School	1974		1975		1976		1977	
	M	F	M	F	M	F	M	F
U. of Florida	1	1	5	1	4	1	5	0
Emory U.	0	0	1	0	1	0	1	1
Medical College of Georgia	18	4	16	4	14	6	9	4
U. of Maryland	33	5	26	9	23	14	25	17
U. of Mississippi	—	—	1	1	2	1	5	4
U. of North Carolina	5	2	8	2	9	5	9	6
U. of Oklahoma	3	0	5	0	5	1	4	2
Oral Roberts U.	—	—	—	—	—	—	—	—
Temple U.	8	2	9	2	10	3	7	4
U. of Pennsylvania	7	0	10	3	9	5	7	4
U. of Pittsburgh	14	4	13	9	9	9	12	10
Virginia Commonwealth U.	9	2	8	2	6	6	6	3
Total by Sex	98	20	102	33	92	51	90	55
Total Black	118		135		143		145	

Source: American Dental Association, *Minority Reports.*
*Historically Black Institution.

Table 26 *(continued)*

1978		1979		1980		1981		1982		1983		1984	
M	F	M	F	M	F	M	F	M	F	M	F	M	F
8	1	5	2	6	3	9	3	11	3	11	3	9	4
1	2	1	4	2	4	2	1	2	0	2	1	2	2
9	6	16	7	20	6	20	8	19	7	11	7	9	7
24	13	25	11	22	7	22	8	19	16	21	19	20	30
9	4	10	5	7	3	5	1	3	2	4	6	4	4
10	6	11	7	10	7	8	6	10	6	11	9	11	8
3	2	4	2	2	2	2	2	4	2	4	2	5	3
—	—	—	—	0	0	0	0	0	0	0	0	0	0
5	6	4	7	5	7	5	5	8	4	8	2	8	5
5	5	5	4	7	5	5	4	3	3	4	1	2	2
12	10	11	5	11	4	10	5	11	4	8	5	5	5
4	2	6	2	7	1	8	2	9	4	12	5	9	6
90	57	98	56	99	49	96	45	99	51	96	60	84	76
147		154		148		141		150		156		160	

Table 27

**Total Enrollment in U.S. Dental Schools in Second-Tier "*Adams* States,"
by School, and Sex, 1980–1984**

Dental School	Fall 1980 M	F	Fall 1981 M	F	Fall 1982 M	F	Fall 1983 M	F	Fall 1984 M	F
U. of Alabama	10	13	8	9	4	9	5	7	2	5
U. of Kentucky	7	5	7	2	5	1	3	0	5	2
Louisville U.	2	2	3	2	4	5	3	5	4	7
Louisiana State U.	4	0	4	2	4	4	6	3	3	5
U. of Missouri/K.C.	8	3	5	3	9	2	8	3	12	4
Washington U.	7	1	5	0	3	0	3	1	3	1
Ohio State U.	12	8	9	6	12	6	10	7	9	8
Case Western Reserve	5	6	6	6	5	5	6	2	6	4
Baylor Col. of Dentistry	2	1	0	2	1	3	0	3	3	2
U. of Texas/Houston	8	10	9	10	10	10	18	10	21	11
U. of Texas/S.A.	6	0	4	1	4	1	5	3	2	5
West Virginia U.	1	0	0	0	0	1	0	1	0	1
Total by Sex	72	49	60	43	61	47	67	45	70	55
Total Black	121		103		108		112		125	

previous administrations. One of the critical factors to bear in mind here is that the cost of dental education exacts a heavy burden on disadvantaged students of all races and on students who are not able to draw on family resources to help defray the costs. Table 28 depicts both current first-year and total estimated costs of dental education for resident students in each of the 59 mainland U.S. dental schools. These costs are not stable and have shown major increases in recent years as a result of uncontrolled inflation and the escalating expenses of dental school training in general. If students are relatively disadvantaged and must seek their financial support outside of family resources, this situation presents staggering problems (see Table 28).

Hence, outside assistance is required by a significant majority of students enrolled in dental schools. As shown in Table 28, the proportion of students receiving loans, scholarships, or both to finance dental education ranges from a low of 25% of students enrolled at Howard University to a high of 100% at the University of Tennessee. First-year costs at the University of the Pacific, the highest in the nation, amount to $19,200 plus fees. First-year resident costs are particularly low at the dental schools of Baylor University ($750), University of Texas at Houston ($400), and

University of Texas, San Antonio ($300). Of these three institutions, the University of Texas/Houston enrolled 11 black students, or 10% of its first-year class in 1984. By contrast, no black student enrolled at the University of the Pacific. The average first-year tuition costs of resident students in schools of dentistry was $6,970 plus an average $267 in general fees in 1984. The combined figure of $6703 in tuition and fees for state residents represented a 10.3% increase over the 1983 costs. Not unexpectedly, nonresident students pay more; their first-year costs in 1984 amounted to $9221 in tuition and fees.[11]

Among institutions in which three-quarters or more of the students received financial assistance are the University of Alabama (75%), University of the Pacific (81%), Georgetown University (85%), Emory University (83%), Northwestern University (84%), Louisiana State University (90%), University of Maryland (79%), Harvard University (75%), University of Detroit (85%), Washington University (78%), Fairleigh Dickinson University (79%), and seven other mainland universities. Of these institutions, the most successful for first-year enrollment of black students were the University of Maryland and Georgetown University.

Since 1978, the parental income of dental school students has changed dramatically. A survey of dental school seniors showed that in 1978 about 36.6% were from families with an annual income of less than $20,000; 36.3% had yearly incomes of $20,000 to $39,000; and 21.7% had annual incomes of $40,000 or more. By 1984, almost half (47.8%) of all seniors in dental schools were from families with a yearly income of $40,000 or more; 38.0% were in the $20,000–39,000 bracket; and only 16.2% had parents who earned $20,000 or less a year.[12] Yet the majority of dental students are compelled to seek financial aid because of the enormity of total yearly expenses incurred through tuition, fees, room and board, and other needs.

With respect to loan programs, dental school students depend heavily on Guaranteed Student Loans (GSLs), their families and other loan sources, National Direct Student Loans (NDSLs), and the Federal Health Professions Loan program. Other loans are made through the Health Education Assistance Loan program and personal bank loans. Members of the 1984–1985 senior class who participated in the survey conducted by the Association of American Dental Schools reported that more than 97% of them borrowed from at least one source to finance their education. The pattern of borrowing showed that the most frequently utilized source is the GSL program. In 1984, some 87.4% of all seniors borrowed through this program, compared to the 54.4% who did so in 1978. The proportion of NDSL users among senior dental students more than doubled between 1978 and 1984, from 18.7% to 39.1%. However, the percentage who borrowed from the Federal Health Professions Loan program declined from 45.5% in 1978 to 38.2% in 1984. During the same period, the percentage who borrowed from parents and other sources rose sharply, from 40.7% in 1978 to 61.7% in 1984.[13]

Table 28
**Financial Assistance Awarded to Predoctoral Dental Students
in the United States, 1982–1983**

Dental School	Number of Applications for Financial Assistance[a]	Number of Applicants Meeting Needs Test
University of Alabama	220	220
University of the Pacific	358	358
University of California/San Francisco	215	194
University of California/Los Angeles	204	204
University of Southern California	N/A	400
Loma Linda University	312	173
University of Colorado	46	36
University of Connecticut	57	57
Georgetown University	563	563
Howard University	229	163
University of Florida	213	81
Emory University	200	251
Medical College of Georgia	168	168
Loyola University	159	159
Northwestern University	306	306
Southern Illinois University	169	46
University of Illinois	573	552
Indiana University	219	219
University of Iowa	N/A	275
University of Kentucky	180	180
University of Louisville	95	220
Louisiana State University	256	256
University of Maryland	496	250
Harvard University	60	59
Boston University	116	116
Tufts University	239	173
University of Detroit	272	267
University of Michigan	392	361
University of Minnesota	N/A	N/A
University of Mississippi	148	123
University of Missouri/Kansas City	486	399
Washington University/St. Louis	N/A	266
Creighton University	141	141
University of Nebraska	219	138
Fairleigh Dickinson University	284	164

Table 28 *(continued)*

Total Amount Requested (thousands)	Number of Applicants Who Received Financial Assistance[b]	% of Students Enrolled Who Received Assistance	Total Amount Awarded (thousands)
$2,509	218	90.83	$1,482
3,351	344	85.36	3,277
1,535	196	47.34	1,216
1,641	335	81.11	2,574
2,617	400	77.22	2,617
3,260	312	85.25	4,320
235	36	34.95	163
351	57	32.39	256
N/A	563	91.54	6,293
871	105	25.55	391
699	217	74.32	1,485
1,500	251	65.88	1,850
1,157	178	78.41	1,205
2,427	159	28.09	595
4,201	306	67.11	4,201
363	169	81.25	659
2,724	552	95.50	3,937
2,054	132	27.97	455
1,770	284	80.23	1,896
1,283	180	84.51	1,238
1,320	211	73.52	1,278
1,395	330	94.56	1,516
1,085	250	50.10	1,085
877	59	81.94	720
2,056	116	48.74	1,224
N/A	159	33.76	551
3,352	263	85.39	2,374
3,068	361	62.78	3,014
N/A	302	54.91	2,007
693	123	71.93	503
N/A	465	78.81	3,256
3,335	266	80.12	2,902
1,602	245	80.86	1,910
920	136	55.06	1,041
4,260	303	94.39	2,927

Table 28 *(continued)*

Dental School	Number of Applications for Financial Assistance[a]	Number of Applicants Meeting Needs Test
U. of Medicine and Dentistry of New Jersey	202	202
Columbia University	216	214
New York University	665	665
State University of New York/Stony Brook	95	95
State University of New York/Buffalo	343	N/A
University of North Carolina	260	204
Ohio State University	450	350
Case Western Reserve University	345	350
University of Oklahoma	208	123
Oral Roberts University	72	12
Oregon Health Sciences University	201	176
Temple University	267	502
University of Pennsylvania	552	540
University of Pittsburgh	288	216
Medical University of South Carolina	190	174
Meharry Medical College	150	148
University of Tennessee	373	494
Baylor College of Dentistry	200	190
University of Texas at Houston	320	127
University of Texas at San Antonio	434	414
Virginia Commonwealth University	334	334
University of Washington/Seattle	283	269
West Virginia University	177	110
Marquette University	516	481
University of Puerto Rico	193	193
Mean	266.6	243.5
Standard Deviation	141.65	146.10

Source: American Dental Association Council on Dental Education Division of Educational Measurement, *1983–84 Annual Report, Dental Education,* p. 23, Table 13.
[a]Some schools reported only students who received aid.
[b]Some schools have reported monies awarded to students who did not have to meet standard needs test.

Table 28 *(continued)*

Total Amount Requested (thousands)	Number of Applicants Who Received Financial Assistance[b]	% of Students Enrolled Who Received Assistance	Total Amount Awarded (thousands)
N/A	202	59.59	1,666
4,255	216	91.14	2,214
11,665	641	90.92	6,770
643	95	90.48	643
N/A	343	98.56	2,489
1,240	237	76.45	1,398
2,391	341	52.70	1,003
2,772	332	84.69	2,652
990	208	80.62	1,412
57	83	85.57	853
1,501	196	68.06	1,488
4,539	511	91.74	4,254
2,700	357	58.81	5,365
2,242	216	50.82	1,784
N/A	174	79.09	1,090
1,881	148	88.62	2,814
3,000	494	101.23	1,619
1,250	190	35.45	1,176
956	318	65.43	1,907
2,673	414	76.67	2,673
2,500	334	78.40	2,444
1,515	240	73.62	1,456
918	157	72.35	1,065
5,204	512	95.70	5,959
1,291	88	33.72	770
$2,164.23	260.5	71.0	$2,056.37
1,789.82	135.33		1,496.40

Scholarship funds from the federal government decreased during the first term of the Reagan administration. In 1984, approximately 32% of dental school seniors received scholarship aid from at least one of five major sources. For example, the percentage of seniors who received scholarships from the U.S. Public Health Service National Health Services Corps Scholarship Fund climbed from 1.6% in 1978 to 2.6% in 1980 to a high of 4.7% in 1982, but was reduced by almost 50% in 1984. An even more dramatic decline was observed with respect to the Armed Forces Health Professions Scholarship participation. In 1978, 6.8% of the seniors received scholarships from this program. A decline to 2.1% was noted in 1981, then to 0.4% in 1982, and downward to 0.2% in 1984. This loss was not compensated for by state scholarships or grants. They also fell, from 13.3% in 1978 to 9.2% of seniors using this source in 1984.[14]

School scholarships or grants as a source of assistance increased between 1978 and 1984. In 1978, some 15.6% of the seniors reported using this source; by 1984, the source had increased to 19.5%. Other scholarship sources showed no appreciable difference between the 9.2% and the 9.3% who helped finance dental education from this source in 1984.[15]

Irrespective of the sources of financial assistance utilized by dental school students, they tend to graduate burdened with an extraordinarily heavy debt. In 1978, only 1 in 4 graduating seniors had accumulated debts of $20,000 or more. By 1984, more than 8 of every 10 graduating seniors in dental schools had debts of this size. In 1978, the average entering indebtedness was only $1600, and the average graduating indebtedness was $12,700. By contrast, in 1984, the average entering indebtedness was $2370, but the average graduating debt was $32,000 for all seniors and $44,300 among graduates from private institutions. The latter figure compares to $25,900 for graduates of public institutions and $36,100 among graduates of private, state-assisted dental schools.[16] Indebtedness has a direct bearing on postdental graduation employment.

Recruitment Programs

Strong recruitment programs are essential for the successful enrollment of significant numbers of black students. Without question, many institutions with a low enrollment of black students recruit with exceptional diligence. Yet they are unsuccessful in attracting black students. For them, the situation is particularly frustrating, since poor results do not adequately reflect the magnitude of their effort nor their overall financial investment in the recruitment process. These recruitment programs include the utilization of minority recruiters, extensive travel to regional centers, visits to historically black colleges and to career days sponsored by other institutions, participation in the Health Professions Summer Program, waiver of application fees, participation in the DDS–Op program, and the availability of a self-paced flexible curriculum. Parenthetically, a few of the institutions have abolished the flexible curriculum in recent years.

Several dental schools maintain that the recruitment and admissions problem is complicated by the small pool of "qualified black students" and the increasing competition for that group. "Qualified," in so many instances, refers exclusively to performance on the DAT. The fact of the matter is that black students, as a group, fall from 1.5 to as much as 2.0 points below the mean DAT scores of the acceptees at several institutions. That is one of the reasons why some institutions, such as the University of Alabama, insist that it is necessary to scrutinize the *entire* profile of the applicant in making admissions decisions, rather than rely exclusively on one or two criteria.

Other institutions candidly admit that their institutional behavior leaves a great deal to be desired regarding black applicants. Institutional behavior may include an intimidating environment within which the personal interview is conducted and the lack of a standardized concept of expectations for the personal interview, which often means that different interviewers are searching for entirely different qualities in the applicant. Frequently, as in any subjective encounter, "people see what they look for and look for precisely what they see."

There may be considerable fallout from the inability of many black students to afford the cost of travel to an institution that expresses an interest in them. Those institutions frequently state that no travel money is available to bring prospective students to the campus. They also fail to draw on alumni in nearby cities or even to send their faculty to cities closest to the candidate to help eliminate travel problems. When they do follow up, several institutions do not provide sufficient scholarship money to enable them to woo capable black students to their institutions.

Further, there is some evidence that institutional commitment is waning. This situation coincides with a rise of the new conservatism in the American society. One dimension of this shift is a disregard for anything more than limited access or tokenism, and some institutions do not even seem committed to that. A few institutions claim that black students are not interested in dentistry and that fact alone accounts for their underrepresentation. This position is unacceptable. While it may be more to the point to assert that the interest in dentistry is not as great as the interest in medicine, which seems to be true for American students in general, the profession of dentistry has to become far more aggressive and less rigid in its practices in order to enroll significant numbers of black students. If it does not enroll black dental students, clearly it cannot produce black dentists.

Graduation Profiles

We have only fragmented data on graduation rates of black students from schools of dentistry before the 1971–1972 academic year. It is evident from historical information that, prior to the 1970s, Howard University and Meharry Medical College produced more black dentists than all other schools of dentistry combined. Between 1972 and 1984, a total of 2296 black students received the Doctor of Dental Surgery (D.D.S.) degree from U.S. schools of dentistry. During the same period, dental colleges produced a total of 64,725 dentists. Black dental college graduates represented a mere 3.5% of the total number of dentists produced in that period. This comparatively low productivity, although resulting in three times the number of black dentists in the work force, accentuates the persistent problem of underrepresentation of blacks in the dental profession.

Table 29 shows that the number of black dental school graduates almost tripled between 1972 and 1974. In that two-year period the absolute numbers rose from 55 black graduates in 1972 to 154 in 1974. The percentage change was from 1.1% of total graduated in 1972 to 3.6% in 1974. The absolute numerical increases in the number of graduates from dental schools among black students continued through 1977. However, the proportion of black students did not reach its peak of 4.1% of total number graduated until the following year, after which a slight decrease in absolute numbers began. That decline was followed by an extremely sharp drop in the number of black students graduated in 1979, as well as a return to the 1976 level in terms of proportion in the total graduating population. The pattern changed in 1980 when the 182 black students graduated from U.S. schools of dentistry represented 3.3% of the total graduating population of 5424 students. This upswing continued to the 1984 graduating class, which produced 219 blacks, 4.1% of the total number of graduates.

This pattern reflects the success and failure of retention programs in dental schools. It may also be instructive on institutional behavior and may be suggestive of the varying quality of students recruited for dental education. Relative to attrition, one would assume that, if attrition were low, well over 90% of the students who entered in 1970–71, for instance, would have graduated in 1974. But 184 black students entered dental school in 1970, and only 154 of them graduated in 1974. That is a loss of 30 students, or almost 16.3% of the first-year entrants. By contrast, total enrollment in the 1970–1971 first-year class was 4565; four years later, 4515 students graduated, resulting in a net loss of 50 students, or less than 1%. Thirty of them were black. Similarly, students who enrolled in 1975 would normally graduate in 1979. In 1975, 298 black students were enrolled in first-year classes. Only 203 received dental degrees in 1979. This was a fallout of 95 students, or 32% of those who entered. By contrast, in 1975,

5763 students enrolled at all schools of dentistry, and 5324 received degrees in 1979. In 1980, 283 black students enrolled in dental schools, but only 219 graduated in 1984. This number represented an attrition rate of 23%. The actual rate may be greater, since repeaters are included in first-year enrollments.

Table 29
Total Dentistry Degrees Conferred, All Institutions Combined, 1968-1984

Year	Total Degrees Conferred	Total Number of Blacks Receiving Degrees	Percentage Black
1969	3457	—	—
1970	3433	—	—
1971	3749	—	—
1972	3775	55	1.4
1973	3961	74	1.8
1974	4230	154	3.6
1975	4515	187	3.4
1976	4969	213	3.8
1977	5336	209	4.0
1978	5177	203	4.1
1979	5324	159	3.8
1980	5424	182	3.3
1981	5550	214	3.9
1982	5371	227	4.3
1983	5756	200	3.5
1984	5337	219	4.1
Total	75,364	2296	—
Total: 1972–1984	64,725	2296	3.5

These findings are also highly suspicious because of the failure to control for institutions with flexible or self-paced curricula. It is not known precisely how many of these students have in fact delayed graduation by a year by taking a reduced load. If these data were known, graduation rates by year might reflect substantial changes in the overall retention or attrition rates. Irrespective of these considerations, there is an apparent problem of retention of black students, one that is of primary importance in the nature of the outcome four years following entry into dental schools.

The first year for which systematic, state-by-state data are available on the race of dental school graduates is 1974. These are the students who entered dental colleges in 1970. In 1974, the 11 schools of dentistry in the 10 first-tier "*Adams* states" conferred a total of 17 degrees on black students, or 12% of all dental degrees received by black students throughout the nation. Almost half of these degrees were conferred by one institution, the University of Maryland, which has consistently led first-tier "*Adams* states" in the number of black dental graduates. Only the University of Georgia approached the University of Maryland in total number of black students graduated between 1974 and 1979 (see Table 29). Between 1980 and 1984, only Temple University among all institutions located in the first tier "*Adams* states" graduated more than one black dental student each year.

The 1984 graduation profile from these institutions attests to the magnitude of the problem of recruitment, enrollment, retention, and graduation of blacks from schools of dentistry in these states. For instance, no blacks received the D.D.S. from Emory University, University of Mississippi, and Oral Roberts University. Only the Medical College of Georgia (6), University of North Carolina (5), and University of Pittsburgh (5) graduated 5 or more blacks with the D.D.S. degree. The remainder of the first-tier "*Adams* states" graduated from 1 to 3 black students (see Table 30).

Second-tier "*Adams* states" have not enjoyed noteworthy success in the recruitment, enrollment, retention, and graduation of black students from dental schools. As shown in Table 31, not a single black student received a D.D.S. degree in 1984 from 4 of the 13 institutions (University of Kentucky, University of Missouri, Kansas City, Baylor College of Medicine, and West Virginia University). No more than three blacks were included in the graduating class of the remainder of the institutions.

A disproportionate number of black dental graduates continues to come from the two historically black dental schools. In 1974 the Dental College at Howard University and Meharry Medical College accounted for slightly more than 50% of all black students who received degrees in dentistry. Their proportions declined slightly to about 50% in 1975, then to slightly more than 49% in 1978 and to 43% in 1977, but climbed to 55% in 1984. These changes suggest that while an increasingly large number of historically white institutions are retaining greater numbers of black students through the year of graduation, the paucity in enrollment and graduation is still troublesome. Only one institution in the United States, the University of Nebraska, failed to enroll a single black student throughout the 1970s. No historically white institutions are even approaching the level of responsibility assumed by Howard and Meharry. Once again, an explanation for their failure to attract and graduate sufficient numbers of black students can be found in institutional behavior as much as in undesirable societal conditions.

Although the University of Nebraska neither enrolled nor graduated a black student, partially because "they did not meet resident requirements,

Creighton University, the private institution in that state, managed to graduate a dozen black dentists between 1974 and 1978. The University of Colorado graduated no black students between 1974 and 1978. Only one black student received dental degrees during that period from Northwestern University and West Virginia University. Table 32 shows an incredibly high number of institutions that graduated fewer than 5 and less than 10 black students during that period.

The most successful historically white institutions outside the "*Adams* states" during this period were the University of Michigan and the University of Southern California. Some institutions, such as New Jersey Dental School, rank relatively high in enrollment but have not been as successful in retaining black students.

The Sex Variable

Dentistry is primarily a male preserve. However, the number of women enrolled in schools of dentistry and graduating from them has increased significantly in the recent past. In 1974, for instance, there were 66 black women enrolled in dental schools. Their absolute numbers and their proportions of all black enrollees increased significantly each year thereafter. By 1978, the 117 black women matriculated in dental schools almost doubled their 1974 enrollment. In 1974, they represented 7.0% of black enrollees. In 1978, they constituted 12.8% of black enrollment in U.S. dental schools. These increases are observed throughout the nation, in "*Adams* states" and elsewhere. In 1984, women constituted about one-third of total black student enrollment in dentistry.

Similarly, black women make up an increasingly larger proportion of graduates. In 1974, there were only a dozen black women who received dental degrees. By 1979, there were 61 black women dental graduates. This number was five times larger than the number who were dental degree recipients in 1974. Although the numbers are extremely small in the "*Adams* states," the data on black women graduates in dentistry show the combined total increasing from 2 graduates in 1974 to 10 graduates in 1979. In all these states as a group, a special effort has to be mounted to improve the ratio of black women graduating from dental colleges. However, only slight improvements in the graduation rates for women were actually registered between 1974 and 1984 (see Tables 30, 31, and 32).

With considerably more aggressive recruitment, appropriate modifications in selection and admissions practices, alterations in institutional behavior in general, the hiring of more black faculty, and substantial increases in direct scholarships to students, dental schools can improve on their success rates in assuring greater equality of educational opportunity.

Table 30
Black Dental School Graduates from Institutions in the First-Tier "Adams States," by School and Sex, 1974–1984

Dental School	1974		1975		1976		1977		1978		1979		1980		1981		1982		1983		1984	
	M	F	M	F	M	F	M	F	M	F	M	F	M	F	M	F	M	F	M	F	M	F
U. of Florida	0	0	0	0	0	0	1	0	0	0	2	0	0	0	2	0	2	1	1	1	1	1
Emory U.	1	0	0	0	0	0	0	0	0	0	1	0	0	0	0	1	1	0	1	0	0	2
Medical College of Georgia	2	1	5	1	5	2	5	1	5	1	0	0	1	2	1	0	1	0	1	0	4	2
U. of Maryland	9	0	6	0	9	0	5	2	5	2	1	3	1	1	1	1	1	1	0	0	3	0
U. of Mississippi	—		0	0	0	0	0	0	0	0	0	0	1	1	0	0	1	3	0	0	0	0
U. of North Carolina	0	0	1	0	1	0	2	0	2	1	4	1	2	1	1	1	0	0	0	0	5	1
U. of Oklahoma	0	0	0	0	1	0	1	0	1	0	1	0	0	0	0	0	0	0	0	0	0	1
Oral Roberts U.	—		—		—		—		0	0	0	0	1	1	1	1	1	2	2	0	0	0
Temple U.	0	0	0	0	0	0	3	0	1	1	2	0	1	1	0	1	2	2	1	0	2	1
U. of Pennsylvania	0	0	5	0	5	0	2	0	0	1	3	1	5	1	1	2	3	2	2	0	2	1
U. of Pittsburgh	3	1	3	0	2	0	1	1	2	2	2	5	1	2	1	0	0	1	1	0	5	0
Virginia Commonwealth U.	0	0	2	0	2	0	1	1	1	0	2	0	2	0	2	0	0	1	1	0	0	0
Total by Sex	15	2	22	1	27	2	21	5	15	9	17	10	19	14	15	9	19	12	14	8	22	8
Total Black	17		23		29		26		24		27		33		24		31		22		30	

Source: American Dental Association, *Minority Reports.*

Table 31
Number of Black Graduates from Dental Schools in Second-Tier "*Adams* States," by School, and Sex, 1980–1984

Dental School	Fall 1980 M	Fall 1980 F	Fall 1981 M	Fall 1981 F	Fall 1982 M	Fall 1982 F	Fall 1983 M	Fall 1983 F	Fall 1984 M	Fall 1984 F
U. of Alabama	0	2	4	2	4	1	0	3	1	2
U. of Kentucky	1	2	1	2	1	1	3	1	0	0
Louisville U.	0	0	0	1	1	0	0	0	1	0
Louisiana State U.	1	2	4	0	4	1	7	2	2	0
U. of Missouri/K.C.	3	0	6	0	0	2	2	1	0	0
Washington U.	0	1	0	1	3	0	1	0	2	0
Ohio State U.	1	0	3	3	1	0	5	2	1	2
Case Western Reserve	2	0	0	2	1	1	1	3	3	0
Medical College of S.C.	0	0	2	0	2	0	0	1	1	1
Baylor Col. of Dentistry	1	0	1	0	0	0	0	1	0	0
U. of Texas/Houston	2	1	3	4	4	3	0	1	2	1
U. of Texas/S.A.	0	0	0	0	1	0	1	0	1	0
West Virginia U.	0	0	1	0	0	0	0	0	0	0
Total by Sex	11	8	25	15	22	9	20	15	14	6
Total Black	19		40		31		35		20	

Table 32
Total Black Dental School Graduates in "Non-*Adams* States"
by School, Sex, and Year, 1974–1984

Dental School	1974 M	1974 F	1975 M	1975 F	1976 M	1976 F	1977 M	1977 F	1978 M	1978 F
U. Pacific	3	0	2	0	0	0	1	0	0	0
U. California/S.F.	6	0	5	0	5	0	3	3	6	0
UCLA	3	1	7	1	4	1	2	0	6	0
USC	0	0	2	0	6	1	7	0	5	1
Loma Linda U.	1	0	1	0	0	1	2	1	3	0
U. of Colorado	—	—	0	0	0	0	0	0	0	0
U. of Connecticut	—	—	0	0	1	0	0	1	0	0
Georgetown U.	—	—	0	0	1	0	1	1	1	0
Howard U.*	42	6	53	8	62	18	49	15	47	13
Loyola U. (Ill.)	—	—	0	0	2	0	0	0	1	0
Northwestern U.	1	0	0	0	0	0	0	0	0	0
U. of Southern Illinois	—	—	0	0	1	0	0	0	0	0
U. of Illinois	7	0	2	1	3	0	3	0	2	1
Indiana U.	2	0	2	0	0	1	1	1	2	0
U. of Iowa	0	0	3	0	2	1	1	0	2	0
Harvard U.	3	1	2	1	1	0	3	0	2	0
Boston U.	—	—	0	0	0	0	0	0	0	0
Tufts U.	1	0	5	1	5	1	4	3	0	0
U. of Detroit	8	0	2	0	4	1	0	0	1	1
U. of Michigan	3	0	5	1	5	1	17	3	8	2
U. of Minnesota	—	—	0	0	1	2	2	0	0	0
Creighton U.	1	0	1	0	4	0	4	0	2	0
U. of Nebraska	0	0	0	0	0	0	0	0	0	0
Fairleigh Dickinson U.	0	0	0	0	1	0	2	0	6	0
New Jersey Dental Col.	0	0	5	0	2	0	2	0	3	1
Columbia U.	1	0	2	1	0	0	2	0	0	0
NYU	2	0	3	1	4	0	1	1	3	0
SUNY/S.B.	0	0	0	0	0	0	0	0	0	2
SUNY/Buffalo	3	0	1	0	2	0	2	1	1	1
U. of Oregon	0	0	1	0	0	0	1	0	0	0
Meharry Medical Col.*	24	1	26	6	23	2	23	6	20	3
U. of Tennessee	4	0	1	0	1	0	1	0	1	1
U. of Washington	1	0	0	0	0	0	0	0	2	0
Marquette U.	0	0	1	0	0	0	0	0	0	0
Total by Sex	116	9	132	21	140	30	134	36	124	26
Total	125		153		170		170		150	

Source: American Dental Association, *Minority Reports for Identified Years.*
*Historically Black Institution.

Table 32 *(Continued)*

1979 M	1979 F	1980 M	1980 F	1981 M	1981 F	1982 M	1982 F	1983 M	1983 F	1984 M	1984 F	Totals Both Sexes
0	0	0	0	0	0	0	0	1	0	0	0	7
2	5	6	4	5	5	0	2	4	0	4	2	67
2	1	4	5	6	5	5	6	4	3	5	2	73
2	0	0	2	4	0	1	0	1	0	0	0	32
2	0	1	1	2	1	1	0	4	1	2	0	23
0	0	1	1	0	0	0	0	1	0	0	0	3
0	0	1	0	0	0	0	0	0	1	0	0	4
3	2	1	0	0	0	1	4	3	2	0	1	21
32	13	35	19	33	21	44	21	37	23	41	32	664
3	1	0	0	0	0	1	3	1	0	1	1	14
0	0	0	2	0	0	1	0	0	0	0	0	4
1	0	0	0	0	0	0	0	0	0	0	1	3
6	6	2	1	1	4	2	2	2	3	3	1	52
1	0	0	1	3	2	2	0	0	0	1	0	19
0	1	1	0	0	0	1	0	2	0	0	0	14
2	1	1	0	2	3	0	2	1	0	1	0	26
1	0	0	0	0	0	0	0	1	0	0	0	2
2	1	2	1	0	1	1	1	0	0	0	0	29
1	0	1	0	1	0	2	0	0	1	0	0	23
3	2	7	6	5	8	0	4	6	4	4	2	96
0	0	2	0	1	0	0	0	2	1	1	0	12
2	1	0	1	0	0	2	1	0	0	1	1	21
0	0	0	0	0	0	0	0	0	0	0	0	0
0	0	0	0	0	0	1	0	4	2	4	1	21
3	2	1	0	4	2	5	3	2	1	2	2	40
0	0	0	1	0	0	0	0	0	0	0	0	7
1	0	2	0	1	0	0	4	0	1	1	0	25
1	0	1	1	1	1	1	0	0	0	1	0	9
1	1	1	1	1	1	1	0	0	0	0	1	19
1	0	2	0	1	1	0	1	0	0	0	0	8
16	1	14	2	22	2	30	13	15	7	30	19	305
1	1	0	0	0	1	0	0	0	1	2	1	16
2	0	0	1	1	0	1	1	0	0	0	0	9
0	0	0	0	0	0	0	0	1	0	0	0	2
91	39	86	50	94	58	103	68	92	51	104	67	1,670
130		136		152		171		143		171		1,670

Notes

1. Clifton O. Dummett and Lois D. Dummett, "Afro-Americans in Dentistry: A Synopsis," *Crisis,* November 1979, p. 398.
2. Ibid.
3. Ibid., p. 379.
4. Ibid.
5. *Admission Requirements of U.S. and Canadian Dental Schools, 1979–80* (Washington, D.C.: American Association of Dental Schools, 1979), p. 3.
6. These issues are a matter of continuing debate between advocates of standardized tests such as the Educational Testing Service and the College Board and by those who have recently challenged the validity of tests, including Ralph Nader, the National Association for the Advancement of Colored People (NAACP), and others. The position of the Educational Testing Service and the College Board is that these factors have minimal effect on the overall performance of the test-taker.
7. American Dental Association, *Trend Analysis, 1977–78* (Chicago: American Dental Association, 1978), p. 1.
8. Ibid.
9. This figure was provided by the American Dental Association. It is based on an address given by Dr. Elijah Richardson, president of the National Dental Association.
10. *Admission Requirements of U.S. and Canadian Dental Schools, 1978–79,* p. 110.
11. ADA, Council on Dental Education, *Annual Report: 1984–1985,* p. 7; and AADS, *Survey of Dental Seniors, Summary Report,* 1984.
12. AADS *Survey,* p. 7.
13. Ibid., p. 9.
14. Ibid.
15. Ibid.
16. Ibid. p. 8.

Chapter 7   MAINSTREAMING BLACK
                            AMERICANS IN OPTOMETRY

Optometric educators claim that a crisis exists in vision care for Americans.[1] This crisis stems from insufficient numbers of trained optometrists to meet the needs of the U.S. population. As Peters argued in 1979, optometric manpower needs have not been given a high priority in the health sciences.[2] Although the 15 schools and colleges of optometry were filled to capacity in 1985, the approximately 1000 optometrists annually graduated from these institutions do not meet national needs. The shortage observed in 1985 results from several additional factors. Chief among them are the fact that demands for vision care have increased; the population is aging rapidly, a fact that heightens demand for better vision care; and there is increased public awareness of the importance of good vision in order to meet the basic needs of a modern, technological society.[3] In addition, many Americans have become more sophisticated about disease prevention in all aspects of health care. Throughout the nation, large numbers of "third-party vision-care programs" have developed.[4] All these factors have raised the demand for optometric care beyond the present capacity of optometrists to respond effectively.

In 1985 there were approximately 23,000 optometrists in the United States. Of that number, approximately 250, or slightly more than 1%, were black Americans. Another 40 or 50 optometrists could be found among the Hispanic and Native American populations. Racial disparities in the manpower crisis can be gleaned immediately from a glance at the ratio between numbers of white optometrists to the size of the white population and numbers of black optometrists to the size of the black population. It is estimated that, among whites in the United States, this ratio is 1 for every 8250 white patients. Among blacks, however, this ratio is 1 black optometrist for every 125,000 blacks in the United States. As established by the American Optometric Association, the optimal ratio is 1 optometrist for every 7500 persons in the population.[5] Clearly, the problem of underrepresentation is considerably more acute among blacks than among whites. It will continue to be so unless there is a dramatic increase in the production of black optometrists.

This chapter describes trends in enrollment of black students in schools and colleges of optometry between 1970 and 1985. It provides substantial

153

support for the hypothesis that the presence of black role models and visible institutional commitment to equal opportunity are directly correlated with growth in access of black students to graduate and professional schools. It points to success models for the recruitment and enrollment of black students in optometry, and to some of the myriad problems confronted by institutions in their attempts to increase access for outsider groups.

The Historical Context

Optometry has always stood in the shadow of medicine and dentistry as a health-care profession. While these fields have enjoyed immense prestige, social status, and financial rewards associated with privilege, that has not always been the experience of optometry. Inducements for selecting optometry as a profession and as a field of scientific study have never been as powerful as have the factors that persuade individuals to enter medicine and dentistry. Further, recognition of optometry as a respectable occupation came considerably later than it did for dentistry, and the prestige granted to the medical profession can be traced back to antiquity.

Programs in optometry undoubtedly began in special colleges during the nineteenth century. In fact, the New England College of Optometry claims to operate the oldest continuous program in optometry in the United States. It traces its origins to the Massachusetts College of Optometry, founded in 1894. However, no formally recognized degree was conferred in its earlier program. The first institution to offer the Doctor of Optometry (O.D.) degree was Ohio State University in 1914. Since that time, 14 additional institutions were organized with degree-granting programs in optometry. Seven of these institutions are private and 8 are public. The 8 public colleges are either components of major universities or are physically and administratively separate state-controlled schools of optometry.

Nine of the institutions were in existence prior to 1960; four opened during the 1960s and 1970s; and two opened in the 1980s. Since there are only 15 institutions in the United States, all of them are essentially regional schools of optometry. That is to say, they have contractual arrangements with other states in their regions for the training of out-of-state residents who wish to pursue a degree in optometry. There are no schools and colleges of optometry located at a historically black medical college. That absence may help to account for the low representation of blacks in this profession.

The 23,000 optometrists in the United States represent a ratio of about 9 optometrists for every 100,000 persons in the population.[6] In 1970, according to Edwin C. Marshall, the ratio between optometrists to population was 1 for 9797 persons. However, the 109 black optometrists then practicing in the United States represented a ratio of 1 black optometrist for every 208,005 black Americans.[7] Because of this immense disparity between the total population and the optimal number of optometrists to provide effective and adequate vision care, the American Optometric Association committed itself to the goal of training a sufficient number of optometrists of all races to attain the optimal level of 1 optometrist for every 7000 Americans.[8] That goal has not been attained despite significant increases in the production of optometrists during the 1970s, and by the mid-1980s.

Recruitment and Enrollment of Black Students

As the 1960s drew to a close, it was apparent to optometric educators that the nation had a serious shortage of black optometrists. Few colleges and schools of optometry had ever given special attention to the recruitment and enrollment of black Americans. One notable exception was the Illinois College of Optometry (ICO). After World War II, capitalizing on educational opportunities provided by the GI BIll, the ICO wooed black students into this field. Consequently, a substantial number of blacks trained in optometry in the post–World War II era were graduates of the ICO. As a result, Chicago in 1985, has the largest single concentration of black optometrists in the United States. More than 30 black optometrists are currently practicing in Chicago.[9]

The National Optometric Association (NOA) was established in 1969. Immediately, the NOA exerted pressure on the predominantly white American Optometric Association (AOA) to assume active leadership and take aggressive action toward the recruitment and enrollment of black students in optometry. The AOA responded to this urgency in three essential ways. First, for the first time in its history, it appointed a black optometrist, Dr. Charles Comer, to one of its major committees. (Dr. Comer served for three years (1970–73) as a member of the AOA Career Guidance Committee.) Second, a minority recruitment officer was appointed; and third, primarily due to the diligence and enthusiastic work of Dr. Henry Hofstetter of the College of Optometry at Indiana University, the AOA allocated some $15,000 for each of two years specifically for the recruitment of minority students. The minority recruitment officer was supported primarily through an Urban Coalition grant of $35,000 to the AOA.[10] This program was jointly sponsored by the AOA and NOA.

In the early 1970s, there was an initial upsurge of interest in the recruitment and enrollment of black students. Inducements for this action came largely from the federal government through capitation money awarded to institutions on the basis of the number of minority students actually enrolled. In addition, "federal giving" to institutions in the health-care fields, including optometry, signaled the availability of federal funds to support affirmative action programs and education in the health fields in general. The institutional behavior suggested an initial commitment to rectifying past injustices and the elimination of discriminatory actions, that had resulted in the critical underrepresentation of black students in this field. In addition to a positive stance assumed by many schools and colleges of optometry, several of the state associations took an active role in the recruitment of black students. For instance, in January 1972, delegates to the AOA Manpower Conference in HEW Region V states (Ohio, Michigan, Indiana, Illinois, Wisconsin, and Minnesota) declared the recruitment of minority students to be a major priority.[11]

The delegates urged their member associations to make optimal utilization of recruitment materials developed by the AOA and NOA. They also recommended a publicity campaign in the state associations' newsletter to call attention to minority recruitment and to establish scholarships specifically for minority students as inducement for them to enter the profession of optometry.[12]

In the early 1970s, in response to NOA initiatives and AOA recommendations, several schools and colleges became far more aggressive in the recruitment of black students than at any time in their history. As early as 1970, the Division of Optometry of Indiana University developed a major recruitment program that was coordinated and administered by black students enrolled in the O.D. program at that time. This committee visited historically black colleges and other universities in Kentucky, Tennessee, North Carolina, and Georgia to inform black students of opportunities at Indiana and to interest them in the optometry program. It sponsored lectures to senior high school College Upward Bound students; participated in Career Day programs, and distributed recruitment materials it had developed. It organized visits to the campus of Indiana University during which prospective students were exposed to the type of training that an optometry degree entails.[13] Importantly, Indiana University's School of Optometry hired black faculty who were visible role models to potential students and who could provide instant evidence of the possibilities of success in this profession.

Other institutions, such as the University of California/Berkeley, University of Alabama/Birmingham, Pennsylvania College of Optometry, Southern College of Optometry, and University of Houston, mounted similarly aggressive recruitment programs to attract blacks and other minority-group students. Invariably, whatever success they experienced can be attributed to some combination of the following factors: (1) the presence of role models (e.g., black faculty in either a full-time university position or a part-time clinical position); (2) the availability and utilization of federal grant money and/or state and institutional funds to provide financial assistance to needy students; (3) the use of flexible admissions criteria; (4) the availability of academic and psychological support services; and (5) evidence that recruitment efforts moved beyond tokenism. Several institutions established an office of minority affairs. Now all 15 colleges and schools of optometry publicly acknowledge a commitment to affirmative action. However, declines in the enrollment of black students suggest a disjunction between articulated policy and actual institutional behavior. Obviously, stating a policy is not necessarily synonymous to its implementation and enforcement.

Institutional efforts in the recruitment of black students were assisted immeasurably through activities sponsored by the National Optometric Association. The NOA not only exerted pressure on institutions resistant to changing the racial composition of colleges of optometry but organized special recruitment programs of its own. For example, the NOA appointed regional directors who were responsible for maintaining direct contacts with selected colleges of optometry and for monitoring their recruitment activities. Whenever they resisted or lagged in their efforts, NOA members reminded them of their responsibilities and commitments consistent with AOA policies. The NOA used some of its members as liaison officers to students and minority affairs at specific institutions. The purpose of this activity was to prevent academic and psychological problems from occurring and to find immediate solutions to problems encountered.

The NOA designed retention programs; offered tutoring, counseling, and psychological support; and its members served as "advocates" before academic boards for students on certain occasions. Local chapters of the National Optometric Association were established on every college campus. These chapters were not only formal associations to which black students could belong but also served a variety of important social and academic functions. For example, white students often studied together and formed working groups to discuss problems encountered in class and in the clinical setting, but black students were often excluded. The black students were also frequently not invited into the cliques, social groups, and informal social activities that contribute to a sense of well-being and that may help create a positive learning milieu. Local chapters of the NOA served these functions and presumably helped reduce attrition and increase retention among black students in optometry.

In the early 1970s, student financial aid consisted of more direct aid and scholarships to students, instead of repayable loans. That pattern contributed in substantial ways to recruitment success. As these funds dried up or were curtailed and increasing reliance on repayable loans occurred, enrollment declines followed. This loss of black students is also attributable to the impression communicated that in the *Bakke* era it was no longer popular to be black. In this period, the federal government was less than enthusiastic in supporting affirmative action in higher education. Consequently, for several institutions, recruiting, enrolling, and graduating black optometrists became a matter of low priority. Declines in enrollment may also be a direct response to a decreasing value attached to being "a doctor of optometry" when some students could very well become doctors of medicine or doctors of dentistry, which offer considerably more prestige than the O.D. carries in the black community.

It is important to note, however, that some schools and colleges of optometry have magnificent recruitment programs on paper, but they fail to implement them. Some have made strong efforts to recruit a critical mass of black students into their programs, but without significant success. Their failure may be attributed in part to inadequate funds contributed from institutional sources. Institutional financial support was, and is, not sufficient to achieve recruitment and enrollment objectives. It may also be explained by the inability to attract federal support for their programs despite the high quality of the recruitment proposals submitted to federal agencies. The lack of commitment of higher-level administrators may also help to explain the failure of these programs. In some instances, too, black students simply do not wish to be what is tantamount to a "first," or a guinea pig, in an institution that has either enrolled no minorities in the past or is without a significant proportion in its total institutional population.

Admissions Criteria

The 15 schools and colleges of optometry employ a combination of cognitive and noncognitive criteria in making admissions decisions. The relative weight assigned to each of the categories by admissions personnel in optometric institutions varies markedly. Shifts in weights plus the flexibility apparent in the utilization of discretionary powers by the admissions committees in assigning differential values to one or both sets of criteria have an unquestionable impact on the enrollment of black students. In some instances, discretionary authority in favoring one set of criteria over the other may have worked to the benefit of both black and white students whom admissions committees deemed worthy of selection.

Cognitive criteria employed in admissions decisions include the scores on the Optometric College Admissions Test (OCAT), gradepoint average in college, and, in some instances, scores on Personality Profiles. Noncognitive factors weighed in admissions decisions include personal interviews, the candidate's autobiography, and letters of evaluation. Several institutional respresentatives maintain that the underrepresentation of blacks in optometry degree programs and their enrollment difficulties may be partially explained by the lack of competitiveness by black students in performance on the OCAT and by their lower college gradepoint averages. An examination of the *Annual Survey of Optometric Educational Institutions* for 1974, 1977 and 1978 shows that only one institution, the Southern College of Optometry, reported that the cognitive portion of the OCAT had no influence on admissions decisions. The number of institutions that reported a "significant" influence exerted by scores on the cognitive portion of the OCAT went from three institutions in 1975 to six institutions in both 1977 and 1978. The number of colleges of optometry that reported a "moderate" influence exerted by OCAT scores dropped from eight institutions in 1974 to five institutions in 1977 and 1978.

Similarly, a noticeable change is observed in the relative importance assigned by schools and colleges of optometry to the noncognitive portion of the OCAT in reaching admissions decisions. In 1974, 7 of the 12 schools and colleges of optometry then in existence reported that the noncognitive portion of the OCAT had no influence on admissions decisions. No significant change in that number was observed for the later years. Between 1974 and 1977, the number of institutions that assigned a "slight" degree of importance to noncognitive performance on the OCAT was reduced by 50%, or from 4 institutions to 2. By comparison, in 1974, one institution, Pacific University, stated that noncognitive aspects were "significant." That institution remained the only one that continued to rate that portion as significant in 1978.

Regardless of the weights attached to OCAT scores, it appears that institutions do utilize their prerogatives and discretionary powers in making decisions regarding the relative importance of this test. Hence, one may justifiably speculate that OCAT scores may be employed as an instrument of exclusion in much the same manner as they can be utilized to include those persons an institution desires or deems otherwise worthy of admission. However, there is an apparent trend in heavier weighting of the OCAT in the 1980s than was the case in the early 1970s.

In Edwin Marshall's 1972 study, 4 of the 11 responding institutions indicated that they made special concessions to minority students.[14] In this study, some institutions reported that they had lowered OCAT minimum requirements for minority or disadvantaged students. However, "relaxing standards," as some referred to this process, resulted in retention problems for these students in later years. It also appears that institutions that claim to be unyielding in their demand that universalistic criteria be applied equally to all students and that are without black faculty and major recruitment programs are unsuccessful in terms of black students. They enroll few black students, and graduate even fewer, than those institutions that are willing to seek black students aggressively and make reasonable adjustments in formal admissions criteria.

As shown in Table 33, mean scores on the Optometric College Aptitude Test (OCAT) vary dramatically among the 15 institutions. The biology mean scores range from a high of 84 at the University of California/Berkeley to a low of 27.5 at Northeastern State University. The Southern College of Optometry did not begin to utilize OCAT scores in making admissions decisions until selection began for the Fall 1986 class. Chemistry scores range from a high of 79 at SUNY to a low of 25 at Northeastern State University. However, the highest mean scores in physics, verbal ability, quantitative ability, and study reading are recorded at the University of California/Berkeley. The lowest mean scores on these measures are registered at Northeastern State University. Given the magnitude of difference in mean scores among the 15 institutions, it is evident that schools and colleges of optometry are compelled to rely on factors other than the OCAT scores in determining who will be admitted.

The gradepoint average (GPA) is often cited as a major determinant in the selection process, and it is sometimes regarded as an impediment to the successful enrollment of black students. Implicit in this argument is that a significant proportion of black students do not qualify for admissions because of poor academic performance in college. A review of *The Annual Survey of Schools and Colleges of Optometry* reveals that the mean GPA for enrolled students in all schools and colleges of optometry was 2.67 (C +) in 1970–1971. In that year, specific institutional means ranged from a low of 2.46 for all entering students at the Illinois College of Optometry to a high of 2.96 at Ohio State University.[15] By 1984, the mean GPA for all 15 institutions combined was 3.18. The mean institutional GPAs ranged from a high of 3.40 at Ferris State College to a low of 2.89 at Southern College of Optometry. In general, institutional mean scores were in the range of a *B* grade; however, it is evident in table 33 that all reporting institutions did admit some students who had achieved a low-*C* average. It is difficult to accept notions of low grades as an impediment of major importance when assessing explanations for the low representation of blacks in these institutions when one reviews the range of GPAs among entering students.

All but two institutions, UC/Berkeley and Southern California of Optometry, interview applicants for admission to the schools or colleges of optometry. The interview and the student autobiography are essential elements in assessment, since they enable selection officers to make some determination of the strengths and weaknesses of the applicant's noncognitive qualifications. The interview may also be utilized to test the applicant's overall ability to relate to other persons, and to ascertain the presence of desirable personality qualities deemed to be salient for successful optometrists.[16]

Since there were only three full-time black faculty members and three black staff members in the 15 schools and colleges of optometry in 1984, it is difficult to assure representation from the black academic community on admissions committees. In those institutions in which blacks are on the

Table 33
Profile of 1984 Entering Class in Colleges of Optometry by Institution, Gradepoint Average, and Mean OCAT Scores

| Institution | Gradepoint Average[a] | | | OCAT Mean Scores | | | | | |
	High	Low	Mean	Bio	Chem	Phy	V.A.	Q.A.	S.R.
University of Ala./B'ham.	3.78	2.20	3.15	56	56	49	48	48	53
UC/Berkeley	3.78	2.14	3.16	84	78	79	75	67	76
Ferris State College	3.90	2.50	3.40	32	50	46	41	58	38
University of Houston	3.97	2.32	3.28	58	50	49	47	48	59
Ill. College of Optometry	4.00	2.41	3.03	39	37	34	36	39	37
Indiana University	N/A	N/A	3.22	50	51	44	43	54	N/A
University of MO/St. Louis	3.95	2.34	3.09	53	56	51	44	43	44
New England College of Optometry	4.00	2.25	3.07	51	45	40	53	44	51
Northeastern State University	4.00	2.82	3.30	27.5	25	30	35	25	35
Ohio State University	3.95	2.74	3.31	48	58	58	48	51	52
Pacific University	3.96	2.29	3.12	49	46	46	45	42	47
Penn. College of Optometry	3.96	2.50	3.08	50	43	40	44	38	46
So. Calif. College of Optometry	4.00	2.75	3.28	64	61	57	52	52	55
Southern College of Optometry	3.93	2.09	2.89	OCAT scores not used until fall 1985					
SUNY	3.98	2.40	3.29	68	79	65	58	58	56

[a]Computed on a 4.0 scale.
OCAT Mean Score Legend: Bio = Biology, Chem = Chemistry, Phy = Physics,
V.A. = Verbal Ability, Q.A. = Quantitative Ability,
S.R. = Study Reading.

Source: *Admissions to Schools and Colleges of Optometry, Fall 1986.* Washington, D.C.: American Optometric Association (Undated).

faculty or staff, blacks do serve on these committees from time to time. Several institutions without black faculty say that they make a sincere and "good faith effort" to recruit black faculty but that they are unsuccessful. They rationalize their failure by assuming that black optometrists are not interested in faculty positions, since the financial rewards of private practice are substantially higher than the actual incomes received by professors, especially those who do not have a simultaneous opportunity to engage in private practice. In some instances, black optometrists in private practice are recruited for an institution's clinical program. Several of these persons occasionally serve on the institution's recruitment and admissions committee. Nevertheless, both the recruitment and admission of black students, important processes in the mainstreaming of outsiders are impaired by the underrepresentation of black faculty members in optometric education programs.

Enrollment Trends

On one level of analysis, an examination of Table 34 leads to the incontrovertible conclusion that significant progress was made during the 1970s in the recruitment and enrollment of black students in schools and colleges of optometry. Significant losses were observed in the late 1970s and early 1980s, however, but upturns in black student enrollment occured in 1983 and in 1984. In 1984, the 98 blacks enrolled constituted the largest number of blacks ever enrolled in optometry. That conclusion is supported by positive trends in absolute numbers of black students enrolled in O.D. degree programs. In 1970, for instance, a total of 15 black students enrolled in all the schools and colleges of optometry. Enrollment of black students increased significantly thereafter. This change was consonant with the recruitment programs mounted by the AOA and NOA. As a result, by 1972, total black student enrollment more than doubled to 38. The success of recruitment is apparant for each succeeding year following 1976–77 when a total of 85 black students were enrolled in optometry degree programs. However, the sharp increases in enrollment during the first half of the 1970s are currently being offset by disturbing enrollment declines since 1976. Total black student enrollment in optometry in 1980 was 22% less than it was in 1976.

On another level, Table 34 shows that at no time during the 1970s and early 1980s did black student enrollment reach 100 students. It is striking that every increase in total black student enrollment is matched by a significant increase in total student enrollment. This suggests that colleges of optometry have not been able to attract black students beyond token numbers. The enrollment data further suggest support for the hypothesis of a positive relationship between the presence of black faculty members and an aggressive recruitment program spearheaded by a minority affairs officer *and* the actual enrollment of black students in professional schools. Nevertheless, colleges of optometry, as a group, expanded both first-year and total enrollment capacities during the period. Further, at no time has total black student enrollment reached a proportion of 3% of total enrollment. In fact, the proportion of total black student enrollment ranged from an abysmally low of .5% in 1970–71 to 2.2% in 1976–77 and 2.1% in 1984–85. Nevertheless, the statistical claim can be made that the proportion of black students enrolled in schools and colleges of optometry increased approximately six-fold during the 1970s. Such assertions border on the ludicrous when one examines both the original numerical base and the absolute numbers represented by such claims. There is no concrete evidence whatsoever to support any argument that black students were enrolled at the expense of white students. The sparsity of their members alone defies that contention. Further, optometry colleges actually enroll from 75 to 84% of all students admitted. There are no reasons to speculate significant departures from this trend in the case of black admittees.

Another observation is that black student enrollment in the 15 institutions varied markedly not only across institutions but over time. For instance, between 1970–71 and 1983–84, the total black student enrollment in optometry at Pacific University never exceeded 2 persons during any one year. By contrast, total black student enrollment was as high as 22 at Indiana University in 1976–77 and as high as 19 at the Pennsylvania College of Optometry in 1983–84. Enrollment in the "*Adams* states" of Alabama and Texas fluctuated markedly during that period. The peak year for enrollment of black students at the University of Alabama/Birmingham was 1977, when 11 blacks were enrolled. Since the dramatic downturn registered in total black student enrollment at that institution in 1979–80, the decline has continued so that the institution's black student enrollment in 1983–84 is precisely the same as it was in 1972, when a total of one black student was studying optometry at that institution. Throughout the period, there was no significant growth in the number of black students enrolled at the University of Houston's college of optometry. Only 3 blacks were optometry matriculants in 1983–84 at that institution (see Table 34).

In 1984, no blacks were enrolled in optometry at Pacific University or Northeastern State University. Essentially token numbers were matriculated at Ferris State College, Ohio State University (located in another "*Adams* state"), and the University of Houston.

These enrollment trends underscore the primacy and importance of role models for successful recruitment and enrollment of black and other minority students in professional schools. A major portion of the success experienced by such institutions as Indiana University, throughout the 1970s and 1980s, and the University of Alabama/Birmingham, at certain points in the 1970s, can be attributed to the presence of black faculty who were aggressive in the recruitment and enrollment process. Although the utilization of black faculty in part-time clinical or adjunct appointments may also facilitate matriculation, that practice, especially when done sporadically, does not seem to have the same quality or as enduring an impact on the recruitment and enrollment process as does the employment of full-time black faculty in tenure-track positions who are available to students throughout the O.D. program. If students are recruited by black faculty, there is good reason to believe that their retention through graduation is also positively affected by their interaction with those black faculty members at critical points in their training. However, sincere, interested nonblack faculty who exact high standards and who evaluate students fairly also play an important role in the retention of black students.

Many of these institutions insist that they are actively seeking "qualified" black students. They insist that finding them is next to an im-

Table 34

Total Enrollment in Colleges of Optometry, by School and Race, 1970–1984

(T = total enrollment   B = black student total enrollment)

Institution	1970–71		1971–72		1972–73		1973–74		1974–75		1975–76		1976–77		1977–78	
	T	B	T	B	T	B	T	B	T	B	T	B	T	B	T	B
Univ. of Ala./B'ham.	28	0	46	1	70	1	85	3	96	4	105	8	112	11	127	11
UC/Berkeley	193	1	212	2	215	6	220	5	229	10	242	10	249	9	254	9
Ferris State College	—		—		—		—		—		—		—		—	
Univ. of Houston	238	2	243	2	250	5	265	4	257	4	258	4	290	3	334	3
Ill. Coll. of Optometry	412	3	455	4	489	4	516	8	529	11	568	7	571	9	584	8
Indiana Univ.	223	4	246	3	253	4	258	5	266	11	276	17	269	22	268	19
New England Coll. of Optometry	197	0	226	1	256	6	281	11	281	12	292	12	313	8	346	6
Ohio State Univ.	190	0	197	1	204	1	210	3	215	3	216	2	220	1	226	2
Pacific Univ.	265	0	273	0	283	0	280	1	289	1	298	1	316	2	329	1
Penn. Coll. of Optometry	429	3	452	4	489	3	513	5	529	6	551	10	530	8	550	8
So. Calif. Coll. of Optometry and LACO	245	1	247	1	260	3	280	0	305	1	344	3	391	3	398	2
So. Coll of Optometry	406	1	479	2	514	4	566	4	559	6	568	5	573	5	580	5
SUNY	0	0	21	0	45	1	65	3	83	4	105	4	149	4	185	5
Univ. of Mo./St. Louis	—		—		—		—		—		—		—		—	
Northeastern State Univ.	—		—		—		—		—		—		—		—	
Total	2826	15	3097	21	3328	38	3539	52	3638	73	3823	83	3983	85	4181	79
% Black	.5		.7		1.1		1.4		1.9		2.1		2.2		1.89	

Source: Association of Schools and Colleges of Optometry, Annual Survey of Optometric Educational Institutions.

Table 34 (*Continued*)

Total Enrollment in Colleges of Optometry, by School and Race, 1970–1984

(T = total enrollment   B = black student total enrollment)

Institution	1978–79 T	1978–79 B	1979–80 T	1979–80 B	1980–81 T	1980–81 B	1981–82 T	1981–82 B	1982–83 T	1982–83 B	1983–84 T	1983–84 B	1984–85 T	1984–85 B
Univ. of Ala./B'ham.	146	10	151	7	161	6	156	6	154	4	156	6	158	4
UC/Berkeley	261	7	266	7	268	8	277	5	267	8	269	10	266	7
Ferris State College	99	1	110	1	409	3	397	3	389	2	378	1	121	2
Univ. of Houston	374	4	405	4	334	4	335	1	334	5	339	3	376	5
Ill. Coll. of Optometry	587	5	596	4	598	3	603	4	537	2	531	6	531	11
Indiana Univ.	258	15	262	10	266	8	272	8	269	11	259	11	257	10
New England Coll. of Optometry	344	4	362	2	359	2	362	3	346	5	354	4	353	4
Ohio State Univ.	229	2	233	2	233	2	236	1	238	2	236	2	236	4
Pacific Univ.	328	1	327	0	119	1	125	1	119	0	119	0	336	0
Penn. Coll. of Optometry	572	5	586	8	586	10	583	8	579	15	584	19	577	25
So. Calif. Coll. of Optometry and LACO	387	2	371	4	367	1	369	5	375	6	382	4	379	4
So. Coll of Optometry	588	4	582	5	582	6	564	6	525	7	478	11	418	8
SUNY	218	2	249	1	258	3	262	3	252	7	239	7	237	9
Univ. of Mo./St. Louis	—		—		—		—		89	2	121	4	120	3
Northeastern State Univ.	—		—		—		—		88	0	94	0	96	0
Total	4391	62	4500	45	4540	57	4541	54	4561	76	4539	88	4461	98
% Black	1.4		1.2		1.2		1.2		1.6		1.9		2.1	

Source: Association of Schools and Colleges of Optometry, Annual Survey of Optometric Educational Institutions.

possibility. It is also argued that most of the black students who are qualified for optometry either are not particularly interested in the profession or use it as a safety valve while they await acceptance into a medical or dental college. The argument posed relative to the lack of "qualified" black applicants raises a number of questions about the meaning of "qualification." Most of these questions were addressed in the section on admissions; however, one unanswered but essential question remains: To what degree are some institutions using the OCAT scores selectively as a means of excluding black students, compared to their assignment of low priority to these scores for students they desire to admit?

Male–Female Ratios

Another significant pattern observed in the total enrollment of black students in optometry is a shift in male–female ratios. The number of black females enrolled in O.D. degree programs, compared to black males, showed striking increases in every year of the decade. In 1970, for example, black males make up almost 87% of black student enrollment, and black females accounted for only about 13%. By 1976, black males represented approximately 52% per cent of all black students in optometry, and black females had climbed to 48%.[17] However, from 1977 to 1981, black female enrollment not only equaled but surpassed black male enrollment so that in 1980 black females represented slightly more than 54% of total black student enrollment. By 1982, however, the situation was reversed; black males once again constituted a majority of black enrollees (see Table 35). Explanations for this trend are ambiguous at best. It may be a function of the degree to which the more qualified black males are drawn to medicine, dentistry, and engineering or the degree to which black females count as a double minority in affirmative action considerations. It may mean that some black females are able to secure sustained parental contributions, compared to black males, or that more black females are better prepared academically for the O.D. degree program than are black male applicants. It could be a manifestation of an actual change in career focus among black females in contrast to black males in comparable age cohorts.

Retention

Retention of black students is facilitated by the maintenance of a variety of academic and nonacademic support services made available to black and other minority students. Mention was made earlier of the retention activities sponsored by the National Optometric Association. Several institu-

Table 35
Total Enrollment of Black Students in Schools and Colleges of Optometry, by Sex and Institution, 1979 through 1984

Institution	1979–80		1980–81		1981–82		1982–83		1983–84		1984–85	
	M	F	M	F	M	F	M	F	M	F	M	F
Ferris State College	1	0	2	1	3	1	2	0	1	0	1	1
Ill. College of Optometry	0	4	0	3	1	3	1	1	4	2	6	5
Indiana University	0	10	3	5	4	4	5	6	5	6	2	8
New England College	2	0	2	0	2	1	4	1	3	1	3	1
Northeastern State College	–	–	–	–	–	–	0	0	0	0	0	0
Penn College of Optometry	1	7	3	7	2	6	5	10	9	10	9	16
Pacific University	0	0	1	0	1	0	0	0	0	0	0	0
So. Calif. College	4	0	3	1	4	1	3	3	1	3	1	3
Southern College	5	0	4	2	4	2	2	5	5	6	4	4
SUNY	1	0	3	0	2	1	4	3	2	5	3	6
Ohio State University	0	2	0	2	0	1	2	0	2	0	2	2
Univ. of Ala./B'ham	3	4	3	3	3	3	2	2	4	2	3	1
UC/Berkeley	2	5	1	4	1	4	3	5	6	4	5	2
Univ. of Houston	3	1	3	1	2	1	4	1	2	1	4	1
Univ. of Missouri/S.L.	–	–	–	–	–	–	1	1	2	2	1	2
Total	22	33	28	29	29	28	38	38	46	42	44	52
Total Black	55		57		57		76		88		98	
% Black	1.2		1.2		1.2		1.6		1.9		2.1	

Source: Association of Schools and Colleges of Optometry.

tions offer tutorial programs, counseling services, and advising through the minority affairs office. Some institutions frequently provide special assistance in the most difficult first– year courses, such as geometric optics and human anatomy, since the highest attrition rates occur during the first year. However, this service is apparently more often provided by interested professors, who are frequently overloaded with other responsibilities.

Hence, there is an urgent need for an organized tutorial program to assist all students with weak academic preparation in most schools and colleges of optometry. An organized program includes not only adequately paid tutorial staff in sufficient numbers but also strong counseling services, a reasonable supply of audiovisual materials that may heighten retention of substantive material in subject matter, the presence of role models with whom students may feel more at ease, and sufficient financial aid to reduce attrition and accelerate the graduation rate of black students from schools and colleges of optometry.

Black Graduates In Optometry

It is especially difficult to obtain data on the precise number of Doctor of Optometry degrees awarded blacks. One reason for this problem lies in the methods of reporting graduation data to the Association of Schools and Colleges of Optometry. The graduation data are not disaggregated by race.[18] Nevertheless, it is estimated that the 15 institutions produce about 26 black doctorates of optometry each year. This number represents a mere 2.6% of the approximately 1000 persons annually graduated from schools and colleges of optometry in the United States. The black students are primarily the products of Indiana University, Pennsylvania College of Optometry, Illinois College of Optometry, and New England College of Optometry. The estimated attrition rate among black students is 20%. Therefore, retention through graduation remains a major problem that deserves special attention, particularly in institutions without solid, comprehensive retention programs. All available evidence suggests that successful graduation is not only a function of the academic strengths that a student brings into the first-year class but also of the overall quality of retention programs and the learning environment of the institution.

Major Problems

Institutions do not claim to have been affected by the 1978 *Bakke* decision because they insist that they never employed admissions quotas or set-asides of any sort for black and other minority students. Indeed, a majority of the institutions seem to have struggled even to enroll two or three black students during any year between 1970 and 1985. However, the lack of a critical mass might be interpreted as a negative quota, which impedes the enrollment of a sizable number of black students. In other words, if the institution has no visible evidence of history of sustained black student enrollment in significant numbers, a negative message might be communicated about the institutional commitment to equal educational opportunity; hence, black students may not be attracted to the school.

Institutions cite as major problems confronting them in their efforts to recruit and enroll black students successfully such factors as lack of minimal qualifications of black applicants; the need for better and more competitive academic preparation among black applicants; well-organized and better-supported recruitment programs with a clear institutional commitment to recruit more minority students; more scholarship money; and the hiring of black and other minority faculty members to serve as role models.

Without question, some black students experience difficulties. A considerable portion of their adjustment problems emanates from attitudes formed during childhood socialization, previous experiences with white power structure, and previous encounters with racist faculty. As a result, many black students, like many white students from the white working-class population, enter a college or professional school without sufficient knowledge of how to work within the educational bureaucracy and often become intimidated by it. Many have never learned to appreciate the value of knowing, or being known by, their professors; or the importance of seeking out assistance before it is too late; or how to be more communicative and self-assertive; or how to rise above the notion that it is a sign of weakness to seek information from others. Because of previous experiences, some black students are suspicious of staff members who offer assistance and then never follow up on appointments. Some black students do not join study groups even when they are open to them. Some are victimized by racism, real or perceived, among their peers and among members of the faculty and university administration.

Such problems notwithstanding, the major problem is finance. With the continuing loss of federal support for higher education, coupled with the escalating costs of higher education in general, the impact of the conditions on black student enrollment is particularly grave in the mid-1980s. Further, the incentive for many institutions to extend themselves to recruit and enroll significant numbers of black students has eroded immeasurably with the loss of capitation grants, which were phased out over a three-year period between 1976 and 1979. Only three or four schools of optometry still have HCOP funds; federal refunding of this program has been tied to demonstrated success in obtaining loan repayments. Low-cost loans are not as available as they were during the early and mid-1970s, and many students are reluctant to subject themselves to a program that will inevitably result in a substantial indebtedness by the time their optometric education is completed. Health Professional Student Loans have also continued to decline. As of 1985, money in this category was generated almost exclusively from revolving funds created by repaid loans from previous borrowers.[18] For students of all races, a plea should be made former students to repay their loans. It is very unfair not to do so.

In the meantime, the cost of optometric education has continued to climb. Between 1977 and 1982, for example, overall educational expenses at public colleges of optometric increased by an average of 70% for resident students and 62% for nonresidents. In the same period, at private schools of optometry, the percentage increases were 73 and 67 for residents and nonresidents, respectively.[19] Annual tution for resident students ranges from a low of zero at the University of California/Berkeley and at Northeastern State University to a high of $9994 at the New England College of Optometry. Tution for nonresident students is lowest at the University of Houston ($1520) and highest at the University of Missouri ($11,163). Similarly, required fees vary markedly among the 15 institutions. No such fees are paid by resident students at Missouri, Ohio State University, and the Southern College of Optometry. Fees are nominal for resident students at the majority of the remaining 12 colleges of optometry. A similar range in required fees is observed with respect to fees charged to nonresident students (see Table 36). As a result, in 1985, some 95% of all optometry graduates had loan indebtedness. Although it is not uncommon for graduates to encumber an indebtedness of $50,000 resulting from training in optometry, the average indebtedness of optometry graduates is about $25,000.[20]

But practicing optometrists compare unfavorably with other professionals in terms of annual salaries. In 1984, the mean net income of all optometrists in their first year of practice was only $27,000. They earned a net income of $55,000 only after nine years of practice.[21] By contrast, physicians reach that level much earlier in their careers. Because of the enormous costs of establishing a practice, only 60% of practicing optometrists are engaged in solo practice. The remaining 40% are distributed in associate practice (HMOs), governmental service, teaching, and research.[22]

The recruitment of blacks to teaching positions in schools and colleges of optometry is another serious problem in the 1980s. Many schools and colleges of optometry do not hire black professionals as either full-time or adjunct instructors. Consequently, black students have few role models in this profession, and white students never have the experience of working under the supervision of a black optometrist. One explanation for the inability of institutions to hire black faculty, even with relatively aggressive faculty recruitment activities, may lie in the unattractiveness of teaching to black optometrists. This situation may result from low salaries paid to university professors, compared to the salaries that can be earned in private practice; the enticements of private practice; the perceptions that black optometrists have of themselves as private practitioners with higher-status rewards than usually achieved through university teaching; and the inability to engage in intramural practice. In other instances, institutions never mount an aggressive recruitment program for the hiring of faculty members from among minority groups, or have no real interest in changing the status quo of white dominance.

Finally, all institutions need to accelerate the pace of recruitment, enrollment, and graduation of black students if, indeed, they are serious about eliminating the underrepresentation of blacks in the field of optometry. It is apparent that what has been done is insufficient to provide an adequate number of black optometrists for meeting the vision-care needs of a major segment of the American population. Consequently, the production of black optometrists in much larger numbers than ever before must become a matter of the highest priority in the second half of the 1980s and beyond.

Table 36
Tuition and Fees, Schools and Colleges of Optometry, Fall 1986

Institution	Tuition* Residents	Required** Fees Residents	Tuition* **** Nonresidents	Required** Fees Nonresidents
U. of Alabama/B'ham	$1400	$ 504	$ 5800	$ 504
UC/Berkeley	none	$1408	$ 3360	$1408
Ferris State College	$3579	$ 15	$ 7239	$ 15
U. of Houston	$ 152	$ 300	$ 1520***	$ 300
Ill. Coll. of Optometry	$8100	$ 99	$ 8100	$ 99
Indiana University	$2236	$ 94	$ 6129	$ 94
Inter American U.	$8000	$ 120	$ 8000	$ 120
U. of Missouri/S.L.	$4663	—	$11163	—
New England Coll. of Optometry	$9984	$ 50	$ 9984	$ 50
Northeastern State U.	none	$1466	$ 1966	$1466
Ohio State U.	$3468	none	$10299***	none
Pacific U.	$8260	$ 115	$ 8260	$ 115
Pennsylvania Coll. of Optometry	$7050	$ 105	N.A.	$ 105
So. Calif Coll. of Optometry	$7500	$ 75	$ 7500	$ 75
Southern Coll. of Optometry	$6615	none	$10915	none
SUNY	$5500	$ 70	$ 8300	$ 70

Source: AOA, *Admission to Schools and Colleges of Optometry, Fall 1986,* p. 16.
*Tuition and fees listed are those at time of publication and may change without notice.
**See page 44 Contract information.
***Admitted contract state students pay resident tuition and fees.
****Out of state tuition for contract students is reduced by the amount of the contract fee, but only to resident level.

Notes

1. Henry A. Peters, O.D., "Critical Optometric Manpower Issues," *Journal of Optometric Education* 4, no. 4 (spring 1979): 8.
2. Ibid., p. 9.
3. *Admissions to Schools and Colleges of Optometry, Fall 1986* (Washington, D.C.: American Optometric Association, n.d.), p. 8.
4. Ibid.
5. Ibid.; and *New England College of Optometry Information* brochure, undated.
6. Information provided by Lee Smith of the Association of Schools and Colleges of Optometry, May 1985.
7. Edwin C. Marshall, *"Social Indifference or Blatant Ignorance" Journal of the American Optometric Association* 43, no. 12 (November 1972): 1261–1266.
8. Ibid.
9. Personal communication with Dr. Edwin C. Marshall, April 1985.
10. According to Dr. Edwin C. Marshall, the $35,000 covered recruitment activities for a period of 12 to 15 months. A consolidated recruitment program was to be mounted by the constituent societies of the AOA, NOA, American Optometric Student Association, and Association of Schools and Colleges of Optometry (ASCO).
11. Ibid.
12. Ibid.
13. Ibid.
14. Marshall "Social Indifference."
15. *Annual Survey of Optometric Education Institutions* (Washington, D.C.: Associations of Schools and Colleges of Optometry). The surveys for each year from 1969 through 1978 were made available for this research by ASCO.
16. *Information for Applicants to Schools and Colleges of Optometry* (Washington, D.C.: Association of Schools and Colleges of Optometry, Fall 1979).
17. See *Annual Surveys and Ethnic Enrollment Data from Institutions of Higher Education.* (Washington, D.C.: HEW Office of Civil Rights), Table 9.
18. Association of Schools and Colleges of Optometry, *Changing Trends in the Financing of Optometric Education,* September 30, 1984, p.6.
19. Ibid.
20. Ibid., p. 19.
21. *Admissions to Schools and Colleges of Optometry,* p. 5.
22. Ibid., pp. 6–7.

Chapter   **8**   THE RECRUITMENT AND
ENROLLMENT OF BLACK
STUDENTS AT SCHOOLS OF
PHARMACY

Pharmaceutical education in the United States is deeply rooted in the historic tradition of institutional segregation, neglect, and controlled access of black students into the profession. This fact is a principal explanation for the current underrepresentation of black Americans in pharmacy. In 1985 there were approximately 3350 black pharmacists in the United States. They constituted 2.0% of the total number of 144,000 pharmacists in America.

A significant majority of black pharmacists received their training at one of four colleges or schools of pharmacy located at historically black institutions: Florida A & M University, Howard University, Texas Southern University, and Xavier University of Louisiana. Although these institutions are historically black universities, founded when blacks were excluded by law from enrolling in traditionally white institutions, their schools and colleges of pharmacy are considerably more desegregated than any of their white counterparts.

This chapter focuses primary attention on recruitment and enrollment of black students in schools and colleges of pharmacy during the 1970s and 1980s. It describes enrollment trends in both graduate and undergraduate pharmaceutical training. Factors associated with enrollment fluctuations are delineated. A case history of the College of Pharmacy of Xavier University in New Orleans demonstrates the success that is attainable in the recruitment, enrollment, and graduation of black pharmacists when institutional commitment is positive.

Recruitment

Organized efforts to recruit more black students into the field of pharmacy have been far from uniform. Recruitment activities in the 72 schools and colleges of pharmacy in the United States may be characterized in one of three ways. The first type of institution may be described as "serious and and committed" in the sense that their academic and administrative leaders

173

facilitate the development of systematized plans for the recruitment of black students, financially support them with staff and program funds, and encourage their actual implementation. These institutions are more aggressive in the overall recruitment process. They do not abandon their commitment in the face of initial failures to achieve articulated goals. They are effective in communicating a sense of integrity and seriousness of purpose to those black students they wish to attract.

The second type of institution consists of those who have "good programs on paper" but fail to operationalize them. They make public pronouncements, either in their literature or proposals to the various funding agencies, about their special concerns for blacks and other minority students underrepresented in pharmacy. However, they quickly abandon the process when their initial results are not commensurate, in their view, with the time and energies expended. As one informant stated, many of these institutions are often interested in the "superblack," but the "superblacks" are not interested in them.

The third group consists of those with "limited or no interest." They are committed to either the maintenance of the status quo or to calculated tokenism. They have no implementable plan for the recruitment of black and other minority students. Nor do they appear to be particularly concerned about changing the racial composition of their institutions. They display little concern about a moral responsibility for making pharmaceutical education more accessible to all Americans.

The enrollment results reflect these varied degrees of institutional commitment during the 1970s and 1980s.

As recruitment is conditioned by institutional behavior and structural factors prevalent in the majority community and the larger society as a whole; so it is also a function of perceptions that individuals in the minority group have about the profession itself. Pharmacy to the professional person is a complex and important component of the allied health science fields. It is substantially more complicated than simplistic perceptions the public has of the profession. Its scope is much broader than what the public believes to be the major function of the pharmacist.

The rank-and-file person in the population is unaware of the six traditional and general fields of specialization: pharmacy, pharmaceutical chemistry, pharmacology, pharmacy administration, pharmacognosy, and Hospital pharmacy. His or her perceptions are influenced by the *man* (because only in recent years have we observed an increasing number of female pharmacists) in the white jacket hidden behind a counter in the rear of the corner drugstore or in the apothecaries of shopping centers. Even then, he or she may not possess a clear understanding of what the pharmacist is doing other than filling physicians' prescriptions for drugs that are already compounded and safely stored in mysterious containers.

Community attitudes are reflected in an invidious occupational ranking system that places pharmacists at a substantially lower level in social status, prestige, and influence than is conferred on physicians and dentists. The pharmacist's position in the social hierarchy has undoubtedly played a significant role in the ability of the field to recruit students in general. Frequently, students who apply for schools of pharmacy do so as a safety valve while they await the results of applications to other professional schools, such as medicine and dentistry. Some go into pharmacy graduate programs, particularly, only after they are not accepted into medicine or dentistry. Other students take an undergraduate pharmacy degree and use it as a major path into dental or medical schools and never practice pharmacy. Some in this group practice both professions.

Ambiguous attitudes about the profession of pharmacy are also prevalent in the black community. These perceptions are strongly shaped by the nature of interaction between community members and pharmacists, their visibility in the community, and leadership roles, and by their success in wearing the mantle of "doctor." Hence, community attitudes are far from uniform. Because there are so few pharmacists in the black community, black Americans may have an even more distorted view of the profession. With such a limited number of role models, recruiters often have to do an exceptionally fine "selling job" regarding pharmacy as a desirable profession for black Americans.

The contextual situation in which blacks see physicians and dentists accentuates their characterization as high-status professionals and stimulates the desire among many black youths to emulate them as professionals. Recruiters must also be adept in convincing black students that pharmacy is not only a profession but offers avenues to other entrepreneurial opportunities.

During the 1970s, organized recruitment programs took a variety of forms. The American Association of Colleges of Pharmacy (AACP) encouraged its member institutions to become more aggressive in the recruitment of underrepresented minorities in the profession. A series of policy statements issued by this association called attention to the escalating urgency of the problem of underrepresentation of minority groups in the field and to institutional as well as organizational responsibilities to rectify past inequities.[1]

In 1971 and 1972, at least 17 pharmacy schools received special grants or funds through the Office of Health Manpower Opportunity explicitly to increase their recruitment activities for minorities into pharmacy. These institutions were the University of California School of Pharmacy, Florida A & M University, Mercer University School of Pharmacy (Georgia), Purdue University School of Pharmacy and Pharmacal Sciences (Indiana), University of Kentucky College of Pharmacy, Xavier University of Louisiana School of

Pharmacy, University of Maryland School of Pharmacy, Massachusetts College of Pharmacy, University of Michigan College of Pharmacy, University of Montana School of Pharmacy, University of New Mexico College of Pharmacy, State University of New York at Buffalo School of Pharmacy, Ohio State University College of Pharmacy, University of Oklahoma College of Pharmacy, Temple University School of Pharmacy (Pennsylvania), Medical University of South Carolina School of Pharmacy, and Texas Southern University School of Pharmacy.[2]

Of these 17 institutions, 6 were located in the "*Adams* states" of Florida, Georgia, Louisiana, Maryland, Oklahoma, and Pennsylvania. Four were located in historically black colleges; 14 were located in states with substantial black populations.

In addition to these institutions, others obtained federal funds and/or institutional financial support for prehealth careers, allied health professional training programs, and general science training. These funds aided the recruitment of blacks and other minorities into pharmacy.

The recruitment program at Temple University's School of Pharmacy illustrates component activities taken by several of the institutions that received Health Professions Special Project Grants for Pharmacy Students. This program, funded initially at $200,000, ran from 1972 to 1975. Its primary goal was the recruitment and enrollment of minority and low-income students in pharmacy schools in order to alleviate shortages in underserved areas (e.g., minority communities and rural areas). The program also provided guidance and counseling services to high school students in urban and rural areas concerning careers in pharmacy. Minority counselors were trained to work with high school, community, or junior college and four-year college advisers in disseminating information about the pharmacy program at Temple University. Numerous visits were made to high schools and colleges to inform individuals of opportunities in pharmacy programs.

During this period, some 258 teachers, administrators, and advisers were either visited or contacted through correspondence. Not only was specific contact by four counselors made with countless students but many students and 15 disadvantaged students from the Appalachian region were admitted to the School of Pharmacy as a result of this organized recruitment program.[3]

In other "*Adams* states," recruitment activities for undergraduate pharmacy programs were reported for this study from Mercer University, a private institution in Georgia; the University of Georgia; the University of Florida; and the University of Maryland. Mercer University received a Special Project Grant for 1973–1974. The school of pharmacy also operated, in cooperation with historically black Clark College in Atlanta, a special manpower program for Nigerian students.

Although the university did not provide a precise description of its recruitment program, one obtains some measure of the program's success by the following enrollment data. In 1972–73, Mercer enrolled 15 black students (9 men and 6 women) in pharmacy. In 1974–75, the enrollment consisted of a total of 11 black students (3 men and 8 women). The number remained at 11 black students in the fall of 1975, but it then included 5 men and 6 women. By 1977, there were 7 black males and 3 black females enrolled in the Mercer University School of Pharmacy. (These data refer to total enrollment figures. However, they suggest that first-year enrollments were minimal following the grant period).[4] A total of 12 black students were enrolled in 1979–80.

Between 1974 and 1978, the school of pharmacy at the University of Georgia had a minority recruitment grant funded by the Health Resources Administration. Previously, during the period of the grant, and into the present time, the recruitment program consisted of contact with the predominantly black schools in the Georgia. Under the grant, a minority recruiter was hired "to generate applications" to the school of pharmacy. However, no special academic support program was offered to black students. One black instructor taught in the school of pharmacy for a short time until she moved out of state. By October 1979, no other black faculty had either applied or been hired in the school of pharmacy.[5]

Between 1968 and 1978, the University of Georgia School of Pharmacy enrolled 1694 white students and 39 black students. Of those 39 black students, 25 were enrolled during and immediately following termination of grant. About 5 black students per year were enrolled during this 11 year period. (In 1979, the total number of black students was 12.) When the program was in full operation, two recruiters were utilized. Financial aid was also provided from state funds. Although Georgia is under litigation to become more desegregated, and even though it was increasing minority presence in pharmacy, the critical variable in the recruitment of black students in general appears to have been both the use of a black recruiter and the presence of a black faculty member, even for a relatively short time.[6]

The University of Florida operated both a special admissions and a regular admissions/recruitment program between 1968 and 1978. Recruitment activities centered on both undergraduate and graduate degree programs in pharmacy. However, based on the data provided for this study, it is not possible to describe fully the precise characteristics of the recruitment program at either the undergraduate or graduate level of pharmacy education. The University of Florida operates a "2–3" program, which involves two years of pre-pharmacy and three years of pharmacy training. In general, the university enrolled all black students who were "accepted." Between 1968 and 1973, when no form of special admissions operated and prior to the full impact of the enrollment mandates consequent to the *Adams* v. *Richardson* litigation, all black students who applied were accepted and enrolled. This number varied from three to a maximum of five in any given year.

The proportion of white applicants ultimately admitted and enrolled was about 95% during the same period. The number of white students enrolled rose from 72 in 1968–69 to an all-time high of 175 in 1972–73. Since 1973, about one-third of all whites who applied were accepted, and approximately 95% of the white acceptees were enrolled. In the same period, when some form of special admissions programs operated for black students, the number of black applicants rose from 3 applicants in 1968 to a high of 8 black applicants in 1977 and 1978. However, the number of acceptances and enrollees for black students has remained fundamentally unchanged. An average of 4 black students are enrolled the B.S. in pharmacy program each year. (The 1979–1980 total black student enrollment was 6.) No black faculty were employed in the school of pharmacy during this period.[7]

The University of Maryland operated a recruitment program under a "Recruitment, Retention and Replacement Grant" for a three-year period from 1972 to 1975. This effort was supported by approximately $80,000 and utilized two full-time staff members for all recruitment functions. The school of pharmacy also received another $30,000 to support recruitment and retention on a two-year grant from 1975 to 1977. One full-time person was employed under this grant. In 1978, the university received $125,000 for its recruitment and retention program in medicine, dentistry, and pharmacy. Six full-time staff persons were hired. At least one full-time black faculty member, who taught pharmacology, was employed throughout the study period. The University of Maryland, like a significant proportion of institutions with colleges or schools of pharmacy, responded to federal capitation programs by expanding overall capacities in the health sciences in order to obtain increased federal government financial support.[8]

Hence, in any overall discussion of enrollment, the actual increases in the total enrollment of black students in pharmacy must be viewed within the context of capitation grants designed to stimulate overall enrollment of a subtantially larger number of students in the health sciences. In the specific case of the University of Maryland, during the recruitment and retention grant periods of 1972 to 1978, the total number of applications increased from 169 in 1972 to a high of 303 applications to the school of pharmacy in 1974, and declined the next two years to an average of 278. It then rose again to 300 applications in 1977 and dropped to 266 in 1978. In 1977, 10% of the applicants were black but in 1978 only 18 of the 266 applicants, or about 7%, were black.

Total enrollment, in the meantime, rose from 77 students in 1972 to 92 students in 1978. First-year black student enrollment increased from 4 students in both 1972 and 1973 to 12 in 1976 (when total enrollment was 94 students) and reached a high of 13 blacks in the first-year class of 1977–1978. However, the 1978–1979 first-year black student enrollment declined to 11. (Total black student enrollment was 31 in 1979–1980.) An important dimension of the Maryland program is that, like the program at Temple University, it combines continuing financial support, good staffing, and the presence of at least one full-time black faculty member, which fosters greater success in the recruitment of black students.[9]

The University of Wisconsin School of Pharmacy is one example of a recruitment program in a "non-*Adams* state." This school also initiated its special recruitment activities in 1972 for the purpose of attracting more minority students into the field of pharmacy. The program was based on five principal goals. These were: to increase the actual number of minority students enrolled in its two-year pre-pharmacy program; number of minority students who complete requirements for admission to the school of pharmacy; number of "qualified" applicants for the school of pharmacy, number of minority students who successfully complete professional degree requirements and number of minority students who actually pursue pharmacy as a career.[10]

Wisconsin employed one director–counselor to administer, coordinate, and implement its program. An allocation of approximately $27,000 was made for financial support of the program in each year. To augment recruitment efforts, the staff director was assisted by campuswide recruiters from the Office of Undergraduate Orientation of the university. The program involved the development and distribution of special bulletins that described opportunities for minority students in pharmacy. An eight-week summer orientation program was initiated. Pre-pharmacy advisers visited Wisconsin high schools with a high proportion of minority students. These advisers also participated in a variety of projects developed by the campuswide recruiters. Financial support provided by the school of pharmacy enabled some of the minority pharmacy students to participate in recruitment activities. The school granted some of the funds required for the establishment of an Office of Minority Programs in the Center for Health Sciences. A coordinated program was not implemented until July 1, 1976.[11]

As a result of these activities, the School of Pharmacy of the University of Wisconsin reported that pre-pharmacy enrollment increased by 100%. The number of minority students who successfully completed admission requirements increased by 50%. The number of minority applicants rose by 25%. However, the original base was exceptionally low. This modest success is attributed to recruiting efforts at college fairs, the publicity generated from the MAPP brochures, and contact developed through the Mid-Western

Pharmacy Consortium. The number of black graduates in pharmacy continues to be noticeably small: one in 1978 and four in 1979.[12]

Nevertheless, it should be stated that the consolidated minority program at Wisconsin includes tutorial assistance, counseling and guidance, financial aid, and work–study opportunities. A possible measure of the program's success is that in 1970, prior to its recruitment activities, there was 1 black student enrolled in pharmacy. In 1979, there were 15. However, there are no black faculty in the school of pharmacy, and this absence may help to account for the limited gains made in the recruitment of black students.[13]

Significant changes in enrollment patterns with respect to the recruitment and enrollment of black students have occurred since 1979 in each of the institutions highlighted above. For example, the School of Pharmacy at Temple University had a black student enrollment in 1979, 1980, and 1981 of 14 for each year. Black student enrollment almost doubled in 1982, when it reached 26. It was virtually unchanged in 1984 at 27 black students (see Table 37).

At Mercer University in Georgia, total black student enrollment remained relatively stable at 22 students in 1981, but a decline to 16 was registered in 1982. In 1983, the enrollment of blacks in Mercer's School of Pharmacy was 18, while in 1984 it was 24 (see Table 37). By 1983, the Pharm. D. had replaced the B.S. as the first professional degree at Mercer.

Total black pharmacy school enrollment at the University of Georgia dropped significantly and dramatically between 1979 and 1982. It fell from 12 in 1979 to 5 in 1982; then it declined to 3 in 1983, but rose to 8 in 1984.

Black students who wish to study pharmacy in Florida are far more likely to attend historically black Florida A & M University than they are to matriculate at the "flagship" University of Florida. The latter institution did not have more than 7 black students in any one year between 1979 and 1982. FAMU enrolls twenty times more black students, and has done a much better job of enrolling "other race" (in this case, white) students than has been the case with the University of Florida (see Table 37).

At the University of Maryland, total black student enrollment dropped from 31 in 1979 to half of that (16) in 1982. Then it climbed to 21 in 1983 and to 25 in 1984. The University of Wisconsin recruitment program seems to have peaked at 19 in 1980. Since that time, total black student enrollment has declined dramatically to only 8 black students in 1984 (see Table 37).

Admissions Requirements

One rationalization offered for the underrepresentation of blacks in health fields such as pharmacy is their inability to meet rigorous admission

Table 37

Black Student Enrollment in First Professional Degree Programs in Pharmacy, 1979–80 to 1984–85 (T = total enrollment, B = black)

Institution	1979		1980		1981		1982		1983		1984	
	T	B	T	B	T	B	T	B	T	B	T	B
Auburn University	337	6	342	6	303	8	251	5	207	5	199	5
Samford University	244	9	191	9	169	8	153	5	170	10	197	20
Arizona, University of	163	1	162	3	151	0	157	1	164	1	183	1
Arkansas Medical Center	207	4	203	6	200	5	200	5	188	3	179	1
California, University of[a]	(329)	26	(340)	21	(329)	15	(325)	9	357[a]	—	355	—
Pacific, University of[a]	164	13	140	17	112	17	90	16	69	2	54	2
So. California University	(439)	5	(359)	4	(368)	5	(436)	7	423[a]	—	412	—
Colorado, University of	205	3	(433)	2	(436)	3	191	2	171	2	175	3
Connecticut, University of	287	2	208	1	199	1	142	1	235	1	218	4
Howard University*	97	54	279	41	59	27	96	45	105	46	143	64
Florida A & M University*	190	134	164	112	137	106	157	152	128	101	133	103
Florida, University of	368	6	360	7	348	6	341	5	330	4	319	6
Mercer University	321	12	325	25	229	22	109	16	134[a]	—	211	—
Georgia, University of	438	12	431	10	379	8	384	5	370	3	391	8
Idaho State University	220	1	173	1	136	—	98	—	87	1	90	1
Illinois, University of	540	24	537	24	538	43	504	47	476	40	323	24
Butler University	250	1	240	3	214	4	171	2	149	1	153	1
Purdue University	483	19	(462)	22	(43)	21	393	11	387	11	408	7
Drake University	237	3	227	6	213	6	186	5	149	5	145	7
Iowa, University	253	2	239	1	215	1	214	1	222	—	233	—

Table 37 (Continued)

Black Student Enrollment in First Professional Degree Programs in Pharmacy, 1979–80 to 1984–85 (T = total enrollment, B = black)

Institution	1979		1980		1981		1982		1983		1984	
	T	B	T	B	T	B	T	B	T	B	T	B
Kansas, University of	242	1	251	2	240	2	219	3	204	3	232	3
Kentucky, University of	248	4	231	2	223	4	233	2	227	1	240	2
Northeast La. University	380	15	399	17	344	15	315	13	299	22	318	23
Xavier University, La	189	118	169	117	172	126	174	126	206	116	222	140
Maryland, University of	273	31	274	20	264	15	247	16	235	21	226	25
Mass. Coll. of Pharmacy	697	15	686	7	670	10	593	14	576	11	528	57
Northeastern University	427	—	352	—	292	—	257	—	231	6	181	—
Ferris State College	448	2	427	7	394	6	363	4	325	3	336	5
Michigan, University of[a]	200	22	156	17	100	12	74	6	14[a]	—	158	—
Wayne State University	332	15	315	16	260	19	235	21	264	26	258	25
Minnesota, University of	344	1	307	2	189	2	129	2	91	—	97	1
Mississippi, University of	306	13	306	14	300	14	294	9	287	18	280	12
St. Louis Coll. of Pharmacy	431	3	435	4	392	3	385	5	376	6	410	8
University of Mo./K.C.	238	6	234	10	236	8	223	10	184	—	169	1
Montana, University of	129	—	122	—	110	—	106	—	96	10	103	—
Creighton University	182	5	171	7	182	15	181	13	181	9	189	7
Nebraska, University of	208	5	(203)	7	(127)	5	(138)	4	143	1	193	—
Rutgers University	378	5	385	3	394	9	367	7	365	—	371	10
New Mexico University	172	2	156	7	131	1	108	1	121	—	122	2
Arnold & Marie Schwartz, LIU	631	30	626	56	544	45	516	51	494	106	485	62

Table 37 (Continued)
Black Student Enrollment in First Professional Degree Programs in Pharmacy, 1979–80 to 1984–85 (T = total enrollment, B = black)

Institution	1979 T	1979 B	1980 T	1980 B	1981 T	1981 B	1982 T	1982 B	1983 T	1983 B	1984 T	1984 B
St. John's University	747	22	774	23	798	41	753	39	727	36	708	28
SUNY/Buffalo	265	5	268	4	271	5	259	5	237	—	234	3
Albany Coll. of Pharmacy	343	1	344	1	335	1	316	2	353	4	374	5
Univ. of No. Carolina	464	15	483	14	495	9	492	7	494	14	457	15
No. Dakota State Univ.	243	—	224	—	197	—	189	—	214	—	201	—
Ohio Northern University	436	4	434	3	408	3	339	2	280	3	270	4
Ohio State University	352	5	350	5	326	2	321	3	323	5	338	8
Cincinnati, University of	197	6	190	10	202	18	192	12	197	14	207	15
Toledo, University of[a]	234	2	237	4	226	8	221	6	205	4	210	3
SW Okla. State University	419	4	343	4	309	5	308	2	311	2	288	—
Oklahoma, University of	260	4	206	4	186	4	158	8	165	9	179	11
Oregon State University	310	1	308	—	275	—	250	—	260	—	236	—
Duquesne University	371	2	377	3	367	—	366	—	336	—	320	—
Phila. Coll. of Phar.	548	5	535	9	553	11	505	8	485	9	463	10
Temple University	402	14	399	14	402	14	400	26	392	23	389	27
Pittsburgh, University of	304	3	287	2	272	2	251	2	265	4	282	6
Rhode Island, Univ. of	306	1	243	1	245	—	266	—	239	—	238	—
Medical Univ. of S.C.	179	10	150	10	129	7	108	9	137	7	147	7
South Carolina, Univ. of	228	8	212	15	202	15	213	19	215	21	196	19
South Dakota State Univ.	135	—	111	—	93	—	111	—	129	—	129	—

Table 37 (Continued)

Black Student Enrollment in First Professional Degree Programs in Pharmacy, 1979–80 to 1984–85 (T = total enrollment, B = black)

Institution	1979		1980		1981		1982		1983		1984	
	T	B	T	B	T	B	T	B	T	B	T	B
Tennessee, University of	289	11	287	10	268	8	254	2	249	8	249	2
Texas Southern Univ.*	230	132	180	98	196	96	209	100	226	99	226	111
Houston, University of	459	26	441	25	343	18	290	26	286	20	286	16
Univ. of Texas at Austin	464	9	448	6	409	10	412	6	388	4	318	6
Utah, University of	193	—	170	1	143	1	137	1	130	—	130	—
Va. Commonwealth U.	276	9	276	11	276	15	281	14	280	19	280	13
Washington, University of	251	9	227	8	197	4	183	5	174	5	176	6
Washington State Univ.	189	1	176	1	170	1	154	1	148	2	148	3
West Virginia University	210	1	205	1	196	3	191	3	188	2	188	2
Univ. of Wisc./Madison	503	16	450	19	396	14	347	12	344	6	344	8
Wyoming, University of	129	1	111	—	105	—	79	—	72	—	72	—
Total	22,560	958	21,628	945	20,132	934	19,027	935	17,127	943	16,772	964
% Black	4.2		4.4		4.6		4.9		5.5		5.7	

Source: American Journal of Pharmaceutical Education, Fall editions, specified years.

[a]Institutions offer Pharm.D. as the first professional degree; they are not included in total figures in this table for 1983 and 1984. Parentheses indicate six year Pharm.D. students.

* 65 schools reporting.

standards. A major impediment often cited is the lack of preparation in basic science courses, such as mathematics, chemistry, and biology, as well as low proficiency in verbal communication. The traditional baccalaureate degree in pharmacy involves what is called a "2–3 program in which two years are in a pre-pharmacy curriculum and the remaining three years are devoted to a pharmacy curriculum. In more recent years, several institutions have offered a "2–4 program," which leads to a Doctor of Pharmacy, or "Pharm. D." degree. In addition, several institutions offer a M.S. degree in pharmacy and fewer offer a Ph.D. degree.[14]

Admission to the B.S. in pharmacy program is generally based on such criteria as gradepoint averages in pre-pharmacy college work. The GPA may be as low as a 2.5 or straight *C* in some institutions, or a *C* + or *B* – average in others. Since 1975, a substantial number of institutions have relied on scores on the Pharmacy College Admission Test (PCAT) in assessing a candidate's application. Interviews are also employed as a means of determining motivation, interest, and commitment or special attributes possessed by the candidate.[15] Reading comprehension and chemistry scores on the PCAT may become central determinants of admission in some colleges of pharmacy. However, the use of this test is so new in several colleges that it is premature to make an assessment of the success of the test in differentiating the quality of applicants compared with the previously employed factors.

Where special admissions programs have operated, they tended to involve a reduction in the expected gradepoint average by a few percentage points for otherwise desirable black students. In this study, there was no evidence that black and other minority students were accepted into the B.S. pharmacy program with less than a *C* average. As in the case of majority-group students, a *C* average was offset by special qualities, such as motivation, perseverance, and interest in the profession that the student displayed during the assessment process.

The most commonly employed cognitive admissions requirement are college gradepoint average and, in 29 institutions, scores on the Graduate Record Examination (GRE). Among the 56 institutions with graduate programs in 1970, as in subsequent years, gradepoint averages expected for admission to graduate programs varied markedly from institution to institution. Thirty-seven institutions were on a four-point (4.0) system. Twenty-one of these institutions required a 3.0, or *B* average but among the remaining colleges of pharmacy, the gradepoint average required ranged from a low of 2.5 to a high of 2.8 on a 4.0 system. Among those institutions on a 3.0 system or a 5.0 system or a 6.0 system, the GPAs expected were consistent with those institutions on a 4.0 system. By 1972, the minimum GPA expected had dropped to 2.25 on a 4.0 system, but a GPA of 3.0 or above was still required by 35 of the 56 institutions with graduate programs. However, the GPA minimum was raised to 2.5 on a 4.0 system in the mid-1970s and has continued to range from 2.5 to 3.0 since that time.[16]

In those institutions requiring the GRE, an average score of 1000, or in the upper 50 percentile was usually expected until about 1975. Since about 1975, cutoff points on the GRE varied from a low of 530 to a high of 1250 in the 25 institutions requiring the GRE. The upper limits include a composite verbal and quantitative score. These requirements are most consistently expected of students who wish to pursue the doctoral degree rather than students interested primarily in the M.S. in Pharmacy degree. About one-half of all graduate students in pharmacy enter with a previous degree in pharmacy. However, the proportion of those entering with a degree in some other field of study increased steadily throughout the 1970s but seems to be leveling off around the 50% mark in the 1980s.[17]

It is not possible to make distinctions between the qualifications brought by black students from those brought by white students in the application, assessment, and admissions processes. These is certainly no rational reasons to assume that the races differed appreciably in qualifications. Wherever special admissions programs existed, they seemed to focus primarily on providing financial aid and special services to minority students, rather than a reduction in academic requirements for graduate study.

Special recruitment efforts, availability of financial aid and scholarship monies, and the presence of black faculty continue to be the most powerful determinants of actual enrollment of black students.

Enrollment: B.S. in Pharmacy Programs

In 1971 the American Association of Colleges of Pharmacy (AACP) directed its Executive Committee to collect information on the racial composition of the student bodies in constitutent colleges. Only one of the 54 colleges of pharmacy failed to report enrollment data by race. In 1971, 618 black pharmacy students represented 3.75% of all students enrolled in B.S. in Pharmacy programs. However, 353 of these students were enrolled in the four historically black colleges of pharmacy. When these students are deducted from the 618, the 265 black students enrolled in the remaining 50 institutions represented a mere 1.0% of enrollment in the traditionally white institutions. In other words, the average number of black students enrolled in pharmacy programs was 5.3 per institutions at the white colleges. However, 12 of these institutions had no black students.

Among black colleges, Texas Southern University enrolled 88 men and 50 women ($T = 138$); Howard University enrolled 63 men and 33 women ($T = 96$); Florida A & M University enrolled 41 men and 18 women ($T = 59$); and Xavier University of Louisiana enrolled 31 men and

29 women or a total of 60 pharmacy students. Among historically white institutions, 9 enrolled 10 or more black students. These were the University of California (11), Mercer University (14), University of Illinois (13), University of Maryland (11), Wayne State University (10), Brooklyn College of Pharmacy (26), University of North Carolina (11), Temple University (11), and Columbia University (15).[18]

The recruitment drive began to show enrollment increases in 1972 and succeeding years. However, because of the overall effort by colleges of pharmacy to enroll significantly larger numbers of students in general, as related to expansion under capitation grants, black student enrollment failed to keep pace with overall enrollment.

In fact, the primary inducement for the spiraling increases in colleges of pharmacy witnessed during the 1970s appeared to be capitation grants. The quota requirements of the Health Manpower Act mandated participating colleges to increase enrollment in whatever class or year they defined as a "first class or year of study" by 10%. This definition referred to the third year of pharmacy in some institutions, while in others it was defined as the fourth year of study. Some colleges of pharmacy ultimately exceeded their capitation quotas; many never did.[19]

In any event, in absolute numbers, black student enrollment increased annually throughout the decade. However, after 1972 when the proportion of black students in colleges of pharmacy stood at 6.6%, the proportion declined dramatically. Thereafter, the proportion dropped by more than 50% to 3.2% of total enrollment in 1974 when 727 black students were enrolled. It rose slightly the following year to 3.8%, which represented an increase of 188 black students when 915 enrolled.

The upward climb continued in 1977 when the 984 black pharmacy students represented 4.2% of total enrollment. It was unchanged in 1979 when 958 black students matriculated in pharmacy school. *Although significant increases in black student enrollment occurred in the historically white institutions, more than one-half (54.3%) of all black pharmacy students are enrolled in the four historically black colleges.*[20]

The number of traditionally white institutions with a black student enrollment of 10 or more reached 15 in 1979, but the proportion of blacks in 68 of these institutions (including Puerto Rico) was only about 2.3% of total enrollment. By 1979, the largest number of black students enrolled in traditionally white colleges matriculated at the University of Michigan (36), Arnold and Marie Schwartz of Long Island University (30), University of Houston (26), University of Maryland (31), University of California (26), and Purdue University (21).

Since 1979, enrollment in the nation's schools or colleges of pharmacy has declined dramatically. For example, 54 schools reported enrollment declines in 1980, while increases in student enrollment were registered in only 15 of these colleges. The net decline was by 4.1% in one year. The decline also worsened within the 4 pharmacy colleges at historically black colleges. By 1980, they constituted only 38.9% of all black pharmacy students, compared to more than 50% a few years earlier.[21]

By 1982, pharmacy school enrollments had declined by 20.7% from their peak enrollment in 1975.[22] Only 19,350 students were enrolled in the 72 colleges of pharmacy. Black student enrollment in the 1980s began with a continuing downturn from peak enrollment in the 1970s, but the 967 enrollees in 1984 approximated 1977 enrollment levels. They constituted 6.1% of total enrollment for the non-Pharm.D first professional degree. They constitute 5.7% of all first professional degree enrollment. However, when the total baccalaureate enrollment of 418 blacks at the four historically black colleges is removed from that number, black pharmacy students comprise a mere 2.5% of total baccalaureate enrollment in the 67 U.S. mainland, traditionally white institutions (see Table 37).

Among the traditionally white institutions in 1984, the highest total enrollment of black baccalaureate students was at Arnold and Marie Schwartz of Long Island University (62), Massachusetts College of Pharmacy (57), St. John's University (28), Temple University (27), Wayne State University (25), University of Maryland (25), University of Illinois (24), Northeast Louisiana University (23), and Samford University (20).

In 1984, 45 institutions or 69% of the 65 traditionally white institutions, had a total black student enrollment of 10 or fewer; 31, or 48% enrolled 5 or fewer blacks in 1984 (see Table 37).

Enrollment in the "Adams States"

The impact of *Adams* litigation on black student enrollment in schools of pharmacy has been mixed at best. While no institution in an "*Adams* state" is without a single black pharmacy student, 15 of the 32 institutions in these states enrolled 10 or fewer black students during the 1984–1985 academic year. Further, the declines registered in pharmacy schools were particularly noteworthy with respect to the fewer black students matriculated in several pharmacy schools in "*Adams* states." Among traditionally white institutions located in these states, the largest enrollments of black students were in schools of pharmacy located at Northeast Louisiana University (23), University of Maryland (25), Temple University (21), University of South Carolina (19), and Mercer University (24) (see Table 38). Clearly, a much more effectively organized enrollment effort, including significant financial support, is warranted if institutions located in the "*Adams* states," as well as other traditionally white institutions, are to succeed in expanding pharmacy career opportunities to black Americans. All the institutions that

Table 38
Average Total Enrollment of Black Students in Schools of Pharmacy in "*Adams* States," 1979–1984 (first professional degree)

Institution	Average Total Black Student Enrollment	Rank in Total Black Enrollment Among *Adams* States
Auburn University	5.8	19
Samford University	10.1	14
Arkansas Medical Center	4.0	24
Florida A & M University[a]	118.0	2
University of Florida	5.6	20
Mercer University[c]	18.5	7
University of Georgia	7.6	17
University of Kentucky	3.0	26
Northeast La. State Univ.	17.5	8
Xavier University[a]	123.8	1
University of Maryland[b]	21.3	5
University of Mississippi	13.3	11
Univ. of North Carolina[b]	12.3	12
Ohio Northern University	3.1	25
Ohio State University	4.6	22
University of Cincinnati	12.5	12
University of Toledo	4.5	23
Southwestern Okla. State U.	2.8	27
Duquesne University	0.8	29
Phila. College of Pharmacy	8.6	15
Temple University	19.6	6
University of Pittsburgh	4.8	21
Med. U. of South Carolina	8.3	16
Univ. of South Carolina	16.1	9
Texas Southern University[a]	106.0	3
University of Houston	21.8	4
University of Texas/Austin	6.1	18
Va. Commonwealth Univ.	13.5	10
West Virginia University	2.0	28

[a] = HBI.
[b] = States formerly under *Adams* litigation.
[c] = Includes Pharm.D. students.

Source: Adapted from Table 37.

responded to the inventory disseminated for the first part of this study indicated a goal of increasing the numbers of black students to a level commensurate with the proportion of blacks in their state populations. However, it is evident that a strong and aggressive recruitment program supported by black faculty in the colleges of pharmacy, adequate financial aid, institutional commitment, and a positive learning environment are all imperative and will continue to be so. The fact also remains that as recently as 1984, 48 of the 70 reporting schools of pharmacy had no more than 10 black students: 32 schools matriculated fewer than 5 black students; and 7 schools enrolled not a single black student.

The number of black faculty averages fewer than one per institution. Even that number is deceptive, since most of the black faculty members represented by it are teaching at historically black colleges. According to studies conducted by Lars Solander, director of the Office of Educational Research and Development of the AACP, full-time black faculty members continue to be underrepresented on the faculties of colleges of pharmacy. This shortage of black faculty remains despite increases in the number of black faculty noted in each of the association's biennial surveys, conducted since 1974. Total black faculty in 1978 was 63, or 3% of the 1914 faculty members in the 72 schools of pharmacy in the United States. In 1974, there were 41 black faculty out of a total full-time faculty of 1621. (Interestingly, 41 of the 63 black faculty in 1978 were males and 22 were females.)[23]

The number of black faculty in schools of pharmacy did not change from 63 between 1980 and 1983. By 1984–85, the number of black faculty had increased by only one, but blacks were still concentrated in the four historically black colleges of pharmacy. Black faculty members constitute about 4% of total faculty; when the 42 blacks employed at historically black institutions are disaggregated from the total number, however, the percentage of black faculty employed falls sharply, to only 1% of the total. It is therefore apparent that the 65 mainland institutions have not been aggressive in the recruitment of blacks for faculty positions in these institutions. Even though the percentage of black students among the total pharmacy student enrollment has risen slightly since 1980, that change is due principally to a total decline of more than 20% in numbers of pharmacy students, while the number of blacks has more or less stabilized, and black institutions are maintaining their enrollments. The presence of black faculty members contributes a considerable amount to this situation. Further, the presence of part-time blacks in clinical faculty roles may be a contributing factor to the success enjoyed by a few traditionally white institutions.

One problem encountered by all institutions with respect to the recruitment of black faculty is their inability to be competitive with the private sector for pharmacy graduates. This situation is especially critical when in competition with job opportunities in industrial, pharamaceutical, and research firms; it is probably less so with the federal government. Nevertheless, the American Association of Colleges of Pharmacy (AACP) reports that the average pharmacist is paid about $25,000 on entering the job market, and most pharmacists in the United States do not earn more than $35,000 per year.[24] Not only do schools of pharmacy have a problem with recruitment, they also have a problem in paying more competitive wages for persons capable of earning significantly more than the national average, should they seek and obtain employment in private industry. In addition, the perquisites ("perks") provided by private industry may increase the attractiveness of such positions, since they are not usually available in colleges and universities.

Sex Ratio

For some time now, black female student enrollment has exceeded that of black male student enrollment. The distribution is depicted in Table 39. From 1979 to 1984, more than three-fifths of the black pharmacy students were women. This disparity may be attributed to a redistribution of black males into other health-related fields or engineering. It further reflects the downward trend in black male enrollment in higher education in general. It may also indicate the degree to which the recruitment and enrollment of women students has paid off in such fields as pharmacy, medicine, dentistry, and optometry. Further, women students are being given more opportunities to demonstrate their academic competitiveness as sex discrimination becomes less apparent. As a result, in many instances, they are more successful in meeting admissions requirements.

Table 39
Black Student Enrollment in Schools of Pharmacy, by Sex, 1979–1984
(first professional degree)

Sex	1979		1980		1981		1982		1983		1984	
	N	%	N	%	N	%	N	%	N	%	N	%
Male	414	43.2	381	40.3	378	40.5	389	40.6	386	40.9	361	37.3
Female	548	57.2	564	59.7	554	59.4	546	58.4	557	59.1	606	62.7
Total												
☐ Black	958	100.4	945	100.0	932	99.9	935	100.0	943	100.0	967	100.0

Source: American Association of Colleges of Pharmacy.

Note: Some percentages do not equal 100% because of rounding.

Table 40

B.S. Pharmacy Degrees Awarded in "*Adams States*," 1974–1984 (*B* = black, *T* = total)

Institution	1974 B	1974 T	1975 B	1975 T	1976 B	1976 T	1977 B	1977 T	1978 B	1978 T	1979 B	1979 T	1980 B	1980 T	1981 B	1981 T	1982 B	1982 T	1983 B	1983 T	1984 B	1984 T
Arkansas University	0	57	0	59	2	60	0	63	2	62	0	51	1	60	1	62	1	58	1	55	2	53
Auburn University	2	71	0	105	0	160	5	98	1	111	1	141	1	103	0	108	2	94	2	97	0	65
Duquesne University	1	56	0	85	0	96	0	184	1	118	1	111	0	104	2	106	0	127	0	126	0	107
Florida A & M Univ.	13	45	21	59	18	44	37	81	47	84	45	67	38	45	36	69	21	45	31	38	29	41
University of Florida	0	104	0	117	3	113	0	138	2	121	3	125	0	122	3	121	1	99	2	109	1	105
University of Georgia	2	156	1	125	1	148	3	145	4	163	2	129	6	132	3	121	2	129	0	128	1	99
University of Houston	2	114	6	108	1	102	1	135	2	138	4	146	4	126	5	131	6	117	5	116	2	76
Howard University	18	37	29	59	22	81	23	71	18	51	20	48	20	50	22	38	7	13	11	21	10	26
University of Kentucky	0	78	0	84	1	87	0	80	1	87	0	72	0	82	1	59	1	78	4	73	1	79
Univ. of Maryland	2	62	1	63	3	76	3	78	6	84	5	94	11	88	7	81	6	86	2	80	3	77
Mercer (Georgia)	8	81	1	95	2	84	4	125	5	93	3	112	0	98	4	96	9	107	11	116	NA	NA
Univ. of Mississippi	0	87	1	106	0	92	1	101	3	92	1	93	1	87	4	99	7	94	2	79	2	90
University of Missouri	1	84	2	62	0	72	1	64	0	72	2	70	1	70	2	68	2	73	1	67	3	66
U. of North Carolina	2	136	3	144	5	132	5	147	5	143	5	137	4	137	7	155	3	160	3	152	4	160
N.E. Louisiana Univ.	2	150	1	152	1	216	1	205	7	196	6	150	5	114	3	142	6	113	3	134	2	113
Ohio Northern Univ.	2	112	0	173	1	108	0	145	0	137	1	120	2	130	0	131	2	160	0	114	0	120
Ohio State University	0	78	1	93	1	128	1	119	3	113	1	115	0	113	2	103	2	105	0	102	1	87
Univ. of Oklahoma	2	61	1	69	0	78	0	120	0	114	3	102	2	84	1	66	0	60	3	45	1	47
Phila. Coll. of Phar.	2	116	4	143	2	159	6	168	1	182	3	179	2	172	1	164	5	176	5	171	5	181
Univ. of Pittsburgh	2	92	0	82	1	96	0	93	0	93	0	93	0	94	1	98	1	83	0	81	1	90
St. Louis University	3	128	1	133	2	141	2	144	5	129	1	126	3	126	0	152	1	152	1	133	2	107
Samford University	0	59	0	73	2	125	0	93	1	116	1	135	1	109	3	102	3	62	2	68	1	50
So. Carolina Medical	0	36	0	38	2	48	0	50	2	62	1	48	4	52	3	58	2	53	3	32	0	31
U. of South Carolina	1	55	4	59	0	58	4	75	3	104	8	79	1	77	3	73	2	68	2	64	9	74
S.W. Oklahoma Univ.	1	148	1	141	2	143	2	165	2	137	0	114	2	147	1	137	3	142	2	86	0	84
Temple University	4	81	4	104	5	106	10	127	6	122	2	123	6	122	3	124	3	132	4	139	6	137
Texas Southern Univ.	26	29	34	45	25	38	41	65	25	47	33	70	24	50	20	36	18	53	20	41	16	50
University of Texas	0	164	1	227	3	234	2	231	3	197	1	204	3	203	2	147	2	155	2	139	1	133
University of Toledo	0	52	1	52	1	77	2	77	0	79	1	80	1	72	0	76	2	78	2	59	3	71
Va. Commonwealth U	1	71	3	92	3	85	3	86	3	89	3	94	2	87	2	99	6	85	2	88	6	84
West Virginia Univ.	1	63	0	70	0	69	1	65	0	65	0	67	0	64	0	71	0	66	1	58	1	60
Xavier of La.	10	30	23	53	21	46	24	57	15	46	43	78	33	78	33	60	38	57	30	45	36	56

NA = Not Available.
Source: American Association of Colleges of Pharmacy.

Enrollment: Pharm.D. and Graduate Programs

The Pharm.D. degree requires six years of training, including two years of pre-pharmacy and four years of coursework in a school of pharmacy. It is not unusual for Pharm.D. degree students to have already received B.S. degree in Pharmacy and to continue for the fourth year of pharmacy training in order to be awarded the Doctor of Pharmacy degree. In 1969, 16 schools of pharmacy offered the Pharm. D. degree. Of that number, five colleges offered it as the first professional degree. During that year, 871 student were studying for this degree as their first professional pharmacy degree, and 154 Pharm.D. candidates already held the B.S. degree. Of that number, 25 were in M.S. degree programs and 16 were seeking the Ph.D. Twenty-one of these students sought degrees in pharmaceutical chemistry. The least selected fields of specialization were pharmacy administration and pharmacognosy, each with two students.[25]

By 1973, the number of students pursuing a M.S. degree in pharmacy had increased to 1035, and there were 957 enrollees in Ph.D. programs. The respective numbers of black students were 20 M.S. students and 12 Ph.D. students, or a net loss of 13 black graduate students in one year. The M.S. students were enrolled at the following institutions: University of California (1), University of Illinois (1), Butler University (2), Purdue University (1), University of Maryland (2), Wayne State University (1), University of Mississippi (1), University of Nebraska (1), Brooklyn College of Pharmacy (4), University of Pittsburgh (2), University of South Carolina (1) and University of Houston (1).[26]

The Ph.D. students were enrolled at Arizona, Georgia, Illinois, Maryland, Missouri/K.C., St. John's, Pittsburgh, Rhode Island, and Wisconsin. In toto, black students represented 1.9% of the M.S. students and 1.2% of the Ph.D. students. Among the "*Adams* states," only in Georgia, Maryland, Mississippi, and Pennsylvania were black students enrolled in a graduate pharmacy program.

An analysis of minority-student enrollment data for 1975 shows a pattern that was prevalent in most institutions both before and after that year. This analysis indicated that non-Americans account for 90.7% of all students listed as minorities; black Americans represented 4.4%; Spanish-surnamed equaled 2.4%; and Asian Americans constituted 1.0% of all persons listed as minority students enrolled in graduate programs. Even when these data are disaggregated by type of degree, non-Americans still constitute almost 89% of doctoral students in the minority student population. However, the proportion of Asian Americans rose dramatically to 5.7% of minority enrollment and Spanish-surnamed declined to 1.2%.

Nine black students were enrolled in master's degree programs. Of that number, one each was enrolled at the University of Florida and the

University of Mississippi, as the only two *"Adams* states" with black students in M.S. programs. Eight black students were enrolled in doctoral programs. These students were distributed at the University of Southern California (1), University of Florida (1), University of Illinois (1), Purdue University (1), University of Nebraska (1), University of Pittsburgh (2), and University of Wisconsin–Madison (1). Again, no institution enrolled a significant number of black graduate students.[27]

The number of black students in M.S. programs fell by 1 student to a total of 8, and the number of doctoral students who were black rose to 12 in the Fall of 1976. The Universities of Connecticut, Kansas, Michigan, SUNY/Buffalo, Ohio State, and Texas/Austin enrolled black doctoral students. These were in addition to Florida, Illinois, Purdue, Nebraska, and Pittsburgh. Florida A & M, Texas/Austin, and Ohio State were added to the list of institutions that enrolled black students in M.S. programs.[28]

In fall 1978, 7 black students were enrolled in doctoral programs, and 20 were enrolled im M.S. degree programs in pharmacy. The doctoral students were scattered in 7 different colleges of pharmacy: Purdue, Kentucky, Michigan, Wayne State, University of Mississippi, University of Kansas, and University of Pittsburgh. Twelve of the 20 black students enrolled in M.S. programs were at historically black Florida A & M University. The remaining 8 were distributed in 8 traditionally white institutions. Forty of the institutions that offer M.S. programs did not enroll a single black M.S. student. Thirty-three of the 40 colleges of pharmacy that offer the Ph.D degree had no black doctoral students.[29]

These data underscore in rather explicit terms the major problem of underrepresentation and token enrollment of black students in graduate degree programs in pharmacy. Once again, it is not possible to produce trained black pharmacists who can meet manpower needs in industry, in educational institutions as university professors and administrators, and in hospitals, or for the corner drugstore, unless they are successfully recruited and enrolled.

In the 1980s, the total number of students matriculated in the 14 institutions that offer the Pharm.D. degree as the first professional degree continued to rise. By 1982, the number of such students had climbed to 2082, which represented a 4.1% increase over such enrollments in 1975. In the fall of 1984, the number of Pharm.D. students was 1874. Black student enrollment in these programs was 81 or 4.3% of that enrollment. The majority of black Pharm.D. students were registered in programs at Mercer University (24), University of Southern California (12), Florida A & M University (11), and the University of California and Pacific University (9 each). Black students enrolled in the Pharm.D. programs at the one historically black college with these graduate programs accounted for 1.5% of total Pharm.D. enrollments and 13.5% of all blacks pursuing this degree.

Similarly, the enrollment pattern with respect to the master's degree in pharmacy did not show appreciable changes. In 1983, only 29 black students were seeking this degree. The one historically black institution that offers the master's degree in pharmacy accounted for 48.2% of all black students seeking this degree.

Including Florida A & M, only 12 schools of pharmacy enrolled black students at the master's degree level. These traditionally white institutions were Auburn (1), Wayne State (1), University of Houston (1), University of Georgia (1), Purdue (1), Northeast Louisiana (1), University of Mississippi (1), A and M. Schwartz of Long Island University (1), Duquesne (1), University of Rhode Island (1), and University of Winconsin (1). Of the 23 black students enrolled in master's programs in 1984–1985, due largely to the enrollment at Florida A & M (an HBI), 18, or about three-fourths of them, matriculated at "*Adams* states" institutions. About three-fourths were seeking the master's degree in Pharmacology (18), and three were enrolled in the master's program in Pharmaceutical Medicine Chemistry. No black student was seeking a master's degree in Pharmacognosy. Only one was enrolled in the Pharmacy Administration curriculum, and only one was seeking a master's degree in Hospital Pharmacy.

Similarly, the 1984–1985 doctoral enrollment of black pharmacy students dramatically illustrated the seriousness of black student representation in pharmacy graduate education programs. In that year, only 13 black students were seeking doctoral degree in schools of pharmacy in the United States. The majority were concentrated in Pharmacy Administration; only 1 student was seeking a Ph.D. in Pharmacology. Only the University of Texas/Austin and the University of North Carolina enrolled as many as 2 black doctoral degree students. The remaining students were distributed at the University of Kansas, University of Kentucky, University of Wisconsin, University of California/Berkeley, University of Oklahoma, Ohio State University, Purdue University, Northeast Louisiana University, and the University of Rhode Island.*

Hence it is evident that no school of pharmacy in 1984–1985 attracted a sufficient number of black graduate students as to approach even a modicum of a critical mass. Enrollment of black students at the graduate level in pharmacy was a barely token representation.

The pattern of enrollment of black students in graduate schools of pharmacy is particularly disturbing in the 1980s. It does not suggest that graduate schools in pharmacy actually made a firm commitment in the 1960s and 1970s to active and aggressive recruitment of black students into this profession. It is as if they expected the students to arrive at a decision by some mysterious osmotic process leading inevitably to their selection of

---

* Since FAMU (an HBI) established a Ph.D. program in 1985, it accounts for more than half of blacks in pharmacy doctoral programs.

pharmacy as a field of graduate study and in that particular graduate school. Therefore, no inducements were necessary. If knowledge about graduate opportunities in pharmacy were limited and if these institutions had no track record of having graduated a sufficient number of black students in the past, that kind of institutional position is clearly untenable. Further, some administrators argue that recruitment and enrollment of black students into graduate pharmacy programs are hampered by salaries and wages that blacks holding an undergraduate degree in pharmacy can earn. Therefore, institutions cannot compete with the lucrative financial incentives offered by the job market. While this argument may have validity if the focus remains solely on the recruitment of students for purely academic positions, it does not have credibility when one begins to focus on the requirements for certain positions in industrial pharmacy, drug research in the pharmaceutical industry, hospital administration, and other occupational areas.

Inability to move beyond tokenism in the recruitment and enrollment of black students is an indictment of negative institutional behavior characterized by either the inability or unwillingness to translate what is tantamount to a "paper-constructed" program into concrete programmatic action. A serious commitment involves a clear articulation of goals and plans from the leadership structure, faculty participation, and an understanding from those unsympathetic faculty that they will not engage in behavior that will ultimately undermine program goals.

It necessitates an ability to *persuade* the ambivalent student that the opportunities in this field are significant, if indeed they are. And they are for some specializations in pharmacy. It may involve "selling the institution and its program," especially when little is known about the institution's commitment to the education of black and other minority students or in those instances in which previous experiences of black students were negative. It necessitates a sufficient financial outlay to support all aspects of the program. Most certainly, it means the enrollment of a critical mass of black students—a missing element in all graduate schools of pharmacy with the exception of the one historically black college that offers the Ph.D. degree. Hence, the important question of the 1980s is: How commited are graduate schools of pharmacy to the goal of enrolling a critical mass of black students and to sustaining that enrollment so that racial parity will be commonplace?

Financing One's Education

As previously argued, recruitment necessitates guarantees that adequate financial assistance will be available to black students, especially at the graduate level. By far the most common method of financial support for graduate students is the acquisition of assistantships and nonservice stipends or scholarships. At the first professional degree level in pharmacy (primarily the

B.S. degree), students depend heavily on Guaranteed Student Loans (47.1% of total enrollment), followed by Pell Grants (28.3%), Health Professions Student Loans (19.7%), National Direct Student Loans (10.9%), and college work–study programs (10.6%). Fewer pharmacy students rely on Supplemental Education Opportunity Grants (9.7%), Health Education Assistance Loans (1.2%), Veteran's Benefits (.8%), and other federal assistance (1.6%). The American Association of Colleges of Pharmacy (AACP) estimated that the total federal aid for pharmacy education in 1983–1984 was approximately $42 million.[30]

In an analysis of President Reagan's FY 1985 budget, the AACP argued that had the President's proposals been fully accepted, the education of at least 11% of pharmacy school students would have been placed in serious jeopardy. The President had proposed devastating cutbacks in Pell Grants, the elimination of SEOG funds, retrenchment in the NDSL program, a major reduction in GSLs, and a dramatic reduction in monies available for the Exceptional Financial Need Scholarship Program.[31] While much of those funds were salvaged by Congress, the FY 88 budget again calls for drastic eliminations and cutbacks that would have enormous consequences for all students, including those enrolled in pharmacy programs.

This situation is further exacerbated by the decision of the federal government to suspend schools from the Health Professions Student Loan (HPSL) program if they have a delinquency loan rate in excess of 5%. HPSL loans are held in a revolving fund so that repayments are used for additional grants to applicants. The assumption is that if schools do not collect overdue payments from their borrowers, the total amount of money available for persons in need will be reduced substantially.

Suspended institutions are no longer eligible for new HPSL monies. They are forbidden to disburse HPSL funds to borrowers. They must meet federally established performance standards for debt collection in order to be reinstated in the program. The implementation of the 5% standard for loan delinquency has had a distressing impact on historically black colleges in which health-profession schools are located. In 1985 suspensions were meted out to Howard University (including schools of medicine, dentistry, and pharmacy), which had a delinquency rate of more than 40%; and to Xavier University's college of pharmacy, which had a delinquency rate of 32%. About 40% of all health-profession programs in the nation were in danger of suspension in December 1984.

The problems are especially acute for minority students, however. The AACP takes the position that the 5% delinquency rate is inconsistent with performance standards imposed in other federal programs, which allow a substantially greater percentage of loan delinquencies before an institution is in default. In addition, the practice of the Department of Health and Human Services (HHS) of counting the entire unpaid amount as delinquent if the borrower fails to make a payment within 60 days on a single payment exacts an undue burden on people with heavy financial responsibilities, huge loans, and low salaries. The situation is likely to be significantly more common among black students, who are largely from families with lower incomes than white student families.

This financial crisis would not be so widespread if black students had a greater opportunity for summer employment to help defray the cost of pharmacy education, and if more realistic financial aid was available to them. In general, fellowships and scholarships, teaching and research assistantships do not go to black students. Consequently they must support their undergraduate and graduate education through repayable loans. But successful enrollment is correlated with good financial assistance available to black students. Without it, irrespective of how sound the recruitment program seems on paper, institutions will continue to fail in their efforts to enroll black students. Obviously, greater amounts of institutional and state funds, in addition to external funds from the private sector, are needed. One example of a positive step in this direction is in Georgia, where the Board of Regents established Regents' Fellowships as an inducement to the recruitment and enrollment of black students. Even there, however, the number of such fellowships permitted yearly must be expanded in order to approximate compelling needs.

Black Graduates in Pharmacy

Although the absolute numbers of black graduates with a B.S. degree in pharmacy have about doubled since 1972, the percentage black to the total number of baccalaureate degrees awarded in pharmacy is less than 4.0% among all institutions combined. As shown in Table 41, the 138 black pharmacy graduates in 1972 represented only 2.9% of total graduates. The 272 black graduates in 1979, the peak number during the 1970s, constituted 3.7%, a fact that exemplified the impact of capitation funds on the recruitment and retention of black students. However, as these funds dissipated and were not replaced by funds from other sources, both enrollment and retention suffered. This fact is perhaps demonstrated by the sharp drop in the number of black graduates to 216 in 1981. By 1984, blacks constituted 228, 4.1% of B.S. pharmacy degrees (see Table 41).

During this 13 year period, the 71 mainland schools of pharmacy graduated approximately 83,757 pharmacists. Of that number, 2636, or 3.1%, were black.

The production of blacks with graduate degrees in pharmacy is abysmal. The nation is not producing an adequate number of blacks per year with either a baccalaureate or advanced degree. At the M.S. degree level, the absolute numbers of blacks increased from 3 to 17 between 1974 and 1981,

Table 41
B.S. Pharmacy Degree Graduates by Race, 1972 to 1984

Year	Total	Black	% Blacks
1984	5546	228	4.1
1983	5919	232	3.9
1982	6448	238	3.7
1981	6869	216	3.1
1980	7091[a]	247	3.5
1979	7383	272	3.7
1978	7613	233	3.1
1977	7803	226	2.9
1976	7611	205	2.7
1975	6559	176	2.7
1974	5788	144	2.5
1973	5070	142	2.8
1972	4802	138	2.9
Total	84,502	2,697	3.13

Source: American Journal of Pharmaceutical Education. [a]Excludes incomplete data from Oregon State (40 graduates) and University of Southern California (125 graduates).

but the production downturn since that time has been staggering. By 1984, the nation was producing only 8 (2.0%) blacks with a M.S. degree in pharmacy. Between 1974 and 1984, the number of blacks who received a Ph.D. degree never exceeded 3 in a single year. In fact, between 1974 and 1984, the nation produced 16 blacks with a Ph.D. in pharmacy (see Table 42).

Table 42
Graduate Degrees in Pharmacy, by Race, Selected Years 1974–1984
(T = total, B = black)

Year	M.S.			Ph.D.			Pharm.D. 1,2[b]		
	T	B	%B	T	B	%B	T	B	%B
1984	394	8	2	227	2	0.9	748	24	3
1983	426	2	b	208	0	0	726	32	4
1982	458	5	1	182	1	*	591	18	3
1981	434	17	4	180	1	*	634	21	3
1980[a]	455	10	2	184	3	2	473	13	3
1977	399	5	1	166	2	1	551	8	1
1974	320	3	1	184	3	2	434	10	2

Source: American Association of Colleges of Pharmacy, *Degrees Conferred by Schools and Colleges of Pharmacy.*
[a]*Excludes one institution that did not provide data.*
[b]*Combines all types of Pharm.D. programs.*

Again, these data depict in dramatic force the immense problem of the underproduction of blacks with pharmacy degrees at all levels of higher education. It is equally evident that traditionally white institutions have a responsibility to expand educational opportunity in pharmacy through outreach programs, aggressive recruitment, mentoring, and institutional support in order to address the problem of the underrepresentation of blacks in this profession.

Xavier University College of Pharmacy*
A Case Study Of Success

As noted, the four historically black colleges of pharmacy enroll about 40% of all black pharmacy students in the United States. They now graduate about 40% of all blacks receiving pharmacy degrees each year. One of the pioneers in pharmacy education for black Americans is Xavier University, located in New Orleans, Louisiana.

Xavier University is a small, black, Catholic university established by Mother Katherine Drexel as a high school in 1915. Mother Drexel also founded the Sisters of Blessed Sacrament, whose mission has traditionally been service to American minorities. By 1917, Xavier had attained a normal school status and was committed to the training of black teachers at a time when state laws precluded them from receiving training at the traditionally white public institutions. Xavier became a four-year liberal arts college in 1925. It established its college of pharmacy in 1927, and a graduate school in 1933.[32]

The founding mission of this university was to offer higher educational opportunities to black Americans. Although white students were prohibited from attending the university by state law, the university's faculty and administrators have always been biracial. Consequently its students, from its inception, were exposed to significant role models in an integrated academic environment and by graduates who frequently returned to the institution for special occasions. The integrated learning environment often was an anomaly to the dual systems of education to which these students were exposed in public high schools. Xavier University, however, operated a "preparatory" school which served as a feeder to the university. Both institutions were nationally recognized for high academic standards, a strong commitment to teaching and the training of students within the academic community, emphasis on self-discipline in the development of study habits, and the success rates of their graduates.

---

*This profile is based on interviews with President Norman Francis, Dean Marcellus Grace, and former Dean Warren McKenna.

Prior to the *Brown* decision by the U.S. Supreme Court, the enrollment of Xavier University stood at 600 black students. Under the dual system of education, Xavier University was immensely successful in the training of black Americans for various occupational roles in a segregated society. It has continued that success rate. For example, a 1965 survey revealed that in New Orleans, 40% of the teachers in the black segment of the public school system were Xavier graduates. Approximately 75% of the black principals and 100% of the guidance counselors in these schools held at least one degree from Xavier University.*

Following the *Brown* decision, Xavier University changed the racial composition of its student body. With the aid of federal funds, the university was able to recruit from an expanded pool of students. Between 1964 and 1979, the enrollment of Xavier University increased from 800 to 1800 students. Most of them were full-time undergraduates. Enrollment rose to 2000 in 1984.

The College of Pharmacy was found in 1927. From the beginning, its pharmacy curriculum was impressive and was bolstered by an equally outstanding premedical program and an excellent curriculum in the basic sciences of chemistry, mathematics, biology, and physics. One measure of the strength of these combined programs is that, over the years, more than 150 of Xaviers's graduates have obtained degrees in medicine. It has an acceptance rate to medical and dental schools of 87% of its graduates who apply. More than one-half of the black physicians now in private practice (22 of 38) and 39% of the black pharmacists in New Orleans alone are Xavier graduates.

The College of Pharmacy is the only private, predominantly black college of pharmacy among the 72 accredited pharmacy institutions in the United States. From its inception, the mission of the College of Pharmacy conformed to the mission of the university: "to increase the level, quality and scope of educational opportunities in pharmacy" for black and other minority students. Recruitment into pharmacy focused largely on (1) counseling and guidance programs with students in Xavier Preparatory High School; (2) dissemination of catalogues and bulletins to predominantly black high schools in New Orleans and elsewhere; and (3) the use of alumni in cities or States outside Louisiana, in high school Career Days, college fairs, and special events.

During the 1960s and into the 1970s, recruitment programs expanded because of the input of federal funds and the attainment of private foundation financial support to increase and strengthen the university's offerings in health sciences. The university, under the new leadership of Norman Francis, an articulate and imaginative lay president, sought much-needed resources

---

*The first two black mayors of New Orleans, their Chiefs of Police and the Superintendant of Schools in 1987 are also Xavier alumni.

that would enable the university to prepare students in areas in which job opportunities existed. Pharmacy, like computer sciences and business administration, was one of the applied sciences targeted for growth and expansion. The funds obtained by Xavier University guaranteed the construction of a new College of Pharmacy building in 1970.

Students were recruited into a "2–3" curriculum, which consisted of two years of pre-pharmacy training in the basic sciences and three years of training in the pharmacy curriculum. In 1970 the College of Pharmacy shifted its emphasis to have clinical pharmacy as its central focus. This change was made in order to provide for students who wanted immediately to enter the job market, as well as those who planned to pursue a graduate degree in this area, opportunities for work experience in a variety of settings. Hence, this curriculum now enables students to receive "on-the-job" training in local hospitals, community pharmacies, drug information centers, and a variety of health clinics as a central component of their undergraduate program.

Despite high operating costs, the university has traditionally committed a substantial proportion of its resources to the College of Pharmacy in order to sustain it as a much-needed facility. This investment, however, reflects positive institutional behavior. Similarly, the emphasis placed on pharmacy as an important component of education in the health sciences and the encouragement given by counselors and admissions and guidance officers, as well as by faculty, in the recruitment process and during freshmen orientation activities to seriously consider pharmacy as one of its professional alternatives, all indicate a quality of institutional behavior that is supportive, desirable , and effective.

Xavier's College of Pharmacy makes exceptionally fine use of its Alumni chapters dispersed throughout the United States in the recruitment process. These chapters conduct programs on a Career Day at various high schools; invite students into the workplaces of their graduates in pharmacy, medicine, and dentistry in order to familiarize them with opportunities available in these fields; and distribute promotional literature to prospective students. Their active participation in the recruitment program has enabled the College of Pharmacy to enroll students of all races and minority groups from 20 states and several foreign nations. Hence, special grant funds, such as the monies received from the Office of Health Manpower Opportunities from 1972 to 1975, were utilized to recruit students from an ever expanding potential pool.

Consequently, total enrollment in the college of pharmacy expanded from 62 students in 1968 to an all-time high of 225 in 1978, but declined slightly to 222 in 1984. This college enrolls more blacks in pharmacy than all others.

The racial composition of the student body in pharmacy changed significantly during the 1970s. As a result, the student body is multiethnic and multiracial. Since 1969, the percentage of black students at the College of Pharmacy has fallen from 100% to 68.9% (1984–1985). For a brief period during the late 1970s, black students actually constituted a "minority" of students in the college. White, Hispanic, Asian, and other students were a majority between 1976 and 1978. During the early part of the 1970s, white students represented more than one-third of the enrollment at the college of Pharmacy. The proportion has dropped significantly since that time; however, white students continue to constitute a critical mass of pharmacy student enrollment (see Table 43). Xavier's success in this regard results not merely from program quality. Xavier is the only pharmacy college located in that part of the state; the only other college of pharmacy in Louisiana is located 300 miles to the north.

Sex Ratio

As is the case with schools of pharmacy throughout the nation, female students have increased their interest in pharmacy, and their access to these colleges has moved considerably beyond token levels. In fact, at Xavier University between 1979 and 1985, the proportion of female students climbed rapidly, from 43.1% of total enrollment to 59.9%. In effect, female students comprise almost three-fifths of the pharmacy enrollment in that institution (see Table 44).

In sum, Xavier University in 1984 enrolled more black students in its College of Pharmacy than did any other institution in the United States. Its total enrollment of 222 students was as much as the combined enrollment of more than 50 of the 67 mainland traditionally white colleges of pharmacy. This fact alone graphically portrays how imperative it is for white institutions to accelerate their efforts to enroll black pharmacy students.

Retention is facilitated by the implementation of a well-coordinated program that involves a strong faculty, reasonably adequate financial assistance, academic and personal advising, counseling, tutorials, a positive learning environment, and the recruitment of outstanding students into the program. Although the faculty is multiethnic, in 1984–1985 it was about evenly divided between blacks and whites. One measure of the quality of the faculty (8 blacks, 8 whites, and 1 Asian) lies in the faculty's ability to garner research funds from external sources. In 1984–85, four faculty members combined had received more than $1 million to support their research. These funds were received largely from the National Institute of Heart, Lung, and Blood; the National Institute of Arthritis, Diabetes, Digestive and Kidney Diseases; the National Institute of Aging; and contractual agreements with the U.S. Navy and the Agency for International Development.

Table 43
Enrollment by Race at Xavier University of Louisiana,
College of Pharmacy, 1968–1984

Academic Year	Total Enrollment	Black Students N	%	White Students N	%	Other Students N	%
1984–85	222	153	68.9	39	17.5	30	13.5
1983–84	206	145	70.3	30	14.6	31	15.0
1982–83	190	136	71.6	30	15.8	24	12.6
1981–82	184	133	72.2	27	14.6	24	13.0
1980–81	180	122	67.8	39	21.7	19	10.5
1979–80	216	136	63.0	54	25.0	19*	8.8
1978–79	225	129	57.3	66	29.3	30	13.3
1977–78	223	107	48.0	74	33.1	42	18.8
1976–77	213	104	48.8	72	33.9	37	17.3
1975–76	160	93	58.1	57	35.6	10	6.2
1974–75	152	106	69.7	46	30.2	0	0
1973–74	131	101	77.1	20	15.2	9	6.8
1972–73	116	95	81.9	11	9.4	10	8.6
1971–72	94	84	89.3	0	0	10	10.6
1970–71	88	88	100.0	0	0	0	0
1969–70	77	77	100.0	0	0	0	0
1968–69	62	62	100.0	0	0	0	0

Source: Marcellus Grace, dean, and Warren McKenna, former dean, Xavier University of Louisiana, College of Pharmacy.

Table 44
Enrollment by Sex, Xavier University, College of Pharmacy 1979–1984

Academic Year	Male N	%	Female N	%	Total Enrollment
1984–85	89	40.1	133	59.9	222
1983–84	89	43.2	117	56.8	206
1982–83	95	50.0	95	50.0	190
1981–82	93	50.5	91	49.4	184
1980–81	95	53.0	84	47.0	180
1979–80	123	56.9	93	43.1	216

Source: Marcellus Grace, dean, Xavier University of Louisiana, College of Pharmacy.

In 1984 the Louisiana Legislature appropriated $1.2 million to the Xavier College of Pharmacy to conduct a clinical pharmacy training program at Charity Hospital in New Orleans. That agreement enabled the College of Pharmacy to hire 12 new faculty members for clinical pharmacy training of its college students in a hospital setting. Aside from the immediate teaching and training benefits derived from the program, in the long run it means that the influence of the Xavier College of Pharmacy graduates will extend even farther into the pharmacy community. As of January 1985, more than 50% of all pharmaceutical hospitals in New Orleans and 90% of all black pharmacists in New Orleans were graduates of Xavier University.

Retention is not only aided by such visible role models. Xavier students have the satisfaction of knowing that its graduates at present serve in high-level academic administrative positions, including a former president of the American Pharmaceutical Association (Mary Munson Runge), serve as directors of advertising for major pharmaceutical companies, and hold important administrative and operational positions in such major companies as Warner Lambert. Also, one-third of all black pharmacists in the nation are Xavierites. Their success serves as an inspiration for students.

Financial assistance for students is received from most of the sources identified earlier. The college also received $600,000 in HCOP funds to cover training over a three-year period, 1984 to 1987. These monies have advanced recruitment and increased enrollment. Xavier University was also one of three historically black colleges (along with Tuskegee Institute and Meharry Medical College) to share $5 million in a special allocation from the Federal Distress Grant Program. Although this program was scheduled to be phased out in 1980, the three institutions continue to obtain such federal support.

Federal capitation grants were phased out in the 1970s, but the College of Pharmacy is awarded a capitation grant of $300 per student in state funds. In addition, funds are received from private sources such as corporations and industry to help defray the tuition of $4,700 per year for students who are largely from low-income families.

Again, retention is strengthened by the day-to-day involvement of the faculty in the educational activity of students at Xavier University. Faculty members extend themselves in the learning and teaching process, and stimulate students to become active learners instead of passive recipients of information. Faculty members take time to talk to students, to listen to problems that evolve as they engage themselves in the subject matter and through social interaction in the learning environment. Rigorous standards are exacted, but the rationale for these standards is clearly and effectively communicated, placed within the context of learning and developing a command of the subject matter so that learning has a purpose and a meaning.

The Xavier University College of Pharmacy has graduated more than 1200 pharmacists since its founding. Between 1980 and 1985, 354 people received degrees in pharmacy from that institution. Of that number, about two-thirds were black. With the anticipated implementation of Pharm.D. program after 1987, it is anticipated that the number of pharmacy graduates will increase sharply at Xavier University.

Although a major share of the historically white institutions are larger, have superior financial resources, and more faculty than does Xavier, none can match Xavier in the production of black pharmacists.

This case history exemplifies the kind and quality of success that an institution can achieve in the recruitment, enrollment, and graduation of pharmacy students in a pluralistic environment if the commitment and necessary resources are present. What happens at Xavier in the training of minority students in pharmacy, is, of course, repeated at Howard, Florida A & M, and Texas Southern universities in the production of blacks in pharmacy. Full access of outsiders to pharmacy education will only be achieved when the traditionally white institutions operate sound programs for expanding equal educational opportunity.

Notes

1. During the 1960s, the American Association of Colleges of Pharmacy urged its member institutions to accelerate access of minority students in schools of pharmacy.
2. Shirley M. Malcom et al., Programs in Science for Minority Students: 1960–75 (Washington, D.C.: American Association for the Advancement of Science, 1976), p. 21-22.
3. Ibid.
4. See Jack E. Orr, "Report on Enrollment in Schools and Colleges of Pharmacy, First Semester, Term, or Quarter, 1972–73", American Journal of Pharmaceutical Education 36 (1972) 138ff; and the same reports for 1973–74, and 1974–75.
5. Abstracted from the Inventory submitted by the University of Georgia.
6. Ibid.
7. Abstracted from the Inventory submitted by the University of Florida.
8. Abstracted from the Inventory submitted by the University of Maryland.
9. Ibid.
10. Abstracted from the Inventory submitted by the University of Wisconsin.
11. Ibid.
12. Ibid.
13. Ibid.
14. Orr, "Report on Enrollment," 1971–72.
15. Ibid.
16. Ibid., 1972–73.
17. John Schlegel, Graduate Enrollment Report, Fall, 1976. (Bethesda, Md.: American Association of Colleges of Pharmacy, n.d.), p. 3.
18. Orr, "Report on Enrollment," p. 1201.
19. Ibid.

20. John Schlegel *et al., Report of Fall Undergraduate Enrollment in Schools and Colleges of Pharmacy* (Bethesda, Md.: American Association of Colleges of Pharmacy, August 1975), p. 3 and Table IX.

21. Bart M. Speedie, "Enrollment Report on Professional Degree Programs, Fall 1980," *American Journal of Pharmaceutical Education* 45 (1981): 400.

22. Steven H. Chasin, "Enrollment Report on First Professional Degree Program, Fall 1983," *American Journal of Pharmaceutical Education* 47 (1983): 275.

23. Orr, "Report on Enrollment," 1971–72.

24. AACP, *Impact of the President's 1985 Budget on Pharmacy Student Financial Aid* (March 8, 1984), p.1.

25. Martin I. Blake's and Jack Orr's reports on "Graduate Enrollment Data" for 1969–70, 1972–73. Both are published in the *American Journal of Pharmaceutical Education.* The respective volumes are 35 (February 1971): 108–127; 37 (February 1973): 138–153.

26. Orr, "Graduate Enrollment Data, 1973–74," *American Journal of Pharmaceutical Education* 38.

27. John Schlegel and Christopher A. Rodowskas, *Enrollment Report of Professional Degree Programs in Pharmacy, Fall 1975* Bethesda, Md.: American Association of Colleges of Pharmacy, August 1976), pp. 1–5 and Tables IV and VII.

28. Ibid.

29. American Association of Colleges of Pharmacy, *Graduate Enrollment Report, Fall, 1978.*

30. Ibid.

31. Ibid.

32. The data in this section are based on reports made available by officials of Xavier University of Louisiana College of Pharmacy in a communication dated February 8, 1980, and 1984–85 interviews with Dean Marcellus Grace.

9 BLACKS IN VETERINARY
MEDICINE

The history of black students in veterinary medical education is a study
of neglect, limited interest, and institutional inaction. Of all the professional areas analyzed in this study, veterinary medicine is among the least
successful in attracting black Americans. Were it not for the systematic
recruitment efforts and demonstrated commitment to enrolling and producing black veterinary medical students evidenced at Tuskegee Institute,
there would be almost no progress made by blacks in this field. In recent
years, however, a significant proportion of the 27 schools and colleges of
veterinary medicine in the United States have organized recruitment programs. Consequently, some of the responsibility for veterinary medical
education of black students has shifted away from Tuskegee Institute.
Nevertheless, a lion's share of that responsibility continues to rest with the
College of Veterinary Medicine at historically black Tuskegee Institute in
Alabama.

This chapter draws attention to the pioneer role of Tuskegee Institute
in training black veterinarians. It examines recruitment practices and
enrollment trends in the 1970s and 1980s. It describes admissions criteria.
Further, it identifies some of the persistent problems frequently associated
with failure of the profession to attract more black Americans to it. Finally,
it focuses attention on some of the concrete efforts to alleviate the problems
of neglect and the underrepresentation of blacks in veterinary medicine.

Tuskegee Institute: Pioneer in Veterinary Medicine

The College of Veterinary Medicine at Tuskegee Institute was established in 1945. Since that year, Tuskegee has graduated approximately
85% of all black veterinarians (holders of the Doctor of Veterinary
Medicine [D.V.M.] degree) in the United States. When this college was
established, minorities were not generally accepted in veterinary medical
programs throughout the U.S. as a consequence of prevailing discriminatory, legal, and social practices and exclusionary educational policies. A
few northern and western institutions admitted a token number of black
students to their programs in agriculture, animal science, and veterinary
medicine.

208

The School of Veterinary Medicine at Tuskegee was founded to assure access of black and other minority-group students to a profession that had not demonstrated any interest in them. From its inception, the school was regional in scope. In addition to the state of Alabama, it recruited minority students from 12 southern states that operated dual, segregated systems of education mandated by state law. Tuskegee admitted white students to its school of veterinary medicine. This act reflected the institution's policy of providing a multiracial student body and pluralistic learning environment for all its students. Consequently, this school of veterinary medicine is the most racially and ethnically integrated school of veterinary medicine in the entire Western Hemisphere.

As a result of its sustained commitment to black Americans, minority students of this and other nations, and disadvantaged students in general, it was estimated in 1974 that of the 400 black veterinarians then in the U.S., who represented 1.3% of the total number of veterinarians, 93% of them were Tuskegee graduates.[1]

Recruitment at Tuskegee[2]

The recruitment program at Tuskegee can serve as a model for successful recruitment for all professional schools and colleges. Its motivating force is a firm, unswerving commitment to provide greater access and equality of opportunity in veterinary medicine. Over the years, recruitment at Tuskegee was predicated on four basic assumptions:

1. There is a dearth in career opportunity information regarding the profession readily available to members of minority groups.

2. There is limited knowledge about the profession of veterinary medicine and a lack of identification with the profession by members of minority groups. This situation of limited knowledge and low identification is a function of the apparent and real underrepresentation of minority groups in the profession. This paucity, in turn, reduces the chances that minority youth will have meaningful interactions with possible role models with whom they can identify or who may influence their aspirations and occupational choices.

3. There is a lack of an organized recruitment program among other schools and colleges of veterinary medicine that could substantially increase the number of black and other minority students in the field or that would offset active recruitment programs initiated and conducted by other professional and occupational groups, and

4. There is a lack of information on financial aid programs available to minority students, as well as inadequate understanding among some institutions about the extensiveness of the need of these students for financial assistance to support their educational pursuits.

Recruitment programs conducted before 1970 were largely supported from university funds. Because Tuskegee Institute is a state-assisted institution with academic programs generally characteristic of a comprehensive university, it has had to be particularly cautious in the allocation of its limited financial resources. Consequently, recruitment was not as extensive as desired as the 1970s began. Those efforts that were undertaken generated approximately 60 to 65 applications from minority students per year.

In 1971 the College of Veterinary Medicine received a recruitment grant from the U.S. Department of Health, Education, and Welfare. The three basic objectives of this grant were (1) to establish a recruitment program specifically designed to search for, identify, and encourage qualified minority-group members to seek admission and, ultimately, to be enrolled in schools of veterinary medicine; (2) to provide financial aid for a limited number of those students who enrolled in order to enable them to pursue a career in veterinary medicine, and (3) to assist these students in their efforts to achieve career objectives by means of a highly structured academic reinforcement program. The objectives were explicit in pointing to the intention of recruiting students who not only sought admission to Tuskegee but who may have desired to enroll in other schools of veterinary medicine.

Another grant was obtained in 1975, which allowed the institution to expand its recruitment efforts and develop additional recruitment strategies. The staff included 4 part-time positions, one materials specialist, one full-time photographer, and one coordinator-secretary. In addition, its 14 full-time faculty and its staff and students committed themselves to play an active role in the recruitment process.

Activities involved in the recruitment process included the following:

1. Preparation of brochures, slide shows, and other materials for distribution to students, alumni, and recruiters. These materials were utilized to heighten minority students' understanding of the profession of veterinary medicine.

2. Visits to 75 campuses of historically black colleges and to high schools that enrolled significant numbers of minority students.

3. Presentation of exhibits on veterinary medicine that showed minority-student activities, at conventions of minority groups, state guidance and personal conferences.

4. Sponsorship of two minority Recruitment Workshops (each of 2 days duration) attended by representatives from all schools of veterinary medicine, the National Urban League (which sponsors a Street Academy program involving a substantial proportion of minority-group students); recruitment organizations; colleges, and high schools. Workshop participants discussed methods and techniques for attracting minority-group

students to the veterinary medicine profession. Each institution shared its experiences in the development of a recruitment strategy and problems encountered in their individual efforts to enroll more minority students.

5. Continuing linkages established between Tuskegee and such organizations as the National Urban League, committed to expanding educational opportunities in the profession for minority and disadvantaged students. The Urban League became a major facilitator of Tuskegee's recruitment drive by its dissemination of Tuskegee's film *Because We Care* to members of its 100 affiliates and educational directors.

6. Recruitment of Upward Bound Students in summer programs on the campus of Tuskegee Institute into the pre-veterinary medicine program of the college.

7. Sponsorship of a Health/Science Career Motivation Fair on the campus. High school students from surrounding counties who were interested in health-career professions were invited to campus and to exhibit their own science work during the fair. Opportunities in the health professions were explored.

8. Linkages with regional and national programs of the State Guidance and Personnel Association and the American Guidance and Personnel Association were both established and strengthened through exhibits at their annual regional and national conferences. Meetings were held with high school counselors and advisers to acquaint them with the field.

9. Information dissemination activities including exhibits on veterinary medicine at national, annual, and local conferences of the National Association for the Advancement of Colored People (NAACP), National Urban League, Shriners, and South Alabama State Fair.

10. News releases to the hometown newspapers of first- and fourth-year students. The purpose of these news releases is to inform local residents of the students' enrollment in the School of Veterinary Medicine as well as to make known the completion of all degree requirements. This is one method of establishing role models in the local community and familiarizing local high school students with the profession of veterinary medicine.

11. The utilization of Tuskegee's film *Because We Care* in recruitment. The importance of the film is multifaceted. For one thing, it portrays the overall educational programs and student life at Tuskegee. It also depicts black students and faculty at work in the School of Veterinary Medicine. In this way it has the impact of demonstrating to students that a full range of educational opportunities with minority-faculty role models are available to them at the institution. And, finally, the film educates students specifically about veterinary medicine as a profession.

12. Establishment of linkages between the School of Veterinary Medicine and science departments of historically black colleges in the development of a "feeder program." By visiting faculty members in such

departments as biology, chemistry, physics, general science, and agriculture, as well as placement officials, their assistance is enlisted in the recruitment process by encouraging them to point to the option of veterinary medicine as a career choice.

13. The utilization of television in aiding recruitment. This activity involves several 60-second spots on stations in Birmingham, Montgomery, and Mobile, Alabama, as well as in Columbus, Georgia. It also includes the showing of a 28-minute film about veterinary medicine on public television stations.

14. Exhibits and film showings at the annual meetings of the major black greek letter organizations.

15. Advertisements in publications that have a wide black readership. These include the major publications of the Johnson Publishing Company, such as *Ebony* and *Jet* magazines. One series of advertisements in these magazines generated approximately 1500 inquiries about veterinary medicine.

16. The dissemination of thousands of leaflets and brochures about veterinary medicine to black and other minority students.

17. Involvement of its 90 Alumni chapters in the recruitment program. The veterinary medical alumni association organized its recruitment committee to assist the overall recruitment activities of the School of Veterinary Medicine. These chapters participate in high school Career Day programs and develop their own special sources to acquaint students with the profession. In so doing, they provide instant role models of the possibilities of success in a career in veterinary medicine.

18. A quarterly newsletter about activities in the School of Veterinary Medicine is mailed to all veterinary alumni, parents of students enrolled in the school, Tuskegee Institute general national officers and alumni chapter presidents, as well as other schools of veterinary medicine.

19. Travel by its members to make presentations to several private groups sensitive to the need for providing financial aid to exceptionally needy minority students. Among the groups that pledged substantial increases in the level of their donations for scholarships/financial assistance were the Ancient Egyptian Order Nobel of Mystic Shrine, Inc., the Order of Eastern Star, and the National Veterinary Medical Alumni Association.

20. Finally, in 1979, a new career motivational film released by Coca Cola, U.S.A. Since a central focus of this film is the School of Veterinary Medicine at Tuskegee Institute, it is particularly important as a recruitment instrument.

The school also conducts a Summer Enrichment Program through which promising students are brought to the campus for an eight-week period. The program consists of an intensive diagnostic testing phase followed by training in "survival skills." Components of the latter phase include test taking, reading comprehension, study habits, note taking, time budgeting, and attitudinal aspects. Contact is sustained through the pre-veterinary medicine phase so that there will be continuity of contact with these students in all phases of their anticipated career in veterinary medicine. Tutorial and counseling services are provided by faculty and professionals with specializations in program areas.

As previously indicated, the School of Veterinary Medicine co-sponsored minority-recruitment workshops with the National Urban League on the campus of Tuskegee Institute. These workshops served to facilitate an understanding of some of the major impediments in the recruitment of black and other minority students into the profession. They also demonstrated to the representatives of institutions in attendance what the possibilities of success were if they mounted aggressive recruitment programs. As a result of these conferences and the model provided by Tuskegee, the American Veterinary Medical Association (AVMA), through its Council on Education, organized a Committee on Minority Affairs. This committee is supposed to assist member institutions of the Association of American Veterinary Medical Colleges in their recruitment programs.

Under its HEW-sponsored recruitment program, the Council established affiliation with two educational assessment programs, the American College Testing (ACT) Assessment Program and the Students Search Service (SSS) of the College Entrance Examination Board (CEEB). These memberships helped raise the number of minority students in the applicant pool by more than 100 students in a single year.

The Four most tangible results of these recruitment activities are these: (1) The number of applicants to the School of Veterinary Medicine tripled in the early years and has continued on the upswing since the program was initiated; (2) enrollment increased substantially; (3) stronger minority-recruitment activities were stimulated at several schools and colleges of veterinary medicine throughout the nation, and (4) an identifiable recruitment model was established for other institutions to emulate.

Admissions Policy And Practices

Admission to the School of Veterinary Medicine is consistent with the philosophy of the institution's commitment to expand educational opportunities to minority and disadvantaged students. Tuskegee Institute was founded specifically to serve the educational needs of black Americans. Over the years, this commitment embraced disadvantaged students in general, irrespective of race or ethnicity. Consequently, the committee on admissions selects students who exhibit intellectual, personal, moral, and social traits that are considered desirable in a Doctor of Veterinary Medicine (D.V.M.). Selection is based on all data submitted by, and on behalf of, the student, not merely on achievement.

In toto, at least six factors enter into admissions decisions: (1) state of residence, (2) quality of the interview; (3) letters of recommendation; (4) academic trend; (5) individual's expressed reason for selecting veterinary medicine as a profession and commitment to the profession; and (6) overall folder evaluation. Since Tuskegee's School of Veterinary Medicine is a regional school, it has contractual obligations to qualified applicants from participating states. Those students are given the highest priority. Next in priority are individuals from states without a college of veterinary medicine. The lowest priority is given to applicants from states that have a school or college of veterinary medicine.

Enrollment at Tuskegee's School of Veterinary Medicine

Since 1968, the School of Veterinary Medicine (SVM) at Tuskegee has received approximately 6900 applications. The majority of applicants were black but an increasingly large proportion were white, and a substantial number were from the Caribbean Islands and West Africa. The college enrolls more Caribbean students in veterinary medicine than any other institution in the mainland U.S. Since 1970, the SVM has increased its space for entering professional students (D.V.M. students) from 37 to 60 a year. The number of applications to Tuskegee increased significantly during the mid-1980s. For example, for the 1984–85 academic year, 412 applications were formally received and processed by the Committee on Veterinary Admissions. One hundred of those applicants were interviewed. The 412 applicants represented a 5% increase over the number received at Tuskegee for the 1983–84 academic year. In effect, the SVM received about 7 applications for every space available in the entering class.

The 1984–85 applicants consisted of 129 black Americans (32%), 242 whites (59%), 1 Native American (Indian), 13 foreign black persons, and 23 applicants from Puerto Rico. Applicants came from Alabama, 12 states that have contracts with Tuskegee, 30 nonregional states, and 5 foreign countries. They included 225 (55%) regional applicants, 174 (43%) nonregional applicants, and 9 (2%) foreign applicants from contract countries.

Black student enrollment at Tuskegee continued to grow throughout the 1970s and 1980s. This growth can be attributed to the successful and aggressive recruitment program conducted by the SVM, the active participation of Tuskegee alumni in the recruitment process, the visibility of black role models at Tuskegee, and the fact that black applicants may feel that the receptivity to black students and the learning environment offered by the school are much more suitable and hospitable than that envisioned at schools of veterinary medicine that do not have even token enrollments of black students. A case in point may be illustrated by nearby Auburn University, which in 1985 had only one black student in its School of Veterinary Medicine. According to informants, this student represents the only black student ever enrolled for a professional degree at Auburn in the history of its veterinary medicine program.

In general, black students constitute approximately two-thirds of the first-year students at the SVM. The white student enrollment about doubled between 1970 and 1979; since that time, white student enrollment has hovered about 30% in each first-year class. Foreign students constitute from 3 to 5% of first-year enrollment. Again, these students are drawn primarily from the Caribbean and West Africa (see Table 45).

Graduation

Since 1969, some 649 students have received the Doctor of Veterinary Medicine (D.V.M.) degree from Tuskegee Institute. Of these graduates, 434 are black and other minorities. Black graduates from Tuskegee are approximately 85% of black D.V.M. graduates in the United States.

Table 45
First-Year Enrollment, Tuskegee School of Veterinary Medicine, 1970–1984

Academic Year	Black Students		White Students		Other Students		Total
	N	%	N	%	N	%	N
1984–85	N.A.	N.A.	N.A.	N.A.	N.A.	N.A.	N.A.
1983–84	N.A.	N.A.	N.A.	N.A.	N.A.	N.A.	N.A.
1982–83	N.A.	N.A.	N.A.	N.A.	N.A.	N.A.	N.A.
1981–82	N.A.	N.A.	N.A.	N.A.	N.A.	N.A.	N.A.
1980–81	N.A.	N.A.	N.A.	N.A.	N.A.	N.A.	N.A.
1979–80	N.A.	N.A.	N.A.	N.A.	N.A.	N.A.	N.A.
1978–79	39	65.0	19	31.7	2	3.3	60
1977–78	34	68.0	16	32.0	0	N.A.	50
1976–77	31	68.9	14	31.0	N.A.	N.A.	45
1975–76	30	66.7	15	33.0	N.A.	N.A.	45
1974–75	29	64.4	16	35.6	N.A.	N.A.	45
1973–74	29	64.4	16	35.6	N.A.	N.A.	45
1972–73	29	65.9	14	31.8	N.A.	N.A.	44
1971–72	30	71.4	12	28.6	N.A.	N.A.	42
1970–71	27	73.0	10	27.0	N.A.	N.A.	37

Source: Dr. Ellis Hall of Tuskegee School of Veterinary Medicine.
N.A = Not available.

A total of 63 females were D.V.M. recipients from Tuskegee between 1969 and 1970. Between 1979 and 1985, female students received 151 D.V.M. degrees there, or 47.3% of the entire number of D.V.M. degrees conferred by the institution. Forty-one women or 65% of the 63 recipients between 1969 and 1979, were black, and 18 (28%) were white. Of the 151 female graduates between 1979 and 1985, 84 (52%) were black, and 50 (33%) were white. The increasing number of women in graduating classes of veterinary schools is consistent with trends observed in other health sciences fields, such as medicine, dentistry, optometry, and pharmacy (see Table 46).

Table 46
Number of D.V.M. Degrees Awarded by Tuskegee Institute, 1969–1985

Year	Total Degrees Awarded	Race Black			White			Other		
		T	M	F	T	M	F	T	M	F
1985	52	25	12	13	12	3	9	15	11	4
1984	51	23	9	14	16	9	7	12	8	4
1983	55	27	11	16	21	12	9	7	5	2
1982	50	25	13	12	19	11	8	6	4	2
1981	44	22	10	12	16	8	8	6	6	0
1980	42	21	11	10	16	10	6	5	4	1
1979	46	24	10	12	15	12	3	7	7	0
1978*	39	24			15					
1977	38	22			16					
1976	40	26			14					
1975	33	21			12					
1974	39	22	NO DATA		17			NO DATA		
1973	16	10			6					
1972	27	21			6					
1971	24	19			5					
1970	23	18			5					
1969*	30	26			4					
Total	649	376			215					
		(57.9%)			(33.2%)					

Source: Dr. Ellis Hall, Tuskegee Institute, School of Veterinary Medicine.
*Gender distribution unavailable for years between 1969 and 1978.

Although Tuskegee Institute produces about 30 black graduates with D.V.M. degrees yearly, that number still constitutes in excess of three-fourths of all black D.V.M. graduates per year. Data generated by AAVMC

Committee on Minority Affairs in response to a 1984 survey of the 27 schools of veterinary medicine revealed that 5 of the institutions did not have a single black student or member of any other minority group in the 1985 graduating class. Two institutions had 1 graduate; 10 institutions had 2; 2 institutions had 3; and 5 institutions reported that from 4 to 7 minorities students would receive the D.V.M. degree in their 1985 class. One institution expected 11 graduates; and one institution, Tuskegee Institute, anticipated that 40 minority students would be in the 1985 class. A major problem seems to exist with respect to how the concept "minority" is applied; that is, who actually constitutes a member of minority group? Because of loose interpretations of that term, the precise number of traditional minority groups (e.g., Blacks, Hispanics, Asians, Native Americans) may be overreported by some institutions. However, at Tuskegee Institute, only those groups usually categorized as minorities are so counted.

Financial Aid

Like students who enroll at Xavier University's College of Pharmacy, the majority of Tuskegee's students in veterinary medicine are from economically disadvantaged families. They require financial assistance to assure their continued matriculation in the institution. This need is substantially more critical in the 1980s, since the basic yearly tuition rose from $1400 in 1975 to $4800 in 1984, and Reagan administration budget cuts have reduced aid. Since approximately 85% of all students require some form of financial assistance, the institution provides as much help as possible from institutional funds. In addition, students may receive assistance through such federal programs as Pell Grants, BEOGs, SEOGs, NDSLs, GSLs, work- study programs, and health-profession scholarships and loans. Many students are hesitant to borrow through the HEAL program because of the enormously high interest rates associated with those loans. However, Tuskegee graduates have been the most responsible of all borrowers of HEAL funds in the nation. In 1984, according to information provided in an interview with Dr. Ellis Hall, that institution had the highest repayment record of all institutions in the United States.

Impact of the *Bakke* Decision

The *Bakke* decision has not had a measurable impact on recruitment and enrollment at Tuskegee Institute. Its program in the School of Veterinary Medicine is consistent with the spirit of the decision by the U.S. Supreme Court in the *Bakke* case, especially regarding opportunities for disadvantaged students regardless of race or ethnicity. It should be reiterated that the *Bakke* decision could serve as an impetus for the recruitment of black and other minority students. This is especially critical since the "race" variable may legally be taken into consideration, under certain circumstances, when making admissions decisions. On the other hand, the *Bakke* decision may also provide a shield for institutions that do not wish to increase minority representation or even include a minority students presence of any dimension. Tuskegee Institute is not one of the latter institutional types, since it is the most thoroughly integrated school of veterinary medicine in this hemisphere. It should be apparent to the reader that the case history of its School of Veterinary Medicine clearly exemplifies the type of progress that is achievable when an institution organizes a sound recruitment program, demonstrates a strong commitment to its objectives, and provides leadership and support for it.

The enrollment data at Tuskegee provide ample support for the hypothesis that the presence of a significant or critical mass of black students in graduate and professional schools is positively correlated with the presence of role models on the faculty. There are 14 black and other minorities on the faculty of the School of Veterinary Medicine. Students see them in action during recruitment, in films about the institution, in their daily work on the campus, in interaction with students of all races, and in leadership positions in the institution. That kind of visibility is a major inducement to go into the profession, since it heightens the level of students' aspiration for a career in a field in which a member of their own racial or ethnic group has achieved notable success.

The graduation data provides substantial support for the contention that the availability of an adequate program of academic and nonacademic support services enhances retention and reduces attrition among students enrolled in a graduate or professional school. Although no data on utilization characteristics are available, impressionistic evidence leads to the conclusion that the availability of organized tutorials, study groups, faculty willing to offer assistance without demeaning the student's capabilities, and on overall positive learning environment are highly salient dimensions of a retention program. All these factors contribute in some way to the retention of students through the completion of their program.

Desegregation Trends

It is estimated that there were 38,000 holders of the Doctor of Veterinary Medicine in the United States in 1985. Of that number, about 800 are black, representing 2.1% of the total number. Whereas in 1974 it was estimated that 93% of 400 black American veterinarians had received their

D.V.M. degree from Tuskegee, that proportion in 1985 stood at or about 80%. This change reflects a small but increasing presence of black students in the remaining 26 schools of veterinary medicine in the United States, which are located at Auburn University, University of California/Davis, Colorado State University, Cornell University, University of Florida, University of Georgia, University of Illinois, Iowa State University, Kansas State University, Louisiana State University, Michigan State University, University of Minnesota, Mississippi State University, University of Missouri, North Carolina State University, Ohio State University, Oklahoma A & M University, Oregon State University, Pennsylvania State University, Purdue University, University of Tennessee, Texas A & M University, Tufts University, Virginia–Maryland Regional College, Washington State University, and University of Wisconsin.

Eight of these institutions have come into existence since 1972, and some have only recently graduated their first class of students. Twelve "*Adams* states" (formerly and currently in litigation) are represented in the group of 27 institutions with schools or colleges of veterinary medicine. The only "*Adams* States" not included here are Arkansas, Delaware, South Carolina, and West Virginia.

Role Of Associations

Compared to other professional organizations, such as the Association of American Medical Colleges, Schools of Law, or Dental Schools, the organizations affiliated with or which accredit schools or colleges of veterinary medicine have been particularly conservative in actively supporting minority-group students. Neither the American Veterinary Medical Association (AVMA) nor the American Association of Veterinary Medical Colleges (AAVMC) has even endorsed a policy statement comparable to the type issued by the Association of American Medical Colleges or the Association of American Schools of Law. The policy statements issued by the latter organizations formally committed their members to increasing their individual and collective efforts to bring black Americans and other minority students into the mainstream of medical and legal education. The lack of pronounced and sustained organizational leadership, which is so essential in speeding up the process of access to equal opportunity in veterinary medical education, helps account for the dearth of aggressive recruitment programs by schools and colleges of veterinary medicine.[3] Hence, some colleges of veterinary medicine reportedly have never enrolled and graduated a black student in their entire history.

This is not to minimize those actions taken by the AAVMC and the AVMA from which minority students have benefitted. In fact, some efforts were indeed initiated during the 1970s in minority recruitment, but the results of these actions fell considerably short of expectations. In the main, it appears that the AVMA was instrumental in facilitating increased visibility of minority recruitment efforts. This effort was primarily in publications about programs in veterinary medical education. It provided a placement service for graduating veterinarians, but its main responsibility lies in the roles it performs as the accreditation body for the schools and colleges of veterinary medicine in the United States and Canada. Through its Council on Education, it considers minority recruitment and other issues relating to the access of minority students to the profession.

Representatives from the American Veterinary Medical Association attended both the 1974 and 1975 Minority Recruitment Conferences at Tuskegee Institute. An expression of commitment to minority concerns was articulated by its representatives. However, it is not clear how that commitment was translated into enduring, influential, significant, viable programmatic actions that lead to major changes in the rate of enrollment of black students to schools and colleges of veterinary medicine.

One of the resolutions the conference proposed in 1975 was that a Minority Affairs Committee be established to deal with the broad problems of access, enrollment, and retention. Such a committee was formed under the ultimate responsibility of the American Association of Veterinary Medical Colleges. The same conference proposed that both the AVMA and the AAVMC waive the residency requirements for admission in all states. This proposal was prompted by the realization that enforcement of residency requirements was a major impediment to successful recruitment of black and other minority students. Similarly, participants agreed that these organizations should obtain "a commitment from veterinary colleges to admit a given number of minority students." Informants report that compliance to these recommendations was threefold. First, the AAVMC did establish a Committee on Minority Affairs. Second, some states relaxed state residency requirements, but others maintain rigid state residency selection and admissions requirements in the mid-1980s. Third, the AVMA continues to include minorities in some of its public relations materials and brochures, and in the film *The Covenant*.

In 1978, following the U.S. Supreme Court decision in the *Bakke* case, the Association of American Veterinary Medical Colleges co-sponsored a workshop conference on Minority Representation in Veterinary Medicine in Washington, D.C. The conference focused on such issues as the legal implications of the *Bakke* decision for minority-student recruitment, the failure of the profession of veterinary medicine to attract black and other minority students, recruitment, admissions, and retention.

One of the most salient conclusions reached by the conference participants was the acknowledgement that "recruitment is a passive activity" at several schools and colleges of veterinary medicine.[5] Since the schools of veterinary medicine have traditionally tended "to act independently and in isolation," they have not developed organized, systematic, and aggressive recruitment strategies learned from the experiences or the successes of other institutions. The passive recruitment stance, it was reported, originates in the perception that the profession of veterinary medicine is free of discrimination.[6] Many persons, both members and nonmembers of the profession, do *not* accept the idea that it is discrimination free.

The participants recognized the tremendous value in the presence of role models on the faculty of colleges of veterinary medicine. That importance is twofold. It provides evidence of the success possibilities for minorities in veterinary medicine. It also creates a more pluralistic and diverse faculty for the benefit of all students in the institution.

Attention was given to actions that may discriminate against minority students and consequently serve as a barrier to their enrollment. Among these were such things as (1) excessive weights given to standardized tests; (2) high value placed on the grade point average (GPA), (3) intimidation and cold indifference that sometimes occur during the interview process, (4) misunderstandings and misinterpretations of behavior that may result from poor interviews; and (5) the rigidity of admissions requirements in some institutions.[7]

Consideration was given to the thesis that retention is, indeed, a multifaceted phenomenon. As such, it involves at least three aspects: academic factors, financial resources, and the sociocultural environment in which learning takes place.[8]

Among the major recommendations made at this conference and which were to have been sent to all college deans and to the president of the AAVMC were the following: (1) a National Coordinator of Minority Affairs should be appointed; (2) each school or college of veterinary medicine should appoint at minimum a part-time Coordinator of Minority Affairs; (3) the meetings of the AAVMC Committee on Minority Affairs should be institutionalized and regularized; (4) stronger linkages should be established between all parties who have responsibilities for recruitment and admissions; (5) an examination of admissions procedures and the elimination of all those that lead to discrimination; and (6) decision makers in the admissions process should have a working understanding of the *Bakke* decision and its impact on institutional policies and practices. In addition, comparative data on admissions and recruitment, covering the years 1976, 1977, and 1978, were to be distributed with the Conference Report.[9]

A National Coordinator of Minority Affairs was never appointed. Several colleges of veterinary medicine either appointed a local minority coordinator or expressed intention to draw more heavily on university-wide minority affairs offices. Some institutions are taking a more holistic view of the applicants' portfolio when making assessments and rendering admissions decisions.

Recruitment of black students in historically white schools and colleges of veterinary medicine has indeed been hampered by the lack of knowledge among black youth concerning the profession. However, that is probably neither the sole nor the primary explanation for their under-representation in these institutions. That situation is undoubtedly more accurately attributed to the quality of recruitment programs at these institutions. Some institutions have no active recruitment program. Others are rather passive in their efforts. Few employ full-time recruitment staff. Often, recruitment programs that are initiated are not sustained for an appreciable period of time. Failure to continue follow-up efforts after visits to recruitment sites does not enhance those steps taken to increase minority enrollment in veterinary medical colleges.[10]

Ten of the 27 colleges of veterinary medicine completed the inventory employed in this study. Among these institutions, recruitment activities included (1) the development of informational materials (e.g., pamphlets, brochures,) for use during recruitment drives; (2) mailings of informational materials to junior and senior high school students; (3) visits to junior and senior high schools to participate in Career Day activities; (4) participation in college fairs on campus and in high schools; (5) visits to predominantly black colleges; (6) the use of alumni in recruiting; (7) the participation of faculty members in visits to other campuses and in on-campus recruitment programs which sometimes include workshops and contact with students enrolled in other science programs; (8) banquets for pre-veterinary medicine students and tours of campus facilities in veterinary colleges; and (9) the use of Tuskegee's mailing list of prospective candidates for admission into veterinary medical colleges.

The only additional recruitment strategy employed by institutions that did not respond to our mailed inventory but that was listed elsewhere was summer employment with practicing veterinarians. This technique provides firsthand knowledge of some of the daily activities of veterinarians and may stimulate greater interest in the profession.[11] Irrespective of the strategy employed, the crucial variable appears to be the strength of the commitment of the institution and its faculty and staff, as measured by the support of recruitment programs through adequate finance and with the employment of minority-group role models. Without these, it is apparent that the recruitment of black students and other minorities is doomed to failure at the onset.

A survey conducted in 1984 by the AAVMC Committee on Minority Affairs revealed that 77.8% of the 27 colleges of veterinary medicine stated that a minority recruitment officer had been hired. However, almost three-fourths of the institutions had no budget item specifically designated to support that office. In fact, colleges were extremely reluctant to indicate the amount of such funds budgeted for minority recruitment. Of the institutions that indicated the existence of such a budget item, the amount set aside for minority recruitment ranged from $2500 to $120,000. Four institutions reported funds of less than $20,000 per year for this purpose. The paucity of recruitment funds appears commensurate with the lack of aggressive recruitment programs.

While more than half the institutions did not enlist the assistance of such well-known groups as the NAACP and the National Urban League in their efforts to attract minority students, 85% said that recruitment was focused on service groups, such as the Scouts. Further, almost all institutions reported participating in Career Day activities at the high school and college levels as components of the recruitment program. More than half indicated that their minority recruitment program did not involve coordinated efforts with recruitment activities in other health-profession schools. Finally, slightly more that one-third of the institutions reported that they were current recipients of extramural funds to be utilized for recruitment and retention of minority students (see Table 47). One item that is not reflected in Table 47 is the fact that one-third of the instituitions had not even applied for such funds during the year prior to the initiation of the survey.

Although these data do show some degree of sensitivity toward a need to accelerate efforts to attract increasing numbers of minority students into veterinary medicine, it is equally apparent that resistance to such programs is pervasive in some institutions. That resistance plus limited budgetary support for minority recruitment efforts help account for the fact that blacks continue to represent only about 2.3% of students applying for the D.V.M. degree in the United States. Consequently, veterinary medicine lags behind all professions in the recruitment and matriculation of black students, even in 1987.

Admissions Criteria

Although admissions requirements vary from institution to institution, there are also similarities between them. One similarity is the lack of "special admissions programs." Another is the institutions' reliance on cognitive and noncognitive (subjective) criteria. The weight assigned to cognitive or traditional factors appears to be contingent on the number of applications received by the institution in relation to available space in the first-year class. Moreover, as the level of competition for limited space rises, one may normally expect stronger reliance on objective measures, since

Table 47
Recruitment Activities, Colleges of Veterinary Medicine, 1984

| | | Presence in Vet Med Colleges | | | |
| | | Yes | | No | |
	Activity	N	%	N	%
1.	College has formal minority recruitment officer	21	77.8	6	22.2
2.	Budget item specifically earmarked for minority recruitment	7	25.9	20	74.1
3.	Recruitment funds available from other budget items	21	77.8	6	22.2
4.	Recruitment involves active aid of external agencies (NAACP, National Urban League)	12	44.4	15	55.6
5.	Recruitment includes participation in high school Career Day programs	26	96.3	1	3.7
6.	Recruitment includes participation in college Career Days	27	100.0	0	0
7.	Recruitment includes minority-specific information	19	70.4	8	29.6
8.	Recruitment includes outreach activities with service groups for minority recruiting	23	85.2	4	14.8
9.	Recruitment involves participation in coordinated minority-recruitment programs with other health professions schools	13	48.1	14	51.9
10.	Current recipient of extramural funds for recruitment and retention of minority students	10	37.0	17	62.3

Source: AAVMC Committee on Minority Affairs, April 23, 1985.

quantifiable data permit cutoff points that may be defended more easily when selection and admissions decisions are called into question.

The College of Veterinary Medicine at the University of Illinois, for instance, announced in its applicant information bulletin for 1980–1981 that there have been "approximately 400 qualified applicants" for the 91 available spaces in the college. Consequently, even if a person completed minimum academic requirements, admission to the college of veterinary medicine was not assured. This college reported a mean GPA of its applicants in recent years to be 4.5 on a 5.0 system. The mean number of credit hours achieved by applicants was 120. This implied that the average applicant was a college graduate. That is significant because it is possible, though increasingly unlikely, for a person to be admitted after having completed only the two or three years of preprofessional training in a pre-veterinary medical program.

Selection criteria at colleges of veterinary medicine usually include (1) college GPA; (2) scores on the Veterinary Aptitude test (VAT); and (3) state residency requirements. Other factors utilized are (4) letters of recommendation; (5) an interview at the college of veterinary medicine; and (6) motivation for a career in veterinary medicine. Some institutions look for the GPA in required science courses, performance on the Graduate Record Examination (GRE); the GRE-Advanced Biology score, animal experience, contact with veterinarians, extracurricular activities, job experiences, leadership ability, effectiveness in communicating with others, maturity, and reliability.

The GPA expected varies from a C+ to a B+ average. VAT scores usually range from 75 to 80%. However, it appears that the heaviest weighting of all traditional factors is assigned to the GPA. Several institutions reported a tendency to deemphasize objective criteria in recent years, to look more toward evidence of personal development, and to place such factors, as GPA, VAT, or GRE test scores in a more balanced relationship to the noncognitive factors employed in selection and admission decisions.

Some institutions have a definite point system that is utilized in determining crucial aspects of eligibility. Under one system, a maximum score of 70% is given to academic criteria and 30% of points are assigned to nonacademic factors. In other instances, each selection category is assigned a maximum of 15 points. A composite score is determined by the total points accumulated in each category. In another institution, a maximum of 55 points may be awarded for objective criteria, while the remaining 45 points are assigned to subjective factors included in the overall evaluation.

Bonus points may be given to an applicant for certain "ancillary factors." Such factors may include quality of course load or taking an extraordinarily heavy course schedule for an extended period of time. On the other hand, bonus points may be awarded minority students as a method of eliminating test bias. Consequently, the number of bonus, or special, points allowed may be equivalent to the value assigned to aptitude test scores.

The majority of these institutions were also reported to have had black faculty involved in the recruitment, selection, and admissions processes or in one or all of these stages.

Each institution reported a strong desire to enroll many more minority students. Each maintained that lack of success arises from the competition for the better-trained black students from other science professions. In effect, these institutions admit that they have not been successful in their overall recruitment program or in attracting blacks to veterinary medicine.

Neverthelesss, there is some general evidence that heavy reliance on high GPAs and high VAT or GRE test scores has indeed militated against the selection of larger numbers of black and other minority students. It may very well be that in the future, as these colleges reexamine their selection and admissions criteria, they will readjust the points assigned to objective and subjective factors in such a manner as to reduce the hasty elimination of otherwise promising students.

The situation with respect to rigid employment of objective admissions criteria was relaxed to some degree during the late 1970s and early 1980s. Between 1976 and 1983, for instance, colleges of veterinary medicine experienced a somewhat alarming decline in applicants. The Tasker Report to the AAVMC indicated that applications dropped from 11,521 in 1976 to 8074 in 1983, Simultaneously, the "accept rate" was rising during that period. For example, the percentage of applicants accepted rose from 30.4% to 39.8% between 1980 and 1983. However, while applications from white students declined, applications from black and Hispanic students rose steadily during that period. Black applicants rose from 2.1% to 2.6% of all applicants to U.S. schools of veterinary medicine between 1981 and 1983.[12] Nevertheless, fewer than 200 black students were enrolled in these institutions in mid-1985.

This national decline in applications to veterinary medicine schools may be attributed to such factors as competition from other science fields, such as computer science and engineering; the possibility of market saturation in the field or an oversupply of veterinarians in the U.S.; and reactions to perceptions of veterinary schools as rigidly selective, since space was traditionally at a premium. As a result of this loss of applicants, many institutions registered serious reservations about their abilities to be as highly selective in their admissions policies as had been the case during the 1970s. One consequence of this decline in applications could eventually be an expansion of opportunities for interested black students who are well qualified but who may have eschewed careers in this field because of the hostile, indifferent, or antiblacks reputation of some colleges of veterinary medicine. This situation, then, may cause any number of institutions to reassess their positions with respect to black and other minority students in order to maintain reasonable enrollments.

Enrollment

Before 1975, the schools and colleges of veterinary medicine reported data about enrollment to the AAVMC that were disaggregated by race and ethnicity. Thereafter, and until 1980, for unclear reasons, institutions not only reported aggregated data on "minorities" but the institutions were scrambled by alphabetical designations, which changed year after year. Consequently it was not possible to discern institutional enrollment data from the files of the AAVMC without a key. That was not available (see Table 48). This decision imperils efforts to engage in research on veterinary medicine that requires ethnic data.

According to Table 48, total black student enrollment in the combined schools and colleges of veterinary medicine declined slightly between 1969 and 1972. However, the significant increase observed first in 1973 has continued. From 1970 to 1974, over 90% of all black students in veterinary medicine were enrolled at Tuskegee Institute. Because of increasing attention given to the recruitment of black and other minority students, this proportion declined to approximately 67.5% in 1985.[13]

Although 12 colleges of veterinary medicine are located in states either currently or formerly covered by the *Adams* litigation, most of these states have not been especially successful in recruiting and matriculating black students. For example, from 1969 to 1979, the University of Georgia enrolled a total of 4 blacks; Ohio State University enrolled 10 but the University of Pennsylvania enrolled 33 minority students. (Inasmuch as this number includes all minority students, the actual number of black students was somewhat fewer.) Between 1973 and 1979, Louisiana State University enrolled 2 black students. Mississippi State University, which opened its College of Veterinary Medicine in 1977, enrolled only 2 black students in two years. The College of Veterinary Medicine at Auburn University has enrolled only 1 black D.V.M. student in its entire history. In 1985, no school of veterinary medicine at a traditionally white institution (TWI) in an "*Adams* state" enrolled black students beyond token numbers.

Since 1978, the number of first-year enrollees in U.S. schools and colleges of veterinary medicine has ranged from 2086 to 2329 (in 1984). The percentage of black students among this group reached its zenith in 1983 when the 63 black first-year matriculants comprised 2.7% of all first-year students. Approximately three-fourths of these black students were registered at Tuskegee Institute.

Between 1971 and 1984, total enrollment in colleges of veterinary medicine rose from 5149 to 8917, a gain of some 2768 students. During the same period; total black student enrollment increased from 96 to 160, a gain of 64 students. However, the percentage of black students in total enrollment in colleges of veterinary medicine actually slipped slightly from 1.9% in 1971 to 1.8% in 1984.

The continued underrepresentation of black students at TWIs is evidenced by the gain of only 6 black registrants in these colleges between 1980 (46 black students) and 1984 (52 black students). Nevertheless, in

Table 48
Total Enrollment in Doctor of Veterinary Medicine Programs,
by Race, 1969–1985, All Institutions Combined[a]

Academic Year	Total Enrollment[b]	Black Students	%	Minority Students	%
1984–85	8917	160	1.8	486	5.5
1983–84	8816	203	2.3	461	5.2
1982–83	8682	161	1.9	426	4.9
1981–82	8447	181	2.1	406	4.8
1980–81	8156	176	2.2	377	4.6
1979–80	7803	N.A.	N.A.	313	4.0
1978–79	7017	—	—	275	3.9
1977–78	7641	—	—	273	3.9
1976–77	6066	—	—	285	4.7
1975–76	7030	—	—	272	3.8
1974–75	6731	121	1.8	141	2.8
1973–74	6408	111	1.7	143	2.2
1972–73	—	90	—	119	—
1971–72	—	90	—	107	—
1970–71	—	91	—	106	—
1969–70	—	92	—	106	—

Source: Dr. Ellis Hall, Tuskegee Institute.
[a]Beginning in 1975, the association began to aggregate all data on minority students; thus ethnic designations were discontinued until 1980.
[b]Includes foreign student enrollment.

1980, Tuskegee Institute, a historically black institution (HBI), accounted for 73.9% of black D.V.M. students. By 1984, its share had dropped to 67.5%. Notwithstanding, the sole HBI with a school of veterinary medicine continues to enroll more black students than all TWIs combined. Therein lies a major failure of TWI schools of veterinary medicine to attract black students beyond a token level, if at all.

The number of minorities in advanced training positions dropped precipitously, from 43 in 1976 to 29 in 1978. This category includes persons seeking other graduate degrees, interns, and residents. In terms of proportions in advanced training, that decline was from 10.7% (of 390) in 1976 to 8.3% (of 359) in 1978.[13]

All the participants in this study indicated interest in enrolling larger numbers of black and other minority students. Only one has definite but minimum enrollment projections mandated by its Boards of Regents, and it is an "*Adams* state." Others do not express goals in numerical terms, while the majority do not have any enrollment goals. Given past experiences that show a clear paucity in number of black students enrolled in veterinary medicine, it seems only logical for schools of veterinary medicine to establish attainable numerical targets or goals for increasing minority student enrollment. This may be the most effective stimulant for concrete action. Ultimately, one outcome may be a more pluralistic and diversified student body as well as greater diversity in the profession itself. It appears that the only effective method for increasing the number of blacks is to target a specific number and direct recruitment toward that goal.

Graduation

Institutional data on graduates from schools and colleges of veterinary medicine are all but impossible to obtain except from cooperating institutions. The HEGIS Reports are of limited value in this regard, for this time period, because in the early years these data were not always disaggregated in the manner required for this analysis. In subsequent years, the data are incomplete. Nevertheless, it can be reported with reasonable confidence that Tuskegee Institute still graduates more than 85% of all black veterinary graduates each year.

Problem Areas

The seven most commonly cited problems regarding underrepresentation of blacks in this profession are (1) the absence of an adequate number of role models; (2) financial aid; (3) limited funding or absence of funding for aggressive recruitment; (4) disinterest of minority students in veterinary medicine; (5) lack of black applicants; (6) competition between the health science areas for the same pool of students, and (7) weak preprofessional training.

Top priority should be given to the recruitment of black faculty members in schools and colleges of veterinary medicine, since their presence has consistently been the most powerful predictor of success in the recruitment and enrollment of black professional students. It is also evident that the larger the number of black faculty members and the more visible they are in recruitment processes, the more successful the institutions are in attracting black students. Tuskegee Institute, as indicated, has more black faculty than any other college or school of veterinary medicine. According to data collected for this study, the following institutions do not have black faculty: Auburn, University of Georgia, Oklahoma State University, Texas A & M University, and the three newest colleges of veterinary medicine:

Tufts University, Virginia Polytechnic and State University, and North Carolina State University. The mean number of black faculty in the remaining schools and colleges of veterinary medicine is one per institution.

Lack of adequate financial aid is another problem that militates against successful recruitment and enrollment. Over half of the veterinary colleges are located in states with high concentration of blacks in the state population. These are also states with high unemployment rates among the black population. High unemployment and comparatively low median family income make it imperative for these students to receive some form of financial aid, even if they enroll in state-supported institutions in which tuition is normally low compared to private institutions.

Unfortunately, scholarships and fellowships are not always available. Of the institutions participating in this study, Ohio State University has had the best record of providing fellowships, scholarships, and teaching assistantships to black students. The number of black student recipients in each of these categories has varied from one to three in each year since 1970. The University of Georgia began to provide two Regent's Scholarships of $5000 each to black students in 1979. Several institutions have now been successful in confronting state legislatures in winning approval to waive residency requirements in order to enhance minority recruitment and, indirectly, assist minority students to overcome the financial barrier to enrollment.

According to AAVMC, the median wage earned by D.V.M.s is about $35,200 per year. This is substantially lower than the median income of physicians, for instance.[15] The veterinarian, too, has to think in terms of the initial costs of private practice, such as the procurement of equipment, facilities, and supplies, and the payment of staff. Even when repayable loans are available, and those loans do not appear to be as readily accessible to veterinarian students as they are to students enrolled in human medicine and dentistry, there is extreme reluctance to subject oneself to long-term indebtedness, especially when the student comes from a relatively poor economic background. This overall dearth of non-repayable loans, scholarships, and teaching assistantships reduces the number of applicants from among otherwise qualified and interested black students.

The "lack of interest" in veterinary medicine by black and other minority students, to which much allusion has been made, is a problem of image of the profession. It also reflects lack of knowledge about the profession and disinterest on the part of white professionals to take the necessary action to alter negative perceptions. Unwillingness to appropriate sufficient funds for the recruitment efforts by interested white faculty at the traditionally white institutions serves only to exacerbate the problem and perpetuate the image, as well as the underrepresentation of blacks and other minorities in veterinary medicine. Medicine, dentistry, and pharmacy will continue to be more successful, regardless of the prestige factor, as long as they provide more resources to attract students. Veterinary medicine must become more competitive, more aggressive, and less conservative in its recruitment programs. In so doing, it can take more concerted action to help strengthen the preprofessional training and preparation received by black and other minority students. Undoubtedly, litigation for inclusion may prove to be another enabling tactic.

Although some of these institutions may have become more skeptical about their activities in view of the *Bakke* decision, others have probably hidden behind the decision as a shield for their own policies of inaction. Of course, the Supreme Court made set-aside quotas of the type formerly employed by the University of California/Davis unconstitutional. Importantly, it left the door wide open for university officials to mount recruitment and admissions programs designed to increase diversity. It was clear in its support of "race," under certain circumstances, as one variable that could be a "plus" regarding admissions decisions. In any event, first and foremost, institutional commitment to the principle of equality of educational opportunity must be present in order for veterinary medicine to move toward noteworthy access to all students, irrespective of race.

Notes

1. Walter C. Bowie, D.V.M., "Opening Remarks," *Proceedings of Minority Recruitment Conference: Tuskegee Institute School of Veterinary Medicine 1974* (Tuskegee Institute, 1974), pp. 10–12.
2. This discussion of the veterinary medical education program at Tuskegee Institute is based on data made available by Dr. Ellis Hall of the College of Veterinary Medicine.
3. According to key informants on recruitment programs in colleges of veterinary medicine, the professional associations in this field never issued policy guidelines of the type articulated by counterpart associations in medicine and law. Individual representatives of the associations in veterinary medicine did express personal beliefs concerning the desirability of increased participation of minority groups in veterinary medicine on several occasions during the 1970s.
4. *Proceedings of Minority Recruitment Conference,* Tuskegee Institute, 1975, p. 54.
5. Donald A. Abt., *Report of the Workshop Conference on Minority Representation in Veterinary Medicine* (sponsored by the Association of American Veterinary Medical Colleges, the American Council on Education, and the Ford Foundation), November 1–2, 1978, p. 4.
6. Ibid.
7. Ibid., p. 5.
8. Ibid., p. 6
9. Ibid., pp. 6–7.
10. Ibid.
11. *Proceedings of the Minority Recruitment Conference: Tuskegee Institute School of Veterinary Medicine, 1974,* Tuskegee Institute, 1974. See also *Proceedings of the Minority Recruitment Conference,* Tuskegee Institute, 1975.
12. John B. Tasker, "An analysis of Applications to United States Colleges of Veterinary

Medicine, 1983: A Report to the Association of American Veterinary Medical Colleges," July 1983.

13. Based on information made available by Dr. Ellis Hall of Tuskegee Institute.

14. Cf. "Trends in Minority Affairs at Schools of Veterinary Medicine", in Donald A. Abt, *Op. Cit.* (Appendix).

15. Based upon telephone conversations with Dr. William Decker, Washington Representative of the Association of American Veterinary Medical Colleges.

Chapter **10** ENGINEERING AND ARCHITECTURE:
PATHWAYS TO PROGRESS

In terms of absolute numbers of students enrolled, no professional area can legitimately claim as much success in changing the racial composition of its field as can the profession of engineering. None can claim as much direct involvement and participation of the corporate structure in concrete programs designed to assure the inclusion of blacks and other minorities in a profession. None can demonstrate so rapid an increase in the actual production of a greater number of minorities for the work force. Although profound and far-reaching changes occurred during the 1970s, much more is now required to assure racial parity in the field of engineering.

Architecture, on the other hand, has not been by any measure, as successful as engineering in mainstreaming outsiders. Consequently, its task is monumental compared to other professions.

This chapter delineates the role of the historically black colleges of engineering in the production of black engineers prior to the 1970s. It describes the primary role played by the corporate structure in accelerating the process of mainstreaming blacks in the field of engineering. It outlines recruitment practices and presents black student enrollment trends during this period. The relationship between enrollment, retention, and the production of undergraduate and graduate degrees and certain predictor variables is explained. Finally, the chapter focuses attention on the central problems of mainstreaming blacks in the field of architecture. All these issues are explored in terms of their relationship to the theoretical notion that institutional behavior is a function of both internal and external pressures as well as societal conditions.

The Production of Black Engineers Before 1970:
Black Schools of Engineering

In 1970, 2.8% of the engineers in the United States came from four minority groups: blacks, Chicano or Mexican Americans, Puerto Ricans, and Native Americans. These four groups constituted slightly more than 14% of the total U.S. population.[1] Blacks alone accounted for 11.1% of the national total. Yet they comprised only about 1% of all the engineers in

233

the nation. Clearly, using the proportion of blacks in the total population as the reference point, their representation in the engineering profession was negligible.

Prior to the 1970s, and especially before 1964, the major responsibility for the training and production of engineers in the black population was left to one or more of six historically black colleges: Howard University, North Carolina A & T, Prairie View A & M (Texas), Southern University (Louisiana), Tennessee State University, and Tuskegee Institute. These six institutions played a unique role in training engineers from the minority population *before* court-ordered desegregation programs were implemented and *before* non-South public or private institutions committed themselves to large-scale recruitment of black students in engineering. They achieved their success despite being persistently understaffed and underfunded. State legislatures did not have a history of treating the education of black students as a matter of high priority. Consequently, historically black institutions were in a constant struggle for funds to support strong educational programs.

The value of the historically black colleges and their schools of engineering in the production of engineers can be gleaned from data that show that, from 1969 to 1973, these six institutions awarded approximately one-half (47%) of all B.S. in Engineering degrees earned by black students. Further, two-thirds of all bachelor's degrees conferred on black students in engineering were from 25 of the 282 schools and colleges of engineering in the United States, including the 6 black institutions.[2] The proportion of blacks who received engineering degrees from these institutions was far greater in earlier years than is represented by the 1969–73 period. In 1969, for instance, the six historically black colleges of engineering awarded 189 bachelor degrees in engineering to black students. According to a survey of the 25 leading schools in the enrollment of black students in engineering, this figure was 93% of all the degrees awarded to blacks. The distribution among the 6 black institutions was as follows: Prairie View A & M (49), Howard University (42), North Carolina A & T (32), Tennessee State (30), Southern University (28), and Tuskegee Institute (8). Purdue University, with a total of seven B.S. degrees conferred on black students in engineering, awarded more degrees to black students than did any other historically white institution that year.[3]

Although a more detailed profile of the role of black colleges in enrolling black engineering students will emerge later in this chapter, mention should now be made of their efforts to stimulate greater participation of black students in engineering programs. During the 1960s, educators and civil rights leaders expressed special concern over the maldistribution of majors selected by black college students. Although black students were obviously underrepresented in literally all fields of study, they tended to concentrate in a few selected majors. Among these fields were education, the social sciences, home economics, and physical education. As efforts expanded to redirect career choices among these students, and as they realized that career opportunities were growing, many black students began to shift to other fields, such as engineering.

Partially because of declining enrollments in white schools of engineering during the 1960s and early 1970s, several of these institutions were excited about the possibilities of saving their engineering programs by enrolling black students in joint-degree programs with historically black colleges. Consequently, a number of joint-degree programs were established in the late 1960s and early 1970s. These programs are labeled "3–2" engineering programs. This designation means that the black student enrolled in a black college spends the first three years of a five-year program taking pre-engineering and liberal arts courses at the parent institution, and the last two years of engineering training at a cooperating white institution. After the successful completion of all degree requirements, the student is awarded degrees from both institutions.

The 1984-1985 list of 32 dual-degree programs located at black colleges is presented in Figure 1. Cooperating traditionally white institutions in 1983–1984 are listed in Figure 2.

Figure 1.
Dual–Degree Programs in Engineering at Historically
Black Colleges in 1984–1985

Alabama A & M University	Morgan State University
Alabama State University	Morris Brown College
Benedict College	Norfolk State College
Bethune–Cookman College	North Carolina Central University
Bowie State College	Oakwood College
Clark College	Rust College
Dillard University	Saint Augustine's College
Florida A & M University	Savannah State College
Hampton Institute	Shaw University
Jackson State University	Spelman College
Kentucky State University	Stillman College
Lane College	Talladega College
LeMoyne College	Tennessee State University*
Lincoln University (Pa.)	Tougaloo College
Livingston College	Tuskegee Institute*
Morehouse College	Xavier University

*Operated dual-degree program with other black colleges.
Source: NACME, *Students Guide to Engineering Schools* (undated).

The implementation of dual-degree programs has enabled a significant number of black students to accomplish objectives of attending historically black colleges and simultaneously taking advantage of professional degree programs not available to them in the parent institution. These programs assist the parent institution to publicize expanded curricula offerings that are often vital for the recruitment of better-prepared students. They were instrumental earlier on in salvaging several engineering programs that were in trouble at traditionally white institutions by helping increase their overall enrollments.

Figure 2.
Cooperating Traditionally White Institutions Dual–Degree Programs
in Engineering with Historically Black Institutions, 1983–1984

Auburn University	University of Kentucky
Boston University	University of Maryland
Brown University	Mississippi State University
Christian Brothers College	North Carolina State University
Columbia University	Old Dominion University
University of Dayton	Pennsylvania State University
University of Florida	University of Rochester
George Washington University	Vanderbilt University
Georgia Institute of Technology	Walla Walla College

Source: NACME, *Students Guide to Engineering Schools* (undated).

The Role Of The Corporate Structure

The progress observed during the 1970s in the recruitment, enrollment, and production of black students in engineering can be attributed both to changes within colleges and universities and to forces external to the institution or within the larger American society, Among the *internal* or institutional factors, at least four stand out: (1) an articulation of the need for expanding access of minority students to a higher education by faculty and administrators of traditionally white colleges and universities; (2) the moral commitment to racial and social justice expressed by many constituents of these institutions; (3) pressures for change by black and white students already enrolled and who were inspired by the civil rights movement; and (4) the need by some decision makers to demonstrate that these institutions do not support policies of racial exclusion.

Four *external* factors also can be identified: (1) demands made by civil rights leaders to expand opportunities in professional education and in graduate schools; (2) pressures explicit in new federal regulations, which affected corporate hiring practices as well as access by universities to higher education funds; (3) affirmative action policies and the possibilities for heavy penalties for noncompliance with regulations and statutes; and (4) pressure exerted by the corporate structure on colleges and schools of engineering to increase the supply of engineers for possible hiring so that they could conform to governmental expectations.

The corporate structure was a prime mover in the rapid growth of black student matriculation in engineering colleges. The concern of corporations was considerably broader than the recruitment and enrollment of students from minority groups or initial affirmative action issues. The fundamental problem was the *inadequate supply* of black and other minority-group individuals who could be hired either for traditional engineering positions in the labor force or for managerial positions in the corporate structure. In the early 1970s, three of every five employees in one representative firm, who occupied the highest positions in that corporation, possessed technical degrees. These top-echelon positions were 99% white and 1% minority.[5] Inasmuch as competition for the few minority group members who were eligible for top-level positions and other jobs that required technical training was widespread and intense, an increasing number of corporations realized that a drastic change in the supply structure was imperative.

Initially, two popular methods for increasing supply were used. One was assisting historically black colleges and cooperative traditionally white institutions to establish dual-degree programs. Another involved financial assistance to the six black colleges of engineering to enable them to produce more engineers. In 1964, the Western Electric Fund made a grant designed to improve the overall "quality performance" of the historically black colleges with the ultimate goal of expanded production of black engineers. This program was coordinated by the Black Engineering College Development Committee of the American Society for Engineering Education (ASCE).[6] This committee focused its attention on methods of expanding enrollment, faculty growth, strengthening the curricula, and ways of improving retention through graduation. Faculty exchanges were sponsored in order to assure adequate course offerings. Even at that time, other companies began to provide increasing financial assistance to black students who attended engineering schools of the predominantly white colleges.[7]

In 1969, the Atlanta University Center, made up of four undergraduate liberal-arts colleges, received a grant of $265,000 from the Olin Charitable Trust Fund to establish a dual-degree program in engineering with the Georgia Institute of Technology (Georgia Tech). In 1970, Howard University was able to establish a chemical engineering facility with the assistance of a grant of $600,000 from the Esso Education Foundation. The Dupont Company made major grants in 1972 to each of the black colleges of engineering to help them strengthen their programs as well as to attract and produce a larger number of black students with engineering degrees.[8]

The major impetus for the organized and expanded involvement of the corporate structure in broadening engineering education opportunities among the minority-group population came from General Electric. Troubled by the "supply imbalance" and the persistance of a condition of minority-group underrepresentation in the population of practicing engineers, General Electric decided to take corrective steps.

In 1972, J. Stanford Smith, senior vice president of General Electric, addressed a meeting of 44 deans of colleges of engineering, at its Management Development Center in Crotonville, New York. He stated that it was necessary to increase the number of blacks in engineering by 10 to 15 times their present number in order to assure the inclusion of a significant proportion of blacks in the top ranks of industry before the century's end. The accomplishment of this goal, Smith asserted, required the combined cooperation of all sectors of the society — public and private; educational institutions at all levels; the entire business community; foundations; professional groups; and minority institutions. He also urged some form of government involvement in what was termed by some a revolutionary enterprise. Otherwise, Mr. Smith admonished, professional education in engineering was entangled in a "formula for tragedy."[9]

Out of the "revolutionary action" proposed by General Electric came the Minority Engineering Effort. Shortly after Smith's urgent call for action, the Conference Board convened a group of executives as members of an informal Minority Engineering Working Committee. Key executives representing General Electric, IBM, Xerox, Western Electric, U.S. Steel, DuPont, and General Motors participated in this working group to study the issues raised by Smith and to ascertain what could be done to translate his ideas into concrete programs. Later, this informal working committee expanded to include the executive director of the National Urban League, the Engineering Council on Professional Development (ECPD), the American Personnel and Guidance Association, the chairman of the Committee on Engineering of the National Academy of Engineering (NAE), and other representatives from the community of engineering educators. These persons became the Council of Minority Engineering of the Conference Board.[10]

Minority Education Engineering Effort (ME³)

Late in 1972, the Task Force of the Engineering Council for Professional Development (ECPD) founded the Minority Education Engineering Effort (ME³). Although ME³ subsequently separated from ECPD, it was an essential component of the early movement to increase the representation of black and other minorities in the engineering profession. This group focused its attention on precollege programs in order to acquaint students with opportunities in engineering and the requirements for admission into college programs. ME³ urged high school students to take courses in mathematics and the general sciences. It advised them to enroll in college engineering programs.[11]

The 1973 National Academy of Engineering (NAE) Conference

Another significant event in the minority engineering effort occurred in 1973 when the NAE sponsored a symposium in which 250 persons participated to discuss further plans for stimulating the effort to broaden the base of participation of minorities in engineering. More specifically, the organizer intended to determine the degree of access of blacks and other minorities to engineering, ascertain the extent and characteristics of existing access programs, promote the development of a coordinated national program supported by institutional and organizational commitment for action, and determine methods of creating new pathways for minority-group success in the corporate world. The participants in this conference agreed to work toward a goal of achieving a tenfold increase in the number of minority engineers within a decade.[12]

National Advisory Council on Minorities in Engineering (NACME)

The Sloan Foundation was instrumental in funding the work of ME³ and the 1973 NAE Conference. This foundation provided an additional $12–15 million to advance the new efforts to produce more engineers from minority groups. It also funded the Planning Commission Task Force in December 1973. The task force urged the achievement of parity in terms of minority-group participation in engineering education and professional development. It also produced an extremely important and influential study called *Minorities in Engineering: A Blueprint For Action.*

As a result of the 1973 symposium, the president of the NAE established an advisory group called the National Advisory Council on Minorities in Engineering (NACME) and the Committee on Minorities in Engineering (CME) of the National Research Council.[13] The central function of the NACME was to advise the NAE president on all matters that pertained to the "specific objective of development career trajectories" for underrepresented minorities toward parity. The concept "parity" referred to a number of minority-group engineers that approximated their proportion in the national population. NACME also functioned to generate financial contributions to the engineering effort from its member companies, which could then be utilized to support the work of the Committee on Minorities in Engineering. These funds are provided to the CME through its parent organization, the National Research Council (NRC).[14]

In 1980, NACME was merged with ME[3], CME, and NFMES. NACME, now an informal organization comprised largely of senior executives of major companies, annually distributes substantial monies in scholarships. The 36 leading corporations and leaders in other business institutions use their influence to mobilize formal and informal support for the effort to create greater parity and strengthen engineering programs.

However, the participation of member corporations in NACME is not uniformly strong. According to the Conference Board, participation in NACME activities by the 36 corporations can be more or less dichotomized in terms of company involvement. One group consists of those whose overall contributions are characterized as "modest." Companies in this category have representatives who attend NACME meetings infrequently and whose own engineering effort shows weak coordination. By contrast, the second group, which contains the majority of the 36 NACME corporations, is especially active, has well-coordinated programs involving a broad spectrum of supportive activities. For instance, they include the utilization of role models from the company as lecturer–teacher on college campuses. In turn, they facilitate recruitment and the overall engineering educational program of some colleges of engineering. Some corporations also assist in organizing community consortia.[15]

Seymour Lusterman points out that degrees of company involvement depend, at minimum, on six external factors: (1) the size of the ethnic population in which the company is located (the assumption here is that the larger the size of the ethnic community, the more active is the company); (2) the existence or absence of an engineering college in the community; (3) the degree of integration in the schools; (4) the degree of the company's own prominence in the community; (5) the number of companies located in the community and the relative importance of the NACME company or firm in relation to others; and (6) the historical pattern of relations between industry and institutions within the community. In any event, as Lusterman maintains, leadership from above, that is, from the top echelon of the corporate structure, is essential for stimulating broad-scale and enduring commitment to the minorities-in-engineering effort in any firm. Where that commitment is absent, suspect, tentative, or in doubt, subordinates do not tend to display much enthusiasm for the program. Strong commitment produces equally sound results.[16] All six external factors are interrelated and affect the course of action taken by firms in any given community. Similarly, they may also be affected by regulatory guidelines issued by the federal government and affirmative action mandates.

Committee on Minorities in Engineering (CME)

The Committee on Minorities in Engineering was offically established in 1974 as a coordinating body for efforts to increase access of minority students in engineering. Its four basic functions are (1) to define needs, identify resources, and make recommendations regarding specific activities that may facilitate its ultimate objective; (2) to construct models of workable approaches for stimulating greater minority-group access to engineering; (3) to serve as a resource center for those interested in learning more about successful approaches to increasing minority-group participation; and (4) to serve as a disseminator of information, data, and research studies concerning the minorities in engineering effort.[17]

The committee consists of two specific classes of members. On the one hand, there are volunteers who are characterized as more deliberate and passive in their approach to the CME's mission. The second group, on the other hand, consists of paid professional staff members who engage in specific actions supportive of the programs proposed and directed by the volunteers. The staff also interfaces with NACME and provides assistance for its endeavors. Volunteer activities embrace a range of programs including conferences, symposia, and promotion of research on critical issues germane to the overall mission of increasing minority-group representation in the engineering profession. The volunteers make a special effort to influence public policy at the federal, state, and local levels through the development of position papers and other documents.[18]

Supportive Organizations

The following list of organizations, corporations, and institutions is intended to be illustrative rather than exhaustive of all pioneers in the effort to broaden participation of blacks and other minorities in Engineering. Omission of other groups here in no way diminishes the value of their roles in this process. Unquestionably, this effort was assisted by such groups as National Executive Committee on Guidance (NECG), the Junior Engineering Technical Society (JETS), the Engineering Joint Council (EJC), the National Scholarship Service and Fund for Negro Students (NSSFNS), the U.S. Chamber of Commerce, the National Association of Manufacturers, the National Alliance of Businessmen, the American Association for the Advancement of Science (AAAS), the National Science Foundation (NSF), the National Institutes of Health (NIH), and the Department of Health, Education, and Welfare.

These groups performed a number of important functions that immediately and in the long run led to significant increases in the enrollment and graduation rates of black students in the field of engineering. Among these were the following:

1. Coordinating efforts by engineering educators and representatives from business and industry and technical organizations in the engineering profession as well as organizations in minority-group communities in working toward the goal of expanded engineering opportunities.

2. Identifying and motivating minority-group students to select engineering as a professional field.

3. Developing motivational materials used in the recruitment process; (including films, slides, pamphlets, brochures, leaflets, circulars, and exhibits), and that may assist counselors and advisers to precollege students.

4. Implementing guidance programs to stimulate engineering careers.

5. Forming high school chapters of student clubs comprised of students interested in the engineering profession. (There are approximately 1500 of these chapters in high schools across the country.)

6. Conducting the National Engineering Aptitude Search (NEAS) to indicate "possible success" in college engineering programs. (Approximately 8000 students in grades 9 through 12 take this test each year.)

7. Providing campus-level support through counseling, tutoring, and advocacy for minority students.

8. Providing role models from the corporate structure for campus recruitment activities, classroom lectures, and temporary faculty in selected pre-engineering and professional degree programs.

9. Visiting college campus fairs, high school Career Days, and general support for recruitment and retention in schools and colleges of engineering.

10. Providing summer jobs and internship programs to further stimulate interest in the engineering profession.

11. Engaging in a broad range of precollege programs including promotion of interest in general science, mathematics, and high school physics, as important preparation for engineering programs.

12. Identifying social, economic, and institutional obstacles to the successful recruitment and enrollment of black and other minority students in schools and colleges of engineering.

13. Assisting high school faculty to improve their own capabilities for providing quality instruction in science and mathematics curricula.

14. Working with parents to promote their interest in engineering as a possible career option for their children.

15. Helping minority faculty in historically black colleges to re-tool themselves for updated curricula in engineering and the supportive science and mathematics fields.

16. Facilitating a more supportive learning environment for black and other minority students.

17. Conducting and/or supporting pertinent research relative to access and expanding equality of educational opportunity in engineering programs.

18. Helping to eliminate the financial barriers to enrollment and retention in schools and colleges of engineering.

The Recruitment of Black Students

Special interest in expanded recruitment of black students, as previously stated, can be traced to efforts in the 1960s to strengthen the engineering curricula of the historically black colleges of engineering. However, these efforts were limited, tentative, and severely underfunded in relationship to the magnitude of the problem. Immediately, they proved inadequate to meet the increasing demand for more blacks in engineering and, later, for the goals of parity within a decade. It soon became apparent that this task exceeded the capabilities of the black colleges. Hence, widespread involvement of white colleges was absolutely imperative even to move one step beyond token levels of minority student access to the engineering profession.

Institutional Strategies

Among the early institutional leaders in predominantly white universities in the effort to increase the enrollment of black and other minority students in engineering were the New Jersey Institute of Technology, University of Bridgeport, Carnegie Mellon, Illinois Institute of Technology, and University of Illinois/Urbana. Their efforts were supported by business and industrial communities, as well as from institutional funds.[19] Recruitment programs in these institutions were initiated between 1967 and 1969.

The program at the University of Illinois/Urbana began in 1969. From its inception, its primary focus was on stimulating wider participation in engineering among those minorities who were grossly underrepresented in the profession. Specifically, the target groups included black, Chicano, Puerto Ricans, and Native Americans. Special minority recruiters were hired. A precollege outreach program became an essential program component for stimulating interest and attracting junior and senior high school students to engineering. The university invited these students to spend two summer weeks on the campus. During this visit, high school students were not only exposed to college life but had an opportunity to study mathematics and engage in analyses of engineering problems. This summer program became the prototype for the Minority Introduction to Engineering program (MITE), which the Engineering Council for Professional Development subsequently established. On campus, a support service system was established for students who needed various forms of assistance toward the completion of degree requirements. Tutorials were at the core of this program.

From the late 1960s into the mid and late 1970s, special minority recruitment programs for undergraduate engineering degree programs continued to expand to the point that almost half of the 282 schools of engineering were actively committed to the recruitment of black and other minority students. In other instances, the degree of involvement ranged from the total absence of a special recruitment program; a passive stance, characterized by reliance on the institution to admit students who might drift into engineering; to relatively moderate, uncoordinated, and disorganized efforts.

The institutions that were heavily involved in special recruitment employed a number of different strategies and frequently a combination of them, such as those listed on pages 242–243.

In addition to these and other recruitment strategies, a number of state and/or regional organizations provided early identification programs, reaching into the junior high school levels, and scholarship monies. Principal among such groups were the Committee to Increase Minority Professionals in Engineering, Architecture and Technology (CIMPEAT) of Atlanta; Philadelphia Regional Introduction for Minorities in Engineering (PRIME); California Consortium for Minorities in Engineering (CCME); Committee for Institutional Cooperation—Midwest Program for Minorities in Engineering, Inroads, Inc.; Engineering Consortium for Minorities; Texas Alliance for Minorities in Engineering (TAME); and the Southwest Consortium for Minorities in Engineering. Generally speaking, all regions of the country were covered by such programs.

Heavily involved institutions also drew on currently enrolled minority students to assist in recruitment. They utilized lists of potential students generated by the ME[3] program, the Student Search List of the College Entrance Examination Board, the American College Test (ACT) list, the National Achievement Scholarship List, and similar sources of potential students.

The salience of a high quality of recruitment is registered in enrollment patterns. The data clearly show that wherever strong, well-coordinated, and organized recruitment programs exist, the enrollment of black students is equally significant and considerably beyond the token stage. In contrast, if recruitment is nonexistent or passive, enrollment is unimpressive or nonexistent.

Even among the largest schools of engineering in the nation, such as the University of Pennsylvania, aggressive action is necessary. This is so even when the institution enjoys high prestige in the engineering profession. High school students rarely know anything about an institution's reputation in the same sense as academicians do. To be passive means that, despite a good reputation, an institution may still enroll only a handful of minority students.

The overall impact of the *Bakke* case was not as severe as some might have anticipated with respect to the use of minority recruitment and special admissions programs. For instance, of the 245 reporting institutions in 1982–1983 NACME survey, 109 or 45% reported special minority recruitment programs; 67 or 27% stated that they conduct special admissions programs in their schools of engineering. Sixteen of the institutions with special admissions programs, or 24%, are located in states that are or formerly were included under the *Adams* litigation. Twenty-nine (27%) of those reporting minority recruitment programs are located in such states. However, several institutions located in the "*Adams* states" were not conducting recruitment programs for minority students at that time. These institutions include the University of Alabama, Arkansas State University, Florida Atlantic University, Florida Institute of Technology, University of Georgia, Louisiana Tech University, McKneese State University, Mississippi State University, Oklahoma State University, University of Oklahoma, University of South Alabama, University of South Carolina, and Virginia Polytech and State University. That failure is often reflected in the scarcity of blacks in engineering at several of these institutions. Further, it is evident from the enrollment data (discussed in a following section) that many institutions have not made substantial inroads into the problem of the underrepresentation of blacks in engineering, despite overall aggressive recruitment programs mounted during the 1970s and 1980s. A number of institutions have good "paper programs," but they are not supported by action. The most fundamental problem is the failure to commit adequate resources, human and financial, to the implementation of these programs.

Admissions Criteria

Undergraduate Admissions

Admission to undergraduate colleges of engineering is not generally done by the engineering colleges. Students are admitted to undergraduate colleges and declare a major field either in the freshmen year or at some subsequent stage. The tendency of many students to explore possible major fields of study before declaring a specific major compounds the issue of comparisons between first-year entry and entry in subsequent years. Nevertheless, institutions most frequently rely on such quantitative assessment factors as SAT scores, the high school GPA, standing in high school graduating class, and rating of the high school from which the student was graduated in determining eligibility for admission.

Qualitative factors utilized include a wide range of criteria that have an impact on the discretionary powers of assessment, selection, and admissions officers in determining who is worthy or desirable. These non-cognitive factors are fundamentally the same as those identified in earlier chapters. However, at the undergraduate level, they may include prowess and special skills in athletics, music, or debating. Motivation, determination, perseverance, and any number of extracurricula activities may be considered. Hence, special admissions in the traditional sense may not be as significant a factor in determining admission as would be the case in some graduate programs. Where it may be salient is in whether or not the student has completed "pre-engineering" requirements, especially in mathematics and science credits, and has a sufficiently high gradepoint average.

Graduate Admissions

At the graduate level, special recruitment and special admissions programs for black and other minority students are rare. Admissions decisions are most frequently based on GRE scores, especially, in the sciences; GPAs in undergraduate colleges; letters of recommendation and sometimes personal interviews. Almost all graduate schools require a B.S. in Engineering, Physics, or a related field. Cutoff points on GRE scores are institution-specific, and no particular pattern is discerned. The minimum GPA required ranges from 2.5 to 3.0 on a 4.0 system. However, many institutions seem more concerned about the quality of academic performance during the last two years of an undergraduate program in engineering. They seek to ascertain patterns of growth in academic performance, and many are willing to take a chance on "late bloomers." Hence, some degree of flexibility in admissions criteria is apparent. In fact, increasing flexibility may become more widespread as larger numbers of graduate schools in engineering begin to be affected by declining enrollments created by financial inducements for B.S. in Engineering graduates from high-technology industries, the business community, or the corporate world.

Enrollment of Black Students

Unquestionably, the efforts initiated by General Electric and the corporate structure, in general, and the external influences on both the business community and institutions, led to major progress toward expanding engineering training opportunities for black and other minority students during the 1970s. While the goal of a tenfold increase within the decade was not attained, significant progress was made toward achieving a greater balance between demand and supply. Once again, increases in enrollment patterns reflect the quality of recruitment, scholarships, financial aid in general, and, most significantly, the presence or absence of black faculty. State totals by year show that being under litigation to dismantle dual systems of education is increasingly correlated with both first-year enrollments and total enrollment of black students.

Nevertheless, relying on state totals alone may be misleading and result in erroneous interpretations of the data. The fact remains that, while substantial numbers of black students have matriculated at the traditionally white institutions in the *"Adams* states," black engineering students in the mid-1980s are still concentrated in the 10 historically black colleges with schools of engineering. (The tenth school of engineering is located at the University of the District of Columbia.) In effect, black students are unevenly distributed in these states. Further, many colleges of engineering, including several in the *"Adams* states," continue to enroll only token numbers of black students.

In this analysis, first attention is focused on trends in enrollment in engineering at the baccalaureate, or first professional degree, level. The period covered is from 1968–1969 to 1983–1984 academic years.

Undergraduate Enrollment Trends

In 1970, 1289 black students enrolled in first-year B.S. engineering programs in the United States. They represented 1.7% of the total enrollment in first-year classes of 71,661. In the following year, engineering colleges experienced a shocking decline in first-year enrollment when they lost approximately 13,000 students. This decline in first-year enrollments continued through the 1973–74 academic year and was followed by a dramatic upturn in 1974 that has continued.

Although engineering educators cannot fully explain this alarming downward trend with complete confidence, they advanced certain possible explanations. This particular trend was attributed most frequently to the Vietnam war. Some students voiced their opposition to science and engineering due to the presumed role this field performed in the continuation of the military effort. Other eligible students were drafted during this period. Still other students believed that a degree in engineering was not marketable. For whatever reasons, the decline in first-year enrollments continued for three years. This drop was partially offset by an increase in total enrollment in 1972–1973 which probably resulted from large numbers of engineering junior college transfers into four-year colleges and universities.

Table 49
First-Year Enrollment in B.S. in Engineering Programs, by Race,
1968–1984, All Institutions Combined

Academic Year	Total First-Year Enrollment	Black First-Year Students	% Black
1983–84	108,763	6,342	5.8
1982–83	114,517	6,715	5.8
1981–82	114,201	7,015	6.1
1980–81	109,314	6,661	6.0
1979–80	103,090	6,339	6.1
1978–79	95,171	5,493	5.7
1977–78[a]	88,780	4,728	5.3
1976–77	81,652	4,372	5.3
1975–76	74,558	3,840	5.1
1974–75	62,582	2,447	3.9
1973–74[a]	51,925	2,130	4.1
1972–73[a]	52,100	1,477	2.8
1971–72[a]	58,566	1,289	2.2
1970–71[a]	71,661	1,289	1.8
1969–70[a]	—	977	—
1968–69[a]	77,484	—	—

Source: Engineering Manpower Commission.
[a] = Total full-time enrollment included University of Puerto Rico *and* mainland institutions.

As first year enrollments dropped off during the early seventies, the actual number of black first year students began a steady climb that continued to the peak year of 1981–82 when the absolute number of blacks in first year classes reached 7015. However, between 1982 and 1984, the absolute number of black students matriculated in first year engineering programs declined by almost 700 students. The 6342 first year black students of 1983–84 approximated the 6339 enrolled in 1979. Similarly, the percentage of black students among all first year enrollees climbed steadily through 1981–82 but that, too, began to fall off slightly thereafter. More specifically, the percentage of black students stood at 1.80% in 1970. By 1979, it had risen to 6.1%, but by 1983, black students constituted only 5.8% of all first-year engineering matriculants (see Table 49).

These data also suggest that one of the central explanations for the comparative ease with which black and other minorities entered colleges of engineering during the 1970s was that engineering colleges had a great deal of space for anyone interested in the field. These colleges were not filled to their capacities as were medical and dental schools; were not pressed for space; and some had difficulty in enrolling a sufficient number of students to maintain credibility within their own institutions. This lack of competition for a resource that was now scarce meant that many institutions welcomed this new source of students, not entirely out of "a new social consciousness," but as a mechanism for halting the downward spiral in enrollments.[20] This fact, coupled with the attractive salaries offered engineering graduates and assurances of jobs, at a time when unemployment rates continued to rise in the nation made engineering more attractive than many career alternatives.

Moreover, the applicant pool among blacks to colleges and universities began to expand significantly during the early part of the decade, and black students entered postsecondary education in unprecedented numbers. In fact, the traditionally white institutions soon outdistanced the historically black colleges in enrolling black students. This should not be surprising, since white institutions outnumber black institutions by almost 50 to 1. Even if all of them went very little beyond limited access, their total enrollment of black students would be significantly greater than that found among historically black institutions. The crucial variable in the access–outcome equation is the difference between these two institutional types in their rate of productivity of black student graduates. In this regard the historically black institutions do a far superior job in terms of absolute numbers produced.

Total Enrollment

Total enrollments refer to the combined enrollments of all classes. Table 50 depicts the trends in these enrollments. According to these data, the declines evident in first-year enrollments were similarly reflected in total enrollment for the period between 1969 and 1973. With the exception of the 1972–1973 academic year, total enrollments dropped alarmingly during this period. There was a loss of approximately 16,000 students between 1969 and 1970; a further loss of about 8000 students occurred the following year. Inexplicably, there was a gain of about 15,000 students in 1973–1974. This upswing in total enrollments continued for the remainder of the decade so that by 1979–1980 the 337,807 students enrolled in all colleges of engineering combined represented an increase of more than 100,000 over the 1970 figure. By 1983, total enrollment had climbed to 402,561. That number was a dramatic demonstration of the increasing attractiveness of engineering as a profession to young American college students.

In absolute numbers, total enrollment for black students also showed a steady climb during the 1970s. In 1969–1970, there were only 2757 black students enrolled in the nation's colleges of engineering. As previously stated, a disproportionate number of these students were enrolled at the six historically black colleges. Because of coordinated and well-organized recruitment programs, the availability of financial aid to assist impoverished students, particularly, and the willingness of colleges of engineering to enroll them, black students entered this field in heretofore unprecedented numbers. As a result, in 1979, the number of black students in engineering represented an approximately sixfold increase over the 1969 figure (see Table 50).

The 2779 black students enrolled in 1969 represented 1.3% of total engineering enrollments. The 14,786 enrolled in 1979 meant that there was an enrollment increase of approximately 600% over the proportions noted a decade earlier. However, it also meant that just as black students entered engineering in exceptionally larger numbers than ever before in their history, so did white students (and, of course, students from other minority groups). Essentially, the entire field of engineering expanded.

Capacities continued to increase, but the demand for engineering graduates in the late 1970s outdistanced supply once again. Consequently, engineering is a critical need area with substantial career opportunities for all those who qualify. A changing technology has now dictated certain manpower needs that must be met. The result is that students trained in engineering, especially in computer, petroleum, and mechanical engineering, are probably the most highly sought bachelor degree recipients in the United States.

This fact helps account for the continued upward spiral in total engineering enrollments into the 1980s. Total enrollment in engineering colleges rose steadily from 337,807 in 1979–80 to 402,561 in 1983–84. Similarly, total black student enrollment increased by more than 3,000, or up from 14,786 to 17,817, during the same period. A significant portion of the rise in total black student enrollment may also be attributed to the development of four additional schools of engineering at historically and predominantly black institutions. Engineering degree programs were established at Morgan State University, Hampton Institute, the University of the District of Columbia, and in the Joint Engineering Institute at Florida A & M University with Florida State University.

Who enrolls black students in engineering? Aside from the four historically black colleges, our data show that the 20 institutions in Figure 3 were the leaders in enrolling black undergraduate students in engineering during the 1970s.

Table 50
Total Engineering Enrollment, by Race, 1970–1984, All Institutions Combined

Academic Year	Total Enrollment	Total Black Students Enrolled	% Blacks
1983–84	402,561	17,817	4.4
1982–83	400,038	17,598	4.4
1981–82	384,162	17,611	4.5
1980–81	362,300	16,181	4.4
1979–80	337,807	14,786	4.3
1978–79	308,556	12,954	4.2
1977–78[a]	289,248	11,388	3.4
1976–77	254,797	9,828	3.8
1975–76	228,183	8,389	3.2
1974–75[a]	197,899	6,319	2.7
1973–74[a]	186,705	5,508	2.9
1972–73[a]	194,727	4,356	2.2
1971–72[a]	210,825	4,136	1.9
1970–71[a]	231,730	2,757	1.1

Source: Engineering Manpower Commission.
[a] = Total full-time enrollment included University of Puerto Rico *and* mainland institutions.

Figure 3
Leaders in the Enrollment of Black Undergraduates in Engineering*

Georgia Tech	Michigan State University
Purdue University	Illinois State University
University of Houston	University of Michigan
University of Illinois/Chicago	North Carolina State University
New Jersey Institute of Technology	University of Illinois/Urbana
Wayne State University	University of Missouri/Rolla
Pratt Institute	University of New Mexico
General Motors Institute	Detroit Institute of Technology
Ohio State University	Drexel
University of Tennessee/Knoxville	Texas A & I

* Historically Black Institutions not included.

In terms of proportion of black students in the engineering college, the latest data available by state, as opposed to institution, show that the following jurisdictions have the largest proportions of black students in their schools or colleges of engineering: District of Columbia (40.6%), Illinois (11.4%), Michigan (11.1%), and Mississippi (6.8%).

In the "*Adams* states," the latest available data provide the ranking in terms of proportion of black students enrolled in all schools and colleges of engineering in the state, shown in Table 51.

Using the definition of total access as a number of black students enrolled that approximates or surpasses proportion of blacks in the state's population, it is evident that black students are far from attaining parity in enrollment. Clearly, at the present rate of matriculation, a massive effort will have to be mounted in order to achieve even the second level of access.

Enrollment in Graduate Programs

In academic year 1969–1970, there were 55 black students enrolled in M.S. in Engineering programs in the United States. The number more than doubled, to 112, in 1971–1972, and continued its upward climb in every year of the 1970s. The 165 black students in M.S. degree programs in 1971 constituted only 0.74% of all M.S. engineering students. By 1976, the 321 black students enrolled in M.S. programs represented 1.2% of the 25,516 students in all institutions seeking that degree. According to the 1979–1980 fall enrollment data, 357 black students were seeking the M.S. degree, out of a total of 27,171, or 1.3% black students in the total M.S. enrollment. The number of black students enrolled in M.S. in Engineering degree programs has risen significantly since the beginning of the 1980s. By 1983, the number had climbed to 587 of 37,969, or 1.5% of all students enrolled in masters programs.(see Table 52). Even with these changes, given the overall paucity of the proportion of employed engineers who are black, black students are grossly underrepresented in graduate engineering programs.

Among the early leaders in the enrollment of black students at the M.S. level were such institutions as Stanford University, University of California/Berkeley, University of Southern California, George Washington University, Howard University, Georgia Institute of Technology, Massachusetts Institute of Technology, University of Detroit, Michigan State University, New Jersey Institute of Technology, New York Polytechnic Institute, and Cornell University. Later in the decade, the University of Pennsylvania, University of Illinois, and Pratt Institute were added to this list.

In the "*Adams* states," Georgia Tech led all institutions in the training of blacks at the M.S. level. Only Pennsylvania, among all remaining colleges of engineering in the "*Adams* states," has enrolled a significant number of blacks at the M.S. level.

The number of black students studying for a Ph.D. degree in engineering in 1979 was five times greater than the number enrolled in this program

Table 51
Current Rank of "*Adams* States" by Number of Blacks Enrolled in
Engineering Schools, 1983–1984 All Institutions Combined
(and Percent Blacks in State Population)

State	Full-Time Students		
	Number of Blacks in Engineering	Rank	% Blacks in State Population
Alabama	1026	4	26.2
(Tuskegee)[a]	(510)		
Arkansas	169	14	16.3
Delaware	68	17	16.1
Florida	322	9	13.5
Georgia	360	7	7.1
Kentucky	75	16	29.4
Louisiana	1071	3	22.7
(Southern University)[a]	(678)		
Maryland	220	12	10.9
Missouri	289	15	35.2
Mississippi	201	13	22.4
North Carolina	1113	2	10.0
(N.C. A&T)[a]	(652)		
Ohio	691	5	6.8
Oklahoma	141	15	8.8
Pennsylvania	582	6	30.4
South Carolina	281	11	43.0
Texas	1363	1	12.0
(Prairie View A&M)[a]	(586)		
Virginia	325	8	18.9
West Virginia	25	18	3.3

[a]Historically black college. (In each case, these colleges account for approximately half of black student enrollment in schools and colleges of engineering within the state of location.)

in 1969. However, the overall trend in the enrollment of black doctoral students did not show a steady or continuous incline. For instance, the number of black doctoral students doubled from 22 to 44 between 1969 and 1971 and increased by 8 students in 1972. However, as the national totals of all students enrolled in doctoral degree programs dropped between 1972 and 1973, so there was a decline in the absolute numbers of black students enrolled in engineering doctoral programs. The erratic nature of the pattern is once again observed in the more than doubling of the number

Table 52
M.S. Degree Full-Time Enrollment in Engineering, 1969–70 — 1983–84
All Institutions Combined

Academic Year	Total M.S. Enrollment	Black M.S. Enrollees	% Blacks
1983–84	37,969	587	1.5
1982–83	33,271	502	1.5
1981–82	31,655	525	1.3
1980–81	29,168	445	1.5
1979–80	27,171	357	1.3
1978–79	25,360	322	1.2
1977–78	26,107	326	1.3
1976–77	25,516	321	1.2
1975–76	N.A.	251	N.A.
1974–75	N.A.	200	N.A.
1973–74	N.A.	220	N.A.
1972–73	22,588	221	0.98
1971–72	22,405	265	0.74
1970–71	N.A.	112	N.A.
1969–70	N.A.	55	N.A.

Source: Engineering Manpower Commission.

of black students studying for the doctoral degree in 1974, followed by a decline that resulted in a loss in excess of 60% by 1976, when only 30 black students enrolled in doctorate programs. The 109 black students enrolled in such programs in 1979 represented 0.81% of the total number of 13,461. Clearly, black students are substantially below parity at the Ph.D. level. This underrepresentation of black doctoral students in engineering continues in the 1980s. For instance, as the decade began, some 109 black students, or less than 1% of the total doctoral enrollment, were pursuing a doctorate in this field. By 1983, the number of black engineering doctoral students had risen to 171, but they still constituted less than 1% of enrollment at that level (see Table 53). Hence, it should not be surprising that the nation produces only 10 to 20 black Americans with a Ph.D. in Engineering each year. Clearly, black students are substantially below parity at the Ph.D. level.

Among the institutional leaders in the enrollment of black Ph.D. students are such institutions as Stanford, MIT, Iowa State University, University of Illinois, University of California at Los Angeles, North Carolina State University, City University of New York, and New York Polytechnic.

Table 53
Doctoral Degree Enrollment in Engineering, by Race, 1969–1984

Academic Year	Total Doctoral Enrollment	Blacks in Doctoral Programs	% Blacks
1983–84	18,540	171	.92
1982–83	16,442	116	.71
1981–82	15,475	116	.75
1980–81	14,465	124	.86
1979–80	13,461	109	.81
1978–79	12,321	100	.81
1977–78	12,369	101	.82
1976–77	10,963	30	.27
1975–76	N.A.	67	N.A.
1974–75	N.A.	71	N.A.
1973–74	11,904	38	.32
1972–73	13,460	52	.39
1971–72	14,100	49	.35
1970–71	N.A.	44	N.A.
1969–70	N.A.	22	N.A.

Source: Engineering Manpower Commission.

With regard to the "*Adams* states," only a single institution enrolled a significant number of black students in Ph.D. programs during the 1970s and 1980s. The notable exception was the University of Pennsylvania, and that occurred during the second half of the period.

At the graduate level, black students tend to enroll in the following engineering specializations: chemical, civil, computer, electrical, mechanical, and nuclear engineering. They do not seem to be attracted at all to such specializations as ceramic, architectural, construction, drafting and design, environmental, metallurgical, and mining engineering.

These enrollment data depict an overall trend of continuous progress in both first-year and total enrollment of black students in schools and colleges of engineering from 1970 onward. Similarly, students of all races have entered engineering in numbers never previously conceived. Yet, there remains a major shortage of engineers for the labor force because of increased demands in the high-technology sector. As a result, graduate enrollments are significantly below the level desired, primarily because of the market situation. There is little or no need for most B.S. degree recipients to think in terms of enrolling in M.S. or Ph. D. programs when the entry-level salaries of this group are often far greater than what a newly minted Ph.D. can expect to receive as an Assistant Professor in most universities and colleges. Many companies in the corporate structure also offer the possibility of graduate training as a fringe benefit in order to attract much-needed skills. This fact holds true for all races and both sexes.

Consequently, it takes an exceptionally motivated student to defer social and economic gratification to study for an advanced degree on a stipend that is from one-seventh to one-fourth of what the starting salary of a B.S. degree holder commands in 1987. Nevertheless, one must take note of the increase by approximately 1000 students in the total number enrolled in doctoral programs in 1979–1980 over the 1978–1979 figure. Further, the 1979 doctoral enrollment of 13,461 is 5079 fewer than the latest enrollment figure, 18,540 in 1983–1984. Again, more must be done to eliminate the shortage of engineers observed during the mid-1980s. It is especially acute in the academic community. This national shortage of engineers for college teaching positions involves a number of complex issues, some of which were mentioned earlier. However, it should be stressed that many persons do not regard the Ph.D. as useful when the market situation is so volatile and weighted so heavily in favor of the first professional degree. Many persons at this level may not appreciate the fact that their quest for upward mobility in high-technology fields may be accelerated by the acquisition of the doctoral degree. There is also a high probability that academic work is undervalued and underappreciated when compared to many dimensions of work in nonacademic settings. To confront this shortage, several major corporations have increased their programs for topping-off salaries of college engineering professors in order to maintain an adequate teaching force, which is so vital for the training of engineers needed in industry, high technology, and other nonacademic settings.

This shortage of engineering professors at the college level provides a major "window of opportunity" for black Americans to gain access to faculty positions. It may be that previously conservative departments, which stand to lose so much because of their inability to staff departments in the numbers required to meet enrollment demands, may reassess their attitudes, subordinate reluctance to practicality, and be willing to hire blacks with an engineering doctorate. If so, and if indeed more blacks are hired in the traditionally white institutions, the visibility of black role models in teaching and administrative positions may attract increasingly larger numbers of blacks into doctoral degree programs and, ultimately, into university teaching positions.

Retention

There is a general agreement that the major problem of the 1970s was the retention of black students enrolled so that the supply side of the equation could be more balanced.[21] The gravity of the situation may be underscored by a single example; The numbers of black graduates with a B.S. in Engineering increased by only 77 students between 1974 and 1977, despite the pronounced increases in first-year and total enrollments in years that should have produced more graduates. We have no precise account of retention rates for every one of the 282 engineering institutions in the nation. However, the Engineering Manpower Commission of the Engineering Joint Council has demonstrated in its research that the graduation rate of minority students is about 54.8% in contrast to 77.8% for white students.[22] This is a highly significant disparity of more than 23%. For black students, the rate may be higher or lower, depending on the institutions selected for analysis. At the current rate of production of black engineers, who make up about 2% of all engineers, massive increases in the total number of black students, both enrolled and graduated, will be imperative over the next 20 years.

According to a study conducted by the task force of the Committee on Minorities in Engineering, the Assembly of Engineering, and the National Research Council and reported in 1977, the causes of the high attrition rate among blacks and other minorities are indeed multidimensional and many faceted. The five most serious factors associated with low retention or high attrition are (1) inadequate precollege preparation; (2) inadequate motivation; (3) inadequate financial assistance; (4) low confidence and self-doubt about one's ability to perform adequately in engineering programs; and (5) personal and family problems.[23]

For several years, the National Action Council for Minorities in Engineering (NACME) has supported a Retention Research Project and encouraged NACME member institutions to support strong minority-retention programs. During academic year 1981–1982, researchers at 11 private and public schools of engineering conducted studies on retention in order to identify factors that seem to be associated with dropout rates. Their findings showed that three factors were positively associated with successful retention programs: (1) the use of an early-warning system that would identify potential problems among students; (2) sustained faculty–student interaction; and (3) the implementation of a summer enrichment program. Though somewhat less powerful as a predictor of success, but nonetheless of importance, was the presence of ethnic student organizations. The results of these studies showed that freshmen retention rates among minority students increased by 13% in one year. At some institutions, success rates were substantially more dramatic. For instance, the retention rate at Lamar University rose from 40 to 79% after a Study Center was established and peer tutoring was provided. At the University of Washington, the retention rate climbed from 62 to 100% when a two-week summer session and extra course sessions were added during the academic year. When similar activities were established at the University of Massachusetts at Amherst, the retention rate rose from 60 to 71%.[24]

In addressing these problems, *it must be reiterated that all black and all minority students do not fall in the category of "underprepared, under-financed and problem-inflicted" students. A significant proportion of these students are more than adequately prepared, often exceptionally well prepared for college programs, regardless of the field of study.* A smaller proportion, as previously stated, come from well-to-do homes and do not ordinarily require substantial financial assistance other than parental resources. *It is a tragic mistake to assume that black or any other minority students represent a homogeneous type, and it is even worse to treat them as if all required special, and all too frequently, demeaning and paternalistic attention.*

Nevertheless, we cannot deny certain demonstratable realities. The school systems of the United States, especially urban public schools, have failed black and other minority pupils. As a group, these students do not have the same quality of preparation in science, mathematical or computational skills, or in the fundamentals of the English language. Self-esteem, often high in the home environment, is forced downward by the environmental and learning conditions within the school. Expectations of some teachers are low regarding black students, and many of them seem anxious to fulfill the prophecy of low performance communicated by teachers. Besides, many black students are literally turned off by racism within the school system.

The home environment, especially parental motivation, may not be conducive to many of these students to develop sound skills. That condition may be a function of many factors, including parental disinterest; lack of parental guidance and influence on the child's behavior; the debilitating consequences of poverty or near poverty, which demand that both parents spend excessive amounts of time away from home, and the absence of learning tools within the home.[25] These situations coalesce to create a total environment in which underpreparedness might be an expected outcome.

This situation is also related to the issue of motivation for a career as an engineer. Without adequate precollege programs and excellent academic counseling in junior and senior high schools, it is unlikely that a sufficient number of black students will learn the essentials required for success as an engineering student. Students frequently do not receive the information even when institutions mail voluminous amounts of leaflets and flyers to high schools. Counselors may not always believe that a black or poor student has the capacity to be an engineer. Therefore, persuaded by his or her own biases, the pupil is encouraged by the counselor to opt for a less strenuous curriculum leading to a less prestigious and less demanding job on graduation from high school.

Finance

A particularly serious impediment to retention through graduation is the financial plight of a disproportionate number of black students. This problem goes considerably beyond having sufficient funds for tuition and books. It extends to worry and the psychological difficulties engendered by excessive anxiety over *how* to obtain the money required to remain in school.[26]

As a general rule, students meet their financial needs in one or a combination of four methods: (1) parental contributions; (2) federal and state programs, including loans, scholarships, and grants; (3) student's/spouse's earnings; and (4) funds from foundations, private business and industry, and individual philanthropists.[27] However, according to a study conducted in 1978, minority students do not generally have the resources required to meet the average tuition costs and other education expenses. The ECDP estimated in 1978 that average tuition cost in public engineering schools (in-state only) was $624, while that of private institutions was $3099.[28] Total costs amounted to $2927 in public institutions and an average of $5620 in private colleges of engineering. In 1985, the average tuition at private colleges is $5418, while that at public colleges is $3719. Given the high proportion of black students who come from families whose median family income is under $10,000 per year, it is evident that most require some form of financial aid. The problem is especially critical for blacks attending private institutions, since their costs are considerably higher.

Recognition of the magnitude of the financial aid problem is not a recent phenomenon. At the inception of the minorities-in-engineering effort, programs to assist black and other minority students were initiated to meet their financial requirements for engineering education programs. Earlier, substantial contributions were made by members of the corporate structure, foundations, and private individuals, which provided much needed scholarships for black and other minority students.

When the Planning Commission for Expanded Opportunities in Engineering issued its highly influential report, *Minorities in Engineering: A Blueprint for Action,* in 1974, it called for the strengthening of financial aid contributions to specified minority groups. It also recommended the establishment of a new fund-raising organization that would be the conduit for all funds raised to support the minorities-in-engineering effort. Out of that recommendation, based on a belief that the quality of financial aid was the major obstacle to accelerating minority-student access to engineering, came the National Fund for Minority Engineering Students. (NFMES).[29] This organization was established in 1975, just as financial aid resources overall began to decline, especially for students in other professions. Its essential functions are to "raise and distribute scholarship funds."[30] Early in 1976, the organization raised over $2 million, one-half of which was distributed to 1000 minority students.[31]

The 54 NACME members, including 34 corporate chairmen, renewed their pledge for support for the engineering effort in 1976. Of 24 NACME members, in a survey conducted under the auspices of the Conference Board and reported in 1978, this commitment was already evident. More than $5 million in total corporate contributions were made in 1977 alone. (In addition, these firms had given generously for the purchasing of school supplies, laboratory and classroom equipment, and books.)

They also contributed 88% of the total amount given by NACME companies to the NFMES. Pledges rose to $9.3 million by June 1979, from some 89 corporations. Private foundations pledged an additional $2 million. It should be noted, however, that three companies gave over $1 million each and that this represented 42% of all contributions from the corporate structure. The top companies accounted for 67% of the total contributions. Without a doubt, these contributions generated considerably more money in scholarship dollars for black and other minority students.[32] Precisely how much more is not known; however, since over 17,000 black students are currently enrolled and since most minority students require financial support, much greater help is at presently needed.

The NFMES initiated a system of "incentive grants" for a school or college of engineering that "committed itself to challenge goals." These goals are enrollment targets mutually agreed upon by the fund and the institution. Awards are granted as these targets are met or approximated, and scholarship monies are made available to support the target group. In 1984, 134 engineering colleges, including the Massachusetts Institute of Technology (MIT) and Illinois Institute of Technology (IIT), participated in the program. About 3700 students currently receive NFMES funds. Awards granted to individual students range from $250 to $2500. The criterion for an award is now "the most qualified students who also need financial aid." When the fund was first established, the criterion was listed as "a needy student."[33] The average award is $735 per year. Awards totaled $2.8 million in 1983–1984.

The fund also sponsors a Summer Engineering Employment Project. This financial aid strategy further enables many black and other minority students to obtain invaluable work experience in an engineering setting, such as in industry or business. Many companies offer jobs to students who participated in summer programs following the completion of the B.S. degree in engineering. Despite the various assistance programs mentioned here, the problem of financing higher education persists for a significant proportion of the black student population. Given current and anticipated shortages of trained personnel, the nation's best interests will be served by providing financial assistance to needy black engineering students.

Self-Confidence

The low level of self-confidence offered as an explanation for the dropout rate among black and other minority students is not only related to underpreparation but to more personal and social factors. While it is quite true that many students do not receive adequate preparation in science and mathematics, many all too early in their lives internalize negative attitudes about these subjects. They come to regard such subjects as too difficult or as subject matter that can be mastered only by bright and gifted students. Similarly, in many instances, students who excel in science and mathematics are placed on a pedestal by their teachers and set apart for special treatment. Those who do not demonstrate the same degree of skill or apparent competence may inadvertently be regarded as "less brainy" or unable to master the most rudimentary science problem. A student who constantly confronts such attitudes, without proper home reinforcement of capabilities, is much more likely to internalize doubts and to develop a lowered sense of self-confidence than would otherwise be the case.

Estrangement

Personal and family problems combined with efforts to adjust to a different social milieu may generate complications in the learning process. When life styles encountered in the colleges' environment, especially for students living in residence, are widely varied from those of the home situations, new adjustments are necessary. Making this transition is sometimes difficult for students. Their reaction may be withdrawal and further isolation from their peers. That isolation is a manifestation of institutional alienation, which, in turn, may become so severe that the response deemed by the students to be most appropriate is simply to withdraw.[34]

Attrition can be controlled. It can be reduced if the early signals of difficulty are immediately recognized and properly handled. But this requires imaginative programs, staff, financial aid, role models, counseling, academic support, a positive and supportive learning environment, reduced racism, and elimination of smothering paternalism disguised as liberalism. It demands recognition of the reality that each black student is a distinct and unique personality—separate and apart from all others. In effect, broadbased retention programs that avail academic and affective support services to all students are vital. In this process, the attitudes conveyed by faculty members toward black students are of special concern. Persistence is directly related to the way students respond to faculty perceptions of them.

Graduation Rates

The number of blacks graduating with a B.S. in Engineering increased by almost 600% between 1970 and 1984. In fact, in 1984 the number of blacks with engineering baccalaureate degrees exceeded 2000 for the first time ever. Although the trend in the production of blacks with the first professional degree in engineering has been upward since 1970, blacks in 1984 still represent less than 3% of all degrees awarded in engineering. Whites continue to be overrepresented, while blacks are underrepresented in the production of engineering baccalaureates. This situation persists despite increasing enrollment and graduation of blacks with engineering degrees. Although, on the surface, it appears that the gains made by blacks are most impressive and significant, relative to the persistence of the white monopoly in the production of engineers, it is perhaps an understatement to argue that blacks have not achieved parity in this profession. Nevertheless, the progress in the production of blacks with engineering degrees over the 10-year period is dramatic. The nation's 282 colleges of engineering produced 1649 more black engineering professionals in 1984 than was the situation in 1974. During that period, some 766,619 engineering baccalaureate degrees were awarded. Of that number, 15,442 were awarded to blacks. Still, blacks constituted a mere 2% of all such degrees awarded (see Table 54).

During any year, as evidenced by the data presented in Table 55, the colleges of engineering located at historically black colleges award about three-fifths of all B.S. degrees received by blacks. The range of this proportion is from 34.2% conferred by Tennessee State University to 89.7% of all engineering degrees received by blacks at institutions located in the District of Columbia (conferred by Howard University and the University of the District of Columbia). Further, of all B.S. in Engineering degrees received by blacks in Alabama, almost two-thirds (63.2%) are earned at Tuskegee University, a historically black institution.

With respect to the production of blacks with engineering degrees in the "Adams states," and the District of Columbia, there is little reason to be optimistic about either the present condition or progress. Without question, some progress has been made with respect to recruitment and production of black engineers in these jurisdictions since the Adams litigation began. However, in 1984, there is no jurisdiction in which the number of blacks graduated with engineering degrees approximates parity. As shown in Table 56, the range in the production of blacks with this degree by all institutions combined within a given state is from a low of .4% in West Virginia to 28% in the District of Columbia. And as previously noted, two predominantly black institutions account for almost 90% of the total number of engineering baccalaureates earned by blacks in the District of Columbia. The continuing underproduction of blacks with engineering

Table 54
Bachelor's Engineering Degrees Awarded, by Race 1970–1984, All Institutions Combined

Year	Total B.S. Degrees Awarded	B.S. Degrees to Blacks	% Blacks
1984	76,576	2,022	2.6
1983	71,591	1,900	2.6
1982	66,652	1,646	2.4
1981	62,935	1,445	2.3
1980	58,742	1,320	2.2
1979	52,598	1,076	2.0
1978	46,091	901	1.9
1977	40,095	844	2.1
1976	37,970	777	2.0
1975	38,210	734	2.0
1974	41,407	756	1.8
1973	43,429	657	1.5
1972	44,190	579	1.3
1971	43,167[a]	407	0.9
1970	42,966[a]	378	.8
Total	766,619	15,442	2.0

Source: Engineering Manpower Commission.

[a]Figures for black students are understated because they do not include data from nonreporting institutions.

Table 55
Black Engineering Baccalaureates Awarded by Predominantly Black Colleges, 1984

Institution	State	Total 1984 Black Graduates in State	Number Produced by Black College	%
Tuskegee University	Alabama	117	74	63.2
Howard University	District of Columbia	127	74	58.2
University of District Columbia	Columbia	127	40	35.5
Southern University	Louisiana	103	57	55.3
N.C. A&T University	No. Carolina	113	56	49.5
Tennessee State	Tennessee	73	25	34.2
Prairie View A&M	Texas	167	97	58.0
Total		700	423	60.4

Source: NACME and Engineering Manpower Commission.

degrees in these states, which also are states in which blacks represent a substantial proportion of the population and in which the pool of black students is comparatively large, indicates that a sustained, aggressive recruitment, retention, and graduation program is mandated by all institutions in these states.

Table 56
Engineering Baccalaureates Awarded in 1984, by Race, in "Adams States" and the District of Columbia

State	Total No. of Graduates	No. of Black Graduates	% Black	Rank in Group
Alabama	1,488	117	7.8	2
Arkansas	359	17	4.7	5
Delaware	268	7	2.6	8
Dist. of Columbia	453	127	28.0	a
Florida	2,001	46	2.3	10
Georgia	1,350	81	6.0	4
Kentucky	556	7	1.2	16
Louisiana	1,465	103	7.0	3
Maryland	1,189	19	1.6	14
Mississippi	550	14	2.5	9
Missouri	1,887	37	1.9	11
No. Carolina	1,414	113	7.9	1
Ohio	3,574	50	1.4	15
Oklahoma	1,002	5	0.5	17
Pennsylvania	4,682	83	1.7	13
So. Carolina	752	26	3.4	7
Texas	4,459	167	3.7	6
Virginia	1,703	32	1.8	12
W. Virginia	617	3	0.4	18
Total	29,769	1,054	3.5	

Source: NACME and Engineering Manpower Commission.
[a]Unranked since the District of Columbia is not an "Adams state."

Graduate Degrees

During the 1970s, graduate schools of engineering in the United States conferred a total of 163,372 M.S. degrees. Of that number, 1240 went to black students. In other words, *black Americans earned less than 1% (0.7%) of all M.S. degrees in Engineering during the 1970s* (see Table 57).

Table 57
Masters's Engineering Degrees Conferred, 1970–1984,
by Race, All Institutions Combined

Year	M.S. Total Total	M.S. Awarded to Black Students	% Blacks
1984	20,992	253	1.2
1983	19,673	258	1.3
1982	18,543	188	1.0
1981	17,914	183	1.0
1980	17,243	167	0.9
1979	16,036	159	0.9
1978	16,182	202	1.2
1977	16,551	147	0.8
1976	16,506	154	0.9
1975	15,773	141	0.8
1974	15,885	158	0.9
1973	17,152	104	0.6
1972	17,356	78	0.4
1971[a]	16,383	47	0.8
1970[a]	15,548	50	0.3
Total	257,737	2,289	.89

Source: Engineering Manpower Commission.
[a]Figures for black students are understated because they do not include data from non-reporting institutions.

Between 1980 and 1984, about 94,365 masters degrees in Engineering were awarded in the United States. Of that number, 1049 or 1.1% were conferred on black Americans. Progress cannot be denied. However, progress is itself highly relative and must be placed in the context of the total number of degrees conferred plus the meanings of the changes observed. Between 1970 and 1984, blacks experienced a 500% increase in the production of M.S. in Engineering, compared to an increase of approximately 33% among whites and others. In absolute terms, this increase means a rise from 50 blacks with this degree in 1970 to 253 with the degree in 1984. Even with what appears to be a dramatic growth for blacks, whatever penchant this evokes for sanguinity must be tempered by the reality that, in 1984, colleges of engineering produced almost 21,000 masters' degrees, but only 1.2% of them were awarded to blacks. That is an intolerable level of underrepresentation.

Only engineering schools at Stanford, George Washington University and Georgia Tech have awarded 10 or more M.S. in Engineering degrees to black students each year since 1980. Several institutions conferred between 5 and 9 M.S. degrees during the same period. These include Catholic University, University of Michigan, MIT, Cornell, Air Force Institute of Ohio, Carnegie Mellon, and Drexel University. Of institutions located in the "*Adams* states," only Georgia Tech, among traditionally white institutions, recruits and graduates substantial numbers of black students at the M.S. level.

The number of black students who earned the Ph.D. in Engineering degree rose steadily from 1 student in 1970 to 19 in 1979. From 1980 onward, the number of doctoral degrees earned by black Americans in engineering has ranged from 16 in 1980 to 29 in 1983 (see Table 58). Again, these numbers often do not exceed even 1% of all engineering degrees conferred on U.S. citizens. As stated earlier, this dearth of graduate engineering degrees earned by black Americans has serious and significant implications for affirmative action—the recruitment and hiring of blacks in positions that demand a graduate degree. The fact that black engineering doctorates constitute not even 1.0% of the total number produced during any given year in the 1980s, reinforces the gross underrepresentation of blacks with this level of training in engineering. Further, it is solid evidence to support the contention that graduate schools can no longer afford to be passive if they are seriously committed to eliminating racial disparities. They must mount aggressive recruitment and training of black Americans for graduate education, whether in engineering or any other field in which the production of black graduates is woefully inadequate.

As with the production of M.S. degrees, only a handful of doctoral-granting institutions have been major centers for the training and production of blacks with engineering doctorates. These include such institutions as Stanford and MIT.

Problem Areas

One of the most important tasks before the engineering education community is to provide more role models for black students in colleges of engineering. Fewer than 20 institutions among the 282 schools and colleges of engineering in the United States have black faculty members.[35] Among these institutions are Stanford, MIT, Northeastern University (Mass.), University of Maryland, Georgia Tech, University of California/Berkeley, and University of Connecticut (whose Dean of Engineering is black). Ten of them are historically black colleges. Especially in highly technical and scientific fields to which so much prestige is attached, it is imperative for young people to have firsthand knowledge that members of their racial or ethnic group have become successful. The absence of black faculty members,

Table 58
Engineering Doctorates Conferred, by Race, 1970–1984,
All Institutions Combined

Year	Total Number of Doctorates Awarded	Doctorates Awarded Black Students	% Blacks
1984	3234	19	.59
1983	3023	29	.96
1982	2887	11	.39
1981	2841	16	.56
1980	2751	19	.69
1979	2815	19	.60
1978	2573	15	.50
1977	2814	16	.50
1976	2977	10	.50
1975	3138	17	.50
1974	3362	12	.30
1973	3687	13	.30
1972	3774	13	.30
1971[a]	3640	8	.20
1970[a]	3620	1	b
Total	47,136	218	.46

Source: Engineering Manpower Commission.
[a]Figures for black students are underestimated because they do not include data from nonreporting institutions.
[b]Insignificant

at the graduate level particularly, may be a major explanatory factor. Black graduate students do not have the option of working and studying with black mentors as do white students. It is in fact a tribute to the recruitment programs and the minority recruiters that they have done as well as they have in producing what is tantamount to a phenomenal increase in the overall number of black students in engineering. The problem here is not only the diminishing momentum observed between the completion of the baccalaureate degree and ability to encourage enrollment in graduate programs. It is a serious indictment of the academic community and state legislators for failing to make academic salaries more competitive with industry and the corporate community.

Another major problem is the disjunction between entry-level enrollment figures and the actual production of engineers among black Americans. The rate of production lags much too far behind enrollment. That is a function of attrition and failure to mount and sustain a sound retention program. Undoubtedly, the two primary aspects of this problem are the quality of preparation in science and mathematics and the availability of a high-quality financial aid package. To resolve the difficulties implicit in these two variables requires an essential linkage between all precollege programs and changes in institutional conditions. Obviously, expanded financial aid is needed now more than ever before.

Most of the institutions surveyed claim that the *Bakke* case will have absolutely no impact on their minority engineering effort.

Architectural Education

A more detailed study of architectural education and the access of black and other minority students than given here is imperative. The Association of Collegiate Schools of Architecture did not provide useful data required to establish 15-year trends. According to one source, "only 20 to 30% of the 87 schools" approved by the National Architectural Accrediting Board (NAAB) report enrollment and graduation data by minority group on a regular basis.[36] This truncated discussion is based largely on information on the period between 1975 and 1978. Limited information is available on the education of black Americans in architecture for the 1978–1984 period. This paucity is due primarily to institutional failures to disaggregate minority student enrollment by specific groups.

Apparently, during the 1960s, professional architects made some efforts toward consciousness raising regarding the status of women and minorities in the profession. Like so many professions, environmental design and general architecture had been, and remains, although to a lesser degree, a white male preserve. Conferences were held on the subject of expanding educational opportunities for minority groups, but there is very little information concerning formal programs that went beyond the talking stage.[37]

It is estimated that fewer than 1% of the architects in the United States are black.[38] Many of them were trained at one of the seven departments and schools or colleges of architecture located at historically black colleges: Florida A & M, Hampton Institute, Howard University, Prairie View A & M, Southern University, Tennessee State University, and Tuskegee Institute. As of the summer of 1984, the program at Prairie View was not accredited by the NAAB, and the program at Tennessee State University was in Architecture and Engineering Technology.[39] Further, Florida A & M's School of Architecture is regarded by some as a white architectural school in a black institution, for it was established primarily by white faculty.

Many historically black colleges are currently experiencing difficulties in the recruitment of students for their programs. Consequently, they have embarked on aggressive recruitment efforts to attract more students and protect their programs. Part of the problem stems from the change in clientele, especially in institutions, black and white, that are in transition from an undergraduate to a graduate school.

Although a few changes may have occurred since *Architectural Schools in North America* was issued, some insight may be gleaned from enrollment data on "ethnic and minority students" reported by the historically black colleges. At that time, the number of students so classified were 23 at Florida A & M, 15 at Hampton Institute, 21 at Howard University, no data on Prairie View A & M, 142 at Southern University, 96 at Tennessee State University and 108 at Tuskegee Institute. Since we normally assume that about 90% of students classified in the category of "racial and ethnic minority" are black, it is safe to assume that Southern University in Baton Rouge enrolled more black students in Bachelor of Architecture programs than any institution in the nation. In fact, of the 52 institutions included in this study, 39 enrolled fewer students in this category than did Hampton Institute.[40]

Efforts to enroll more black students in schools of architecture throughout the nation seemed to have peaked during the mid-1970s. It is claimed that only about one-third of the 87 NAAB accredited schools now make a special effort to attract black students to this profession, and most of them are private institutions. In general, public institutions have larger numbers of applicants and, judging from past history, have not been as inclined to expend the necessary energy to assure a more heterogeneous mix among the student body of colleges of architecture.[41]

Nevertheless, in academic year 1977–1978, it was estimated that 1300, or 8% of the 14,000 students enrolled in B.A. in Architecture programs in the 87 schools of architecture in the nation were from minority groups. The largest numbers of these students appeared to have matriculated in institutions in which minorities were faculty members of the schools. By 1984, the 4083 minority students enrolled in the baccalaureate architecture programs constituted 24.5% of the 16,651 B.A. in Architecture enrollees. Due to the failure of the 89 schools of architecture to differentiate between minority groups, no definitive statement can be given with respect to absolute numbers of blacks enrolled in accredited schools of architecture. However, it is known that five HBIs had accredited schools of architecture in 1984: Howard University, Florida A&M, Hampton Institute, Southern University, and Tuskegee University. Baccalaureate enrollment data were available on only three of these institutions, and graduate data were available on two.

In 1984, blacks made up 269 of the 281 architectural baccalaureate enrollees at Howard University. They accounted for 146 of the 165 baccalaureate matriculants at Hampton, and 156 of the 244 students enrolled in the B.A. in Architecture program at Southern University. Exactly one-half (4 of 8) of the masters' degree enrollees at Florida A&M, and 65% (13 of 20) of the masters' degree students at Tuskegee, were black. The HBIs that had the largest numbers of blacks providing instruction also enrolled the greatest number of black students. For instance, 15 (60%) of Howard's 25-member faculty in architecture were black; 100% (8 of 8) of those at Southern University were black; 50% (5 of 10) of those at Tuskegee; one-fifth (2 of 10) at Hampton, and 1 of 18 of the architecture faculty at Florida A&M were black. The HBIs graduated approximately 100 blacks with the B.A. in Architecture degree in 1984. Howard University accounted for almost 50% of this cohort.[42]

This sketchy overview raises a number of questions concerning access and production of black students in architecture that cannot be addressed here. We need far more disaggregated data and more specific institutional information concerning precise programs that these colleges operate now or have conducted in the past in order to assess fully their roles in the mainstreaming of blacks in architecture.

Notes

1. *Minorities in Engineering: A Blueprint For Action* (Report of the Planning Commission for Expanding Opportunities in Engineering. Alfred P. Sloan Foundation, New York, 1974), p. 1.
2. Ibid., pp. 96–97.
3. Ibid., p. 99.
4. Ibid., p. 188.
5. Seymour Lusterman, *Minorities in Engineering: The Corporate Role* (New York: The Conference Board. 1979), p. 2.
6. Ibid.
7. Ibid.
8. Ibid.
9. Ibid.
10. Ibid., p. 3.
11. Ibid.; see also *The Committee on Minorities in Engineering: Scope and Activities* (Washington, D.C.: National Research Council, n.d), p.3.
12. Ibid.
13. Ibid.
14. *Committee on Minorities in Engineering*.
15. Lusterman, *Minorities in Engineering*, p. 3.
16. Ibid.
17. *Committee on Minorities in Engineering*.
18. Ibid., pp. 3–7.
19. Interview with Levoy Spooner of the Committee on Minorities in Engineering, June 1979.
20. *Minorities in Engineering: Blueprint for Action*, p. 9.
21. See *Retention of Minority Students in Engineering* (Washington, D.C.: National Academy of Sciences, 1977).
22. Ibid., p. 2.
23. Ibid.

24. NACME, *Increasing the Yield, 1981–82* (New York: NACME, 1983), p. 13.
25. James E. Blackwell, "Social Factors Affecting Educational Opportunity for Minority Group Students," in *Beyond Desegregation: Urgent Issues in the Education of Minorities* (New York; College Board, 1978), Chap. 1.
26. NACME, *Op. Cit.*
27. *Financial Aid Needs of Undergraduate Minority Engineering Students in the 1980s* (New York: National Fund for Minority Engineering Students, December 1978).
28. Ibid.
29. Ibid.
30. *Minorities in Engineering: A Blueprint for Action*, pp. 134–135.
31. Ruth G. Schaegger, "Corporate Leadership in National Program," *Conference Board Record* 13, no. 9 (September 1976): 9.
32. Ibid.
33. Lusterman, *Minorities in Engineering*, p. 42.
34. *Retention of Minority Students in Engineering.*
35. Ibid.
36. From an interview with Dr. Lucian Walker, dean of the Howard University School of Engineering, June 1979 and June 1985.
37. Personal interview with Dr. Hugo Blasdel of the National Architectural Accrediting Board, September 1979.
38. Ibid.
39. Ibid.
40. Ibid.
41. *Architectural Schools in North America.*
42. Blasdel, *Op. Cit.*

11 THE LEGAL PROFESSION AND
BLACK AMERICANS

The primary focus of this chapter is on legal education for black Americans during the 1970s and 1980s. It examines the impact that policy changes in legal professional associations enunciated during the 1980s have on the inclusion of black and other minority students in law schools. It describes enrollment trends and some of the more salient factors associated with these changes. Special attention is given to issues of conflict and confrontation evidenced in special admissions and the *DeFunis* case; the role of the Council on Legal Education Opportunities Program in mainstreaming blacks, and persisting problems that impede progress in increasing the representation of black Americans in the legal profession.

A Historical Overview

Any assessment of changes in the status of black Americans in the legal profession or of efforts to increase their representation in schools of law must be placed in the context of overall enrollment changes during the period under review. In that regard, it should be stressed that law schools have experienced phenomenal growth and an unparalleled demand for space since the end of World War II. This exceptional demand for space in schools of law is at the core of many of the dominant issues regarding the paticipation of blacks and other minority students in legal education. It is the cutting edge of issues pertinent to admission to the practice of law, for this growth in demand stimulated the movement to develop quantitative measures for a more restrictive determination of eligibility.

The instrument of *exclusion* sought was attained with the development of the Law School Admission Test (LSAT) in 1947. (Others may perceive the LSAT as a determinant of *inclusion;* that is a point of major contention, especially since so many persons regard the LSAT, like all objective admission tests, as a primary method devised for the benefit of professional schools to exclude persons they do not want.) Nevertheless, the LSAT was not immediately embraced by American schools of law. In fact, according to Franklin R. Evans, only 18 law schools utilized this test in its assessment processes in 1948, the first year it was administered.[1] However, with the realization of its immense utility, its popularity grew widely and spread to cover approximately 90% of all entering law school students by 1967. In 1980 the American Bar Association, which sets the standards for accreditation for law schools and accredits them, required law schools to *demand* that students seeking admission to the schools present their LSAT scores.[2] Even with this requirement, the power of the test for inclusion or exclusion was never revealed until the unprecedented numerical growth of law applications began about 1953.

As is detailed in a subsequent section, total enrollment in schools of law, approved by the American Bar Association, has tripled since 1950, when it stood at 43,685 compared to a total enrollment of 125,689 in 1984. Since 1962, or even 1965, total enrollment has more than doubled in ABA-approved law schools.[3] Although the enrollment of black students in schools of law was highly significant during this period and also more than doubled, it did not keep pace with the upward spiral witnessed among white applicants who were successfully admitted to law schools.

Notwithstanding, there can be little doubt about the veracity of the viewpoint that as pressure for space in law schools mounted, the utilization of quantitave determinants as a defensible solution to the problem and as justification for decisions to *exclude* accelerated. This position has never achieved unequivocable and universal support. To the contrary, opponents to this exclusionary quality of cognitive measures attacked them with the same vehemence employed by their defenders, who proclaimed their unimpeachability as gatekeepers of the meritocracy. The latter group ultimately argued their sacrosanct character as the primary safeguard against the lowering of admissions standards and as the protectors of quality of the product graduated by schools of law.

Proponents of so-called meritocracy often advocated cognitive measures as a front-line defense against affirmative action, special admissions, special programs, and special scholarships for black and other minority students. Some opponents to this perception of a "strict meritocracy" based solely on objective or mathematically constructed criteria countered with the assertion that this sudden attachment to cognitive devices was a mask either for a resentment of the efforts to include blacks and other minorities or for subliminal racism.

Despite the decision by the U.S. Supreme Court in the *Baake* case, the arguments remain, organizational and individual polarization persists, and suspicions of motives of various groups pervade social relationships and intergroup interactions. Minority students suffer because of the racism in American society that permits individuals to asume that simply because the person is a lawyer from a minority group, the credentials he or she has legitimately earned, frequently with honors and distinction, are necessarily suspect. Hence, these persons are called on to *prove* their mettle in ways never demanded of other groups in this country.

Another aspect of the historical context is the central role performed by schools of law located at historically black colleges and universities in the training of lawyers from minority groups. These institutions arose during the pre-*Brown* period; that is, prior to 1954. They were established largely by state legislative mandates, often hurriedly, as a means of keeping the existing public schools of law "for whites only." Some came into existence at the public historically black institutions on the insistence of black educators in the state who wished to elevate their colleges to university status by the establishment of professional colleges or schools.

Over time, schools of law were developed at Texas Southern University (Houston), Southern University (Baton-Rouge, Louisiana), South Carolina State College (Orangeburg), North Carolina Central University (Durham), Lincoln University (Jefferson City, Missouri) Florida A & M University (Tallahassee), and Howard University (one of the oldest in the nation, established in 1869, in Washington, D.C.). Of these institutions, only four remain as viable schools of law in 1987: Howard University School of Law, which is the oldest and perhaps most prestigious of this group; Thurgood Marshall School of Law at Texas Southern University; Southern University School of Law; and the School of Law of North Carolina Central University. Although established primarily to serve the needs of black Americans during the period of de jure segregation, each one of these law schools is considerably more racially integrated than is any other institution, public and private, in the state or jurisdiction in which it exists. Generally, each produces more white graduates than the number of black law students graduated from the traditionally white law school in the same jurisdiction.

Graduates and faculty members of these institutions are among the more distinguished members of the legal profession. They include judges, prosecutors, public officials, law school professors, college presidents, members of the president's cabinet (the late Hon. Patricia Harris), and a member of the U.S. Supreme Court (Associate Justice Thurgood Marshall). Without a doubt, these historically black schools of law, like their counterparts in medicine, have performed a major service to the nation as a whole. Without them, the proportion of blacks in the legal profession, minute as it is, would be considerably less than the 2% representation of blacks in law in 1987.

The Impact Of Professional Associations

The major thrust of the 1960s regarding equality of access was on how to include more black and other minority-group members *within* the system. That was indisputably an integrationist perspective, which demanded that groups denied democratic privileges of citizenship now be granted all such rights and privileges. These groups demanded to be "in," and being "in" meant access to the entire institutional fabric of the social system, as well as equality of rewards for services rendered.

Including previously excluded groups necessitated major policy changes and unequivocable leadership among the various professional associations that would direct the course of action taken by their appurtenant or constitutent subgroups. By the early 1960s, the American Bar Association had dropped its membership barriers to black Americans. The persistence of these barriers had earlier on led to the founding by black lawyers of the National Bar Association. The ABA committed itself in policies promulgated at this time to ending discrimination based on race or ethnic origin. What these policies meant was that blacks and other minority groups were no longer to be denied membership, by official decree, in law schools or any ABA-sanctioned activity on the basis of race or national origin.[4]

The American Association of Law Schools (AALS) issued an "Anti-Discrimination "Article" that was included in the Articles of Association in 1963. This article demanded that member institutions provide or maintain "equality of opportunity in legal education" and terminate all aspects of discrimination based on race or color. This position was affixed in the "Approved Association Policy" that was annexed to that provision. This policy left no doubt that its central concern was with ending discrimination in *admission* to law schools.[5] In effect, this policy was a reaffirmation of some of the recommendations made earlier by the AALS Committee on Racial Discrimination to end restrictive barriers to equity in the admissions process. That committee also warned in 1963 of current and impending problems blacks faced in being admitted to the practice of law and to the future problem of persuading blacks even to apply to law schools.[6]

Under the leadership of the AALS president in 1963, Walter Geilhorn, a number of far-reaching changes were in the offing. In his presidential address in Los Angeles in December 1963, President Geilhorn advanced a number of what could then be described as "bold plans" for the more effective inclusion of black Americans in legal education and for the removal of impediments to the practice of law. Three of his eight proposals had a direct bearing on the legal education of black Americans. They were projects that the AALS could support immediately: (1) a study of the major social, economic, financial, education, and other structural impediments to the enrollment of black students in schools of law; (2) a study of the imbalanced delivery of legal professional services to the needy and disadvantaged population; and (3) a study of the strengths, weaknesses, and problems associated with part-time legal education. A grant was obtained from the

Ford Foundation to support the study envisioned in the first project. A Special Committee on Provision of Needed Legal Services was created to implement the second project, and a special project on part-time legal education was organized with the appointment of a full-time project director.[7]

Both the ABA and the AALS are among the sponsors of the Council on Legal Education Opportunity Program (CLEO), which has assisted an average of 200 minority students each year since 1968 to enroll in schools of law. In addition, both groups established special committees to address primary concerns of minority groups. The ABA's legal consultant issues an annual report that updates enrollment data on blacks and other minority students by class for all approved schools of law. A Review of Legal Education in the United States, published annually, also describes specific kinds of institutional data. These data may include enrollment and graduation statistics, tuition per year, admissions requirements, and other information of special interest to a potential applicant. The Pre-Law School Handbook is considerably more detailed in this regard, since it often expands on the specific institutional characteristics.

The AALS established a Standing Committee on Minority Groups. This committee has over the years addressed a number of issues related to the AALS policy enunciated in the "Principals of Non-Discrimination" and its "Equality of Opportunity" provision that was amended on December 30, 1970.[8] Of special concern are issues such as conformance among the various law schools to the principles of unbiased admissions procedures and policies, unbiased allocation of financial assistance, the recruitment and hiring of minority-group members as law professors, and assurance from the committee on accreditation that standards of fairness and unbiased actions are indeed upheld by all ABA-approved institutions. These concerns suggest a high degree of suspicion that conformity to these principles has not always been uniform from law school to law school.[9]

Minority-group members serve on a number of standing and special committees of the AALS, and under the auspices of the Committee on Minority Groups, they have played a special role in enhancing the overall policy of equality of opportunity and full participation of minority lawyers in the affairs of the association. One of the committee's major efforts, in addition to stimulating greater access of black and other minority students to law schools, is the Registry of Minority Faculty, which is published annually by Derek Bell, dean of the Law school at the University of Oregon.* This annual publication serves a dual purpose. First, it enables the AALS to have a quick reference guide to minority faculty by institution. Second, it enables the Committee to monitor the hiring and promotion practices of institutions with special attention to the status of racial and ethnic minorities in law schools.

*In 1986 Derek Bell resigned his position at the University of Oregon and returned to the Harvard University Law School.

In addition to these activities, the professional associations played a major role in the establishment of the Law School Data Assembly Service (LSDAS). Through this service, applicants may have one set of their admissions profile, transcripts, test scores, and so forth centralized for circulation to interested institutions that participate in this service. This program, in turn, enables applicants to save enormous sums associated with paying for multiple transcripts when they apply to several law schools during the course of a single year.

One special case deserves extended discussion at this juncture. That is the case of *DeFunis* v. *Odergaard* described in Chapter I. This case was important because of the issues it raised regarding both constitutional law and its focus on special efforts undertaken in the 1960s to accelerate the process of achieving equity in the admission of minority students to law schools. When the case reached the Washington State Supreme Court, about 30 *amicus curiae* were filed.[10] Reaching a consensus on the position to be taken by the AALS involved consideration of several issues of enormous importance for higher education; for instance, preferential admissions, discretionary authority of law schools admissions committees, the appropriateness of judicial intervention on "single-factor (e.g. race) issues," the question of how standardized tests should be characterized, and how to handle the question of the validity of the LSAT. Ultimately, dissensus on those matters was resolved to the satisfaction of the members of the Executive Committee of the AALS, and its name was attached as one of the four organizations represented in the brief sponsored by the Council on Legal Education Opportunity.[11]

It should be pointed out that the AALS never opposed a hearing on the *DeFunis* case, neither in the Washington courts nor before the U.S. Supreme Court. Whereas the Executive Committee of the AALS had joined four other groups in an *amicus* brief in the lower court, it presented a separate brief before the U.S. Supreme Court. When the Supreme Court handed down its decision in this case on April 23, 1974 in which it held that the case was moot because DeFunis was already enrolled in law school and was about to be graduated, the AALS felt that its position was vindicated.

The AALS also filed one of the 62 *amicus curiae* briefs in the *Bakke* case. In effect, it reiterated its position on the continuing need to rectify past practices of segregation and discrimination, which resulted in the present underrepresentation of blacks and other minorities in the legal profession. However, the AALS appears to be quite deliberative in its approach to the difficult issues, and some individual members continue to be conservative and to promote principles of gradualism.

The ABA assumed a new posture on affirmative action at its 1980 meeting in Honolulu. Its House of Delegates passed Amendment 212, which requires law schools, as a condition of accreditation, to substantiate evidence that they "provide full opportunities" to minority students who wish to study law. This amendment thus became incorporated into the ABA's standards for the approval of law schools. The amendment, passed on the recommendation of the ABA's Section on Legal Education, represented a particularly powerful instrument for enforcing an implicit educational policy of long standing.

The National Bar Association, the historically black association of lawyers, was formed to carry out essentially the same functions as the originally all-white American Bar Association. It holds annual meetings that serve as a forum for addressing current issues that black lawyers confront in the profession. It sponsors seminars through which practicing lawyers can be updated on elements of the law affecting their practice, and its members engage in a number of social action programs. The NBA has been supportive of efforts to increase the representation of black Americans in the legal profession initiated in the early 1960s. It should also be stressed that among its members are black lawyers who argued most of the cases spearheaded by the National Association for the Advancement of Colored People and the Legal Defense and Educational Fund, which led to far-reaching decisions by the U.S. Supreme Court. Its members have, therefore, served as role models of special significance to minority students. By itself, this function has had an immeasurable impact on successful endeavors to attract more black Americans to the legal profession.

Council On Legal Education Opportunity (CLEO)

CLEO was organized in 1967 for the expressed purpose of strengthening efforts to enroll more minority students in the legal profession and to increase the probability that those accepted for admission would have an excellent chance for successful completion of a law school career. The establishment of CLEO came as a result of a study by the Committee on Minority Groups of the AALS, sponsored by the Ford Foundation, which demonstrated a dismal profile of the representation of minority-group students in the law school student population. The study also provided significant data that showed that the low production rate of minority-group lawyers was an outcome of certain forms of institutional behavior, as manifested, for instance, in admissions practices.[12] When CLEO was founded less than 1% of all lawyers in the nation were black Americans. Further, due to maldistributions, some states had a single black lawyer for every 30,000 black residents.[13]

CLEO operates on the premise that the traditional methods of assessing the potential of students for study in schools of law and for their possible success as lawyers do not always work for all groups of minority and disadvantaged students. It further maintains that the successful completion of special preadmission and preenrollment programs may be a more effective and appropriate assessment technique for making selection decisions than strict reliance on LSAT scores and GPAs. The third aspect of the CLEO program is its emphasis on the value of financial assistance to minority students who seek admission to law schools so that they may be encouraged actually to enroll once they are admitted.

When CLEO was established in 1967, it was sponsored by the American Bar Association, the American Association of Law Schools, the National Bar Association, and the Law School Admission Council. Later, in 1972, a new sponsor was added to this list, the La Raza National Lawyers Association. The membership of the council is made up of delegates from these bodies including student representatives.[14]

The major program efforts of CLEO are the identification, selection, and enrollment of minorities and disadvantaged students in summer institutes; the conduct of these institutes; and the awarding of annual stipends to students who participate in the program. Seven regional summer institutes are held each year. These sessions are designed to familiarize students with the demands of law school, to introduce them to the study of law through minicourses, and to help them correct certain identifiable deficiencies in their educational backgrounds.[15] Each of the seven institute sites represents one of approximately seven geographic areas into which the country is divided for administrative purposes by CLEO. The institute sites vary each year within a region, but their host institution is always an ABA-approved school of law. Courses are taught in the main by law school professors committed to the CLEO goal of strengthening the capabilities of these students to become successful matriculants in the law school of their choice.

Student participants in CLEO programs and activities are primarily, but not exclusively, from the underrepresented minority groups: blacks, Chicanos/Mexican Americans, Puerto Ricans, and Native Americans. The average number of participants per year since 1967 has been about 200 students. Between 1968 and 1985, about 5000 students had participated in the CLEO program. Of that number, 4725 completed the summer institute program. By 1985, 98% of this group had entered law school. In the first four years, 69% of CLEO students graduated from law school. The present retention rate is approximately 95%. They have enrolled in over 140 ABA-approved law schools. About 50% of CLEO students are black.

The general status of these students, regarding the admissions process, varies and may be mixed even within a particular cohort. That is to say, among the 200 institute participants may be students who have already been accepted to law schools but who want the institute experience. There may also be students who have a conditional acceptance with the final decision awaiting the outcome of their performance in the CLEO program. Also included are students who may not be accepted into a law program but who are in the process of applying.[16]

Since 1967, CLEO estimates that approximately 50% of its students have been accepted outright by schools of law and that the remaining 50% are divided between those with conditional acceptances and those who were applying but subsequently accepted. In the post-*Bakke* era, it appears that more and more law school are looking to the CLEO program and its summer institutes to assist them in reaching final decisions regarding certain students. More specifically, the CLEO performance evaluation or the CLEO endorsement serves as that *additional* factor needed to achieve a positive selection or admission decision.[17] What is apparent here is that many schools of law are increasingly reluctant to take the chances they once took regarding the use of certain predictive measures. Others are cautious, because of the ever-present danger of legal entanglements, that their selection procedures can be rationalized. Still other law schools may very well be using the *Bakke* decision as a justification for retrenchment or inaction regarding the recruitment and selection of minority students for law school.

The funding of the CLEO program has always been inadequate to fulfill the goal of providing *adequate* financial assistance to its students. Funds to support program operation and administration, including salaries for professional staff and program activities such as prelaw recruitment and the summer institutes, were initially supported by annual grants from the Legal Services Division of the Office of Economic Opportunity (OEO). In 1971 this grant was supplemented by another one from the Special Student Services Division of the Office of Education in the Department of Health, Education, and Welfare. The annual federal appropriation ceiling for CLEO's entire operation has been $1 million since 1967. In fact, the monies from the two sources meant that a total of $950,000 was received from the federal government for its operations. As a result, CLEO, which provides annual stipends of $1000 to each of its students, was at precisely the same funding level in 1985 as it was in 1967, and the federal government has made no allowances for depreciation of the dollar. However, the federal appropriation generated $3 million dollars in institutional support.[18]

CLEO officials have been forced to make annual treks to Congress to justify its existence and to fight for its $1 million, despite all the evidence of the program's success in achieving its objectives. There were years in which its continuation was in doubt, largely because of congressional indifference, and in one year it probably would have been sacrificed had it not been for timely intervention from then Senator Walter Mondale. The program is funded through 1986 pursuant to provisions of Title IX, Part D, of the Higher Education Act of 1965, as amended. But, once again, CLEO stipends are limited to $1000 per year per student. This is in sharp contrast to the stipends of $4500 per student per year permitted to other programs funded under the same act, such as the GPOP and Public Service Scholarships. However, there is a possibility that CLEO scholarships might be increased when Congress reconsiders the 1965 Higher Education Act once again in 1987. Under its FY 86 budget, CLEO received $1.5 million from the federal government.* This increase permitted an increase in annual stipends of $750, or $1750 on average for each of the three years in law school. CLEO has requested a ceiling of $5 million, which would enable it to raise the level of its stipends consistent with the present dollar value and to continue to strengthen its program, as well as to broaden the scope of its activities to include a more representative number of minority students.[19]

None of the sponsoring organizations has made substantial financial contributions to CLEO over the years, even though they have provided other advice and support of immeasurable value. In contrast, several major foundations and corporations have given direct financial assistance for the maintenance and support of CLEO's program. Among these are such groups as the following:

Ford Foundation	IBM
Rockefeller Brothers Fund	RCA Corporation
American Bar Endowment	Xerox Corporation
General Electric Foundation	General Motors
Celanese Foundation	International Mining & Chemical
Standard Oil of Indiana	Ford Motors Company Fund
Alcoa Corporation	Singer Corporation
Standard Oil	Western Electric
P.P.F. Industries	Jones & Laughlin Corporation
Philip Morris Corporation	CBS Corporation

Despite the constant struggle over funding, CLEO has functioned as a major organizational structure for increasing the number of black and other minorities in the legal profession.

The Recruitment Of Black Students

In the mid-1960s, following the articulation of positive policy changes and the enunciation of Articles of Anti-Discrimination by the ABA and the AALS, most law schools began to seek out students from previously excluded populations. For many of these institutions, the process of actively recruiting students was an entirely new experience. Earlier, they had relied on their reputation or on their position as the flagship public institution as inducements for students to seek admission. As a result, the law school community, like the subcommunities of the entire institution, was a homo-

---

*The 1987 appropriation remained fundamentally unchanged. However, the 1988 budget proposed by President Reagan eliminates the CLEO program.

geneous unit comprised of a population dominated by white males in the student body, white male faculty, administrations, and white male boards of trustees. The 1960s demanded a change in this situation—the creation of more racially and ethnically heterogeneous communities in which men and women of all groups could have equal access.

The various steps taken to increase the representation of black students in schools of law may be better understood by focusing on specific examples of institutional activities reported for this study.

The University of Wisconsin Law School at Madison established its Legal Education Opportunities Program (LEOP) in 1967 to assist minority and disadvantaged groups to obtain legal education. One of its major activities is the recruitment of minority students, both resident and nonresident. As a result of its recruitment program, the annual enrollment of black students in this law school rose from 6 per year in 1968 to an average of 18 per year from 1972 to 1980. Recruitment here involves information dissemination, visits to various colleges and universities, use of role models from faculty and minority student body, provisions for financial assistance, campus visits, and many other activities described in other chapters. In terms of proportion of enrollment, black students constituted 2.4% of enrollment in 1968. However, in 1979, they represented 6.2% of enrollment in the school of law at Wisconsin. This change was the direct consequence of the recruitment component in the LEOP program. Black student enrollment reached an all-time high of 35 students in 1973, which then represented 11.7% of enrollment.[20]

An affirmative action program was inaugurated at Ohio State University College of Law in 1968. It embraced active recruitment as one of its central components. The College of Law carried on much of its recruitment activities during the 1970s at historically black colleges and at other institutions, which had a significant concentration of minority students. In early years, recruitment responsibilities were shared by the Dean of Admissions, faculty members of the College of Law, and representatives of the Black Americans Law Student Association (BALSA). In 1977, the College of Law added another staff person to share the recruitment effort, assist in enrollment, and strengthen the retention program. The use of the interview became more pronounced in the recruitment process, primarily to supplement information provided in the applicant's file. The college also recruits students enrolled in the midwest CLEO Institute and now extends its efforts to the precollege level.

The success of its recruitment is also measured by the change in enrollment of black students between 1968 and 1978. In 1968, the 3 black students enrolled in the College of Law represented 1.8% of enrollment of 166 students. In 1978, the 21 enrolled black law school students represented 8.2% of the total enrollment of 254 students. The largest number of black students ever matriculated was 27, in 1974. This cohort represented 11.4% of enrollment at that time.[21]

In addition to these activities, others include such strategies as open-house sessions (University of Oregon), participation in recruitment conferences and follow-up activities (Case Western Reserve University), counseling prospective applicants about law careers (University of Washington), the use of the 13 College Program and the College Board's Locater Service (American University), the utilization of a law school pre-start program that was a prototype for CLEO (Emory University), and continuing use of CLEO programs (University of Richmond).

In general, recruitment programs were immensely successful during the 1970s in seeking out, identifying, and encouraging significantly larger numbers of black and other minority students to enroll in colleges of law. However, success was neither constant nor uniform from institution to institution. Nor did it lead to racial parity in access to legal education. In fact, during the 1980s, emphasis on the recruitment of minority students has diminished significantly. Authorities at some law schools have expressed the view that it is no longer necessary or desirable to use their recources for this purpose. Consequently, the presence of black students remains at token and limited-access levels in the overwhelming majority of American schools of law. Further, as we see in the section on enrollment, a downward trend has begun that will have to be redirected in order for black Americans to attain parity in admissions and productivity even by the end of the century.

Admissions Requirements

The major controversy in law schools during the 1970's regarding black and other minority students arose over the issue of admissions standards. Heated debates centered on special admissions programs; preferential admissions procedures (which presumably favored minority students); the utilization of the LSAT as a major determinant of admission; the relative weights assigned to *quantitative* assessment measures, admissions goals, and set-aside programs; and other special programs for minority-group students. At some point during the decade, each aspect of the admissions issue came under a relentless attack by their opponents that transcended mere intellectual discourse. There were outright demands for the immediate dismantling of all programs organized to strengthen minority-group access.

In order to redress past inequities in admissions policies, which had clearly prevented the selection and enrollment of minority students for law schools, it is estimated that approximately 60% of all ABA-approved law schools constructed special admissions programs of one kind or another during the 1970s. The specific characteristics of these programs varied from law school to law school. In most instances, the development of these programs was motivated by identifiable educational values, and for explicit political, economic and social reasons. In terms of their operation, they ranged from set-aside arrangements, or clearly defined goals for the number of black and other minority students who should be admitted to each entering class, to more flexible arrangements, which included adjustments in standard admissions requirements.

Among the prominent colleges of law with special admissions programs during the period were the University of Washington, Temple University, Boalt Hall of the University of California/Berkeley, Ohio State University, University of New Mexico, New York University, University of Denver, University of Colorado, Florida State University, Indiana University, University of Iowa, the University of Wisconsin, Rutgers University, and University of Texas/Austin.

Although it is not possible to describe each program here, a brief discussion of three of the programs will illuminate processes involved in special admissions.

The College of Law of the University of Washington initiated a special admissions program in 1973. Its goal was to include "a reasonable representation of minority students" in each entering class and to assure increasing diversity in the legal profession. Under this program, black and other minority students were evaluated in a separate tract from all other applicants. LSAT scores and undergraduate GPAs were modified in order to achieve the goal of admitting "academically qualified minority applicants despite records of less strength" on these measures than other applicants. Other, noncognitive factors that were strong in the minority applicant's portfolio enabled them to advance above the mathematical cutoff levels of rejection. The process was effective in changing the racial and ethnic composition of the law school. However, since the *DeFunis* litigation the number of black students in entering classes had fallen from a high of 14 in 1970 to only 5 black students in 1978.[22]

The admissions programs at Ohio State University gave special consideration fo minority identification, and disadvantages experienced by virtue of that status and experience with testtaking and its impact on the LSAT score. Compensations derived from these considerations enabled the college to admit more disadvantaged students than otherwise would have been the case.[23]

The University of Wisconsin used recommendations from both LEOP committee and its admissions committee. The admissions committee considered the applicant's file independently of the recommendations made by the LEOP committee but then made its final decision on the basis of recommendations submitted by both committees. A number of both academic and nonacademic factors entered into the admissions process for all students.

However, minority students benefited, but not unfairly, from the employ-ment of "nontraditional" criteria such as diversity of experience and background factors.[24]

The admissions process at the University of Texas Law School was es-pecially noteworthy. Its admissions committee, like many during the 1970s, was composed of law school faculty members, members of the student body, and regular admissions or administrative personnel. The college employed what it calls an "administrative mode" and a "committee mode" in deter-mining eligibility for admission. The administrative mode was based on the "presumption of qualification." In this mode, the two objective factors that were weighed, assigned a numerical value, and combined for an index number, were the LSAT score and the undergraduate GPA. An adminis-tratively predetermined range of acceptable index scores was established. If a student's index score fell within that range, qualification was assumed.[25]

On the other hand, the committee mode is utilized to consider "evidence of qualification." In this situation, either the admissions committee or a subcommittee analyzed all data accumulated in the applicant's file and evaluated this information to determine suitability for its program and to make an assessment of the potential of that student to serve the legal needs of society.[26]

Admissions decisions were made after careful scrutiny of all relevant factors, including the number of available seats, fairness to all applicants, and the importance of diversity in the educational setting. All factors, tradi-tional and nontraditional, were subjected to intense evaluation. For exam-ple, the LSAT score was evaluated in relationship to scores received on other objective tests, such as the SAT, the ACT or the GRE. In this way, it was possible to ascertain relevant information about test-taking ability and the degree to which test scores were consistent or inconsistent with perfor-mance on LSATs and in undergraduate courses. Hence, a suggestion regarding the overall potential for success in law school might be made in a rational manner. The academic record was also evaluated in terms of the curriculum chosen by the applicant and the relative strength or reputation of the institu-tion attended. The committee looked for growth, progress, change, maturity, and other factors that were indicative of quality in the academic perfor-mance.[27]

Subjective measures also included a sense of creativity, leadership in extracurricula activities, postgraduate experiences, and evidence of energy and determination. The applicant's own personal history was subjected to a systematic and rigorous assessment in order to give the candidate the benefit of any doubt.[28]

As a result of this process, the total number of black students specially admitted to the University of Texas School of Law has been significant in every year since 1973.

For instance, in 1976, special admissions offered to black students numbered 35, while 65 were made to Mexican Americans. In that year, 3 blacks and 13 Mexican Americans were "regularly admitted." Eighteen of the black students admitted under special admissions and 2 admitted under "regular" procedures actually matriculated. (The numbers for Mexican Americans were 45 and 16, respectively.) In 1977, 47 special admissions were awarded to black students, and 57 went to Mexican Americans. The numbers of regular admissions increased for both groups. For black Americans the number was 7, and for Mexican Americans it rose to 16. Of the 47 black students admitted under special admissions arrangments, 23 actually matriculated, while 35 of the 57 Mexican Americans matriculated in the school of law. Three of the 7 regularly admitted blacks and 10 of the 16 Mexican Americans regularly admitted matriculated in 1977.[29]

According to objective data provided from the School of Law at the University of Texas, approximately 318 of the 6,000 students admitted during the 1970s were members of minority groups. *More than 98% of the minority students have succeeded as law students.*[30] Although this is significant evidence of the exceptional quality of a sound special admissions program, total access was not attained, since blacks constitute 12.5% of the population in Texas.

The experience of these four institutions with special admissions programs is instructive regarding a number of issues pertinent to the entire admissions process. For instance, it is apparent that the LSAT, while a highly useful and important predictive device for performance in the first year of law school, should not, in and of itself, be used as a reliable predictor of overall success during the entire law school career. Certainly, no valid claim can be made that LSAT scores have significant predictive power regarding success as a practicing lawyer.

According to a study made of performance on LSAT tests, black and Chicano/Mexican American applicants showed lower LSAT and lower undergraduate GPAs than did white students as a group. However, both black and Mexican American students were accepted at higher rates than white students, even though the "rate of acceptance" for white applicants was higher overall.[31] This difference reflects institutional consideration, in the main, of applicant's racial or ethnic background when selecting students during that period. However, as Evans asserts, one cannot regard the accepted minority students as anything less than fully qualified for law school. When employing the major objective predictors of success in the first year of law school, the mean GPA and the LSAT scores for minority students are higher than the mean for *all* (emphasis added) who were enrolled in 1962.[32] The meaning of this observation should not be dismissed. What is suggested here is that, as competition for limited space accelerated, law schools raised the cutoff points for undergraduate GPAs and LSAT scores higher and higher.

Consequently, some students who were highly admissible in 1962 are below eligibility levels by 1985 cognitive standards. And that is where the major problem with these measures lies.

Albeit, Evans maintains that blacks would experience a reduction rate of 60% and Mexican Americans a reduction rate of 40% if they were accepted at the same rates as majority students "at the same level of LSAT" and undergraduate gradepoint average.[33] Law schools report that if the same levels of expectations were applied universally, all things equal, and without consideration to subjective measures of evaluation, the percentage of black students in the first-year classes would fall to less than one-half of what it was in 1977, or from about 5.3% to between 1 and 2%. And this would have a national impact and widespread ramifications not only for matriculation but for, among other things, the structure of financial aid programs.[34] That is one reason why the adjustments made by law schools in the wake of the *Bakke* decision are of special salience in view of the possible "chilling effect" that misinterpretations of the Supreme Court's decision could have on the enrollment of minority students.

Responses to the Bakke Decision

Several institutions found creative methods of assuring that the full range of their assessment, selection, and admissions procedures conformed to the legal mandates of the *Bakke* decision. For example, in November 1978, the law school faculty of Rutgers University voted to modify its admissions program by expanding to 30 places the number of seats allocated for its special admissions program. This was done to assure greater inclusion of *disadvantaged* white students in the program. As a result, all seats in the entering class are open to all groups, irrespective of racial or ethnic designations.[35]

The University of Washington eliminated its two-tiered or separate evaluation system but does take race into consideration as one of many factors employed in the evaluation of an applicant. Ohio State University utilizes several of the factors reported by the School of Law at the University of Texas/Austin. So does Stanford University employ a combination of quantitative and nonquantitative factors while stressing the primacy of the former over the latter in making these decisions.[36] The impact of the collective weight of special and regular admissions programs can only be assessed in the cumulative growth or changes in the number of students enrolled since 1970. Our focus is solely on the number of black students. Although many of the trends demonstrated for black students were observed for other minority students, space does not permit an equal treatment here of these groups in this study.

Enrollment of Black Students in Law Schools Since 1970

First-Year Enrollment

First-year enrollments of black students in law schools almost doubled between 1969 and 1979 (see Table 59). However, observations of the absolute numbers of black students portray a condition of steady progress, followed by enrollment fluctuations. As the 1970s began, 1115 black first-year students were enrolled in schools of law. They represented 3.8% of all first-year enrollees. The peak in proportion of black students of all students in first-year classes was not achieved until 1978 when it reached 5.9%. However, the highest absolute number was in 1976, but this was followed by a decline of some 85 black students in the next first-year class. In 1978 there was a gain of 79 black students, but this was followed by another loss, of 19 black students in the 1979 first-year enrollment.

Table 59
First-Year Enrollment in J.D. Programs, Approved Law Schools, by Race, 1968–1984, All Institutions Combined

Academic Year	Total Enrollment	Black Student Enrollment	% Blacks
1984–85	40,747	2,214	5.4
1983–84	41,159	2,247	5.4
1982–83	42,034	2,217	5.2
1981–82	42,521	2,238	5.2
1980–81	44,296	2,144	4.8
1979–80	34,632	2,002	5.7
1978–79	34,118	2,021	5.9
1977–78	39,670	1,943	4.9
1976–77	39,996	2,128	5.3
1975–76	39,038	2,043	5.2
1974–75	38,074	1,910	5.0
1973–74	37,018	1,943	5.2
1972–73	35,131	1,907	5.4
1971–72	36,171	1,715	4.7
1970–71	34,713	N.A.	N.A.
1969–70	29,128	1,115	3.8
1968–69	23,652	N.A.	N.A.

Source: A Review of Legal Education in the United States — Fall 1985 (Chicago: American Bar Association Section on Legal Education and Admissions to the Bar).
N.A.: Not Available

Undoubtedly it is this inability to *sustain* a steady, upward trend that led to allegations of a retreat by law schools from the commitment to move forward toward parity. This assertion underscores the immense disillusionment among many black Americans over what they perceive to be failures in legal education. It is apparent that, despite the progress made and the high-quality recruitment programs established, law schools in the United States are currently enrolling only 1100 more black students in first-year classes than they did in 1969. Hence, the progress achieved is substantially less than what it may appear to have been at first glance.

Total Enrollment

The total number of black students enrolled in the 164 ABA-approved law schools more than doubled between 1969 and 1978. Specifically, the total number of black students enrolled increased from 2128 in 1969 to 5257 in 1978 (see Table 60). There was a steady rise in tht total number of black students with increases in every year through 1976. In the following year, there was a loss of 202 black students, but this was followed by a slight increase of some 45 students. However, as the decade closed, there was another loss of 93 black students in total enrollment. These losses are accounted by both declines in first-year enrollment and by attrition beyond the first year of law school.

Because of the accusations that black and other minority students entered professional schools, such as law schools, at the expense of white students, it is imperative to stress the rapid acceleration of the total number of students enrolled in law schools during the 1970s and 1980s. As Table 60 shows, the total enrollments for *all* students in law schools rose in every year of the study period. Specifically, it jumped from 62,779 in 1968 to almost 128,000 students in 1982–1983. Not until the 1979–80 academic year did minority students represent 8.1% of total enrollment. That proportion is neither equivalent, nor tantamount, to equality of opportunity and equality of access in law schools. Consequently, the issue of "reverse discrimination" looms larger and larger as a red herring constructed to forestall efforts to assure equality of opportunity to underrepresented minority groups.

However, as shown in Table 60, total black student enrollment began another upswing in 1980 when the 5506 matriculants surpassed the previous peak of 5350 black students in law schools in 1978. That increase continued through 1984, the last year for data which are available; in the academic year 1985, total black law school enrollment was 5955. In part, these increases also reflect an expansion of slots, since the number of ABA-approved schools of law had increased to 174.

Table 60
Total Enrollment in J.D. Programs, Approved Law Schools, by Race,
1968–1985, All Institutions Combined

Academic Year	Total Enrollment	Black Student Enrollment	% Blacks
1984–85	125,698	5,955	4.74
1983–84	127,195	5,967	4.69
1982–83	127,828	5,822	4.55
1981–82	127,312	5,789	4.55
1980–81	125,397	5,506	4.39
1979–80	122,860	5,257	4.20
1978–79	121,606	5,350	4.40
1977–78	118,557	5,305	4.40
1976–77	117,451	5,503	4.60
1975–76	116,991	5,127	4.40
1974–75	110,713	4,995	4.50
1973–74	106,102	4,817	4.50
1972–73	101,664	4,423	4.30
1971–72	93,118	3,744	4.00
1970–71	82,041	N.A.	N.A.
1969–70	68,386	2,128	3.10
1968–69	62,779	N.A.	N.A.

Source: A Review of Legal Education In the United States — Fall 1985 (Chicago: Americal Bar Association Section on Legal Education and Admissions to the Bar).
N.A.: Not Available

The peak for the proportion of black students in total enrollment during the 1970s was 4.6%, which was attained in 1976. For the remainder of the decade, the percentage of black students among total enrollment declined each succeeding year, to 4.2% by the end of the decade. However, as total enrollment increased for the law school population as a whole, so did the number and percentage of black students in each year between 1980 and 1984. Nevertheless, it was not until 1984 that the proportion of total enrollment attributed to black law school students again matched the 4.6% observed in the 1976 peak year. This enrollment pattern suggests that there cannot be a withdrawal of demonstrable commitment to produce a sufficient number of black attorneys. Otherwise, the nation will never advance beyond the level of calculated tokenism regarding opportunities for minorities and, therefore, will accentuate the disillusionment of the present moment.

Enrollment in Historically Black Law Schools

As noted earlier, the historically black schools of law tend to enroll proportionately more white students than is the case regarding black students in the traditionally white institutions in the same jurisdiction or state. In 1970, for example, of the 61 black students enrolled in law schools in Louisiana, 45 were enrolled at Southern University and only 4 were enrolled at Louisiana State University School of Law. In the same year, 92 of the 99 black law students in North Carolina were enrolled at North Carolina Central University, while only 7 were enrolled at the University of North Carolina/ Chapel Hill. About 150 of the 177 black students in Texas law schools were enrolled at the Texas Southern University School of Law.[37]

In 1979, 147 of the 210 students enrolled at Southern University were black, while only 23 of the 876 law students at Louisiana State University were black and other minorities. Loyola and Tulane universities enrolled 49 and 29 *minority* students, respectively. Over 90% of these students were black. Although these numbers represent improvements in the representation of black students, their overall distribution remains fundamentally unchanged. In North Carolina, North Carolina Central University School of Law was 64% black but 36% white. The University of North Carolina Law School at Chapel Hill was 95% white and 5% black.

As recently as 1983, historically black institutions (HBIs) with law schools continued to be substantially more successful than publicly supported, traditionally white institutions (TWIs) located in the same state in enrolling both black and "other race" students. For example, in Louisiana, 62.7% of total enrollment at Southern University School of Law (HBI) was black, and 33% was white. By contrast, at publicly supported Louisiana State University, a TWI located in the same city, 97% of the law school enrollment was white, and only 3% was black and other minorities. Similarly, in North Carolina, 50% of the law school student body at North Carolina Central University (HBI) was black, while 50% was white. However, at publicly supported University of North Carolina (TWI), 94% of the law school enrollment was white, whereas blacks and other minorities constituted only 6% of total enrollment. In the same year, in Texas, white students represented about one of every five (19.1%) law students enrolled at Texas Southern University (HBI), while black students made up 80.9% of the total law school enrollment. By comparison, blacks and other minority students (including a substantial proportion of Hispanics in this category) represented only 6.3% of law school enrollment at Texas Tech, 16% at the University of Houston, and 21% at the University of Texas/ Austin. Note in this discussion of institutional enrollment and other characteristics, the 1984 *Review of Legal Education* does not disaggregate minority students. Minorities in the institutions cited here are predominantly black and/or Mexican American.

In the District of Columbia, the site of Howard University (HBI) and five law schools located at TWIs, a situation exists that is virtually identical to that observed in Louisiana, North Carolina, and Texas. Eighty-nine percent of the law school enrollment at Howard University is black, and 11% is white. Among the five TWIs, the highest proportion of black and other minority students is found at the Antioch School of Law at which minority students represent 34.3% of total enrollment. By contrast, black and other minority students constitute 17.4% of total enrollment at the law school of Georgetown University; 9.6% at George Washington University; 8.4% at Catholic University, and 7.9% at American University. In the District of Columbia, where all the TWIs are private, the TWIs are more effective with respect to the matriculation of black students. Location and aggressive recruitment help to account for their success.

Each institution enrolled larger numbers of black students during the early 1980s. However, it is evident that the four historically black law schools have been considerably more effective in increasing access to students of all races than have the traditionally white institutions. In most of the 174 ABA-approved law schools, integration of black students remains at the token level in the mid-1980s. Each institution enrolled larger numbers of students during the early 1980s; however, it is evident that the historically black institutions have done a better job of increasing access to all students than have the historically white institutions. Further, integration remains at essentially a token level of access in most traditionally white institutions.

Special Programs

Once black students matriculate, *some but not all of them* require either academic or nonacademic support systems, or both, as ways of fostering retention through graduation. Academic support is provided in part by faculty members who take an interest in sharpening the intellectual tools of students. Many institutions offer formal and informal tutorials. Learning centers assist students to sharpen their communication skills. Special orientation programs are conducted for newly matriculated students to help them attain a better understanding and appreciation of what is involved in the study of law and how to complete registration procedures, become acquainted with other students, and meet their first-year professors.

Some institutions offer special courses, such as the one on Legal Methods at Ohio State University, to students who have completed the first year of study but who have an apparent need to sharpen writing and oral communications skills. Sometimes these students are permitted to carry a reduced academic load. Special study sessions and tutorial and voluntary review sessions are conducted by BALSA and/or the minority-student organizations in the law school. BALSA also offers test-taking exercises.

Nonacademic support activities encompass a range of services including scholarships and financial aid and psychological support. Many law students receive varying amounts of direct and indirect financial aid. These monies may be provided through the CLEO program, grants from the local chapter of Bar Associations, special institutional grants, faculty contributions, state-authorized tuition waivers, federally subsidized work–study programs, and repayable loans. In addition, since 1972, the NAACP–LDF has awarded over 2700 law scholarships. Many institutions have been especially instrumental in finding new sources of financial assistance as original sources dried up or were reduced. However, much more has to be done, given the economic disabilities of a substantial proportion of black students.

BALSA, Black Student Unions, black faculty, and other minority-group organizations perform an immensely valuable service in the affective support they provide some students. For this group, it is comforting to know that there is a critical mass of students of one's own racial or ethnic group or that there are black law professors who care about their welfare and are willing to spend time in informal discussions with them as individual students. There is special strength gained from the informal social contacts provided in social interaction with black students at social functions, the cafeteria, lunchrooms, or in intramural sports activities. All these activities form a cohesive network of nonacademic support services that have a positive impact on the overall well-being of black students in a predominantly white institution.

Problem Areas

Still, major problems remain. Although the topic of applications to law schools was not explored here, there is no question about the need to expand the application pool among black students. The pool question is inextricably tied to both the expanded career options that open other opportunities for black college graduates and the specific need to enroll and graduate larger numbers of black college students. Even if this were done, other structural inequities that impede access would have to be eliminated and the economic problems of financing three years of legal education would have to be confronted head-on.

Comparatively few black students can afford to support themselves in law schools through their own funds. Many potentially successful students are unwilling to subject themselves to a major debt through repayable loans in order to attend law school when other options are available. Others pay a heavy price in lowered performance when they are compelled to take on substantial employment in order to provide for themselves and their families while enrolled. Grades often suffer, and many professors are not inclined to take the psychological problems or pressures induced by home situations into consideration when reviewing a student's performance. This situation may lead to abandonment of the immediate goal of a law degree. The financial aid problem could be alleviated in a large measure through more governmental intervention—federal or state—with broader coverages under the Graduate and Professional Opportunities Program (GPOP), and a graduate system similar to the undergraduate BEOGs and the SEOGs.

Although a far greater number of exceptionally well qualified black students could be recruited for law school programs than currently, the fact remains that all too many black students are still victimized by weak preparation in elementary, secondary, and collegiate education. Too many suffer from deficiencies in oral communication and writing skills. There are problems of personal confidence, of sophistication, and of lack of ease in dealing with others. Without a doubt, the deliberate intimidation of students by prejudiced, insecure, and power-hungry professors does not allay the fears that some students already have of active participation in classroom discussions. Further, the lingering problem of racism, subtle as it may be from time to time, must still be confronted. And racism is not always subtle! In fact, it sometimes is bold and direct. It is evidenced in the attitudes that some professors have toward black and other minority students and faculty, in their treatment of minorities, in their deliberate attempts to subject minority students to public embarrassment or ridicule, in their harsher grading of minorities, in their unwillingness to make the same kinds of exemptions or special dispensations for black students that they freely grant to white students, and in their beliefs that all blacks students are necessarily less competent than even the average white student.

That schools of law have made some inroads in dealing with the problem of the underrepresentation of black faculty in them cannot be dismissed as liberal rhetoric. However, that progress is but one step in the right direction. The need for increasingly larger numbers of black faculty and administrators is evident, particularly since there are only approximately 250 black and other minority faculty in all schools of law in the United States.[38] But the issue of black faculty does not end with their hiring. It extends to promotions and the granting of tenure. Comparatively few law schools have tenured minority faculty. Nor do the majority of ABA-approved law schools have significant numbers of blacks in visible, decision-making administrative positions. Observation of the special difficulty for members of minority groups to receive tenure is a reality that does not attract black lawyers to the academic life. It is incumbent on law school deans, other administrators, and professors to socialize black students into the fundamental requirements for positions as law school faculty early in their careers and to do all they can to motivate those who show a special interest toward teaching as a career. However, it may be necessary to reassess the reward structure so that rewards associated with academic life may compensate for whatever sacrifices may be made by abandoning private practice, wherever that is required.

Retention, of course, persists as a major issue and it is currently being addressed, however unevenly, in methods discussed under the heading of special programs. The point is, nevertheless, that larger numbers of black lawyers ought to be produced each year. It appears that, from an examination of the numbers of black law students in third-year classes, *law schools are producing about 1,800 black law graduates per year.* But that number is reduced each year by the disproportionate number of black students who fail to pass bar examinations. That failure further hampers the productivity rate and delays substantial increases of black lawyers in the labor force. *Nevertheless, it is estimated that in 1985, there are some 17,000 black lawyers in the total number of 653,687 lawyers in the United States* (2.6%). Clearly, it is necessary to move far beyond the educational paralysis that has so far guaranteed a negligible representation of black Americans in the field of law.

Notes

1. Franklin R. Evans, *Law School Admissions Research* (Princeton, N.J.: Law School Admission Council, 1977), pp. 569–71.
2. Ibid.
3. In the interest of space, this assessment is based solely on events within ABA-approved institutions and not on the non-ABA-approved schools of law dispersed throughout the United States.
4. Michael Cordoza, *The Association Process, 1963–1973* (Washington, D.C.: American Association of Law Schools, 1974), p. 18.
5. Ibid.
6. Ibid.
7. Ibid., p. 47.
8. See Walter Leonard, "Report on the Committee on Minority Groups," *Proceedings of the 1972 Annual Meeting, Section I* (Washington, D.C.: American Association of Law schools), pp. 65–69. Appendix to this report carries the reference Amendment to the Principals of Non-Discrimination. This amendment connotes a more inclusive policy statement than the policy statement enunciated in 1963.
9. Special Services of the ABA and the AALS also include task forces and committees established to offer concrete resolutions to the problems of underrepresentation and retention among minority students.

10. Cordoza, *The Association Process,* p. 61.
11. Ibid., p. 62.
12. Ibid., p. 66. Also former President Walter Leonard of Fisk University; former chair of the AALS Committee on Minority Groups.
13. Wade J. Henderson, *Statement on Behalf of the Council on Legal Education Opportunity Before the Subcommittee on Post Secondary Education,* U.S. House of Representatives, June 13, 1979.
14. Ibid.
15. Ibid.
16. Ibid. See also, "Report of Activities of the Council on Legal Education Opportunities for the Period Ending, 1972," *AALS Proceedings of 1972 Annual Meetings,* pp. 123–124.
17. Henderson, *Statement.*
18. Ibid., and Lawrence Dark, Director of CLEO.
19. Ibid.
20. From Data Provided by the University of Wisconsin-Madison.
21. From data provided by The Ohio State University.
22. From data provided by the University of Washington; and from Allen P. Sindler, *Bakke, DeFunis, and Minority Admissions* (New York: Longman, 1978), pp. 31–38, 41–42, 118, passim.
23. From data provided by the Ohio State University.
24. From data provided by the University of Wisconsin / Madison.
25. From data provided by the University of Texas / Austin.
26. Ibid.
27. Ibid.
28. Ibid.
29. Ibid.
30. Ibid.
31. Evans, *Law School Admissions.,* p. 566.
32. Ibid., pp. 567–568.
33. Ibid.
34. Ibid.
35. *New York Times,* November 1978.
36. From data Provided by Stanford University.
37. James E. Blackwell, *The Participation of Black Students in Graduate and Professional Schools* (Atlanta: Southern Education Foundation, 1977).
38. Section on Minority Groups, Association of American Law Schools, *1979–80 Directory of Minority Law Faculty, ed. Derek Bell* (Washington, D.C.: Association of American Law Schools, 1980), and telephone interview with Dean Derek Bell, University of Oregon School of Law, January 24, 1986.

12 THE SOCIAL WORK PROFESSION:
PARITY ATTAINED AND LOST

The only profession in which black Americans have ever attained parity of access and equity in graduation rates is that of social work. This chapter explores the approaches taken by the social work profession to provide equality of educational opportunity. It examines enrollment and graduation trends, and faculty distribution. It also offers explanations to account for the current decline in the enrollment of black students in graduate schools of social work.

Historical and Societal Contexts

Unlike other major professions, social work began to take steps to correct racial inequities in its profession in the same year that the *Brown* decision was pronounced by the U.S. Supreme Court. In 1954, the Commission on Accreditation for Schools of Social Work "adopted a mandatory standard" that required assurance of nondiscriminatory practices be assured in all schools of social work. According to this policy change, all schools of social work were to conduct their programs without any form of discrimination based on race, ethnic origin, creed, or color. This policy had universal applicability in that it covered selection and admission of students, conduct in the classroom and in field practice assignments, and the organization of a school's program.[1] This fundamental principle of nondiscrimination in social work has been national policy since 1954.

With the promulgation of the new policy, and given the nature of the profession itself, an influential leadership role assumed by this profession in the mainstreaming of blacks should move it forward. As the civil rights movement picked up momentum, social work practitioners, educators, and policymakers vocalized the urgency of producing more black social workers. In principle, social work had always embraced the idea of inclusion and openness for persons who wished to be trained in the technology of human services delivery and in the methodology of helping others to realize their greatest potential. But principles and practices are sometimes inconsistent and strangely contradictory.

The profession, however, suffered from a credibility gap that centered on its image with black and other minority groups. On the one hand, its practitioners were committed to the principle of providing assistance to the disadvantaged and to persons in need of various human services. It aimed to acquaint others with the strategies designed to help them organize their lives for more effective and orderly living. The population, in general, had an image of social workers, what Andrew Billingsley once labeled "the public assistance worker"[2]—an image that was sometimes favorable and sometimes unfavorable, depending on the contacts and types of experience that potential students had with social workers. Social work as a profession did not enjoy the prestige and status ordinarily accorded science and technology fields by the American public. In the 1950s and early 1960, some of the misinformed expressed a view that social work, like elementary school teaching, was "woman's work," "something people did when they could not do anything else." This image problem did not reflect a view unique in the relationship between the profession and the black population. It was shared by others who knew little about the profession and the human services objectives it encompassed.

The recruitment of black Americans into the profession necessitated a confrontation with the image issue by social work educators and practitioners. The success of the community of social work educators, administrators, and practitioners in addressing this problem is evidenced by the profound changes in the racial composition of social work schools during the 1960s. Before then, the primary hope that black Americans had for admission to a graduate school of social work rested on actions taken by the two historically black institutions that had schools of social work. Atlanta University, headed for several years by Whitney Young, and Howard University led the way in the training of black graduate students in this field. Had it not been for their efforts, there would have been considerably fewer social workers from the black population. Early failures to expand social work opportunities underscored the inconsistencies between the practice of middle-class whites administering social services to the poor and minorities and the importance of having more representatives from the social work clientele involved in decisions that affected their own well-being.

The problem of underrepresentation of black Americans in white colleges of social work was critical, although in 1960, 13% of all first-year graduate students in social work were black.[3] In fact, few white institutions admitted black students, and in most of those who did permit black students to enroll the representation in the total school population was at best a token one. Therefore, the Council on Social Work Education began to urge its member institutions to become more aggressive in the recruitment of black and other minority students. In some instances, because of the insistence of black faculty, individual schools of social work took the initiative to develop constructive "manpower production programs" designed to produce a greater supply of black Americans with graduate degrees in social work.

The Berkeley Model

Although a number of institutions took initiatives, we can describe the program at the University of California at Berkeley as a proto-type of efforts initiated in the 1960s for the integration of blacks in social work, which, in turn, strengthened the mainstreaming process and led to parity in both access and production during the 1970s. This description draws heavily on the historical overview provided by Andrew Billingsley, a former member of the faculty of the School of Social Work at the University of California/Berkeley. His seminal article, which forms the basis of this analysis, is entitled "Black Students in Graduate Schools of Social Work."[4]

Before 1963, there were many years in which black students were not included in the yearly social work admissions. In 1963, only two black students were enrolled in the school of social welfare at the University of California/Berkeley. This token enrollment was inconsistent with the ideals and goals of the Graduate Council at the university, which expressed a commitment demonstrably to expand educational opportunities in its graduate programs for minority-group students. This commitment was explicated in a memorandum issued by the Administrative Committee of Graduate Council in the spring of 1964 to deans and department heads. The memorandum called for special efforts to seek, identify, and encourage the enrollment of "disadvantaged minorities" in graduate programs on that campus. As Billingsley states, most schools and departments ignored the recommendation by taking no concrete action that would change the status quo. However, the dean of the School of Social Welfare appointed a committee of faculty members in the fall of 1964 to take what would become pioneer efforts to include more black and minority students in graduate schools of social work.[5]

It should also be noted here that during this period a number of terms presumed to characterize the conditions, status, and learning abilities of black and other minorities were either coined or popularized. Among these were the following: "culturally deprived," "educationally deprived," "culturally neglected," "culturally disadvantaged," and "educationally disadvantaged." Although deeply embedded in the professional jargon, the popularity of these terms diminished over time as their negative connotations were increasingly rebuked. Many rejected the notion of "cultural or educational," if not "individual," *deficit* implicit in them. Unfortunately, academicians and administrators were so vociferous in their labeling of blacks and other minorities as "educationally disadvantaged" that the American public tended, mistakeingly and sometimes conveniently, to perceive *all* black Americans as educationally inferior.

The development of a minority recruitment program in the School of Social Welfare at the University of California/Berkeley was an innovation in education. From its inception, it enjoyed three of the essentials for success. First, it had unqualified support from the top echelon of administrative leadership within the university. Second, it had the commitment of the immediate leadership of the unit that housed the program. In this case, it meant the dean of the School of Social Welfare. And third, it established a faculty committee to guide and direct the recruitment process. This "racially balanced" faculty committee was committed to the principle of widening the door of opportunity for minority students.[6]

The Berkeley faculty, at one point, was trapped in conceptual difficulties that dramatized the terminological dilemmas and ambiguities to which intellectuals are prone: Who is a minority? Who is "educationally disadvantaged"? Should all blacks be admitted because of their past history of segregation and discrimination? Are middle-class blacks to be given the same treatment as "authentic ghetto types," since they may not be as "educationally disadvantaged" as lower-class blacks in the ghetto? Should the focus be on the "authentic ghetto type," who is the epitome of the "culturally deprived" and the personification of the "educationally disadvantaged"? Or should the term minority be perceived in much broader terms so as to include certain segments from the population as a whole that might have shared similar experiences to black Americans because of ethnic group or socioeconomic status?

With these questions resolved to the faculty committee's satisfaction, the committee established important linkages with the institutional structures whose actions affected outcomes of their own deliberations and policies. These were such groups as the Executive Committee of the School of Social Welfare, the Admissions Policy Committee of the School of Social Welfare, and the minority faculty of the school, who ultimately played a crucial role in the program's overall development.[7]

In organizing this program, the Minority Students Committee dealt with a number of concerns described in previous chapters. These include (1) the image and knowledge of the profession in the target population; (2) the lack of financial aid sufficient to support graduate or professional education; (3) adademic qualifications for graduate or professional school admission; (4) motivation for a career in the profession; and (5) special admissions and special support services to strengthen the possibilities of graduation for those in need of academic and special assistance. The latter involved finding ways to support financially the special programs of counseling, guidance, and other services that might be required.

On the recommendation of the Minority Students Committee, the School of Social Welfare established a minority recruitment program. This action exacted not only a change in policy but fostered a major shift in faculty attitudes. This meant a shift away from the notion of "selecting only from those who seek us out" to actively recruiting students not generally included in the school's population. This list of recruitment activities is consonant with those strategies followed by the School of Veterinary Medicine at Tuskegee Institute, especially in the utilization of faculty, alumni, and minority students in the distribution of promotional materials, the high school visitation program, and special activities at historically black colleges.

The committee's recommendation for establishing counseling and advising services as an integral part of the program was also approved by the faculty. However, the minority faculty, who served as important and invaluable role models in the initial recruitment efforts, played a vital role in this component of the program.

On the recommendation of the Minority Student Committee, the School of Social Welfare made the critical decision to change its admissions criteria. For instance, a minimum GPA of *B* in college work was no longer required for admission. In fact, according to Billingsley, a few students with a GPA of *C*, but who possessed other qualities desired in social welfare students at Berkeley, were accepted. In effect, there was a major shift from the utilization of purely cognitive determinants to noncognitive factors in making admissions decisions.[8]

At the suggestion of the Minority Student Committee, the School of Social Welfare hired more minority faculty members. The number of black faculty in the School rose from 2 in 1963 to 7 in 1968, and the first faculty of Mexican American origin was hired in 1968. In addition, black professionals served as visiting lecturers or as part-time faculty during this period. Since the total number of faculty within the School at this time was 60 to 64, the minority faculty represented a significant proportion, or a critical mass, within the School. Hence, an essential program component was assured.[9]

However, it is important to note that, despite the admission of students with less than a *B* average from college, "virtually no academic assistance" was provided to minority students from 1964 to 1968. There was no organized tutorial program, for example. These students were successful in completing the program primarily through their own efforts. This fact notwithstanding, it should be stressed that there was a critical mass of black students at Berkeley, and the black faculty constituted a significant segment of the total social work faculty. Further, there were other psychological support mechanisms within the school environment on which students could draw as needed.

Financial support for the program came initially from the California Department of Social Welfare, which provided stipends to students who agreed to work for the state following the completion of their degree requirements. Some students were supported through the work– study program of the Office of Economic Opportunity of the U.S. Department of Health, Education, and Welfare. Others received fellowships under funds made available from NIMH, the Children's Bureau, and other federal agencies; and some were supported through funds provided by private foundations such as Carnegie, the San Francisco Foundation for the Aged, and the Stern Family Fund.[10]

The outcomes of these efforts were particularly gratifying in terms of increasing access to black students. Over a five-year period, from 1964 to 1969, total enrollment in the School of Social Welfare increased from 272 to 375. The total enrollment of black students climbed from 7 in 1964 to 52 in 1968 or from 2.5% to 13.9% of total enrollment. Minority enrollment jumped from 5.0% to 23.7% within that period.[11] Clearly, parity was attained in the School of Social Work in a relatively short time. This was accomplished on the strength of the program and the commitment to it manifested in the leadership, faculty, presence of role models, financial support, and adjustments in traditional admissions requirements that did not compromise the integrity of the institution despite initial repudiation by some faculty members. Minority graduates of the School of Social Welfare at the University of California/Berkeley during this period now hold some of the more important positions in the professions.

During the 1970s, profound changes occurred at Berkeley. For one thing, black students enrollment in the School of Social Welfare dropped by almost 50% between 1970 and 1978. The once sizable number of black faculty declined to two persons in 1978. Even by fall 1983, only three blacks held full-time faculty positions in Berkeley's School of Social Welfare. Seven black students were enrolled in the M.S.W. program. Hence the situation in the 1980s continues to reflect the downward spiral of the 1970s. These changes raise the questions whether the initial commitment and programatic strengths were sustained and whether the black faculty were victims of a revolving-door syndrome: hired but lost through denial of tenure.

Recruitment, Admissions Criteria, and Special Admissions

According to a study reported by Arnulf Pins for the Council on Social Work Education in 1963, the 326 black students enrolled in all schools of social work in the United States that year represented 13% of total enrollment. Further, there was an upward turn in enrollment in graduate schools of social work during the remainder of the 1960s. But the enrollment of black students, while continuing to grow, did not keep pace with overall enrollment. Harold Greenberg and Carl Scott reported that by 1968, black students represented only 10% of total enrollment in social work schools.[12]

Given that decline, demands grew for mainstreaming outsiders, and for integration and inclusion of a diverse student body; as a consequence, most social work schools initiated programs to assure increases in minority-student enrollment. Many of these institutions, like the University of California at Berkeley, quickly grasped the apparent compatibility of their professional goals and the commitment of black and other minority students to social change. They realized the basic issues involved in meeting fundamental survival needs as well as enhancing upward mobility aspirations of a large segment of the population, who made up such a substantial proportion of their clientele. It was imperative to include larger numbers of these groups in order to fulfill a wide array of social and educational goals. Numbers of students from these groups demonstrated that the traditional social work curriculum, for instance, was not always appropriate in addressing the problems of the real world. Therefore, the educational benefits resulting from the infusion of students from the social work clientele could be enormous and far-reaching. Consequently, many institutions initiated special minority recruitment programs. They could no longer rationalize the apparent contradictions between basic social work philosophy and existing educational policies. How could a helping profession with a focus on urban problems and the conditions of the poor justify the exclusion of students from among its clientele? Could not substantial institutional and professional benefits be reaped by their inclusion?

According to a 1969 survey, 48, or 75% of the 64 schools of social work then in existence, had recruitment programs in operation or were planning them for implementation in the 1969–1970 academic year. Over 80% of these institutions had already designated a specific person to be in charge of recruitment programs. In about one-fifth of the cases that person was either the dean or a member of the dean's immediate staff. Slightly less than half of the institutions established special committees chaired either by a member of the administration or by a special recruitment officer secured for this purpose.[13] Essentially, this pattern continued throughout the 1970s; that is, recruitment was conducted under the auspices of the dean, a special recruitment officer, or a minority recruitment committee with faculty participation.

However, during the 1970s, greater efforts were made toward the development and implementation of coordinated recruitment programs. These ranged from individual institutional efforts, such as the program implemented in the School of Social Work at Western Michigan University, to a consortium model established at Texas.

At Western Michigan University, the first recruitment committee had an ad hoc status as a "committee on minority concerns" when established in 1972. A year later, the committee was changed to a standing status with recruitment designated as one of its central functions. Full-time faculty members carried on recruitment responsibilities in addition to their regular teaching load. The limited funding made available to the committee had to be utilized primarily for recruitment trips. An optimistic goal of one-third minority student enrollment was initially set, but never attained. Enrollment did increase, but declined again to about 6% in 1978. Once again, the school reaffirmed its commitment to the goals of the program. Since 1978, a faculty member, with released time and aided by a graduate assistant, has assumed primary recruitment responsibilities.[14]

The University of Texas/Arlington participates in the Texas Consortium of Graduate Schools of Social Work organized in 1968. This consortium was established for the expressed purpose of expanding opportunities for minority students in graduate schools of social work. Since its inception, it has been supported by the National Institute of Mental Health. Under the shared funding arrangement, participating institutions receive funds for recruitment programs and special stipends. For instance, in 1972, the first year in which the University of Texas/Arlington participated, the institution received approximately $40,000 to support student stipends and a full-time recruiter. Since that time, the university has not only had a full-time recruiter but has provided from three to eight stipends a year.[15]

Over half the schools of social work have flexible admissions criteria. The implementation of these criteria is not viewed as a compromise of standards; rather, it is a mechanism for creating equity in the admissions process and for a more careful and systematic evaluation of all strengths that a potential student brings to the institution. The Graduate Record Examination (GRE) may or may not be required; it may be waived for students whose college GPA is 3.0 or above. It may be required but not weighted disproportionately among all the measures employed for evaluation. Few institutions actually employ inflexible, absolute, quantitative admissions standards. Frequently, schools of social work scrutinize very carefully and give greater weight to the quality of academic performance during the last two years of undergraduate work and the performance exhibited in courses in related fields (e.g., sociology and psychology).

Schools of social work stress evidence of ability to perform at the graduate level and potential for success as a social worker. The former may mean an overall college GPA of C; or a C+ in the last two years of undergraduate study, or a cumulated B average or above, or a C+ average with good GRE scores; or a C average combined with excellent potential as revealed through noncognitive measures of evaluation. The latter may include motivation for a career in a human services profession; leadership ability, evidence of having overcome undue hardships and the maintenance of motivation in the face of great adversity, relevant work experience that demonstrates a commitment to helping others; sound judgment, and the maturity to understand the complexities of interpersonal relationships and interactions with diverse groups of people. These attributes become a major focus of the applicant's personal statement, the interview, and references to each of them is evaluated.

In order to minimize expenses to students, many schools of social work draw on their alumni for assistance in local or regional interviewing. Frequently, these persons are in a much better position to evaluate the nature of the work experience that the applicant reports because of their knowledge and proximity to the locale in which the experience occurred. It is therefore likely that any number of very promising students who may not ordinarily have been accepted have been admitted because of this participation of alumni.

Financial Assistance

During the late 1960s and until the middle of the 1970s, funds to support educational programs were reasonably adequate. Schools of social work obtained significant funding through direct grants, research projects that carried monies for student stipends, assistantships and fellowships, and substantial foundation support. Various branches and agencies of the federal government were particularly supportive. Among them were NIMH, the Children's Bureau, the Social and Rehabilitation Service, the National Institutes of Health, the National Institutes of Education, the Office of Economic Opportunity, and the various manpower branches of the U.S. Department of Labor. State health and welfare departments, as well as alumni groups, also provided major financial support for efforts to expand opportunities for black and other minority students in social work.

Many of these efforts, as already reported, came under a brutal attack by individuals and some formal organizations who charged that they discriminated against white students, or were tantamount to "reverse discrimination," and that their constitutionality was highly suspect. The same allegations were levied against the Minority Fellowship Program of the American Sociological Association, funded initially by the National Institute of Mental Health (NIMH). In fact, a few members of the American Sociological Association either resigned or threatened to resign in protest over the establishment of its minority program.

Coincident to these attacks, institutions with professional programs witnessed a significant decline in financial aid, scholarship monies, and general financial support. This curtailment, if not total dissipation, of financial support had a deleterious impact on recruitment and enrollment efforts. In fact, in some instances, among them social work, many of the gains achieved in the late 1960s and early 1970s were lost or difficult to maintain.

The problem continued into the 1980s. For example, the number of grants from NIMH in 1983 was approximately 50% of grants to graduate students in social work in 1983. Increasingly, students are compelled to depend on loans to finance their social work education. In fact, in 1983, loan programs constituted the most common source of financial support among masters' students; 35.2% depended on loan programs. This source was followed by school or university funds, which accounted from 23.7% of grants to M.S.W. students. The third most frequent source of funds for these students was through work–study programs (11.4%). A significant portion of funds to graduate students in social work is distributed through various kinds of grants from field instruction agencies. These funds are obtained from state and local governments and work–study appropriations, voluntary social welfare agencies, foundations, and other voluntary associations.[16]

The most prominent sources of funds for doctoral students in social work are loan programs (25.7%), school and university funds (24.9%), research and graduate assistantships (23.5%), and federal government sources (13.3%). NIMH funds account for 5.8% of funds provided D.S.W. students, but NIHM grants represented only 52% of those awarded in 1983.[17] This distribution seems to have become the pattern for the foreseeable future.

While this retrenchment may not have been the sole determinant of the enrollment decline registered in the 1970s and 1980s, it was unquestionably a major contributor to this loss of black students in graduate social work education programs.

Enrollment of Black Students

At no time in this century has the census-counted black population of the United States exceeded 12% of the total population. Throughout the 1970s, the reported black population ranged from 11.1% to 11.6%. (Many persons, lay and professional, however, argue that every U.S. census misses a significant number of blacks. If that is so, the proportion of blacks in the total population may exceed 12%.) Using our definition of total access or enrollment parity, black students in first-year M.S.W. classes not only reached parity but exceeded it in all but the three final years of the decade. Declining enrollments, first observed in 1983, have continued and show no evidence of slowing down. However, the decline in black student enrollment in graduate social work education is consistent with the overall downturn in the number of students attracted to social work since 1978. Part-time enrollment has been increasing in social work at the graduate level.

First-Year Enrollment

First-year enrollment in schools of social work increased at a steady rate for all students between 1969 and the 1972. The peak for first-year enrollment among black students was reached in academic year 1972–1973 when the 1226 first-year black students represented 15.7% of all students enrolled at that level. In both absolute numbers and proportionate enrollment in first-year classes, the increases observed for black students in the three preceding years were noteworthy. As the 1970s opened, black students constituted more than 14% of all first-year M.S.W. students.

First-year M.S.W. enrollments declined for all students between 1974 and 1977, and enrollments still seem to be sporadic. By contrast, the downward trend in absolute numbers as well as in proportion of all students in first-year classes witnessed among black students in 1973 has continued unabated. As a result, fewer black students were in first-year M.S.W. classes in 1983 than there were before 1969. The percentage of black students in first-year M.S.W. classes dropped significantly, from 14.2% in 1969 to 9.3% in 1979 and 9.0% in 1983 (see Table 61).

Hence, the optimism of full integration in schools of social work reflected in percentage distributions through 1975 has been replaced by trepidation and alarm that some institutions have already reneged on their original commitment and that the dissipation of funds for stipends, scholarships, and general financial aid is having a negative impact on black students' presence in graduate schools of social work. Another explanation for the declining enrollment of black students in first-year M.S.W. classes lies in expanding career choices for black students; some students who would ordinarily have selected social work have enrolled in more prestigious and lucrative professions.

Total Enrollment

A similar trend is observed in total enrollment in M.S.W. degree programs for the nation as a whole. Total enrollment climbed steadily throughout the 1970s, without declines in any single year. In contrast, total enrollment for black M.S.W. students peaked in 1972 but has continued downward since that time. Black student enrollment held at parity or above-parity levels through 1975 and was near parity in 1976. But the trends set in

Table 61
First-Year Enrollment M.S.W. Programs, Schools of Social Work,
by Race, 1969–1983, All Institutions Combined

Academic Year	Total Enrolled	Number of Black Students	% Blacks
1983–84	6526	N.A.	N.A.
1982–83	6339	N.A.	N.A.
1981–82	7514	679	9.0
1980–81	N.A.	N.A.	N.A.
1979–80	8056	799	9.3
1978–79	8197	844	10.3
1977–78	8510	864	10.1
1976–77	7951	836	10.5
1975–76	7840	933	11.9
1974–75	7935	1004	12.6
1973–74	8235	1070	12.9
1972–73	7788	1226	15.7
1971–72	7137	1067	14.9
1970–71	6699	975	14.5
1969–70	6241	888	14.2

Source: Statistics on Social Work Education (New York: Council on Social Work Education, 1970–1983). Reprinted with permission of publisher. N.A.: Not Available.

motion in 1977 signaled serious problems in the 1980s. This situation not only foretold a loss of parity but was suggestive of impending difficulties in attracting black students to social work in significant numbers. The enormity of the problem can be noted by the fact that total black M.S.W. enrollment in the mid-1980s approximates black enrollment before 1970. Hence, the loss of black students in social work in the past 10 years has been staggering (see Table 62).

Using biennial data for comparative purposes, it is evident from Table 63 that the enrollment of black students in 25 of the largest schools of social work has been uneven at best since 1970. Over 90% of these institutions do not currently enroll as many students in social work as they did in 1970. It is also evident from this table that the major thrust for recruitment and enrollment seemed to have peaked once again in 1972 through 1974, followed by a continuing downward spiral. The data provided on such institutions as Florida State University, University of Chicago, Wayne State University, Adelphi, Columbia, University of California and UCLA all illustrate this point.

In fact, by 1983 black student enrollment had fallen so rapidly that 50% of the 86 mainland schools of social work had 5 or fewer blacks

Table 62
TotalM.S.W. Enrollment in Schools of Social Work, By Race,
1969–1983, All Institutions Combined

Academic Year	Total M.S.W. Enrollment	Number of Black Students	% Blacks
1983–84	14,225	1247	8.8
1982–83	15,131	1435	9.5
1981–82	16,552	1475	8.9
1980–81	17,122	N.A.	N.A.
1979–80	17,397	1722	9.9
1978–79	18,493	1894	10.2
1977–78	18,399	1921	10.4
1976–77	17,638	1969	11.1
1975–76	17,388	2149	12.3
1974–75	17,238	2210	12.8
1973–74	16,716	2217	13.2
1972–73	15,596	2352	15.8
1971–72	14,456	2116	14.5
1970–71	13,205	1847	13.9
1969–70	12,061	1495	12.4

Source: Statistics on Social Work Education (New York: Council on Social Work Education, 1970–1984). Reprinted with permission of publisher. N.A.: Not Available.

matriculated in first-year classes. Twenty-five institutions (29%) enrolled at least 10 blacks in their first-year classes. Of these institutions, the "*Adams* states" were represented by schools of social work at the University of Georgia (17); Atlanta University, an HBI (38); University of Maryland, a former "*Adams* state" (21); Norfolk State University, an HBI (19); University of Pennsylvania (11); University of Pittsburgh (19); University of South Carolina (10); Temple University (22); and University of Virginia (12).

These diminishing numbers and proportions of black students in first-year enrollments raise significant questions about institutional behavior and external conditions that might account for the changes observed. What has happened to institutional behavior? Has the commitment of an earlier period vanished, or are there uncontrollable external and internal forces that render it difficult to sustain institutional commitment in measurable or identifiable ways? How successful are black faculty in affecting decisions? Have their internal pressures paled in significance as they mobilize their energies to achieve the personal goal of gaining tenure? Where is the money needed to fund social work education? Why is this money not available?

Table 63
First-Year Black Student Enrollment, M.S.W. Programs, Twenty-Five
Largest Schools of Social Work, Selected Years, 1970–1981

Institution	1970	1972	1974	1976	1978	1979	1981
Univ. of Alabama	14	15	12	5	16	16	3
Univ of Calif./Berkeley	13	11	7	5	7	7	4
Howard University	32	53	53	67	79	72	54
Florida State University	24	18	11	2	1	3	3
Atlanta University	61	61	61	40	53	62	38
Univ. of Chicago	45	44	26	17	14	6	16
Univ. of Kansas	15	15	25	10	11	14	7
Univ. of Illinois/Urbana	20	55	16	8	12	4	6
Boston University	15	18	7	11	10	5	10
Univ. of Michigan	42	28	22	27	25	23	7
Wayne State University	29	41	32	27	11	10	6
Univ. of Maryland	19	24	26	17	14	17	21
Rutgers University	27	40	38	36	25	29	26
Adelphi University	18	14	3	6	6	8	3
Columbia University	51	50	44	33	39	27	25
Fordham University	43	24	17	17	14	26	12
Hunter College	17	41	19	15	17	12	13
New York University	45	24	26	13	17	13	24
Case Western Reserve	17	29	19	15	17	11	9
Bryn Mawr College	13	19	10	9	10	8	2
Univ. of Pennsylvania	44	45	31	28	17	8	11
Univ. of Pittsburgh	45	57	23	23	15	22	19
Va. Commonwealth Univ.	12	24	24	14	11	9	12
Univ. of Southern Calif.	13	11	7	8	11	5	7
Univ. of Calif./Los Angeles	23	22	17	10	8	4	11

Source: Statistics on Social Work Education (New York: Council on Social Work Education, 1970–1981). Reprinted with permission of publisher.

The "Adams States"

The "*Adams* states" had mixed results in the enrollment of black students during this period. According to Table 64, the University of Oklahoma was the least successful in enrolling black students. The two largest public schools of social work in these states are located at the University of Maryland and Virginia Commonwealth University. In general, each institution sustained an enrollment of black students considerably above 10% of the total number of first-year students enrolled in every year of the 1970s. The same was true at the University of North Carolina, whose school of social work is considerably smaller than the two institutions just described.

No steady trend can be discerned at Florida State University, University of Georgia, or Louisiana State University. The University of Southern

Mississippi just opened its school of social work in 1974. However, it should be pointed out that in 1978, Florida State University enrolled ½₂₄ the number of black students it did in 1970. The first-year enrollment of black students at the University of Georgia, on the other hand, reached the 10% level in seven of the nine years on which data were reported. LSU achieved a similar but somewhat higher proportion in eight of the nine years. However, these proportions must be viewed in the context of the proportion of blacks in the total population of the state. When, this is done, we see that none has achieved total parity (see Table 64).

When one examines the total enrollment of black students in the "*Adams* states" during the 1980s (see Table 65), certain patterns are striking. In the mid-1980s, one-third of the 30 schools of social work located in current or former "*Adams* states" had a black student enrollment of fewer than 10%. These schools were University of Arkansas, Barry College; Louisiana State University; University of Maryland; University of Missouri; Ohio State University; University of Oklahoma; University of Texas/Arlington; University of Texas/Austin, and Virginia Commonwealth University.

Enrollment in Doctoral Programs

The black student enrollment in doctor of social work (D.S.W.) programs increased steadily throughout the 1970s (see Table 66). The only exception to this generalization was in the 1976–1978 period, which showed a slight decline. Nevertheless, a major absolute increase followed this downturn.

In every year of the decade, the proportion of black students in D.S.W. programs exceeded their proportion in the national population. In terms of percentage of total D.S.W. students enrolled, the enrollment of black students peaked in 1974 when 123 students represented 17.4% of total D.S.W. enrollment. According to the latest available data, black students represent 11.9% of these enrollments. This is clearly open access and above-parity levels. It should also be noted that the number of institutions offering post–M.S.W. graduate work increased from 23 in 1970 to 46 in 1983. This growth in the number of doctoral degree programs helps account for the numerical increases in student enrollment.

The description so far pertains exclusively to national totals. Only through an analysis of institutional data can one discern either institutional behavior or characteristics of specific states. Trends in the "*Adams* states" are illustrative in this regard. In 1970, when the "*Adams* states" represented 13% of the doctoral degree institutions, they enrolled 11.1% of black D.S.W. students. In 1972, these states had 16% of the institutions, but 13.8% of black D.S.W. students. Their proportions of these students

Table 64
First-Year Enrollment in Primary Public Institutions, Schools of Social Work, "*Adams States*," by Race, 1970–1979

Institution	1970	1971	1972	1973	1974	1975	1976	1977	1978	1979
Florida State University										
Total enrollment	112	91	97	75	67	79	95	113	83	89
N black students	24	13	18	6	11	2	2	6	1	3
University of Georgia										
Total enrollment	58	69	111	43	37	43	39	47	89	53
N black students	5	4	15	5	8	8	7	8	20	4
Louisiana State University										
Total enrollment	92	80	112	90	106	115	106	87	93	75
N black students	8	11	14	11	17	10	9	2	17	8
University of Maryland										
Total enrollment	117	211	207	198	186	173	187	169	203	153
N black students	19	41	24	27	26	24	20	13	14	17
So. Mississippi University										
Total enrollment	—	—	—	—	—	—	51	47	57	50
N black students	—	—	—	—	—	—	11	4	6	14
University of North Carolina										
Total enrollment	66	65	80	49	60	53	41	44	45	41
N black students	9	6	9	6	8	6	4	7	6	2
University of Oklahoma										
Total enrollment	27	49	61	61	75	49	43	57	48	—
N black students	1	5	4	2	5	2	3	3	2	—
Virginia Commonwealth University										
Total enrollment	78	73	111	119	135	101	120	123	111	91
N black students	10	10	24	20	24	10	14	13	11	9

Source: Statistics on Social Work Education, (New York: Council on Social Work Education, 1970–1979). Reprinted with permission of publisher.
Note: No data available on the University of Arkansas

Table 65
Full-Time M.S.W. Enrollment, Institutions in "*Adams* States,"
by Race, 1981, 1982, 1983[a]

Institution	1981 Total	Black	1982 Total	Black	1983 Total	Black
Alabama	89	18	90	11	88	10
Arkansas	36	5	45	5	38	2
Atlanta[b]	93	75	96	84	74	62
Barry	129	9	140	N.A.	94	4
Bryn Mawr	150	6	141	10	108	11
Case W. Res.	208	30	162	24	147	14
Cincinnati	34	10	39	11	47	11
Florida	161	11	134	6	122	12
Houston	125	10	107	11	123	16
Howard[b]	130	111	119	98	118	96
Georgia	229	23	231	45	146	23
Kentucky	90	5	74	5	67	N.A.
Louisiana	153	18	131	13	164	14
Louisville	125	16	104	11	97	N.A.
Maryland	328	33	292	34	229	16
Missouri	77	8	80	6	77	5
Norfolk[b]	97	33	92	29	86	27
N. Carolina	153	17	120	16	127	16
Ohio	226	26	190	22	187	17
Oklahoma	109	4	102	2	107	3
Penn.	137	18	114	14	114	14
Pittsburgh	219	26	232	29	240	40
St. Louis	97	8	62	7	53	8
S. Carolina	106	17	81	9	87	14
So. Miss.	53	10	60	16	51	23
Temple	218	49	188	59	125	44
Tex/Arlington	186	13	148	15	134	9
Tex/Austin	107	4	116	6	116	6
Tulane	147	15	108	24	82	9
Virginia	231	22	220	14	213	17
W. Virginia	97	2	81	1	65	N.A.

Source: Council on Social Work Education *Statistics on Social Work Education* (New York: The Council, 1981, 1982, 1983).
[a]Full-time and at least 50% in social work program.
[b]Historically black institution.

declined in 1974 when, with 13.7% of the institutions, they enrolled 12.3% of black D.S.W. students. The downward trend continued in 1976 when they represented 14% of the institutions but only 10% of the black students. An upswing occurred in 1978, in both number of institutions (8 of 40)[18] and the absolute number and proportion of black D.S.W. students. In 1978, these 8 institutions enrolled 23 of the 127 black students enrolled in D.S.W. programs, or 18.7% of the students. Finally, in 1983, 19 students were enrolled in D.S.W. programs in the 11 schools in "*Adams* states." The students represented 18.6% of enrollment at that time.

Therefore, it appears that enrollment increases among black doctoral students in these states occurred only as the number of doctorate-granting institutions increased. There is little indication that specific institutions made appreciable gains in the total number of blacks matriculated in doctoral programs.

Table 66
Enrollment in Doctor of Social Work Programs, by Race, 1970–1983, All Institutions Combined

Academic Year	Total Enrollment	Number of Black Students Enrolled	% Blacks
1983–84	855	102	11.9
1982–83	922[a]	130	14.1
1981–82	868	120	13.8
1980–81	825[a]	107	12.9
1979–80	954[a]	119	12.5
1978–79	821	127	15.5
1977–78	866	116	13.4
1976–77	769	120	15.6
1975–76	712	123	17.3
1974–75	648	113	17.4
1973–74	617	104	16.8
1972–73	565	87	15.4
1971–72	504	70	13.3
1970–71	462	54	11.7

Source: Statistics on Social Work Education (New York: Council on Social Work Education, 1970–1983). Reprinted with permission of publisher.
Note: For this analysis, D.S.W. enrollments are subsituted for the designation "post–M.S.W."
[a]One school unreported.

The Production of Black Social Work Professionals

Most graduate students in social work are enrolled in M.S.W. degree programs. About half of the of the 87 accredited schools of social work in the United States also offer the D.S.W. degree. At the beginning of the 1970s, only 23 institutions offered post–M.S.W. studies; by 1980, that number had grown to 38. For purposes of this analysis, attention is first drawn to the production of black students with the M.S.W. degree. Unfortunately, the only usable data available are for selected years between 1970 and 1984 (see Table 67).

Table 67
M.S.W. Degrees by Race, 1970–1984, All Institutions Combined

Year	Total M.S.W. Degrees	M.S.W. Degrees Awarded to Black Students	% Blacks
1984	N.A.	N.A.	8.3
1983	9,034	731	8.1
1982	9,556	755	7.9
1981	9,750	867	8.9
1980	9,850	N.A.	N.A.
1979	10,080	937	9.3
1978	9,476	881	9.3
1977	9,254	971	10.4
1976	9,080	1,007	11.0
1975	8,824	1,071	12.1
1974	8,005	1,246	15.5
1973	7,387	N.A.	N.A.
1972	6,909	N.A.	N.A.
1971	6,284	N.A.	N.A.
1970	5,866	N.A.	N.A.

Source: Statistics on Social Work Education (New York: Council on Social Work Education, 1970–1984). Reprinted with permission of the publisher.
Note: One institution not included.
N.A.: Not Available.

After an initial increase in the number of black students who earned the M.S.W. degree, in recent years there has been a decline in both their absolute numbers as well as their proportion of all M.S.W. degrees earned in the United States. In 1974, black students earned 1246 (15.5%) of the total of 8005 M.S.W. degrees. The production rate of black students with M.S.W.

degrees continued above or near parity levels for the next three years, but the downward trend that began in 1975 has continued relatively unchecked. In the 1980s, approxmately 8% of M.S.W. degrees are awarded to blacks (see Table 67).

Although the numbers of black students who earned the D.S.W. is small, their proportion of all D.S.W.s earned stood at or above parity in the mid-1970s. It began a process of decline in 1977, and dropped abruptly below black representation in the total population to the 6.7% level in 1978. As a result, only a dozen or so black persons with the D.S.W. degree were produced. Another upswing occurred in 1979 when the 18 doctorates earned by blacks represented 10.9% of the total. The absolute number (35) and percentage (15.5) peaked in 1981 (see Table 68).

Table 68
Doctor of Social Work Degrees Awarded, by Race, 1970–1984, All Institutions Combined

Year	Total D.S.W. Degrees Awarded	D.S.W. Degrees Awarded to Black Students	% Blacks
1984	N.A.	N.A.	15.5
1983	227[b]	26	11.4
1982	284	24	8.5
1981	226	35	15.5
1980	213[b]	N.A.	N.A.
1979	174	18	10.9
1978	178	12	6.7[a]
1977	177	18	10.1
1976	179	23	12.8
1975	155	19	12.6
1974	157	18	11.4
1973	112	N.A.	N.A.
1972	149	N.A.	N.A.
1971	148	N.A.	N.A.
1970	89	N.A.	N.A.

Source: Statistics on Social Work Education (New York: Council on Social Work Education, 1970–1984). Reprintd with permission of the publisher.
[a]This drop may be explained by the failure of 7.3% of the institutions to report.
[b]One institution did not report.

These downward trends mean that a critical shortage of trained black social workers may be on the horizon because the present production level cannot keep pace with retirement losses and the demand for social work personnel in teaching and administratiion, and in state, local and federal government positions.

Black Faculty

Of all the disciplines offered in graduate and professional schools, social work has been the most successful at achieving racial and ethnic integration. Although some institutions have only one or two black faculty members, there is a visible presence of black faculty in most of the 87 social work institutions in the United States. In 1980, only a half-dozen schools were *without* a single black faculty member, and in several schools black faculty members represented a substantial proportion of total faculty. Aside from the three historically black institutions (Atlanta University, Howard, and Norfolk State University), the following institutions led all others in total number of black faculty: Case Western Reserve University, University of Pennsylvania, University of Pittsburgh, and University of Maryland.

In 1983 seven institutions did not have a single black on the social work faculty. Blacks constituted a significant proportion of faculty in several schools of social work: Adelphi; University of Alabama; Boston College and Boston University (both have blacks as deans of the School of Social Work); California State University/Sacramento; Case Western Reserve University; University of Pennsylvania; University of Pittsburgh; San Francisco State University; Southern Mississippi University; Temple University; University of Washington; and Wayne State University.

During this period, several schools of social work hired black professionals in key administrative positions, such as the dean of the school. Examples include Case Western Reserve University, Boston University, and Boston College.

The number of black faculty members increased through most of the period (see Table 69). It did not peak in absolute numbers until 1979 when 389 black faculty members were teaching in all schools of social work in the nation. In academic year 1973–74, an earlier peak was achieved when absolute increases in the numbers of black students were enrolled. Expanding schools of social work hired more faculty, majority and minority. A downward turn occurred the next two or three years, but this was followed by notable increases. The decline in absolute number of blacks teaching full-time in schools of social work registered at the beginning of the 1980s was halted in 1983 when the total number climbed to 313.

Table 69
Number of Full-Time Black Faculty in Schools of Social Work,
1970–1984, All Institutions Combined

Academic Year	Total Faculty	Total Black Faculty	% Blacks
1983–84	1931	313	16.2
1982–83	2016	319	15.8
1981–82	2240	339	15.1
1980–81	N.A.	N.A.	N.A.
1979–80	2387	389	16.3
1978–79	2253	336	14.9
1977–78	2149	328	15.5
1976–77	2058	317	15.4
1975–76	2180	323	14.8
1974–75	2185	330	15.1
1973–74	2309	341	14.8
1972–73	2341	316	13.5
1971–72	2248	276	12.2
1970–71	2199	259	11.7

Source: *Statistics on Social Work Education* (New York: Council on Social Work Education, 1970–1984). Reprinted with permission of the publisher.

The national proportion of black faculty has always been above the proportion of blacks in the population. It reached its highest level in 1979 when the 389 black faculty members represented 16.3% of the 2387 faculty employed in all schools of social work in the United States. A caveat must be inserted regarding these proportions, since they include black faculty employed at Atlanta University, Howard University, and Norfolk State University. When their numbers are removed from the totals, the proportion of black faculty falls to about 12%. In the majority of social work institutions, the proportion of black faculty members does not apporoximate even this level.

There are notable exceptions. For instance, throughout much of the period, black Americans represented approximately one-third the social work faculty at the University of Pittsburgh. They were fairly close to this level at the University of Pennsylvania from 1974 onward. That proportion (or higher) has existed at Temple University since 1972. In constrast, since 1970 the number of black faculty declined at Virginia Commonwealth, while the number at the University of North Carolina has remained static (4 of 26) since 1978. The number dropped from 3 to 2 at Louisiana State University between 1978 and 1983; remained unchanged at 2 of 19 at Florida

State University and the University of Georgia; but declined from 3 to 1 at the University of Oklahoma (see Table 70). In general enrollment patterns among black students within these schools of social work seem to reflect the losses in the number of blacks on the faculty.

Although some of these proportions are unimpressive, the incontrovertible fact is that social work has achieved far more success in providing role models than has any other profession. The presence of visible role models in the classroom, in administrative positions, as field supervisors, and as directors of agencies in which field assignments are made has a profoundly positive impact on efforts to expand and retain educational opportunities in this profession. It is sound evidence of the results that may be attained when institutional commitment is strong. It suggests what results are probable when a variety of role models are present to help create a positive image of the profession, as well as to attract a sufficient number of black students and black faculty.

Problem Areas

The problems facing the recruitment of black students into social work in the 1980s are not rooted in the *Bakke* decision. These institutions long ago implemented modified admissions criteria with sufficient flexibility to accommodate potentially excellent social work professionals from all races. A major problem is suggested in declining enrollments. Social work has difficulties of serious proportions in competing with professionals whose earning capacity is considerably higher than that which the average social worker earns in most states. In general, social workers are underpaid for the services they perform, and in many cities, towns, and states, increasing their salaries or wages is not a matter of the highest priority. This poses a major threat to efforts to attract strong individuals to the profession.

The limited or dwindling pool of black applicants suggests that recruiters can no longer afford to rely so heavily on college students who major in the social and behavioral sciences. That pool is also dwindling. It is now incumbent on schools of social work to establish outreach programs and implement stronger recruitment activities in the high schools so that information about the field can be disseminated at earlier levels of secondary school studies.

There are also problems of retention in some institutions because of a lack of preparation, weak study skills, communication inadequacies, and writing deficiencies of some students. But there are equally grave problems intrinsically associated with low retention. They encompass alienation and isolation within schools in which black students are in very small numbers and without psychological support, cultural reinforcements, social bonds,

Table 70
Full-Time Black Faculty, Schools of Social Work in
"*Adams* States," 1981–1983

Institution	Total Faculty			Black Faculty		
	1981	1982	1983	1981	1982	1983
Alabama	30	28	25	6	4	4
Arkansas	13	11	13	3	2	3
Atlanta[a]	11	15	15	10	14	14
Bryn Mawr	22	19	19	4	4	5
Barry	20	20	19	3	3	2
Case Western	30	24	26	6	4	5
Cincinnati	11	10	9	4	4	4
Florida State	22	22	19	3	2	2
Georgia	27	24	21	3	2	2
Houston	19	19	19	2	2	2
Kentucky	18	18	17	2	2	2
Louisiana	28	24	19	3	2	2
Louisville	28	21	15	3	3	3
Maryland	60	51	49	8	8	10
Missouri	16	13	11	2	1	1
Norfolk[a]	14	18	21	9	13	16
No. Carolina	29	27	26	4	4	4
Ohio State	31	32	32	7	6	6
Oklahoma	16	18	15	1	2	1
Pennsylvania	26	26	15	8	8	5
Pittsburgh	38	33	33	13	11	11
St. Louis	21	13	14	1	0	0
So. Carolina	18	18	17	3	3	3
So. Mississippi	11	10	11	6	5	5
Temple	28	27	37	10	9	13
Tex/Arlington	37	30	31	4	4	3
Tex/Austin	27	26	28	2	1	1
Tulane	18	14	13	2	1	1
Virginia	43	43	38	6	7	7
W. Virginia	18	18	17	2	2	1
Florida Intern'l		13	11		3	2

Source: Council on Social Work Education, *Statistics on Social Work Education*, 1981, 1982, 1983.
[a]Historically black institution

and the affective ties necessary for survival in what they may perceive to be a hostile or unwelcoming environment. Of special note is that some faculty members are still prone to lower their expectations for black and other minority students. Regardless of the motivation for this inexcusable and intolerable behavior, the damage done to the graduate students can be all but insurmountable in future years. Each of these issues can be remediated or remedied through skillful institutional and societal intervention.

The problems of financial aid will not disappear so long as black families earn only 55% of the income that white families earn. It will not vanish so long as black students are not awarded fellowships, scholarships, and adequate financial aid so that they will not be saddled with life-long debts. High-interest, repayable loans are not the answer, especially when the expected earning power is comparatively low. Subsidization of graduate and professional studies should be based, of course, on both need and merit. But full financing of students in these educational programs should be based most extensively on a commitment to serve in the under-served areas as its quid pro quo.

Notes

1. Kurt Reichert, "Survey of Non -Discriminatory Practices in Accredited Graduate Schools of Social Work," in *Ethnic Minorities in Social Work Education,* ed. Carl Scott (New York: Council on Social Work Education, 1970), pp. 39–51.
2. Andrew Billingsley, "Black Students in Graduate School of Social Work," in Scott, *Ethnic Minorities in Social Work Education,* pp. 23–38.
3. Harold I. Greenberg and Carl A. Scott, "Ethnic Minority Recruitment and Programs for the Educationally Disadvantaged in Schools of Social Work," in Scott, *Ethnic Minorities in Social Work Education,* pp. 11–22.
4. Ibid.
5. Ibid., pp. 28–31.
6. Ibid.
7. Ibid.
8. Ibid.
9. Ibid.
10. Ibid.
11. Ibid.
12. Ibid., p. 11.
13. Ibid., pp. 12–14.
14. Data provided by Western Michigan University.
15. Data Provided by University of Texas/Arlington.
16. *Statistics on Social Work Education* (New York: Council on Social Work Education, 1983), pp. 44–45.
17. Ibid.
18. *Statistics on Social Work Education* (New York: Council on Social Work Education, 1970–1978), passim.

Chapter **13**   THE PRODUCTION OF BLACK
DOCTORATES

Few areas in the academic community have stirred as much controversy or created a crisis of such monumental proportions as has that of the production of doctoral degrees among black Americans. The production rate and the actual number of persons awarded the doctorate each year have had many serious implications. The production of Black Ph. D.s has raised a number of questions about the "actual or potential pool" of candidates for positions. This issue is often expressed today in terms of "the available pool," which begs the question of what should be the basis for affirmative action goals and guidelines. It has created others questions: Should the number of blacks and other minorities sought as a goal be equal to their proportion in the total population of a given area, their proportion in the state population, or their representation in the national population? Or should it be tied to their proportion in the "available pool" of actual doctoral degree holders?

Resolution of these questions has never been satisfactory to all sides in the disputes they generated. Nevertheless, these issues reveal a much deeper problem: the continuing shortage of black Americans who hold the doctorate. This fundamental and pressing problem remains in the 1980s despite significant increases in the absolute numbers of blacks awarded the doctorate during the 1970s.

Because of the scope of the doctoral fields encompassed, it is not possible to provide a detailed analysis of enrollment data field by field. However, it is essential to note that the actual number of black Americans enrolled in doctoral degree programs is minuscule when measured by any of the traditional standards. For instance, blacks are underrepresented in enrollment whether or not such measures as the following are employed: number of black Americans in the doctoral age group; proportion of black Americans in either the city, state, or national population, proportion of black Americans who are college graduates.

It should be reiterated that this disproportionately low number of black students enrolled in doctoral degree programs continues even as the pool of blacks who have graduated from college and who, theoretically, could be eligible for advanced degrees expands. The existence of an expanded pool of potential candidates for doctoral degrees among blacks with college degrees suggests that any number of barriers must be operating that effec-

322

tively prevent them from enrolling in doctoral degree programs. Attention is given to some of these impediments to enrollment in a subsequent section. The principal concern of this analysis is on the actual production of black doctoral degree holders.[1] Another primary concern is with their distribution by field of study. Inasmuch as the economic disabilities of black Americans may prevent them from pursuing the doctorate as quickly as white students generally do, it is imperative to examine differences between white and black Americans who are successful in becoming doctoral degree recipients specifically in sources of financial support while in graduate school.

An Overview

The proportion of black students enrolled in graduate schools increased throughout the 1970s; since that time, the number and proportion of black graduate students have fallen sharply. In 1972, black graduate students represented 4.2% of total graduate school enrollment in the United States. There was an increase to 5.2% in 1973.[2] By 1975, blacks represented 6.4% of graduate student enrollment.[3] Between 1972 and 1980, the absolute number of full-time black graduate students rose only by 600. The magnitude of the problem of declining black student enrollment in graduate schools may be discerned even more clearly by a disaggregation of full and part-time matriculants. For instance, in 1972, 21,500 blacks were full-time graduate students. That number represented 5.3% of the total full-time enrollment. In 1978, the number of black graduate students fell to 21,000, or 4.9% of full-time matriculation. The erosion continued in 1982 as the number of full-time black graduate students dropped to 18,887, or 4.2% of full-time graduate enrollment. And in 1984 the preliminary estimates of the number of blacks in our nation's graduate schools constituted no more than 4% of full-time enrollment at that level.[4]

A similar pattern occurred with respect to blacks as part-time graduate school matriculants. Consistent with national trends, and as commonly observed among graduate students in general, the majority of blacks in graduate school are part-time enrollees. Nevertheless, a downward spiral in the number of part-time black students continues at an alarming rate. This fact may be illustrated from 1976 data, which showed part-time black student enrollment in graduate schools as 43,300, or 6.6% of part-time enrollment. By 1980 the number of such students had fallen to 37,800, or 5.8% of total part-time enrollment. In 1982 the downward slide continued so that the 35,920 blacks registered as part-timers represented only 5.0% of enrollment. In 1984 preliminary estimates of the number of black part-time registrants in graduate schools constituted less than 5% of all such students.[5]

At the same time that the decline in black graduate student enrollment has occurred, the pool of black baccalaureates has increased significantly. For instance, in 1976 the nation produced 59,000 blacks with baccalaureate degrees, or 6.4% of all bachelors' degrees conferred. In 1981 the number of blacks climbed moderately to 61,000 or 6.5%. In 1984, it is estimated that the number of blacks graduating with a bachelor's degree constituted 6% of the total number.[6] This expansion of black baccalaureates would seem to suggest that the available pool of blacks to graduate or professional school programs should increase. Instead, dramatic losses of black graduate students have created special concern in graduate schools across the nation. That concern is further complicated by the reality that inattention to the problem in the late 1970s and early 1980s is coinciding with a shrinkage in the percentage of black high school graduates who enroll in college. That situation may exacerbate even more seriously the probability of recruiting from a shrinking pool of blacks for graduate education in the late 1980s and early 1990s unless baccalaureate fallout is curtailed.

The loss of black graduate students at some of the major graduate centers has been especially disconcerting. For instance, between 1978 and 1984, the number of black graduate students at the University of Pittsburgh fell by 14%, or 520 from a total graduate enrollment of 9900.[7] At the University of Michigan, the number of black graduate students dropped from 459 in 1979 to 234 in 1984. Similar declines were registered at such major institutions as the University of Chicago, Stanford University, Princeton University, Harvard University, and University of California/ Berkeley. Retrenchments continue to be national in scope, not limited to any one section of the country nor any particular type of institution.[8] In 1985, it was estimated that, of the 1.2 million graduate students, less than 5% were black.

When analyzing total enrollment of black students by state, it is necessary to keep in mind that their distribution within state or publicly controlled institutions will vary widely whenever the state has a historically black college with a graduate degree program. At present, 34 historically black colleges, dispersed throughout the southern and border states, offer at least one graduate degree. Programs in education are prominent among the disciplines in which a master's degree is offered at the HBIs; matriculants may study for that degree in at least 22 disciplines at the 34 HBIs. The doctorate is offered at Howard University, Atlanta University, Meharry Medical College, Texas Southern University, Jackson State University, and Morgan State University.* Howard began to offer a doctoral degree in 1957. Eleven years later, Atlanta University offered its first doctorate, although it had offered the master's degree for several years. Meharry, Texas Southern, Jackson State, and Morgan State universities are relatively new in providing opportunities for doctoral studies. About 10 disciplines—primarily educa-

* Note: Florida A&M University began a Ph.D. in Pharmacy program in 1985.

tion, biological sciences, home economics, and communications—are represented in doctoral degree programs offered at the HBIs.

At the doctoral level, there is a paucity of black students enrolled in every field in all States. This observation holds true even when confronted with the data on enrollment of black students in doctoral programs in education. Even in this field, an incontrovertible fact is that black Americans are underrepresented in both enrollment and in the number of doctoral degrees they earn. The critical issue here: Why have not our nation's graduate schools attracted sufficiently large enrollments of black students for them to approximate parity or to move beyond a level of tokenism in the number of doctoral degrees produced annually? Another unresolved issue: Why do not larger numbers of black students enroll in doctoral programs?

A partial answer to these questions is that graduate schools, unlike professional schools, have not in the past mounted well-organized and systematic recruitment programs specifically designed for black and other minority students. Most of them rely on their reputation, "old boy networks," ill-defined programs, limited scholarships and feeble announcements that their institution is "an equal opportunity" institution. Often these words are shallow, empty pronouncements, with little or no intent to implement their full meaning.

An indisputable fact is that many black students failed to satisfy cutoff points on the Graduate Record Examination (GRE) where it was a standard admissions requirement. Weaknesses on the GRE occurred sometimes when college grade-point average (GPA) suggested that the students should have performed at a substantially higher level on this test. In many of these instances, especially in the early 1970s when capitation funds were distributed in part on the basis of the number of students enrolled and when grant/research money was more plentiful, some graduate departments were more willing to "take a chance" on students whom they perhaps classified as "high gain, minimum risk" if they came close to GRE cutoff points. Undoubtedly, a few who never should have been admitted were enrolled.

The influence factor suggested by the concept of "old boy network" seems to work most effectively for black students matriculated in predominantly white institutions. Further, letters of recommendation on behalf of black candidates help when they come from a faculty member who is either well known by scholarly reputation or well known to one or more members of the department's admissions committee. In this regard, it is important to keep in mind that the *number* of "admissions committees" usually approximates the *number of departments* or special programs that exist within the institution. Hence, a student may be "admissible" to the university but not necessarily "admissible" to a given department. Being "admissible" to both is a prerequisite for most fellowships and scholarships awarded through institutional funds. But the "old boy network" cuts through these problems.

To take note of the paucity of departmental minority recruitment committees is not to suggest that all departments were and are insensitive to the issue of enrolling more black students in graduate schools. Many are and were committed to this goal during the 1970s. Their admissions committees did their best to "flag" a black student when assessing applications. This process was not approached in any systematic manner. It often took the form of trying to establish racial or ethnic identity by examining the name of the institution from which the baccalaureate degree was earned; the name of the student (was this a common "black name" or not?); the identity of persons who wrote letters of recommendation; or membership in black-oriented student groups or civic organizations.

Another explanation of this underrepresentation in enrollment lies in the reputation of apathy and disinterest, lack of sensitivity, or racism attributed to a faculty member of some departments by students who had experience in the department. A reputation of indifference or racism does not attract black students to the department. Neither does the absence of a critical mass, which presumably may be explained by indifference or racism. While it is also true that some students may misinterpret strict adherence to academic standards as racism, that alone does not disprove the presence of faculty members who do not believe that their department is the "right place" for black students. Many black students report encounters with majority professors who inform them, directly or in subtle ways, that they feel that these students would be more "comfortable" in another department or institution. In any event, this reputation becomes widely disseminated in the network of black students, who refuse even to apply to such departments or institutions.

Further, there is the apparent problem of lack of interest among many black college students in pursuing graduate studies. This low commitment to graduate studies may exist because it never occurs to students who are first-generation college students to think beyond obtaining a college degree. It may occur because of improper counseling and guidance programs in their undergraduate colleges.[9] They may not have adequate knowledge of the process of applying to graduate schools, of locating adequate funding, or of how to select an area of specialization within a broad major field. Importantly, they do not think of graduate school at the moment because of staggering financial obligations accrued during four years of college. While neither factor is necessarily peculiar to black or other minority students, each one is undoubtedly far more serious for these groups than it is for the average middle-class white college enrollee or for poor white students whose professors take a special interest in them. Hence, all these factors may act as a strong deterrent to the pursuit of graduate studies, or at least strong enough to persuade black students to defer graduate work until a later time.

Doctorates Awarded to Black Americans

According to a detailed analysis of doctorates earned by women and minorities made by Dorothy M. Gilford and Joan Snyder, between 1950 and 1954 only 139 black persons with doctoral degrees were in the labor force. During the next five years, following the *Brown* decision, that number rose to 277. In the 1965–69 period, when federal enabling legislation was enacted that fostered greater access of black students to higher education, the total number of black persons who held a doctorate and were in the labor force climbed to 586.[10]

These data are instructive in understanding the results of historical patterns of segregation, discrimination, and racism that had operated to reduce the numbers of black persons with the doctorate. At no time during this period did the number of black Ph.Ds rise above 1% of all doctorate holders in the labor force.

Although no systematic reliable national data for 1970 to 1973 are available, the data on the production of blacks with doctoral degrees between 1973 and 1984 may be illuminating. They show a pattern of increasing absolute numbers and the proportion of total degrees awarded that coincided with successful attacks on exclusionary barriers. For instance, the 581 doctorates produced among black Americans in 1973 alone approximated the total number in this category for the combined five-year period of 1965 to 1969. (see Table 71).

An examination of Table 50 shows a near doubling of the number of doctoral degrees earned by blacks in a seven-year period. A peak in the number of doctorates was reached in 1977 when this group earned 1109 doctoral degrees. Since that time, with only two exceptions, the absolute number of doctoral degrees earned by black American citizens has been in a downward spiral. Hence, as shown in Table 72, the number of black doctorates in 1983 went below 1000 for the first time since 1975. In 1983 blacks received 918 doctorates, or 3.2% of all doctoral degrees conferred on U.S. citizens. In 1984, 948 blacks (3.7% of total to U.S. citizens) received doctoral degrees. Again, less than 4% of all doctorates earned by Americans are earned by black citizens. This pattern is graphically depicted in Table 72.

In 1973, the 581 degrees awarded to black Americans represented 2.4% of the 27,129 doctorates conferred on U.S. citizens in all institutions combined. The percentage of all degrees earned by black Americans was uneven over the next five years. They fluctuated from a low of 3.3% to a high of 4.5% of all degrees awarded U.S. citizens during the period. Blacks earned 3.9% of all doctorates awarded in that seven years.

Table 71
Doctorates Awarded to Black Americans, 1973–1979

Year	Total Doctorates Awarded	% Black of Total Awarded, All Races	Black Men	%	Black Women	%
1979	1055	5.0	551	52.2	504	47.8
1978	1029	4.5	581	56.5	448	43.5
1977	1109	3.7	681	61.4	428	38.6
1976	1085	4.9	647	59.6	438	40.4
1975	989	3.3	642	64.9	347	35.1
1974	846	3.8	580	68.6	264	31.4
1973	581	2.4	N.A.	N.A.	N.A.	N.A.
Total	6694[a]	3.9	3882[a]	60.2	2929[a]	39.8

Source: Constructed from data provided by the National Academy of Sciences, Commission of Human Resources.
[a] Figures are for 1974–1979 only. They may be inflated by 2 in toto after rounding off.

Between 1977 and 1979, an uninterrupted increase in these proportions occurred so that the number of doctorates earned by black Americans rose from 3.7% in 1977 to 4.5% in 1978 and 5.0% in 1979. The 1979 figure was the largest representation of blacks ever among doctorates awarded to Americans. Yet, as the decade ended, all the doctorate-granting institutions and all their departments combined produced only slightly more than 1000 black Americans with a doctoral degree. Since 1980, the fluctuations observed, plus the drop in the number of black doctorates below the 1000 level, dramatize the overall severity of underrepresentation in the production of black doctorates in the United States.

Between 1973 and 1984, black Americans were awarded a total of 11,795 doctorates. This number represented a mere 3.7% of the 314,985 doctorates conferred on U.S. citizens of all racial and ethnic groups. The gender gap began to be narrowed in the late 1970s. Earlier, as in 1974, black males received more than two-thirds of all doctoral degrees conferred on black Americans. But with the gradual breakdown of sex-based inequalities and barriers with respect to recruitment and admissions practices, the gender gap not only narrowed but was finally reversed. In the mid-1980s, more than half of all doctoral degrees earned by black citizens are earned by

Table 72
Doctorates Awarded U.S. Black Citizens by Field, Percent of Total Doctorates, Percent of Total Awarded Black Americans by Years, 1973–1984

Field	1973	1974	1975	1976	1977	1978	1979	1980	1981	1982	1983	1984
Physical sciences												
Total degrees	4338	4892	4760	4445	4369	4193	4298	4114	4168	4288	4424	4453
Black citizens	45	46	36	27	41	51	48	29	39	36	32	44
% of degrees/Blacks	6.1	5.4	3.6	2.5	3.8	5.0	4.6	2.4	3.1	3.4	3.4	4.9
Engineering												
Total degrees	2738	3144	2959	2791	2641	2423	2494	2479	2528	2655	2780	2915
Black citizens	27	16	11	12	11	9	17	18	19	20	29	15
% of degrees/Blacks	1.0	1.9	1.1	1.1	1.1	.9	1.6	1.1	1.6	1.9	3.1	1.4
Life sciences												
Total degrees	4073	4894	5022	4971	4767	4887	5076[b]	5305	5461	5565	5540	5745
Black citizens	96	69	55	63	55	59	52[b]	68	80	72	74	97
% of degrees/Blacks	13.1	8.2	5.6	5.8	5.3	6.7	5.0	5.7	6.3	6.9	8.0	9.2
Social sciences												
Total degrees	4796	6156	6307	6583	6504	6543	6379[b]	6253	6505	6250	6055	5895
Black Citizens	87	107	159	172	179	191	206[b]	222	223	244	199	222
% of degrees/Blacks	11.8	12.6	16.1	15.9	17.9	18.6	19.6	19.3	19.6	23.5	21.6	21.1
Arts and sciences												
Total degrees	4461	5174	5046	4883	4559	4235	4143	3863	3745	3560	3494	3528
Black citizens	74	75	89	91	96	75	119	103	93	103	79	101
% of degrees/Blacks	10.1	8.9	8.9	8.4	8.6	9.8	11.3	9.4	8.3	9.9	8.6	9.6
Education												
Total degrees	5670	7261	7349	7727	7448	7190	7370	7576	7489	7256	7147	6780
Black citizens	382	501	605	667	665	583	556	602	582	606	516	509
% of degrees/Blacks	52.0	59.2	61.2	61.5	60.0	56.7	53.0	57.4	55.6	58.4	56.2	48.5
Professions												
Total degrees	1151	1421	1446	1474	1340	1454	1414[c] (1413)	1345	1388	1491	1728	1917
Black citizens	24	32	34	53	41	46	52	53	59	52	69	61
% of degrees/Blacks	2.4	3.8	3.5	4.9	3.7	4.5	5.0	4.7	5.6	5.0	7.5	5.8
Total degrees U.S. citizens	27,129	26,827	27,009	27,195	26,007	26,529	25,369	26,394	26,262	25,533	25,564	25,167
Total degrees Black & Black U.S. citizens	581	846	989	1,085	1,109	1,029	1,050	1,095	1,007	1,037	918	948
% Black U.S. citizens	(2.1)	(3.1)	(3.6)	(4.0)	(4.2)	(3.8)	(4.1)	(4.1)	(3.5)	(3.6)	(3.2)	(3.7)
All persons combined	32,727	33,000	32,913	32,923	31,672	30,850	31,200	30,982	31,319	31,048	31,190	31,253

Source: Compiled from data provided by the National Academy of Sciences; Commission on Human Resources.
[a] Totals include degrees awarded to all students in these fields, irrespective of citizenship.
[b] These numbers may be slightly inflated due to rounding.
[c] The number in parenthesis refers to degrees classified this year as in the teaching fields.

black women. The loss of black males, however, may reflect something more than a closing of the gender gap. It may be indicative of a fallout pattern among black males that reduces their overall proportion in the educational pipeline at a much earlier age. This underproduction of black males with doctorates might also be attributed in part to a higher dropout rate from doctoral studies and/or to their selection of other options and job opportunities in the marketplace. Nevertheless, the black male dropout rate from high school and college severely restricts the pool available for doctoral studies.

The closing of the gender gap in the production of doctorates is observed in the total population as well. Again, this pattern is indicative of the increased access of women to previously excluded or limited dimensions of the opportunity structure. Among blacks, however, even with the upsurge in the proportion of females among black doctoral degree recipients, the relative paucity of blacks with doctoral degrees underscores how serious is the actual shortage of black professionals. Entirely too few black men and women are recruited, admitted, and matriculated in doctoral programs. Clearly, too few are produced during any given year.

Distribution by Field

In many institutions and many fields of study no doctoral degree was awarded to a black American. The result is a highly distorted distribution of black doctoral degree holders in the major fields of study.

The Commission on Human Resources of the National Academy of Sciences aggregates earned doctorates into seven or eight major fields. For most of the decade, the category "teaching fields" was added to the list. The areas are Physical sciences; Engineering; Life sciences; Social sciences; Arts and Sciences, or Humanities; Education; Professions; and Teaching Fields. The numbers of degrees reported is based on self-reports; that is, on the number of persons who received the doctorate in each of these fields who returned a completed and usable mailed questionnaire. It is therefore possible that this number may be somewhat at variance with those reported from other sources, such as Engineering, for instance, whose data are submitted by deans to an accrediting agency or body.

Examples of subfields in the *Physical Sciences* include Mathematics, Physics and Astronomy, Chemistry, Earth and Environmental and Marine Science. *Engineering* comprises all the specializations listed in Chapter 9. *Life Sciences* refer to the Biological Sciences, Agricultural Sciences, and Medical Sciences (e.g., Pharmacology, Parasitology, Environmental Health, and Veterinary Medicine). *Social Sciences* encompass the traditional social science fields and Psychology with its various branches or divisions. In the social sciences are such subfields as Anthropology, Economics, Econo-metrics, Sociology, Statistics, Political Science, Urban and Regional Plann-ing, and Public Administration.

Examples of the *Humanities* include Art, History, Theater, Religion, Philosophy, Linguistics, Comparative Literature, and Music. The *Profes-sions* are represented by Theology, Business Administration, Home Economics, Journalism, Social Work, Speech, Law and Jurisprudence, and Library Science. *Teaching Fields* include a combination of several subfields in other larger fields mentioned above. They are represented, inter alia, by Agriculture, Art, Business, English, Foreign Languages, Industrial Arts, Mathematics, Reading, Physical Education, Vocational Education, Health and Recreation, and General Science. *Education* includes a number of specializations ranging from Elementary Education to Higher Education.

During the 1970s and 1980s, Education dominated the fields in which doctoral degrees were earned by blacks. As a result, the impression is often given and allegations are frequently made to the effect that there "were too many blacks in Education." While more than half of all doctorates earned by blacks remained consistently in Education, black Americans represented 1.8% or slightly more among all Education doctorates conferred between 1973 and 1979. The range in rate of all degrees conferred on blacks was from 61.5% in Education in 1976 to 52% in 1973. Thus, during the middle years of the 1970's, approximately 6 of every 10 doctorates received by black citizens were in the field of Education. Since 1980, the 5106 degrees earned by blacks in Education comprise only 3.96% of all such degrees conferred on U.S. citizens.

With such a comparatively high concentration of black Americans in one field, fewer than 4 of 10 degrees had to be distributed among 6 or 7 fields. The obvious consequence of this maldistribution is a substantially greater distortion of proportions of all doctorates. There are some fields in which not one doctoral degree was received by a black American. But be-tween 500 and 600 degrees are awarded to blacks in Education each year.

The second most common field of doctoral study among black Americans is the Social Sciences, including Psychology. The absolute number of degrees earned in these disciplines increased without interruption until 1983 when the 199 black doctorates was the lowest number conferred on blacks in that area since 1978. Further, there was a loss of 45 social science/psychology degrees among blacks between 1982 and 1983. Even with that loss, the 199 degrees represent 21.6% of the 918 degrees conferred on black citizens in that year. In 1984, the 222 degrees earned by blacks in the social sciences/psychology remained approximately one-fifth (21.1%) of doctorates earned by blacks. The third concentration of black doctorates is in the Arts or Humanities. The range in absolute numbers of degrees received by blacks in these fields from 1973 to 1984 was from 74 to 119.

Only in 1979, 1980, 1982, and 1984 did the number of Arts and Humanities doctorates conferred on blacks reach or exceed 100 for the year.

The production of blacks in the Physical and Life Sciences has always been abysmal and far below either need or expectation. These disciplines happen to be areas in which the shortage of blacks is especially acute. Although many blacks have been reluctant to enter these science fields, the problem is much more complicated. For one thing, academic departments in these specializations have been among the more resistant to the recruitment and training of black graduate students and are among the most defiant with respect to the hiring of blacks for faculty positions. Many black graduate students report feelings of alienation, encounters with perceived racism, and extreme difficulties in obtaining interested advisers when studying for the doctorate in several of these disciplines.

Given these problems, it is less surprising to note that there were fewer than 30 blacks with doctorates in Engineering; fewer than 40 with doctorates in the Physical Sciences; and fewer than 75 with a doctorate in the Life Sciences in each year of the 11-year period under review. The notable exceptions in the Life Sciences occurred in 1973 when 96 blacks received degrees in these fields and again in 1981 and 1984, when they were awarded 80 and 97 Life Sciences doctorates, respectively. Even then, blacks earned about 1.4% of the doctorates in Life Sciences; .9% of those conferred in Physical Sciences; and .7% of all Engineering doctorates earned by U.S. citizens (see Table 72). Without question, the black student participation rate in these fields of doctoral study strains credibility to be labeled even "token participation."

Even though percentage changes from year to year might appear impressively positive in some areas, the actual production rate must be viewed in the context of the proportion of all degrees awarded U.S. citizens and requirements for parity. It is evident that with a production rate of less than 4% of all doctorates received by U.S. citizens during the review period, it is virtually impossible for black citizens to catch up in the forseeable future. To reach parity will require a massive influx of black students in doctoral programs and an equally all-encompassing revolution in the production rate of doctorates. Unfortunately, such profound changes in higher education do not appear to be in the offing. The future is bleak, and the underrepresentation currently observed will continue without major and sustained intervention by relevant decision makers unafraid to use their power, influence, and resources to induce structural and policy changes.

According to the Carnegie classification of doctorate-granting institutions, universities fall into one of eight rated types. They are (1) Research I (institutions are the most researched-oriented); (2) Research II (or more moderately research-orientated institutions); (3) Doctoral I; (4) Doctoral II; (5) Comprehensive I; (6) Comprehensive II; (7) Liberal Arts I, and (8)

Liberal Arts II. All other doctorate-granting institutions are categorized as "other" or as "unrated universities or colleges."[11]

According to one major research study on institutions from which black Americans received the doctoral degree, the proportion of black Americans awarded the doctorate from Research I institutions is smaller than the proportion for all doctoral degrees earned. On the other hand, black Americans rank first among U.S. citizens of all racial and ethnic origins in the proportion who earned doctorates from Research II universities. They also rank high in the proportion of doctorates conferred in the "other" category.[13]

Sources of Funds For Graduate Education

Major differences exist between black and white students in how they finance their graduate education. As indicated in earlier studies, these differences lie almost entirely in the heavier utilization of loans by black students and the significantly greater proportion of white students who are awarded teaching and research assistantships.[14] However, as Table 73 is analyzed, not only are these differences apparent but other variations in financing graduate education are especially evident.

White graduate students were considerably more successful during any period in obtaining fellowships and trainee grants through federally subsidized projects. Only in the very last year of the 1970s was the gap between these groups narrowed by any appreciable degree. By contrast, black students received more support in the category of "other fellowships", which refer to monies granted from nonfederal sources and noneducational institutional grants. The percentage point differences between the two groups are significant and favored black students, proportionately, throughout the review period.

However, in the categories of teaching and research assistantships there can be no equivocation about the disproportionate benefits and successes experienced by white students compared to the limited proportions of assistantships awarded black students. Approximately half of all white students financed their graduate education through teaching assistantships in every year under review, compared to approximately one-fourth of black students who were able to use this means of financial support. Similarly, in every year under review, the proportion of white students awarded research assistantships more than doubled the proportion of black students who received this form of support.

Since teaching and research assistantships are invaluable for graduate students, lack of black students support in these two areas continues to be an issue of major concern among black educators and civil rights groups.

Table 73

Sources of Support for Doctoral Students, by Race, 1974–1984, and Percentage Using Sources

Source	1974 %	1975 %	1976 %	1977 %	1978 %	1979 %	1980 %	1981 %	1982 %	1983 %	1984 %
Federal fellow/trainee											
Black	33.7	28.7	30.2	24.3	19.3	19.0	19.1	17.8	17.9	17.9	17.7
White	40.5	38.1	34.1	28.3	23.8	21.8	21.7	21.0	19.6	18.5	16.6
GI Bill											
Black	17.3	13.9	15.9	12.9	11.7	8.7	6.5	6.9	5.8	4.9	5.2
White	12.4	13.2	13.5	12.4	11.1	9.9	8.5	7.9	6.3	5.4	5.2
Other fellowships											
Black	26.6	26.1	25.3	28.0	24.6	24.0	26.6	22.3	23.7	26.1	10.4
White	21.7	22.8	23.0	21.0	19.9	19.8	19.9	20.4	20.9	22.1	4.3
Teaching Assistantships											
Black	28.8	30.1	27.6	25.9	23.6	23.8	24.8	25.7	25.3	23.9	30.6
White	49.1	52.0	51.5	48.7	46.8	47.2	47.3	47.4	47.6	47.8	48.4
Research Assistantships											
Black	15.1	17.2	15.8	15.0	15.2	14.9	14.0	15.4	14.4	15.8	20.1
White	30.3	34.5	35.4	33.9	33.0	34.4	34.1	35.1	36.4	37.0	38.2
Educational/institutional funds											
Black	14.1	17.0	15.2	12.2	11.7	12.1	10.8	11.7	11.5	13.1	N.A.
White	12.1	13.2	13.2	11.3	9.7	10.2	10.8	10.7	11.0	11.8	N.A.
Own/spouse earnings											
Black	49.9	69.5	67.1	67.4	65.9	68.4	72.6	73.3	70.7	70.3	81.0
White	52.1	64.3	74.0	72.3	69.8	69.5	70.2	70.4	69.6	69.8	82.2
Family contributions											
Black	3.3	9.3	10.4	9.3	7.9	8.7	10.6	10.8	10.6	13.6	
White	7.2	14.8	17.5	15.6	14.0	14.4	15.8	16.6	16.9	17.6	
National Direct Student Loan											
Black	—	13.2	16.9	14.8	12.9	14.3	18.8	17.6	16.2	19.2	25.0
White	—	9.1	11.6	10.2	9.4	10.0	11.1	12.8	15.1	16.8	22.0
Other loans											
Black	18.6	15.9	14.4	14.6	12.8	13.5	16.0	17.7	18.1	18.0	20.3
White	14.0	13.6	13.9	11.5	9.9	10.0	10.7	12.0	13.1	13.0	13.9
Other											
Black	4.3	6.8	6.6	5.7	4.8	7.4	5.1	5.3	4.5	4.1	3.9
White	3.7	4.7	5.3	4.7	4.4	4.2	4.0	4.3	4.0	3.8	3.5
Unknown											
Black	5.0	2.8	2.7	2.3	3.2	2.5	1.8	1.6	2.1	2.6	1.3
White	2.3	1.2	1.1	1.2	1.2	1.0	1.0	1.0	1.0	1.0	.7

Source: Compiled from data provided by the National Academy of Sciences; Commission on Human Resources.

Both forms of assistantships provide immeasurable on-the-job training and practical experience, which may prove of immense value in preparation for doctoral examinations, in developing mentors among the full-time faculty, in sharpening pedagogical and research skills, in becoming more sophisticated in the intricacies of laboratory research, and in demonstrating special personality traits or characteristics that can be highlighted when the doctoral recipient attempts to move into the labor force. Further, these assistantships often provide an opportunity for undergraduate students to be exposed to graduate students of their own racial or ethnic groups. In turn, this exposure may serve as a prime inspiration for members of that group to major in the same field or to think more positively about pursuing graduate studies. Equally important is the exposure that they provide nonminority students to minority graduate students, which in turn may force them to overcome any demeaning stereotypes they may hold about the intellectual abilities of minority groups. Hence, the salience of assistantships is a multifaceted or multidimensional phenomenon. Throughout the period under review, black graduate students were shortchanged in these areas.

Black graduate students fared slightly better in funds received from educational and institutional sources. The major advantage experienced by black students in this area occurred in 1975. This situation coincided both with the recession (whose effects were devastating to minorities in general) *and* with losses of federal funds to support graduate and professional education. Apparently, several educational organizations and institutions assumed more of the responsibility for assisting black students to finance graduate education at this time. However, the gap between black and white graduate students was narrowed each year thereafter.

The economic predicament of most black students is reflected in the larger proportions of black students who must resort to some form of loan in order to finance their education, in contrast to a smaller proportion of white students who use this funding source. As indicated in the percentage of both groups in this category in Table 73, the differences are significant. The gravity of this problem increases in severity when the loan profile is viewed in terms of how much support a graduate student can expect to receive from family contributions. In every year, white students were considerably more successful in obtaining family contributions than were black students. The peak year for both groups coincided with the recessions and declines in federal fellowships and trainee grants. The years 1975 and 1984 are especially noticeable.

A high proportion of both groups receive financial assistance through personal earnings or from spouse's earnings. While racial differences fluctuated during the 1970s, it is evident that in the 1980s blacks have relied more than whites on this source of support. This pattern reflects greater gains by whites in other sources of financial aid and the necessity of blacks to depend on family for whatever assistance is possible in order to achieve their goals.

The difference between the two groups on the proportions who receive GI Bill benefits are relatively minor. The remaining two categories are not of major consideration.

Graduate and Professional Opportunities Program (GPOP)

Title IX, Part B, of the Higher Education Act initiated the Graduate Professional Opportunities Program (GPOP) of fellowships. The purpose of these fellowships is to assist underrepresented minorities and women "to prepare for academic and other fields." These fellowships, which provide a 12 months stipend of $4500, are awarded for graduate study. Recipients are remitted institutional tuition and mandatory fees.[15] These awards were made for the first time in 1978–79, when Black students received 293, or 53% of the 553 fellowships awarded.

Fewer white and other minority students received GPOP fellowships compared to the rate of success for black students. However, white students were more successful than either Hispanic, Asian American, or Native American students. The 1978 and 1979 rates for white students were 26.1% and 22.6% of the total, respectively. This translates into a total of 204 white GPOP recipients. The 1978 and 1979 percentages of total fellowships were 16.5% and 16.4%, respectively, for Hispanic doctoral students. Hispanic students, therefore, received 141 of all GPOP fellowships. Asian Americans received 48 of the total number awarded during the first two years, and Native Americans were awarded a total of 28 fellowships. The percentages for Asian Americans were 6.9 and 4.9 respectively, while they were 3.6 and 3.1 for Native Americans in 1978 and 1979, respectively.[16]

For 1980, the renewed fellowships totaled 789, while 213 new fellowships were awarded. The number of participating institutions has more than doubled (114 in 1980) over the 55 who participated during the first year of the program. Yet despite its success, the GPOP program was immediately targeted for elimination in the very first year of the Reagan administration, and in each year thereafter. The GPOP budget ultimately was saved; however, the program has struggled to survive with level funding under a Reagan administration that is hostile to higher education. Since 1981, the appropriation has ranged from $10 million to $11.7 million in 1985. In 1984, the last year for which we have systematic data, the distribution of 1054 recipients was as follows: blacks 52% of the total number of awards; Hispanics, 21%; Asians 4%; Native Americans, 3%; and white women, 19% of the total.

The GPOP program is only one of several federal sources of financial aid for doctoral students and graduate education in general. Not only is the Office of Education involved in these efforts, but so are other agencies and branches of the federal government. For instance, financial aid programs or fellowships are awarded through such agencies as the National Science Foundation, the National Institute of Education, the National Institutes of Health, the National Institute of Mental Health, and the Health Resources Administration. However, it is rare for blacks to receive fellowships in open competition through such programs as the NSF Fellowships. For example, H.A. Neal reported that not a single black received an NSF regular (open competition) award in 1981, 1982, or 1983.[19] The general NSF practice is to eliminate applicants who do not have competitve GRE and GPA scores. Heavy reliance on the GRE is injurious to blacks, since mean scores for blacks as a group are substantially lower than those for whites.

An example of an organizational program to assist black and other minority graduate students to pursue a doctoral degree is the Minority Fellowship Program of the American Sociological Association (ASA). This program was developed at the insistence of the Caucus of Black Sociologists of the ASA in 1970. By 1973, the Center for the Minority Group Mental Health Programs of NIMH gave a six-year grant to establish and fund a program for the recruitment and financial support of minority students who wished to pursue a doctoral degree in sociology. Since that time, additional support for the program has come from the National Institute of Education, and the Cornerhouse Fund and through tuition remissions from some of the participating institutions.[20]

A full-time project director was hired for the program, through a national search in which the ASA and the Caucus of Black Sociologists participated. The project director is housed in the national headquarters of the association. Not only is he responsible for initiating recruitment activities, he also works with the ASA Comittee on Minority Fellowships in the selection process, visits minority fellows at their institutional location; serves as a visible role model for the Fellows, and provides important nonacademic support for students who sometimes need someone to listen to their experiences as they become adjusted to the rigors of a doctoral degree program in an alien environment.

In the 12 years of the program's operation, under the able leadership of such program directors as Maurice Jackson and Paul Williams (who held the directorship for 10 years), approximately 220 black and other minority students have been supported by the program. Of that number, one-third (82) had received the doctorate in sociology by 1984. Although this cohort represents one of the highest completion rates among the five minority fellowship programs operated by the NIHM, funding from that source is not sufficient to meet the needs of eligible applicants. In part, this problem reflects an increase in the number of academically strong and otherwise eligible applicants. Significantly, it also reflects the tremendous retrenchment in NIMH funding for fellowships that do not conform to a much tighter and more restrictive definition of mental health studies. Inasmuch as sociology is an immensely diversified discipline, it is not possible, under highly circumscribed definitions of mental health, for applicants interested in other subspecializations to be funded by NIMH for their graduate studies. Thus, the ASA looked to other sources, such as the Cornerhouse Fund and membership contributions. Even these sources are not sufficient to meet increasing requests for doctoral fellowships in sociology from larger numbers of eligible applicants. Therefore, in 1985, the ASA organized a Task Force on Financial Support for Minority Fellowships. One of the special functions of this group is to identify potential sources of fellowship funds for minority students.[21]

The American Sociological Association established, again at the insistence of the Caucus of Black Sociologists, an executive associate for minorities and women. The importance of the office is measured by both the stature of the person recruited for the position and the overall quality of the work performed by the office. One of the most effective incumbents of this position in recent years was Dr. Doris Wilkinson, a former professor of sociology at McAllister College. As the Executive Associate for Minority and Women Affairs, her office addressed such issues as career opportunities for minority social scientists in nonacademic settings; the location of fellowship monies and training seminars, special projects of interest to minority and women sociologists. Summer institutes in research techniques, innovations, and strategies were organized. And the practice of a column devoted to these concerns, initiated by the first person who held this position, Professor Maurice Jackson of the University of California/Riverside, was continued in *Footnotes*.[22] This office over the years initiated broad contacts wtih other foundations and governmental agencies in the Greater Washington community. The early work done by previous incumbents—Dr. Jackson, Dr. Lucy Sells, and Dr. Joan Harris—was essential in this regard. Since black Americans constitute only about 3% of all sociologists in the United States, and since women sociologists, like minority-group members, still encounter formidable barriers in hiring, promotions, and tenure, the continuing need for this office is real and obvious. Similarly, there is a need for minority fellowships and minority–women affairs officers in all of the professions to stimulate the process of increasing doctoral degree production among these groups. The Minority Center of the NIMH has also assisted four other associations with similar programs, including social work and social science fields.

This list of financial contributors is by no means exhaustive. The work of the private sector, the foundations, and individual philanthropists was just as important in these areas as in the professions discussed in earlier chapters. The Ford Foundation, for instance, began its minority fellowship programs in the early 1960s. Its most important predoctoral program, begun in 1967, has been instrumental in helping at least 1800 minorities receive the doctorate through its support of about $50 million. Other foundations, such as Carnegie, Mellon, Rockefeller, Exxon, IBM, and Lilly, assisted blacks and other minorities in the 1970s.

While all sources of financial assistance are of immense importance to black and other minority students as they embark on their doctorate, the size of most grants is grossly inadequate. The enormity of the problem is captured by the full realization of the economic disabilities under which most black and other minority students labor. Earlier, it was pointed out that the median black family income in 1985 is only about 55% of that of white families. It is less for Puerto Rican families and still worse for Native Americans. Rectification of these inequities demands substantially larger financial outlays to assure support for a larger cohort of students who could be recruited for all graduate fields of study. If the nation is indeed, committed to the achievement of parity between the races in the number of doctorate holders in the labor force, it will have to do nothing less than make a gargantuan increase in financial support for graduate education. Further, it will be absolutely necessary to avoid the kinds of legal challenges to these efforts that resentful groups are likely to organize against the existence of programs designed to assist minority students.

Time Lapse between the Baccalaureate and the Doctorate

Unquestionably, the magnitude of the economic problems encountered by black students helps to account in a measureably significant way for the longer time that black doctoral recipients take to obtain this degree. Consequently, black doctoral recipients are usually older as a group when they receive the doctorate than are all other groups, including whites, Chicanos, Asian Americans, and Native Americans.

Regarding the age at which the doctorate is granted, black recipients average about five years older in every year than both white recipients and the aggregate of all doctoral recipients (see Table 74). Blacks may delay entry into a doctoral degree program following receipt of the baccalaureate degree because of the need to work. Or they may work part-time on the degree while being employed full-time, and this practice inflates the median time lapse. The registered time it takes to earn the doctorate is not statistically different between black Americans, white Americans, and the aggregate of all American recipients. It takes from 5.8 to 6.8 years in registered time between the baccalaureate and the doctorate. One should be mindful that some students also work toward a master's degree in the interim, stop-out for a while, and work for a time before renewing doctoral studies. This pattern also adds to the time lapse.

The five-year age difference between black and white doctoral recipients has a number of implications for postdoctoral employment. The higher age of black doctoral recipients may help explain their lower representation in postdoctoral fellowships, but that is not the sole explanation for this under-representation. The fact that many black doctorate holders of an older age search for, and are attracted to, higher-paying positions in administration, industry, and government service may be attributed to the age factor. Their income demands may be higher given the need to provide for their children, who are likely to be older than those of younger doctoral recipients. In such instances, some departments within universities encounter major problems in competing for black Americans with doctorates because of salary demands. Many are unwilling to offer substantially higher salaries to black doctorates for fear of alienating white faculty, who may allege unfairness and deeply resent black faculty members hired at somewhat higher salaries. Still another fact must be considered. Many black persons who receive the doctorate have already had several years of full-time teaching experience, either in a historically black college, a small and predominantly white liberal arts college, or a community college. The problem faced by some departments is how to evaluate years of "college teaching experience" in relationship to the salaries demanded by newly minted doctorates who are five years older *and* black. Few black Americans with this type of experience are willing to enter an institution at "entry-level" salaries or ranks. Thus, controversies having broad ramifications may follow, regardless of the decision reached, unless a clearly defined institutional policy is articulated and has support from a significant consensus.

Special Problems and Issues

In recent years, there has been a decline in the production of doctorates among black Americans. Simultaneously, significant increases, with few fluctuations, have occurred in the number of other minority-group members who have earned the doctoral degree. For example between 1980 and 1984, the number of black citizens who received a doctorate fell from 1095 to 948. Among Puerto Ricans, the number awarded the doctoral degree more than doubled between 1980 (69 degrees) and 1982 (140 degrees), but fell again in 1984 to 133. Yet the production represented a dramatic increase.

The production pattern for Mexican Americans was similar to that noted among Puerto Ricans. For instance, in 1980, the nation's graduate schools

Table 74

Median Age at Doctorate and Median Time Lapse from Baccalaureate to Doctorate, by Race, 1973–1984

	1973	1974	1975	1976	1977	1978	1979	1980	1981	1982	1983	1984
Age at doctorate (all students)	31.3	31.4	31.5	31.6	31.6	31.7	31.9	32.2	32.4	32.6	32.9	33.2
Black	N.A.	36.7	36.3	36.2	35.9	36.0	36.4	36.9	37.3	37.5	37.0	37.4
White	N.A.	31.3	31.4	31.5	31.4	31.5	31.7	32.1	32.2	32.3	32.7	33.0
Median time lapse												
Total	8.4	8.6	8.7	8.8	8.8	9.0	9.2	9.4	9.6	9.7	10.0	10.3
Black	N.A.	8.5	8.5	8.7	8.7	8.9	9.1	12.9	13.0	13.0	13.2	13.8
White	N.A.	12.4	12.4	12.5	11.9	12.3	12.2	9.3	9.3	9.6	9.8	10.2
Registered time												
Total	5.8	5.9	6.0	6.0	6.1	6.2	6.3	6.4	6.5	6.6	6.8	7.0
Black	N.A.	5.9	6.0	6.0	6.1	6.2	6.2	7.0	7.1	7.4	7.5	7.6
White	N.A.	5.9	5.8	6.0	5.9	6.4	6.5	6.4	6.4	6.6	6.8	6.9

Source: Constructed from table reported in *Summary report of Doctorate Recipients from United States Universities* (1973–84); Commission of Human Resources, National Research Council; National Academy of Sciences.

conferred 109 doctoral degrees on Mexican Americans. That number rose to an all-time high of 182 in 1982, but declined to 173 in 1983, and then rose slightly to 178 in 1984. The pattern among Native Americans was somewhat more erratic. Doctorate production among this group was highest in 1980, when 106 Native Americans received the degree. However, a significant downturn occurred in 1981 when only 89 degrees were conferred on Native Americans. The decline continued in 1982 (77 doctorates), but reversed in 1983 (81 doctorates), and declined in 1984 (73 doctorates). While aggregated data would suggest overrepresentation in the receipt of doctorates among Asians, disaggregated data reveal a most startling finding: during any given year, Asian Americans received only about one-seventh of the doctoral degrees conferred by American graduate schools to persons of Asian ancestry. An overwhelming majority of Asian doctorates produced annually are conferred on non-U.S. citizens. For example, in 1982, Asian citizens received only 430 of the 2898 doctoral degrees earned by Asians. In 1983, they received only 490 of the 3120 doctorates awarded persons of Asian ancestry. In effect American minority groups are still underrepresented with respect to their proportions among annual recipients of doctoral degrees.[23]

The problem of the inordinately restricted size of the applicant pool for graduate studies among black students is persistent and widespread. Some dimensions of this problem were highlighted in other segments of this chapter and in previous ones. Nevertheless, when discussing the applicant pool, the disparity between the rate of production of college graduates who are black from historically black and historically white colleges emerges as a factor of profound importance.

According to accumulated college enrollment and graduation data, the historically black colleges now matriculate only about 20% of all black students in colleges across the nation. But almost half (42%) of all black students are enrolled in a community or junior college, and many of these students are in programs not transferable to a four-year college or university. Further, the majority of black students graduated with a baccalaureate degree each year are produced by the historically black colleges, which have only about 20% of the students.[24] This fact suggests that a major crisis exists in the traditionally white institutions regarding not only the production of black college degree holders but their failure to expand the pool of potential applicants among black students for graduate and professional degree programs.

The central and compelling issue here regarding actions of policymakers and other officials is that they must raise questions and examine institutional behavior and the quality of the teaching or learning environment in traditionally white institutions that render them singularly less successful in the production of black college graduates. The dropout rate among black students is considerably higher in these institutions that is the case in the historically black colleges. Why this problem is so pervasive in white institutions is a question that is still begging careful scrutiny.

A related issue is that of the recruitment and retention of black faculty for graduate faculty positions. Clearly, a part of the problem is the continuing underrepresentation of black Americans in all academic disciplines and fields of specialization. But there is another equally pressing matter—that in a period of retrenchment, union shop principles often take effect in the academic world, too: The last hired shall be the first fired. Since black and other minority faculty members fall into the category of last hired, they are relatively unprotected when anything approaching a seniority principle is enforced. That situation is further exacerbated by the "revolving door" syndrome. According to this principle, black faculty members are hired and retained long enough for institutions to satisfy requirements of being "an equal opportunity employer" and, in the view of many black faculty victimized by the process, with little intention of ever retaining them, regardless of the exceptional quality of their overall performance. Many are retained for five or six years. They are forced out to search for another position, and the process continues with another black or minority faculty member.

Tenure is theoretically denied because of weakness in one or more of three areas: teaching, research, and service. In many major institutions, service is a criterion of the lowest priority. Yet that is where the strengths of many minority faculty lie, because every conceivable committee within the university wanted them as a "minority presence." Acceding to these requests meant that precious little time remained for the scholarly research and productivity required for tenure. Some may argue that black and other minority faculty members made a "rational choice" to perform these services. That may very well be the case. However, a "minority presence" is essential on decision-making committees whose decisions affect the educational programs and quality of learning for minority students.

There is ample evidence to support the contention that black and other minorities do not have equal access to the research funds and postdoctoral fellowships that strengthen research capabilities. If they do not have access to these funds, then engaging in the type of research that generates thousands of dollars for the department and that may enrich a person's career or increase the probability for tenure is virtually impossible.[25] To alleviate the problem of fewer minority researchers, the Ford Foundation in 1985 announced a multimillion-dollar postdoctoral fellowship program for minorities. This program is directed by the National Science Foundation.

Frequently, when tenure has been undertaken and articles published, the quality of the journal is seriously questioned. In the view of some white faculty members, an article published in a "white-oriented" or "mainstream" journal in existence only 2 years counts for more points than an article published in a journal with 50 years of history that carries a "black label."

Not infrequently, when books are published, the issue then focuses on the quality and prestige of the publishing house rather than the quality or merit of the book itself and the contribution that it makes to the literature in that particular field. In other words, too many minority faculty members are subjected to unfair and inappropriate tenure evaluations that escalate the revolving-door syndrome. Having said all these things, it should be absolutely clear that *incompetence should never be rewarded, regardless of race, color, ethnicity, sex, or creed. However, faculty members should have the same opportunities to meet the criteria for tenure in an equally wholesome environment, irrespective of race, color, ethnicity, sex, or creed.* Further, and without equivocation, they should be evaluated fairly in all decisions affecting their performance as scholar–teachers.

The shortage of black faculty can be alleviated in part by more aggressive recruitment by the various departments. They can identify early promising students in their own colleges, encourage them to pursue the doctorate, assist them in funding their graduate education, and then hire them in full-time teaching positions. This process may mean making exceptions to the general practice of not immediately hiring one's own graduates. Doing so may be one of the efficacious remedies for the problem of underproduction.

Coordinated recruitment necessitates major transformations in institutional commitment to the goal of increasing larger numbers of black and other minorities for graduate education. That commitment means strong and assertive leadership throughout the academic community. It demands that departmental racism, indifference, and apathy be subordinated to the will of the institution to accelerate educational opportunities for all groups in every department and in every program of the college or university. It means demonstrated evidence, across the entire structure of the institutional community and by academic and administrative leaders, that no manner of racial bigotry and intolerance will be condoned. Coordinated recruitment also necessitates the appropriation of funds sufficient to support an adequate staff and an aggressive recruitment program. Such programs recognize the fact that thousands of highly competent and eager graduates are produced annually by small liberal arts colleges and universities. Many may never perceive graduate or professional education as a viable option. Their counselors and advisers may not have sufficient knowledge of potential opportunities that may await them. This rich source of untapped talent should be sought as a mechanism for increasing both minority presence in graduate and professional schools and, ultimately, for the production of larger numbers of minorities with a doctorate or other professional degree.

Most important, sustaining a renewed commitment is an absolute imperative, a sine qua non, if you will, for success in the production of doctoral degrees among blacks and other minorities.

Notes

1. The production of black graduates with masters' degrees rose dramatically during the 1970s. Although this growth is recognized, a detailed attention to this level of graduate education is not within the purview of this study. Nevertheless, programs designed to increase the production of black doctorates will benefit from tapping that comparatively large pool of black Americans who hold the masters' degree and from regarding this group as a potential pool for doctoral-level training.
2. See *Racial and Ethnic Enrollment Data from Institutions of Higher Education* (Washington, D.C.: Office of Civil Rights, Department of Health, Education, and Welfare, 1972–1978); and Elaine H. El-Khawas and Joan Kinser, *Enrollment of Minority Graduate Students in Ph.D. Granting Institutions* (Washington, D.C.: American Council on Education, August 1974). "Ph.D. Manpower Employment Demand and Supply 1972–1985." *Bulletin No. 1960,* Department of Labor, Bureau of Labor Statistics, 1973, p.9.
3. Data Provided by the National Center for Educational Statistics.
4. James E. Blackwell, "The Declining Presence of Black Faculty on White Campuses," *Proceedings of the Second Annual Conference on Black Administrators at Predominantly White Colleges* (Cambridge, Mass.: MIT, 1985),
5. Ibid.; and 1984 data provided by the National Center on Educational Statistics.
6. Ibid.
7. Linda Watkins, "Losing Ground. Minorities' Enrollment in College Retreats after Its Surge in '70s," *Wall Street Journal,* May 29, 1985; p. 1.
8. Ann McKay-Smith, "Large Shortages of Black Professors in Higher Education Grow Worse," *Wall Street Journal,* June 8, 1984 p.1.
9. See U.S. Commission on Civil Rights, *Toward Equal Opportunity: Affirmative Admissions Programs at Law and Medical Schools* (Washington, D.C.: U.S. Government Printing Office, June 1978); *Social Indicators of Equality for Minorities and Women* (Washington, D.C.: U.S. Government Printing Office, August 1978); and James E Blackwell, Maurice Jackson, and Joan Morre, *The Status of Racial and Ethnic Minorities in Sociology: A Footnote Supplement* (Washington, D.C.: American Sociological Association, August 1977).
10. Dorothy M. Gilford and Joan Snyder, *Women and Minority Ph.D.s in the 1970's: A Data Book* (Washington, D.C.: Commission on Human Resources, National Research Council, National Academy of Sciences, 1977), p.18.
11. Ibid., p. 122.
12. James E. Blackwell, *Networking and Mentoring: A Cross-Generational Study of Black Experiences in Graduate and Professional Schools* (Atlanta: Southern Education Foundation, 1983).
13. Ibid.
14. Ibid.
15. *Program Support of Graduate Education* (Washington, D.C.: U.S. Office of Education, May 1, 1980).
16. Ibid.
17. Anne S. Pruitt, " Does Minority Graduate Education Have a Future?" *Planning and Changing* 14, No. 1 (Spring 1983): 15–21.

18. Data provided by the U.S. Office of Education.

19. H. A. Neal, "Critical Issues Facing Minority Graduate Students in Science and Engineering" (Paper presented at the Annual Meeting of the Association of Graduate Schools, College Park, Md., October 1983); and *Footnotes* 13, No. 5 (May 1985): 1.

20. Personal communication with Dr. Paul Williams, director of the Minority Fellowship Program of the American Sociological Association, July, 1980.

21. Ibid.

22. Doris Wilkinson, "Federal Employment for Sociologists," *Footnotes*, March 1980; "Percentage of Women Doctorates in Sociology Increases," *Footnotes*, December 1977; and "Careers, Minorities and Women," *Footnotes*, 1977–1980, passim.

23. *Summary Report of Doctorate Recipients from United States Universities* (Washington, D.C.: National Academy of Sciences, 1980–1984).

24. National Advisory Committee on Black Higher Education and Black Colleges and Universities, *Access of Black Americans to Higher Education: How Open Is the Door?* (Washington, D.C.: U.S. Government Printing Office, January 1979), p. 20.

25. Stephen S. Wright, *The Black Educational Policy Researcher: An Untapped National Resource* (Washington, D.C.: National Advisory Committee on Black Higher Education and Black Colleges and Universities, Department of Health, Education, and Welfare, 1979).

Chapter **14** POLICY IMPLICATIONS IN
MAINSTREAMING OUTSIDERS:
OUTLOOK FOR THE FUTURE

Few objective analysts deny that some progress was made between 1970 and 1987 toward increasing educational opportunities for black Americans. The magnitude of that progress is a matter of serious debate within the black community. The data presented in this study and the analysis of enrollment and graduation trends dramatize the unevenness and episodic nature of the efforts made toward "mainstreaming Americans." Although the climate of hostility, indifference, and erosion of commitment to the ideals of a just and fair society generated by the leadership of President Ronald Reagan is a serious threat to the mainstreaming of blacks, successes experienced to the end of 1986 could provide a bulwark of opposition to the tactics of retrenchment promoted by the Reagan administration. This chapter reviews the progress achieved over a 15-year period to enhance the status of black Americans in graduate and professional education. In addition, some attention is devoted to projections about the future of blacks in higher education in relationship to national, social, economic, and political conditions.

Asserting that some degree of progress was made toward better access to graduate and professional education is not to claim that the progress actually achieved fulfills enunciated goals and collective aspirations. Without a doubt, the nation has not achieved educational parity. In fact, in most fields and in most insititutions, the educational establishment has fallen far short of public goals and expectations.

The 1970s began with a high level of expectation and some evidence that expanding educational opportunities to include black Americans and other minorities had substantial national support. Federal intervention in educational policies had already achieved great significance. This situation was primarily a consequence of publicity given to actual enforcement of affirmative action policies, the utilization of capitation grants to facilitate minority-student enrollment in professional schools, and student aid programs, as well as the encouragement given to individual institutions to expand their educational facilities.

Enrollment in graduate and professional schools was on the upswing. It is important to reiterate that black and other minority students benefited from an educational policy that mandated enrollment expansion in general

347

and that they did not precipitate that expansion. White students were the primary beneficiaries of this policy since a far greater number of students from this segment of the population actually enrolled in graduate and professional schools during the 1970s than was the case with black and other minority students.

The corporate structure and private foundations have played a profound role in expanding educational opportunities. The services rendered by them in the process of mainstreaming outsiders, described in earlier chapters, were not only extensive but far-reaching in their implications for educational change. Incontestably, their collective involvement was stimulated in part by external pressures for positive action. It was, significantly, a manifestation also of the sensitivity among many leaders and lower-level decision makers in the corporate and foundation sectors to the moral responsibility that these groups have to create a larger pool of professionally trained persons among the minority population. Consequently, they drew on their financial resources and professional expertise to support the establishment of an impressive array of educational programs designed to increase educational opportunity, parity, and a larger supply of professionals in the American population.

At the beginning of the review period there was a certain amount of ambivalence among the leadership and other functionaries in graduate and professional schools about appropriate actions to accomplish equality of access. For many, the actions undertaken and the programs implemented represented movement on an unchartered course. This uncertainty reflected the absence of a critical mass of minorities in such institutions, as well as limited experience with minorities. In many instances, these were persons who had fought earlier against racial inclusion, but who in the 1970s and 1980s were expected to lead their institutions in the construction of programs to assure equality of access, substantially improving the rate of producing black professionals. Consequently, many early programs were grounded on ambiguous educational policies.

Although laws may not change attitudes, they are a powerful instrument for transforming behavior. Responding to federal laws and statutes to terminate discriminatory behavior, many institutions did indeed take a number of steps toward expanding educational opportunities in graduate and professional schools for minority-group students. Steps were taken to improve the institutional climate in ways that would foster racial accomodation, reduce personal anxieties, and promote a positive orientation toward learning. The motivation to engage in these expansion processes and to mount new programs was concrete evidence of the commitment of some faculty members, administrators, and legislators to the overarching principle of racial equality and social justice.

The success experienced during the review period in moving toward the production of a larger number of professionals in the black American population can be attributed to at least five interrelated factors. These include roles played by (1) the federal government, before 1981; (2) the private sector (as represented by the corporate or business world and foundations); (3) institutions themselves in seeking out black students with potential to become professionals; (4) the relentless determination of students to succeed even in the face of various forms of adversity; and (5) sustained pressure.

Success was by no means total. Institutional involvement was by no means ubiquitous, as the media would have the American public believe. On the contrary, institutional commitment was too often equivocal. Institutional policies too frequently vacillated in response to public opinion. Comparatively few institutions produced the lion's share of black Americans trained in the professions. As noted, when the historically black professional institutions are excluded from the analysis, it becomes especially clear that most of the historically white institutions failed to move beyond token levels regarding the admission, enrollment, and graduation of black Americans. Further, some professional schools enrolled as few as a dozen black students during the entire period. Some never enrolled a single black student. While the situation may reflect the size of the black population in these states, the issue is considerably larger in scope. There is no state in the United States without *any* black citizens, and no state without black school-age children. Then why is it that states with only a few blacks in the total population cannot approximate even that representation in their graduate and professional schools?

Another illustration of the tendency for a small number of professional schools to enroll a majority of the black students may be drawn from medical education. According to data collected for this study, approximately 44 of the nations's medical schools in existence at the beginning of the 1970s enrolled fewer than 50 black students in first-year medical classes throughout the decade. That is, when all black students actually enrolled in first-year medical schools classes were totaled for the decade, about 44 medical schools had enrolled no more than 50 black students in first-year classes. Even though the medical colleges of Howard University, Meharry Medical College, and Morehouse enrolled only about 20% of all black medical students in 1987, compared to over 80% by Howard and Meharry in 1970, there is still a serious problem of token access to most medical institutions. As in other fields included in this study, many institutions have excellent "paper programs" and claim to make "good faith" efforts toward expanding educational opportunities, but have no discernible commitment to translate pronouncements into viable programs.

Despite these observations, as a result of affirmative efforts by several educational institutions and federal, state, and local administrative bodies, and because the federal government, prior to the election of Ronald Reagan, was supportive of these endeavors, the production of black professionals by graduate and professional schools did increase. Between 1970 and 1984, the nation's graduate and professional schools did produce 9124 more black physicians; 2296 more black dentists; 300 more black optometrists; 15,451 more blacks with the first professional degree in engineering; and about 10,000 more blacks with at least a master's degree in social work, And between 1973 and 1984, there was an increase of 11,795 blacks holding the doctoral degree, and about 3000 more blacks with law degrees.

A sad truth is that, despite such notable increases in the production of black professionals, the percentages of black Americans in most professional fields are still about as shocking as they were in 1970. For instance, in 1987, black Americans still constitute about 2.0% of the nation's physicians, 2.1% of the veterinarians, 1.0% of the optometrists, 2.0% of the pharmacists, 2.3% of the dentists, 2.6% of the lawyers, and 2.1% of the engineers. At the current rate of production of black professionals, at least four decades will be required to attain racial parity in most professions. The nation cannot afford such a snail's pace of production toward equality of educational opportunity. Given the demographic trends among all sectors of the population, the nation cannot afford the calculated indifference and insensitivity characteristic at the federal level with respect to the development of black talent as a much needed national resource. However, the establishment of major scholarship programs by such philanthropic organizations as the McKnight Foundation's program in Florida and the Ford Foundation Fellowships are encouraging counterpoints, indeed.

Hence, there is little reason to be sanguine about absolute numerical changes. Unfortunately, several danger signs inform us that serious trouble lies ahead. These include (1) a declining or unchanging black student enrollment; (2) a decrease in the commitment to aggressive recruitment strategies; (3) fallout from the Bakke case, which encourages some institutions to reduce their programs for minority students and increase the weights assigned to objective admissions criteria when confronted with difficult choices; (4) a reluctance by the federal government to take the necessary leadership to persuade institutions to draw on that portion of the Bakke decision that can facilitate racial heterogeneity in graduate and professional schools; (5) a shift in federal policies away from direct student grants to repayable loans and the implementation of federal policies and practices that make it increasingly difficult for eligible students to obtain information about available financial aid; (6) a shrinkage in role models as black faculty members fail to receive academic tenure; and (7) opposition to minority-student programs by the public and by influential special-interest groups.

Needed Policy Changes (How To Succeed By Really Trying)

Clearly, educational parity has not been achieved. American black professionals are not produced at a rate commensurate with the total population of either the state in which they reside or the nation as a whole. Evidence presented in earlier chapters shows that the nation is far from reaching educational parity between the races and equality of opportunity for black and other minority-group citizens. *Consequently, policy changes are necessary in three levels, at minimum: (1) the governmental level; (2) the private and corporate levels; and (3) the institutional level. In addition, major changes are vital in the home, social and school environments in order to increase the level of motivation for learning among greater numbers of black students and to strengthen their determination to succeed.*

Substantial improvement in the rate of access of black students to graduate and professional schools and in their production as professionals can be made if institutions renew their commitment to fulfill the real promise of equality of opportunity. That commitment encompasses a search for funding sources and maintainance of provisions for financial aid, scholarship monies, educational outreach programs, college enrichment and academic support services, programs to reduce attrition and to enable all students to complete their training successfully with confidence that they are capable of being highly competent professionals. It means *more* than so-called good-faith efforts to recruit and enroll more black students and to hire more black faculty members. It demands actualization and success in these endeavors so that all students will benefit from a racially and ethnically heterogeneous learning environment.

Institutional commitment is evidenced in receptivity to the concept of heterogeneity and to a positive orientation toward the steps necessary to achieve it. That change often requires a willingness to reevaluate admissions requirements and sometimes to make them more flexible and amenable to policies of *inclusion.* An appropriate mix of both traditional (objective) admissions criteria and nontraditional or (subjective) criteria can be developed that will satisfy the constitutional requirements or the legal boundaries imposed by the *Bakke* decision. This can occur only if institutions actually *desire* to enroll more minority students.

Similarly, the hiring of more black faculty members, who may be percieved as positive role models and as evidence that the negative stereotypes internalized by some students are totally unfounded can become a reality only through institutional will, determination, and creativity. Clearly, the production of enlarged numbers of black professionals is a first major step in this direction. But if the nation's graduate schools are annually producing only 10 mathematicians, 10 physicists, 20 chemists, 20 agricultural scientists, 1 anthropologist, 2 art historians and no biomedical engineers with doctoral degrees from the black American population, they have a monumental task before them if they want to rekindle this institutional commitment.

An expansion of educational outreach programs is imperative. These programs require joint enterprises with junior and senior high schools on a scale never before undertaken and with an intensity perhaps not fully understood. Secondary school counselors and college or professional school advisers should interact with a greater degree of regularity in order for students to become more familiar with changing career opportunities and with new requirements for admission into professional degree programs. Outreach programs embrace motivational activities that stimulate students to learn and provide them with the personal strength to withstand peer-group pressures to take the easy way out of high school or college.

The institutional climate may have to be transformed in order to increase the probability of potential role models for students and of students themselves wanting to accept a job or to enroll at the institution. Reputations of racism, institutional hostility, and prejudice in the classroom spread with extraordinary speed and are often difficult to overcome. Consequently, it is not unreasonable for the institutional leadership to enunciate policies against all forms of racial and ethnic prejudice and to specify clearly penalties for violations of these policies. Neither is it unthinkable in the 1980s for institutions to sponsor racial awareness programs in which the participants are faculty administrators and students. These may be one instrument for understanding *how* subtle racial animosity, prejudice, and overt racial antagonisms may be attacked in order to create a more harmonious learning environment. By the same token, it must be recognized that racism may be alleged where it does not exist, and when it does occur, it often may be difficult to substantiate.

If the institutions are receptive to change, they may welcome some form of federal intervention to assure that they will achieve their goals of equality of educational opportunity within a reasonable time frame. Similarly, they will be more likely to cooperate with corporations and private foundations regarding suggestions for changes in educational policies.

Skeptics may view the emphasis on changes in institutional behavior as something akin to a liberal's dream or unlikely to be realized without significant alterations of institutional power, external pressure, and internal demands from a coalition of enlightened faculty and students of all races. In view of apparent attacks on minority programs, allegations of "reverse discrimination," the insistence on the objectification of merit, and the willingness of some institutions to interpret legal mandates in ways that are deleterious to minority-group interests, there is great force behind such arguments. However, some professional schools have made good-faith efforts, with and without apparent success, in opening their doors to minority students. Several achieved success despite lukewarm leadership from the top echelon of university administration and impediments created by hostile faculty and faculty who genuinely believe that the most promising students are always those who score the highest on admissions tests. For all these reasons, governmental intervention in educational policies should become more widespread in the 1980s than at any time in the history of American higher education. It may be absolutely necessary if states and institutions continually fail to commit themselves and their resources toward the realization of educational equality.

Hence, federal and state governments must commit themselves to an unyielding and uncompromising policy of equality of educational opportunity. This policy considers not only the 18 states under litigation in the *Adams* v. *Bennett* case (formerly *Adams* v. *Richardson, Adams* v. *Califano, and Adams* v. *Bell* at one or more points during the study period), but all the states in the nation. Equality of educational opportunity means much more than dismantling a dual system of education in formerly de jure segregated states. It also attacks the exclusionary policies and practices promoted by many institutions in states characterized by de facto segregation and discrimination. The commitment given by the federal government, its leadership, and its myriad agencies for the enforcement of sound educational policies regarding equality of opportunity cannot be any less than that given at institutional and private levels. In fact, the government's commitment should establish a national standard of determination to achieve educational opportunity for all Americans. It should be sufficiently strong, pronounced, and visible to the public so that even the most resistant actors fully understand that equality of educational opportunity is unequivocably national policy and that blacks, Hispanics, Native Americans, and Asians have the same opportunities for access and graduation as do white students in our nation's graduate and professional schools.

Unfortunately, the fears registered by black Americans when Ronald Reagan was elected president in 1980 are becoming reality. Instead of the federal government's being perceived as the "government of all the people," under President Reagan the federal government is increasingly viewed by a significant portion of the black population as the "enemy of black people," and Ronald Reagan is seen as the "white man's president." During the first six years of his presidency, Mr. Reagan has failed to assert the kind of forceful leadership required for improving the educational and economic status of black Americans. Not only has he forcefully articulated his opposition to affirmative action, he has supported the efforts of the attorney general of the United States and the chief of the Office of Civil Rights to dismantle all affirmative action programs. Further, he has attempted to persuade the U.S. Supreme Court to declare all such programs unconstitutional.

These actions represent a vigorous and determined effort by President Reagan and his administration to reestablish a segregative society, a society in which opportunity is restricted and limited for black Americans. Clearly, he has not advanced the fundamental principles of educational opportunity. Nor has he advanced the fundamental precepts of civil rights in ways that support the spirit of the decision rendered by the U.S. Supreme Court in *Brown* v. *Board of Education of Topeka, Kansas*. Many blacks argue that no president and administration have been so blatantly opposed to the advancement and aspirations of blacks and to their citizenship protections guaranteed under the Fourteenth Amendment to the Constitution as have President Reagan and his Administration. It is claimed that the aspirations of blacks for equality of access to graduate and professional schools, just as their desire to escape poverty through more beneficial employment programs, have been sacrificed on the altar of political expediency. Further, instead of using federal leverage to compel institutional compliance to dismantle dual systems of segregation, the Reagan administration supports state systems that oppose even the basic mandates of *Adams* v. *Bennett,* when powerful political forces within the white population demand compromises not supported by the black population. For instance, the federal government under President Reagan has a penchant for settlements in desegregation cases that do not fully comply with the proscriptions laid down by the federal government itself and the federal courts during the administrations of Presidents Carter, Ford, and Nixon. Hence, instead of influencing policy changes at the state level that are supportive of vigorous recruitment, admission, and enrollment of specified numbers of black students, and of a more equitable distribution of financial aid, graduate assistantships, and an accelerated pace for the recruitment and hiring of black professors, the policies and practices of the Reagan administration will result in rollbacks unless institutions and states disregard recommendations by the federal government and accede to the demands made by blacks at state, local, and institutional levels.

These facts notwithstanding, the federal government *can* be an instrument for positive and creative change. It can influence states and institutions to expand educational opportunity, provided the leadership in this regard is strong, persistent, and supportive. It can also be a mechanism for stagnation and retrogression if the leadership is indifferent or is vigorously opposed to positive federal intervention on behalf of previously *excluded* segments of the population.

Evidence from earlier times, especially during the 1970s, showed how powerful the federal government can be for creating an atmosphere of positive change. The use of capitation grants, a commitment to affirmative action in higher education, and the expressed willingness of the federal government to cutoff funds to institutions not in compliance with court orders, reinforced by the moral leadership of the presidency to enforce the law, all facilitated expanded access to graduate and professional schools. Inasmuch as a commitment to such affirmative efforts is lacking in the presidency of Ronald Reagan, it seems even more incumbent on the Congress of the United States and the Supreme Court of the United States to protect the rights of all citizens for equal access to higher education. It is imperative for the Congress to enact measures that will safeguard existing rights from the onslaughts of a hostile administration *and* to enact legislation where necessary to clarify and strengthen existing laws.

Title III funds, as well as other resources, can be expanded and more judiciously utilized to enhance the educational programs of the historically black colleges. Support for the maintenance and survival of historically black colleges, such as Meharry Medical College, has been the single most important contribution of the Reagan administration with respect to access of black Americans to higher education. This support for black colleges, most of which still have enrollments that are at least 90% black, widens the pool of potential black students for graduate and professional schools. However, the hand that giveth is too often the hand that taketh away. Hence, the largesse demonstrated with respect to the survival of historically black colleges is not extended with equanimity to methods that foster access and retention of blacks in traditionally white institutions and significant enrollments of white students at the historically black colleges.

Most important, the federal government must take the leadership in eliminating the debilitating social and structural barriers to equality of access among black and other minority students. The impediments to access and successful outcomes so widely encountered by blacks are imposed by an unemployment level twice the rate of the national average, or an income that is only about 55% of the median family income of white families, or a teenage unemployment rate that is three or more times that of the national average. All these take a heavy toll on black Americans. They render far too many black families incapable of providing the quality of support needed by their youth to survive or succeed in postsecondary education. High dropout and pushout rates among black high school students result; they become a potent barrier that the federal and local governments can address through enrichment programs that will create and sustain interest in learning.

In each of the above ways, the federal government especially can have a profound impact on institutional behavior and educational policy. That impact also extends to exacting assurances from institutions that just as they will no longer utilize set-aside programs of the type questioned in the *Bakke* case, their educational policymakers must be equally as committed to that portion of the *Bakke* decision that legitimates diversity and heterogeneity and the use of *race* as one important variable in deciding who shall be *included* in graduate and professional schools.

Another level of policy concern is in the private sector. It is addressed specifically to the corporate structure, private foundations, and the professional associations. While each of these units of the private sector has contributed an immense amount of financial resources and expertise in the past to promote programmatic efforts that assure greater access and educational opportunity for minority students, this is not the time for retrenchment. Not only is it necessary to to sustain the level of commitment to this goal, they must raise and articulate their efforts more forcefully.

There is a need, therefore, for the continued involvement of the private sector in the granting of both need-based scholarships and financial awards predicated on merit to minority students who have demonstrated exceptional academic promise. There is also a need for the private sector to assume greater leadership roles in establishing their own outreach programs, as well as cooperative enterprises with specific institutions in the form of early-identification programs. There is abundant evidence that it is important for students to learn about career opportunities and their requirements as early as possible in their educational career, as well as to have concrete proof that members of their group can be successful in these occupations.

The need for precollege programs, summer internships, college workshops, and informal encounters with members of the corporate structure is real. Earlier chapters mentioned the success of some of these programs. The quality of those successes suggests that many of them should be expanded and that they should get greater financial and human resource support.

Without a doubt, minority students and their families must do something for themselves. Families have the responsibility for establishing a learning environment in their home, for stimulating an interest in learning, for imposing the discipline and respect for authority that create self-discipline in the person. Families, too, have a responsibility to motivate their children by whatever ways known to them and through cooperation with elementary and secondary school systems. There is ample evidence of success from generations of black persons who have achieved that success despite origins in economic poverty and initial training in less than exceptional schools. They had determination, perseverance, self-discipline, and an orientation to achievement that was instilled by parents who wanted them to be successful and by *significant others* interested in their welfare. The same can be done on an even broader scale today.

Family responsibility includes observation of the educational activities of children—whether or not they have homework, library assignments, or special projects to complete. It also means paying attention to attendance at school and to membership in peer groups that reinforce self-discipline, respect for the authority structure, and a desire to learn, rather than to those that encourage opposition to learning. There is no reason to assume that the middle and upper-class members of the dominant group in American society must have a corner on the market for the development of sound skills. Just as hundreds of thousands of minority students, all from disadvantaged socioeconomic groups, have developed these skills in the past, so can students from these origins today profit, in large numbers, from such practices learned and reinforced at home and at elementary and secondary schools. Becoming more academically competitive is also a responsibility of the students themselves.

Elementary and secondary school systems have an equal responsibility to minority pupils. It involves sound teaching, adherence to academic standards, compassion, racial awareness and understanding, and a belief in their students' capacity for learning. It means helping to strengthen self-esteem and personal confidence and a willingness to engage those subjects presumed to be "tough." And success should be recognized, praised, and rewarded.

These are joint efforts and joint actions that require mutual support and understanding. But this emphasis on home and school factors is not intended to communicate an impression that the kinds of programs, recommendations, and courses of actions proposed for the institutions, government, and private sectors must await radical transformations in the overall quality of precollege education or major changes in orientations toward education in the home. The 1970s taught us, if not reinforced the belief, that concerted action is a necessary precondition for advancing beyond token levels of access to graduate and professional schools or for moving forward in the production of doctorates among minority populations.

Beyond Tokenism: Five-Year Plans

A standard practice in foreign aid, modernization, and development is to persuade developing nations to construct five-year development plans. An explicit purpose of these plans is to establish carefully conceptualized goals that may by achieved by a definite target date. These plans include a specification of the resources required as well as their probable sources. Methods or courses of action are articulated in a series of phases or stages particularized for each goal. A monitoring mechanism is incorporated for identifying obstacles and problems, as well as for ascertaining success at critical junctures in each phase. Monitoring also permits an evaluation of the methods employed and the quality of resources specified to accomplish the original purposes of each five-year plan. As a result, corrective steps may be taken to eradicate problems believed to impede progress.

Obviously, academic institutions, corporations, and private foundations frequently construct such plans. During the 1970s, plans were indeed developed for the purpose of increasing minority-student enrollment in professional schools (e.g., Project 75 in medicine and the Engineering Effort). The implementation of these plans played a major role in stimulating the quest for equality of educational opportunity in specific professional fields. This work should be continued by the professions.

Similarly, institutions should develop new plans that involve further joint ventures and cooperation with the federal government, the business community, private foundations, and professional associations with the same purposes of producing significant numbers of professionally trained persons from minority populations. The conceptualization of these plans should likewise be a joint enterprise and should reflect greater commitment by each of the cooperating sectors to increasing educational opportunities for outsider groups.

It is time for a renewal of a national consensus that the training of all the nation's talent is of compelling urgency. That consensus should be based on basic American values of social justice, equality of opportunity, and the universality of democratic ideals. It is further predicated on basic issues of pragmatism and selfish interests that point to demographic changes occurring in the United States. If Hodginson is correct,[1] the aging of white America and the declining birthrate among white Americans, coupled with expanded birthrates among blacks and other minorities, will compel the nation to depend more heavily on a well-trained minority population of blacks, Hispanics, Native Americans, and Asians to meet its most basic human resource needs. Thus, it is in our national and our selfish interests to be certain that the people on whom the nation will depend for expertise in the future be as thoroughly trained as possible.

Specifically, there should be a national understanding that there is a critical need for a far greater array than now exists of experts in each of the areas covered in this study—people who can expand the delivery of health-care services, extend legal and social services to all persons in need, and respond positively and creatively to the demands of an increasingly technological society. Further, opportunities for college and university teaching–research functions should increase significantly in the 1990s by virtue of the retirement of those individuals who entered the profession during the 1950s and 1960s. Hence, expanded opportunities for trained members from minority groups should be accelerated in the 1980s. The issue is also one of process and methodology. That is why the cooperation of all levels of policy and decision making is required to attack this immense problem of underrepresentation of minorities in the professions.

Interorganizational cooperation can provide the financial and human resources for attaining specific goals during each five-year phase. A mechanism for accountability should be clearly incorporated and carefully monitored. What is learned to this point should be a basis for determining what actually worked or is workable if appropriate support is given to those strategies. Hence, the cooperating organizations might lend varying types of support, coordinated by the academic institution, to specific programs.

A comprehensive program necessarily embraces a positive and psychologically supportive institutional climate, a sound recruitment strategy, well-coordinated outreach programs that extend into the institutions's target area, early-identification activities, assessment, selection and admission policies based on a good mix of objective and subjective criteria, ability to attract students to graduate or professional school, utilization of summer institutes for both precollege and pre-professional programs, continuing use of self-paced curricula as appropriate, availability of academic and nonacademic support services at both collegiate and professional school levels, and systematic, unbiased evaluation of students so that those with the potential to succeed may be re-assured of their progress and those without such potential can be counseled out of the program.

The hiring of blacks for faculty and administrative positions in the traditionally white institutions should be a matter of the highest priority. This study has shown that the presence of black faculty is the most powerful predictor of enrollment and graduation of blacks from professional schools. There is equally compelling evidence that black students want and need black mentors, as well as a critical mass of black graduate and professional school students sufficient to enable them to form viable networks that will facilitate their progress as students and in the professions. Earlier research[2] shows that black students are not likely to be selected as protégés by potential mentors and that they often experience numerous problems attempting to forge social networks on predominantly white campuses. Yet, they deeply feel a need for mentors and a system of social networks.

The financial costs for support, operation, and management of programs should also be borne jointly by the federal government, the corporate sturcture, private foundations, and the institutions themselves. For feasibility and management purposes, some 100 institutions could be selected as cooperating institutions for the first phases of the five-year plans. The number allocated to a given state may be based on the size of the minority populations in that state or jurisdiction and the quality of the plan developed by competing institutions at the state level.

Precedents for joint ventures already exist (e.g., health services centers that incorporate medicine, dentistry, optometry, pharmacy, nursing, biomedical sciences, and other health-related fields). Such models could be applied to other professional fields where individuals or independent units operate within the same institution. This would provide more effective coordination and better cost control. What's important is that the result should be a substantially improved mechanism for increasing access beyond the token level, an enriched quality of training provided to students; improved intergroup understandings among students, faculty, administrators, and executives of diverse racial or ethnic heritage; as well as the production of professionally trained minorities in numbers that would reach educational parity in the not too distant future.

How soon this change occurs may very well be contingent on profound alterations of the power structure in the educational establishment. It may depend on both internal and external pressures exerted on state systems of higher education and specific institutions for policy changes. It may be accelerated by the determination of minority students themselves to become more competitive in largers numbers, and by their demand that graduate and professional schools create a more positive learning environment in which a greater production of black professionals can take place.

In the final analysis, some essentials cannot be missed: black students have strong desires to become physicians, dentists, lawyers, engineers, architects, optometrists, and social workers, and to earn doctoral degrees. They have equally strong desires to work and earn sufficient funds to finance their graduate or professional studies. Related goals can be accomplished only if the economic and educational barriers against access to equal schooling, jobs, and wages are eliminated. That will occur only through sustained leadership; federal and state intervention; cooperative undertakings between colleges, professional schools, high schools; and the corporate world combined with a genuine realization of equality of opportunity.

Even though black Americans may be extremely pessimistic about the future, it is imperative for them to take control of their own fate. Blacks should become even more self-assertive and determined to gain constitutionally legitimate rights. Now is the time for strong national and grassroots leadership that is able to utilize the many strengths and resources within the black community. More so than at any time in the recent past, the need for unity, group discipline, focus on concrete objective, and clearly articulated strategies for the maintenance of past civil rights achievements is paramount.

Black people must not permit attacks against affirmative action, whether in higher education or in equal access to employment opportunity, to continue unchecked. Clearly, many of these attacks are a mask for the single purpose of dismantling the economic, educational, and social remedies established during the past three decades. Coalitions with other minority groups and with persons within the white population committed to expanded opportunity across racial and ethnic lines may be necessary. However, the primary responsibility for the continuation of this quest for equality rests squarely on the shoulders of black people.

Finally, despite the persistence of social, economic, and educational barriers to mainstreaming, black students cannot afford to acquiesce to apathy, indifference, self-centeredness, and withdrawal. It is imperative for them to commit themselves in larger numbers to intellectual rigor, self-discipline, the value of learning, and the continued development of those skills vital for incorporation into the mainstream.

Notes

1. Harold Hodginson, in *Demographic Imperatives: Implications for Educational Policy* (Washington, D.C.: American Council on Education, 1983).
2. James E. Blackwell, *Networking and Mentoring: A Study of Cross-Generational Experiences of Blacks in Graduate and Professional Schools* (Atlanta: Southern Education Foundation, 1983).

Bibliography

1. Abt, Donald A. *Report of the Workshop Conference on Minority Representation in Veterinary Medicine* (Sponsored by the Association of American Veterinary Medical Colleges, The American Council on Education, and the Ford Foundation), November 1-2, 1978.
2. Admission Requirements of U.S. and Canadian Dental Schools, 1970-85, Washington, D.C.: American Association of Dental Schools, 1970-1985.
3. Admissions to Schools and Colleges of Optometry, Fall 1986, Washington, D.C.: American Association of Optometry (undated).
4. Albarnel, Karen, "Is a Relapse Ahead for Minority Medical Education?" *Foundation News* (March, 1977), 24-27.
5. American Association of Colleges of Pharmacy, *Graduate Enrollment Report,* Fall, 1978, 1979, 1980, 1981, 1982, 1983, 1984, 1985.
6. _____, Tables IV and VII, Vol. 40, August, 1976, p. 1-5. Bethesda, Maryland.
7. _____, "Impact of the President's 1985 Budget on Pharmacy Student Financial Aid," March 8, 1984.
8. American Dental Association, *Trend Analysis, 1977-78.* Chicago: American Dental Association, 1978.
9. _____, Council on Dental Education, *Annual Report: 84-85.* and AADS Survey of Dental Seniors, *Summary Report,* 1984.
10. *Annual Survey and Ethnic Enrollment Data from Institutions of Higher Education.* Fall 1976, Washington, D.C.: U.S.H.E.W.: Office of Civil Rights, Table 9.
11. *Annual Survey of Optometric Education Institutions.* Washington, D.C.: Association of Schools and Colleges of Optometry. The surveys for each year from 1969 through 1978-84 were made available for this research by ASCO.
12. Association of Collegiate Schools of Architecture, *Architectural Schools in North America.* Washington D.C.: The Association of Collegiate Schools of Architecture, 1979.
13. Association of American Medical Colleges, *Minority Students in Medical Education: Facts and Figures,* November, 1983.
14. _____, *Minority Students in Medical Education: Facts and Figures II.* Washington, D.C.: AAMC, Office of Minority Affairs, March, 1985.
15. Association of Schools and Colleges of Optometry, *Changing Trends in the Financing of Optometric Education,* September 30, 1984.
16. Atelsek, Frank J. and Gomberg, Irene L., *Special Programs for Female and Minority Graduate Students.* Washington, D.C.: American Council on Education, HEP Report, Number 41, 1978.
17. Bardolph, Richard, *The Civil Rights Record.* New York: Thomas Y. Crowell, 1970.
18. Bell, Derek, ed., *Directory of Minority Law Faculty.* Section on Minority Groups, Association of American Law Schools, 1979-80, Washington, D.C.: Association of American Law Schools, 1980.
19. Bennett, Lerone, *Before the Mayflower: A History of Black America.* Chicago: Johnson Publishing Company, 1969.

20. Bennett, William, *To Reclaim A Legacy.* Washington, D.C.: The National Endowment for the Humanities, 1984.

21. Bierstedt, Robert, "An Analysis of Social Power," *American Sociological Review* 15 (December 1950): 730–738.

22. Billingsley, Andrew, "Black Students in A Graduate School of Social Work," in Carol Scott, (ed.), *Ethnic Minorities in Social Work Education.* New York: Council on Social Work Education, 1970, pp. 23–28.

23. Blackwell, James E., *Access of Black Students to Graduate and Professional Schools.* Atlanta: The Southern Education Foundation, 1975.

24. _____, and Philip Hart, *Cities, Suburbs and Blacks.* Bayside, NY: General Hall, 1983.

25. _____, "Correlates of the Scholastic Aptitude Test," an unpublished paper presented at the annual forum of the College Board, October 1983, Dallas, Texas.

26. _____, *Desegregation of State Systems of Higher Education: An Assessment.* Atlanta: The Southern Education Foundation, 1984.

27. _____, *Networking and Mentoring: A Cross-Generational Study of Black Experiences in Graduate and Professional Schools.* Atlanta: Southern Education Foundation, 1983.

28. _____, *The Black Community: Diversity and Unity.* Second Edition. New York: Harper & Row, 1985.

29. _____, "The Declining Presence of Black Faculty on White Campuses," Proceeding of The Second Annual Conference on Black Administrators at Predominantly White Colleges. Cambridge, Mass.: M.I.T., 1985, pp. 132–137.

30. _____, *The Participation of Black Students in Graduate and Professional Schools.* Atlanta: The Southern Education Foundation, 1977.

31. _____, "The Power Basis of Ethnic Conflict in American Society," in Lewis A. Coser and Otto N. Larsen (eds.) *The Uses of Controversy in Sociology.* New York: The Free Press, 1976, Chapter 10.

32. _____, "Social Factors Affecting Educational Opportunity for Minority Group Students," Chapter I in *Beyond Desegregation: Urgent Issues in the Education of Minorities.* New York: The College Board, 1978, 1–12.

33. _____, Maurice Jackson and Joan Moore, *The Status of Racial and Ethnic Minorities in Sociology: A Footnote Supplement.* Washington, D.C.: The American Sociological Association, August 1977.

34. Blake, Martin I. and Jack Orr, reports on "Graduate Enrollment Data" for 1969–70 and 1971–72, 1972–73, respectively. Both are published in the *American Journal of Pharmaceutical Education.* The respective volumes are 35 (February 1971):108–127; 138–153 and 37 (February 1983).

35. Blalock, Hubert M., cf., "A Power Analysis of Racial Discrimination," *Social Forces* 39 (1960):53–69 and _____, *Toward a General Theory in Intergroup Relations.* New York: John Wiley & Sons, 1967.

36. Bowie, Walter C., D.V.M., "Opening Remarks," Proceedings of Minority Recruitment Conference: Tuskegee Institute School of Veterinary Medicine, Tuskegee Institute, 1974, pp. 10–12.

37. Bowles, Frank and Frank A. DeCosta, *Between Two Worlds: A Profile of Negro Higher Education.* New York: McGraw-Hill Co., 1977, p. 32 and Appendix B–34.

38. *Bulletin 1960.* Washington, D.C.: U.S. Department of Labor, Bureau of Labor Statistics, 1973.

39. Cordoza, Michael, *The Association Process, 1963–1973.* Washington, D.C.: American Assocation of Law Schools, 1975.

40. Chasin, Steven H. "Enrollment Report on First Professional Degree Program, Fall 1983." *American Journal of Pharmaceutical Education,* Vol. 47, 1983.

41. Collins, Randall, "Some Comparative Principles of Educational Stratification," *Harvard Educational Review* 47; No. 1 (February 1977): 1–29.
42. Commission on Human Resources, *Minority Groups Among United States Doctorate Level Scientists, Engineers and Scholars, 1983*. Washington, D.C.: National Academy of Sciences, 1984.
43. Crain, Robert L., " School Integration and Occupational Achievement Among Negroes." *American Journal of Sociology* 75 (1970):593–603.
44. Curtis, James L., *Blacks, Medical Schools and Society*. Ann Arbor: University of Michigan Press, 1971, p. 57–58.
45. Dubois, W.E.B., *The Souls of Black Folk*. Chicago: A. C. McClury Co., 1903.
46. Dummett, Clifton O., and Lois D. Dummett, "Afro-Americans in Dentistry: A Synopsis," *Crisis* (November 1979):398.
47. Edwards, Harry, *Black Students*. New York: The Free Press, 1970.
48. El-Khawas, Elaine H. And Jean Kinser, *Enrollment of Minority Graduate Students in Ph.D. Granting Institutions*. Washington, D.C.: American Council on Education, August 1974.
49. *Enrollment of Minority Graduate Students in Ph.D. Granting Institutions*. Washington, D.C.: American Council on Education, August 1984.
49b. _____, "Ph.D. Manpower Employment Demand and Supply 1972–1985." Washington, D.C.: American Council on Education, 1976.
50. Evans, Franklin, F., *Law School Admissions Research*. Princeton, NJ: Law School Admission Council, 1977.
51. Evans, Gaynelle, "Social, Financial Barriers Blamed for Curbing Blacks' Access to College," *The Chronical of Higher Education,* (August 7, 1985):1.
52. Franklin, John Hope, *From Slavery to Freedom*. New York: Alfred Knopf Co., 1952.
53. *Financial Aid Needs of Undergraduate Minority Engineering Students in the 1980s*. New York: The National Fund for Minority Engineering Students, December, 1978.
54. Gilford, Dorothy M. and Joan Snyder, *Women and Minorities Ph.D.'s in the 1970s: A Data Book*. Washington, D.C.: Commission on Human Resources, National Research Council, National Academy of Sciences, 1977.
55. Gillespie, Donald A. and Nancy Carlson, *Trends in Student Aid: 1963–1983*. Washington, D.C.: The College Board, 1984.
56. Gordon, Milton, *Assimilation in American Life*. New York: Oxford University Press, 1964.
57. Greenberg, Harold I. and Carol A. Scott, "Ethnic Minority Recruitment and Program for the Educationally Disadvantaged in School of Social Work," in Carol Scott (ed.) *Ethnic Minorities in Social Work Education*. New York: Council on Social Work Education, 1970.
58. Guren, Patricia and Edgar Epps, *Black Consciousness: Identity and Achievement*. New York: John Wiley & Sons, 1975.
59. Henderson, Wade J., Statement on Behalf of the Council on Legal Education Opportunity Before the Subcommittee on Post Secondary Education. U.S. House of Representatives, June 13, 1979.
60. Hill, Robert, *Illusions of Black Progress* (Washington, D.C.: National Urban League, 1979).
61. Hodginson, Harold, presentation in *Demographic Imperatives; Implications For Educational Policy*. Washington, D.C.: American Council on Education, 1983.
62. *Information for Applicants to Schools and Colleges of Optometry*. Washington, D.C.: Association of Schools and Colleges of Optometry, Fall, 1979.
63. "Information for Minority Group Students." *Medical School Admissions Requirements,* Washington, D.C.: American Association of Medical Colleges, 1976.
64. Johnson, Davis C., et al., "Recruitment and Progress of Minority Medical Schools Entrants, 1970–72, *Journal of Medical Education* 50:721, 1975.

65. Johnson, David F. and William E. Sedlacek, "Retention by Sex and Race of 1968–1972 U.S. Medical School Entrants," *Journal of Medical Education* 50:932, 1975.

66. Jolly, H.P. and Thomas Larson (of the AAMC), "Participation of Women Minorities in U.S. Medical Faculties." Washington, D.C.: Department of Health, Education and Welfare, Publication No. (HRA) 76–91, 1976.

67. *Journal of American Medical Association* 243:9 (March 7, 1980):853.

68. Kuhli, Ralph C. "Education For Health Careers," *Journal of School Health* 41 (January 1971):17.

69. Leonard, Walter, "Report on the Committee on Minority Groups," *Proceedings* of the 1972 Annual Meeting, Section 1, Washington, D.C.: The American Association of Law Schools, pp.65–69.

70. Lusterman, Seymour, *Minorities in Engineering: The Corporate Role.* New York: The Conference Board, 1979.

71. Malcom, Shirley M. et al., "Programs in Science for Minority Students: 1960–75. Washington, D.C.: American Association for the Advancement of Science, 1976, p. 21–22.

72. Marshall, Edwin C., "Social Indifference or Blatant Ignorance," *Journal of the American Optometric Association* 43:12 (November 1972):1261–1266.

73. *Minorities in Engineering: A Blueprint For Action* (A Report of the Planning Commission for Expanding Opportunities in Engineering). New York: Alfred P. Sloan Foundation, 1974.

74. National Advisory Committee on Black Higher Education, *Increasing the Yield, 1981–82.* New York: NACME, 1983.

75. _____, and Black Colleges and Universities, *Access of Black Americans to Higher Education: How Open is the Door.* Washington, D.C.: U.S. Government Printing Office, January 1979.

76. National Medical Fellowships, Inc., *Annual Report, 1983.* New York: National Medical Fellowships, Inc., 1984, p. 22–26.

77. _____, *Informational Brochure.* New York: National Medical Fellowships, Inc., 1984.

78. Neal, H.A., "Critical Issues Facing Minority Students in Science and Engineering." Paper presented at the Annual Meeting of the Association of Graduate Schools, College Park, Md., October, 1983 and *Footnotes,* 13:5 (May 1985).

79. *New York Times,* November 25, 1978.

80. Orr, Jack E., "Graduate Enrollment Data, 1973–74. *American Journal of Pharmaceutical Education,* Vol. 38.

81. _____, "Report on Enrollment in Schools and Colleges of Pharmacy, First Semester, Term or Quarter, 1972–73," *American Journal of Pharmaceutical Education.* Vol. 36, 1972, p. 138ff; and the same reports for 1973–74 through 1985–86.

82. Peters, Henry A., O.D. "Critical Optometric Manpower Issues," *Journal of Optometric Education* 4:4 (Spring 1979):8.

83. *Proceedings* of the Minority Recruitment Conference; Tuskegee Institute School of Veterinary Medicine, 1974. Tuskegee: Tuskegee Institute, 1974.

84. *Proceedings* of the Minority Recruitment Conference: Tuskegee Institute School of Veterinary Medicine, 1975. Tuskegee: Tuskegee Institute.

85. *Program Support of Graduate Education.* U.S. Office of Education, Washington, D.C.: May 1,1980.

86. Pruitt, Anne S. "Does Minority Graduate Education Have a Future," *Planning and Changing* 14:1 (Spring, 1983)15–21.

87. *Racial and Ethnic Enrollment Data from Institutions of Higher Education, Fall, 1970.* Washington, D.C.: Office of Civil Rights, Department of Health, Education and Welfare, 72–8, 1973.

88. *Racial and Ethnic Enrollment Data from Institutions of Higher Education, Fall 1982.* Washington, D.C.: DHEW, ORC – 72-78, 1978.

89. Reichert, Kurt, "Survey of Non-Discriminatory Practices in Accredited Graduate Schools of Social Work," *Ethnic Minorities in Social Work Education,* (ed.) Carol Scott, New York: Council on Social Work Education, 1970, p. 39–51.

90. Reitzes, Dietrich C. *Negroes and Medicines.* Cambridge, Mass.: Harvard University Press, 1958.

91. *Report of the Association of American Medical Colleges Task Force on Minority Student Opportunities in Medicine.* Washington, D.C.: Association of American Medical Colleges, 1978.

92. *Report of the AAMC Task Force on The InterAssociation Committee on Expanding Education Opportunities in Medicine for Blacks and Other Minority Students.* Washington, D.C.: April 22, 1970.

93. *Retention of Minority Students in Engineering.* Washington, D.C.: National Academy of Sciences, 1977.

94. Schaegger, Ruth G. "Corporate Leadership in a National Program," *The Conference Board Record* Vol. XIII, No. 9, (September 1976).

95. Schlegel, John and Christopher A. Rodowskas, *Enrollment Report of Professional Degree Programs in Pharmacy.* Fall 1975.

96. _____, et al., *Report of All Undergraduate Enrollment in Schools and Colleges of Pharmacy.* Bethesda, Maryland: American Association of Colleges of Pharmacy, August 1975, p. 3 and Table IX.

97. _____, *Graduate Enrollment Report, Fall, 1976.* Bethesda, Maryland: American Association of Colleges of Pharmacy, (no date), p. 3.

98. Sorenson, A.A., "Black Americans and the Medical Profession, 1930–1970," *Journal of Negro Education* 41 (Fall, 1972):337–342.

99. Sindler, Allan P., *Bakke, DeFunis and Minority Admissions.* New York: Longman, 1978.

100. Smith, Ann McKay, "Large Shortages of Black Professors in Higher Education Grow Worse," *Wall Street Journal* (June 8, 1984), p. 1.

101. Speedie, Bart M., "Enrollment Report on Professional Degree Programs, Fall 1980," *American Journal of Pharmaceutical Education,* Vol. 45, 1981, p. 400.

102. *Social Indicators of Equality for Minorities and Women.* Washington, D.C.: U.S. Government Printing Office, August 1978.

103. *Statistics on Social Work Education.* New York: Council on Social Work Education, 1970–1978.

104. _____, New York: Council on Social Work Education, 1979–1984.

105. *Summary Report of Doctorate Recipients From United States Universities.* (for 1980–84), Washington, D.C.: National Academy of Sciences.

106. Tasker, John B., "An Analysis of Applications to United States Colleges of Veterinary Medicine, 1983: A Report to the Association of American Veterinary Medical Colleges," July 1983, (Unpublished).

107. The Association of American Colleges, *Integrity in the College Curriculum,* Washington, D.C.: The Association of American Colleges, 1984.

108. The College Board, *Academic Preparation for College.* New York: The College Board, 1983.

109. _____, *Report of the National Blue Ribbon Panel on Declining Test Scores.* New York: The College Board, 1979.

110. _____, *Project Equality,* New York: The College Board, 1983.

111. _____, *Update From Washington.* November 1984, p.3.

112. The National Commission on Excellence in Education, *A Nation At Risk.* Washington, D.C.: U.S. Government Printing Office, 1983.

113. The National Institute of Education, *Involvement in Learning*. Washington, D.C.: The National Institute of Education, 1984.

114. U.S. Commission on Civil Rights, *Toward Equal Opportunity: Affirmative Admissions Programs at Law and Medical Schools*. Washington, D.C.: U.S. Government Printing Office, June 1978.

115. U.S. Department of Commerce, *America's Black Population: A Statistical View*. Washington, D.C.: Bureau of the Census, Special Publication PIO/POP-83-1, 1983.

116. _____, *The Social and Economic Status of the Black Population in the United States: An Historical View, 1970–1978*. Washington, D.C.: Bureau of the Census, Special Studies, p. 23, No. 80, 1979.

117. _____, *Population Profile of the United States: 1982*. Washington D.C.: Bureau of the Census, Current Population Reports, Special Studies Services, p. 23, No. 130, U.S. Government Printing Office, 1983.

118. Watkins, Linda, "Losing Ground: 'Minorities' Enrollment in College Retreats After Its Surge in 1970s," *Wall Street Journal*, May 29, 1985, p.1.

119. Wilkinson, Doris, "Federal Employment for Sociologists," *Footnotes*, Washington, D.C.: American Sociological Association, March, 1980.

120. _____, "Percentage of Women Doctorates in Sociology Increases," *Footnotes*, Washington, D.C.: American Sociological Association, December 1977.

121. _____, "Careers, Minorities and Women," *Footnotes*, 1977–1980, Supra.

122. Wright, Stephen S. *The Black Educational Policy Researcher: An Untapped National Resource*. Washington, D.C.: National Advisory Committee on Black Higher Education and Black Colleges and Universities, Department of Health, Education and Welfare, 1979.

ABOUT THE AUTHOR

James E. Blackwell (Ph. D. Washington State University; M. A. and B. A., Case Western Reserve University) has been a Professor of Sociology at the University of Massachusetts/Boston since 1970. Dr. Blackwell has taught at Case Western Reserve University, San Jose State University, Washington State University, Grambling State University, Tribuvhan University (Nepal) and the University of East Africa (Tanzania).

Among the honors received and positions held in professional organizations are: The DuBois–Johnson–Frazier Award (1986) and the Spivak Award (1979) of the American Sociological Association; membership in the Sociological Research Association; *President* of the Eastern Sociological Society (1981–82); *President* of the Society for the Study of Social Problems (SSSP) (1980–81), and Founding *President* of the Caucus of Black Sociologists (1970–72).

During the Sixties, he directed Peace Corps activities in Tanzania and in Malawi and was a member of the U.S. Foreign Service Officer Corps in Nepal. Dr. Blackwell has been an Invited Member of the White House Conference on Aging; Member, Advisory Board and Consultant – United Board for College Development; Member, Research Study and Review Panel, Social and Rehabilitation Service, Department of Health, Education and Welfare. Member of Special Task Force Conference on "Dismantling Dual Systems of Higher Education;" Member of Special Task Force on "Equality of Opportunity to Graduate and Professional Schools;" Member, "Critical Issues in Higher Education;" and Appointed to the Advisory Committee on Research of the College Entrance Examination Board.

His scholarly research and publications have focused on racial and ethnic minorities, race relations theory, desegregation, and the social dynamics of the black community. His major books include *The Black Community: Diversity and Unity; Cities, Suburbs and Blacks* (with Philip Hart); *Black Sociologists: Historical and Contemporary Perspectives* (with Morris Janowitz); *The Power Basis of Inter-Ethnic Conflict in American Society;* and *Networking and Mentoring.* In addition, he has published numerous journal articles, chapters for textbooks, and research monographs.

In his view, Black Americans continue to be outsiders in graduate and professional education, despite significant gains achieved during the 1960s, 1970s and 1980s. He documents enrollment and graduation trends by race and shows how specific factors are correlated with both success and failure in the recruitment, admissions, enrollment and graduation of Black students from graduate and professional schools. Specific attention is focused on Engineering, Dentistry, Medicine, Veterinary Medicine, Law, Optometry, Pharmacy, Social Work and Doctorate Degrees Granted in the Physical Sciences, Education, Humanities and Arts, Life Sciences, Social Sciences and the Professions.

Name Index

Abarnel, Karen 11n, 362
Abt, Donald A., 231n, 362
Al-Amin, Karema, XVIII
Atelsek, Frank J., 112n, 362

Bardolph, Richard, 27n, 362
Bell, Derek, XIX, 41, 296n, 362
Bennett, Lerone, 26n, 27n, 362
Bennett, William, 71n, 363
Bierstedt, Robert, 34, 47n, 363
Billingsley, Andrew, 299–302, 321n, 363
Blackwell, James E., XVI, XVIII, 19, 26n
    27n, 47n, 73n, 111n, 112n, 271n,
    296n, 345n, 361, 363
Blake, Martin L., 207n, 363
Blalock, Hubert M., 34, 47n, 363
Blasdel, Hugh, 271n
Bowie, Walter C., 231n, 363
Bowles, Frank H., 4, 26n, 363

Chasin, Steven H., 207n, 363
Collins, Randall, 47n
Comer, Charles, XIV, 155
Cordoza, Michael H., 295n, 296n, 364
Coyle, Susan, XIX
Crain, Robert L., 16, 17, 364
Cureton, Mary, XIX, 101
Curtis, James L., 111n, 364

DeCosta, Frank A., 4, 26n, 363
Decker, William, XIX, 232n
DuBois, W.E.B., 6, 26n, 364
Dummett, Clifton O., 152n, 364
Dummett, Lois D., 152n, 364

Edwards, Harry 14, 27n, 364
El-Khanas, Elaine H., 345n, 364
Epps, Edgar, 16, 17, 27n, 364
Evans, Franklin R., 272, 286, 287, 295n,
    296n, 364
Evans, Gaynelle, 28n, 334, 364

Ferguson, David A., 115
Foster, Luther M., XIX

Francis, Norman, XIX, 41, 200
Franklin, John Hope, 6, 26n, 27n, 364

Geilhorn, Walter, 275
Gilford, Dorothy M., XIX, 327, 345n,
    364
Gillespie, Donald A., 73, 364
Gomberg, Irene L., 85
Gordon, Milton, 26n, 364
Grace, Marcellus, XX, 42, 200, 207n
Graham, James W., XIX
Greenberg, Harold I., 303, 321n, 364
Gurin, Patricia, 16, 17, 27n, 364
Gyorfy, Pilar, 85

Hall, Ellis, 41, 216, 217, 228, 231n,
    232n
Hart, Philip, 111n, 363
Henderson, Wade J., XIX, 41, 296n
Hill, Robert B., 19, 21
Hodginson, Harold, 358, 361, 364
Hofstetter, Henry, 155

Jackson, Maurice, 337, 338, 345n, 363
Johnson, David F., 364
Johnson, Lillye Mae, XIX
Johnson, Mordecai W., 114
Jolly, H. P., 112n, 365

Kendall, Maurice E., 365
Kramer, Gene A., XIX
Kuhli, Ralph C., 111n, 365

Larson, Thomas A., 112n, 365
Leonard, Walter J., 295n, 296n, 365
Lusterman, Seymour, 240, 270, 271n,
    365

Malcolm, Shirley M., 206n, 365
Marshall, Edwin C., XX, 154, 159,
    172n, 365
McKay-Smith, Ann, 345n, 366
McKenna, Warren, XX, 41, 200
McMillan, Elridge W., XVI

Meredith, James, 13
Meuller, John H., 336
Mirandi, Luis, XIX
Mishell, Robert L., 335
Moore, Joan M., 363

Nader, Ralph, 152n
Neal, H. A., 346n, 365

Orr, Jack E., 206n, 207n, 365

Payton, Benjamin, XIX
Penna, Richard, XIX
Peters, Henry B., 153, 172n, 365
Pins, Arnulf W., 302
Posner, Ruth, XIX
Pratt, John Judge, 23
Prieto, Dario, XIX, 96, 103
Pruitt, Anne S., 345n, 365
Purvine, Margaret, 337

Reichert, Kurt, 321n, 366
Reitzes, Dietrich C., 12, 27n, 366
Richardson, Elijah, 152n
Rudd, Millard, XIX
Runge, Mary Munson, 205

Scott, Carl A., 303, 321n, 364
Schaegger, Ruth G., 271n, 366
Schlegel, John L., 206n, 207n, 366
Sedlacek, William E., 107, 112n, 364
Sindler, Allan P., 86, 112n, 366
Smith, J. Stanford, 238
Smith, Lee, XIX, 172
Solander, Lars, XIX, 190, 338
Sorenson, A. A., 27n, 366
Snyder, Joan, 327, 345n
Speedie, Bart M., 207n, 366
Spooner, Levoy, 270n
Stuart, A., 64, 365
Syverson, Peter D., XIX

Tasker, John B., 231n, 366
Thompson, Vertis, 112n

Walker, James K., XIX
Walker, Lucian, 271n
Washington, Booker T., 6, 366
Watkins, Linda 345n, 366
Wellington, John S., 85
White, James, XIX
Wilkinson, Doris Y., 338, 346n, 367
Williams, Paul, 337
Wooten, Daniel, 112n
Wright, Stephen J., 346n, 367

Subject Index

Access
and Civil Rights Movement, 13–15
and institutional behavior, 352, 353
barriers to,
defined, 44–45
types of, 44–45
Adams v. *Bell*, 23, 353
Adams v. *Bennett*, 13, 353
Adams v. *Califano*, 23, 59, 130, 353
Adams v. *Richardson*, 23, 178, 353
"*Adams* States", 23, 80, 122–123, 130,
131, 132, 146, 147, 176, 188–190,
193, 219, 245, 247, 252, 255, 262,
266, 309, 311, 314
Admissions Programs, 69–71
American Association of Colleges of
Pharmacy, 42, 175, 186, 190, 191,
197
American Bar Association, 41, 273, 275,
277, 278, 289
American Dental Association, 39, 113,
115, 116, 133
American Indian Students
GPOP recipients, 336, 342
in Engineering, 233
in Law, 279
in Medicine, 80, 107
American Medical Association, 76–79
Architectural Education, 268–270
Association of American Dental Schools,
39, 113, 116, 137
Association of American Law Schools, 15,
41, 219, 275, 277, 279
Association of American Medical Colleges,
15, 39–40, 76–79, 82–85, 86, 107,
219
Association of American Veterinary
Medical Colleges, 41, 213, 216, 219,
220, 221, 222, 226, 227, 230
Association of Collegiate Schools of
Architecture, 42
Association of Schools and Colleges of
Optometry, 42, 155–156, 162, 168

Subject Index

Bakke Case, 23, 24, 25, 30, 70, 85–88,
95, 98, 103, 110, 118, 128, 220,
231, 245, 277, 352, 356
Berkeley Model in Social Work, 299–
302
Black Colleges
graduate schools, 324–325
of Architecture, 268–269
of Engineering, 233–236, 250, 262,
263
of Law, 274, 291–292
of Pharmacy, 180, 186–187, 200
of Social Work, 298, 309
of Veterinary Medicine, 208–219, 228
Black Doctorates, 322–346
Black Students
and Civil Rights Movements, 13–15
and career choices, 15–17
and college-going rates, 22–23, 70–71
Brown v. *Board of Education*, 9, 12, 13,
87, 297, 354
Career Choices of Black Students, 15–19
Civil Rights Movement, 13–15
Charles Drew Medical Center, 76, 104,
110
CLAST, 68
Committee on Minorities in Engineering
(CME),
Competency Examinations, 67, 68
Council on Legal Education Opportunity,
(CLEO), 41, 272, 278–283
Council on Social Work Education, 15,
39, 298, 302

Data Analysis of Survey Findings, 46–47,
48–64
Correlates of Black Student enrollment
in professional schools, 51–56
First year black student enrollment in
professional schools, 56–60
Most powerful predictors, 56–64
Specification of variables, 48–51
Total black student enrollment in

professional schools, 60–63
Total black graduates from professional schools, 60
Types of data, 35–43, 48
DeFunis Case, 23, 24, 25, 30, 70, 85–88,
272, 276
Dentistry
dental education of blacks, 113–152
admissions criteria, 118–119
applicant activity, 117–118
enrollment trends, 119–133
first year and total by race, 121–131
trends, in "*Adams* States", 122–131
national trends, 119–127
factors affecting enrollment trends,
133–143
financial aid, 133–142
graduation trends, 144–147
historical overview, 113–115
professional associations, 115–116
recruitment programs, 142–144
sex variables in dentistry, 147–150
total enrollment of black students,
131–133
Dubois-Washington controversy, 6–7

Education
and black colleges, 6–7
and doctoral level, 324–325
and doctoral recipients, 322–346
changing rates of, 66–70
crisis in, 65–73
dual systems of, 6–13
economic barriers, 17–23
Engineering and training of black
Americans, 233–271
admissions criteria and policies, 245–
246
undergraduate admissions, 245
graduate admissions, 246
dual degree programs, 235, 238
enrollment by race, 246–256
undergraduate enrollment, 247–252
"*Adams* States",
graduate enrollment trends, 252–256
finance, 259–260
estrangement, 261
graduation and production rates by
race and degree, 262–266
problems of students, 266–268
production in black colleges, 233–236

recruitment, 243–245
retention, 256–261
role of corporate structure, 236–243,
348
self confidence of students, 261

Financial assistance patterns, 71–73

Graduate and professional opportunities
program, 25, 294
Graduate education and doctorate
production, 322–346, 350
distribution by fields, trends in, 330–
333
distribution by degree and sex, 327–
332
doctorates awarded blacks, 327–330
graduate and professional opportunities
program (GPOP), 336–339
median age of doctorate recipients by
race, 341
overview, 323–327
production of doctorates among
blacks, 324, 327–330
sources of funds for graduate study,
333–336
special problems, 340–345
time lapse between B.S. and Ph.D.,
339–340

Hocut, Thomas, 8
Howard University, 4, 7, 12, 75–76, 93,
95, 97, 100, 101, 104, 107, 110,
113, 114, 115, 117–118, 120–121,
129, 136, 138, 144, 146, 173, 186,
197, 349

Legal Education of black students, 272–
296
admissions policies and practices,
283–287
CLEO, 41, 272, 278–283
enrollment by race, 12, 288–292
first year enrollment trends, 288–289
total enrollment trends, 289–290
enrollment in black colleges, 291–292
graduates, 295
historical overview, 272–274
impact of professional associations,
274–278
problem areas, 293–295

responses to *Bakke* decision, 287
special programs, 292–293

Mainstreaming, 126
  definition, 1–2
  historical context of, 1–6
  in Reconstruction period, 3–6
Maryland v. *Murray*, 9–11
Medical education of blacks, 74–112
  "*Adams* States", 80
  admissions criteria, 88–92
  application activity, 92–97
  black faculty in, 109–111
  DeFunis and *Bakke* cases, 85–88
  enrollment trends, 12, 97–102
  graduation trends, 106–107
  Howard University and Meharry
    Medical College, 75–76
  Implications of *Bakke* decision, 86–88
  Problems: retention and social
    barriers, 107–109
  role of professional associations,
    76–85
  sex ratio, 104–105
  total enrollments, 102–105
Meharry Medical College, 7, 12, 75–76,
  93, 95, 97, 100, 101, 104, 107, 110,
  113, 114, 115, 117–118, 120, 121,
  129, 140, 144, 146, 349, 355
Methodological issues, 29–47
Mexican American Students,
  GPOP recipients, 336, 340, 342
  in Engineering, 233
  in Law, 279, 286
  in Medicine, 80, 107
McLauren v. *Oklahoma Regents*, 9–11
Minority Fellowship Program, 305, 337,
  338
Missouri ex rel Gaines v. *Canada*, 9–11
Morehouse Medical College, 76, 104, 110

National Academy of Engineering (NEA)
NAACP, 8, 211, 223, 278
NAACP-LDF, 8, 9–11, 24, 86, 293
NACME, 239, 241, 245, 257, 260
National Bar Association, 275, 278
National Dental Association, 115, 116
National Fund for Minority Engineering
  Students, 259, 260
National Medical Association, 76, 79, 82
National Medical Fellowships, 79, 82, 108

National Optometric Association, 155,
  157, 162, 166

Optometric Education of Blacks, 153,
  172
  admissions criteria, 158, 161
  Black graduates, 167, 168
  enrollment trends, 155, 158, 162–166
  national trends, and "*Adams* States",
    162–166
  sex ratios, 166
  historical context, 154–155
  major problems, 168–171
  recruitment, 155–158
  retention, 166–167

Plessy v. *Ferguson*, 5, 7, 114
Pharmacy Education and Blacks, 173–207
  admissions requirements, 180–186
  Black Graduates in, 198–200
  enrollment by degree program, 186–
    188, 193–194
  enrollment in "*Adams* States",
    188–191
  overview of problem, 195–198
  recruitment, 173–178
  "*Adams* States", 176
  institutional profiles, 176–180
  Xavier University School of Pharmacy:
    Case Study of, 200–206
  sex ratios, 191
Policy Implications of Mainstreaming,
  347–361
  a review of the 70s, 347–351
  beyond tokenism, five year plans,
    recommendations, 357–361
  policy changes needed, 351–357
  governmental, 351, 353–356
  corporate and foundation changes,
    351, 358
  home and pre-college environment,
    351, 356–357
  individual responsibilities, 351–356
  institutional responsibility, 351,
    358–360
Project Equality, 67
  Project, 75–79, 82, 97, 358
Puerto Rican American Students,
  GPOP recipients, 336, 340
  in Engineering, 233

in Law, 279
in Medicine, 80, 107

Raise Bill, 68
Reagan Administration, 24, 25, 133–134
199, 347, 354–356

Sipuel v. *Board of Regents of Oklahoma,*
9–11
Social Work Education and Black
Americans, 297–321
admissions and recruitment, 302–305
Berkeley model, 299–302
Black faculty, 317–319
enrollment trends by race, 306–314
first professional degree, 307–309
enrollment in "*Adams* States", 309–
311, 314
enrollment in doctorate programs,
311–314
total enrollments, 307–410
historical overview, 297–299
problems, 319–320
graduation rates by race and institutions, 315–317

sources of financial aid, 305–306
Sweatt v. *Painter,* 9–11

Tuskegee Institute,
and veterinary medicine, 208–219
and Engineering, 233–236, 250, 262,
263
Tuskegee Institute Case Study, 208–219

Unemployment and income, 18–22

Veterinary Medicine and Black
Americans, 208–232
admissions policies, practices, and
criteria, 213–214, 223–226
desegregation trends, 218–219
enrollment trends, 214–215, 226–229
graduation trends, 215–216, 229
historical overview, 208–209
impact of *Bakke* decision, 217–218
Problem Areas, 229–231
recruitment practices, 209–213
role of professional associations, 219–
223

Xavier University College of Pharmacy,
200–206